≺≻

THE STATE AND FREEDOM
OF CONTRACT

THE MAKING OF MODERN FREEDOM

General Editor: R. W. Davis
Center for the History of Freedom
Washington University in St. Louis

THE STATE AND FREEDOM
OF CONTRACT

< >

Edited by Harry N. Scheiber

STANFORD UNIVERSITY PRESS
STANFORD, CALIFORNIA
1998

Stanford University Press
Stanford, California
© 1998 by the Board of Trustees of the
Leland Stanford Junior University
Printed in the United States of America

CIP data appear at the end of the book

<>

Series Foreword

THE STARTLING AND moving events that swept from China to Eastern Europe to Latin America and South Africa at the end of the 1980s, followed closely by similar events and the subsequent dissolution of what used to be the Soviet Union, formed one of those great historic occasions when calls for freedom, rights, and democracy echoed through political upheaval. A clear-eyed look at any of those conjunctions—in 1776 and 1789, in 1848 and 1918, as well as in 1989—reminds us that freedom, liberty, rights, and democracy are words into which many different and conflicting hopes have been read. The language of freedom—or liberty, which is interchangeable with freedom most of the time—is inherently difficult. It carried vastly different meanings in the classical world and in medieval Europe from those of modern understanding, though thinkers in later ages sometimes eagerly assimilated the older meanings to their own circumstances and purposes.

A new kind of freedom, which we have here called modern, gradually disentangles itself from old contexts in Europe, beginning first in England in the early seventeenth century and then, with many confusions, denials, reversals, and cross-purposes, elsewhere in Europe and the world. A large-scale history of this modern, conceptually distinct, idea of freedom is now beyond the ambition of any one scholar, however learned. This collaborative enterprise, tentative though it must be, is an effort to fill the gap.

We could not take into account all the varied meanings that freedom and liberty have carried in the modern world. We have, for example, ruled out extended attention to what some political philosophers have called "positive freedom," in the sense of self-realization of the individual; nor could we, even in a series as large as this, cope with the enormous implications of the four freedoms invoked by Franklin D. Roosevelt in 1941. Freedom of speech and freedom of the press will have their place in the narrative that follows, certainly, but not the boundless calls for freedom from want and freedom from fear.

We use freedom in the traditional and restricted sense of civil and political liberty—freedom of religion, freedom of speech and assembly, freedom of the individual from arbitrary and capricious authority over persons or property, freedom to produce and to exchange goods and services, and the freedom to take part in the political process that shapes people's destiny. In no major part of the world over the past few years have aspirations for those freedoms not been at least powerfully expressed; and in most places where they did not exist, strong measures have been taken—not always successfully—to attain them.

The history we trace was not a steady march toward the present or the fulfillment of some cosmic necessity. Modern freedom had its roots in specific circumstances in early modern Europe, despite the unpromising and even hostile characteristics of the larger society and culture. From these narrow and often selfishly motivated beginnings, modern freedom came to be realized in later times, constrained by old traditions and institutions hard to move, and driven by ambition as well as idealism: everywhere the growth of freedom has been *sui generis*. But to understand these unique developments fully, we must first try to see them against the making of modern freedom as a whole.

The Making of Modern Freedom grows out of a continuing series of conferences and institutes held at the Center for the History of Freedom at Washington University in St. Louis. Professor J. H. Hexter was the founder and, for three years, the resident gadfly of the Center. His contribution is gratefully recalled by all his colleagues.

R.W.D.

≺≻

Contents

<>

Acknowledgments

The contributors to this volume and the editor are indebted to Prof. Douglass C. North of Washington University, who conceived of the project for essays on the state and freedom of contract. His challenging prospectus, though meant to be preliminary and tentative, largely shaped the project's initial agenda and served well to provide a basic conceptual framework for the book. Professor Richard Davis, director of the Center for the History of Freedom at Washington University, was a constant source of fresh ideas, encouragement, and guidance as the project went forward. The editor and authors benefited greatly also from comments at a conference held at the Center at an early stage of the project, and also from discussion at faculty seminars at Boalt Hall School of Law, University of California, Berkeley, and at an annual meeting session of the American Society for Legal History. We are especially indebted to Professors Robert Gordon and Carol Rose, Yale Law School; Lawrence M. Friedman, Stanford Law School; and David Konig, Department of History, Washington University. Also, the authors regularly exchanged views and offered comments to the volume editor on the drafts circulated by the others; and so while each chapter stands on its own as an individual's work, the volume as a whole is in a real sense a collaborative project.

H.N.S.

CONTRIBUTORS

James Gordley
University of California, Berkeley

David Lieberman
University of California, Berkeley

Charles W. McCurdy
University of Virginia

Arthur F. McEvoy
University of Wisconsin

John V. Orth
University of North Carolina

Donald J. Pisani
University of Oklahoma

Harry N. Scheiber
University of California, Berkeley

Martin Shapiro
University of California, Berkeley

A. W. B. Simpson
University of Michigan

≺ ≻

THE STATE AND FREEDOM
OF CONTRACT

≺ ≻

Introduction

HARRY N. SCHEIBER

A VITAL ISSUE IN THE HISTORY of how freedom has been established in the modern world is the proper place of "economic
liberty" in relation to the classic civil and political liberties such as
freedom of religion, press, speech, and assembly and the right to participate as a voter in the political process. The chapters in this volume seek to provide fresh interpretive perspectives on this issue by
examining the place of economic liberty in the development of Anglo-American law from the end of the feudal era to the present day.

The phrase "freedom of contract," used in our title, is dealt
with by the authors in two ways. First, there is the institution of
"contract" itself, and its strict meaning in law—that is, contract as
the legal form in which agreements and promises are made, with
the purpose of making them enforceable by the courts. Some of the
chapters in this book are indeed specifically concerned with the institution of contract in this stricter legal meaning. They address
from various perspectives questions of when contract appeared in
the common law of England, as a legal category and institution distinguished from property law; of how social and economic change
generated a need for, was influenced by, and thus provided the context of, innovations in the legal understanding of contract; of the
degree to which the emergent concept of contract absorbed or retained elements of legal doctrine that served to qualify and hedge
the economic liberty advanced by freedom of contract.

The second way, which has been commonly deployed in the
rhetoric of Anglo-American law as well as in political theory and
political economy, is as a shorthand expression referring to economic liberty in a large and embracing sense, that is, the idea of
economic individualism. This idea places a high value upon the
goal of maximizing the control that private individuals and firms

are permitted to maintain over their property and other vested interests, with a concomitant minimizing of governmental interventions that trench upon private rights. In this sense, as some argue, freedom of contract not only is "a tool of change" but also is an instrument for "self-determination and self-assertion" of individuals, groups, and firms that make use of it in their private activities.[1] Economic liberty in this sense affords free play to individuals to use their "faculties"—their born talents and educated skills, which James Madison and other leaders in America's Revolutionary and Founding periods declared to be a vital aspect of their "property," and as such fully as deserving of the state's protection as were their chattels, or physical property. Our intention, in dealing with freedom of contract in this broader sense, is to consider from the perspective of legal history what Richard Davis, the series editor, has termed the "freedom of the individual from arbitrary and capricious authority over persons or property, and the freedom to produce and to exchange goods and services." We consider those concepts both as they have developed historically in our law and as they have reflected the larger objectives and values of freedom in an open society.

It is important to note, in this regard, one special feature of the rhetoric. In the United States, the term "liberty of contract" was designated by the courts as a constitutional concept, and as such it became a touchstone doctrine by which the constitutionality of various types of social and regulatory legislation was judged. The courts used the word *liberty* in this instance because it appeared in the federal Constitution's fifth and fourteenth amendments (referring to the protections to be afforded to "life, liberty, and property" interests). In popular political discourse, however, "liberty of contract" came to be used interchangeably with "freedom of contract." It is often employed similarly in scholarly writing as well, not only with reference to American law and policy but more generally in the study of legal systems and doctrine; and it is so used by several of the authors in this book.

The commonplace nature of the saying, "A bargain is a bargain" reminds us of how ingrained in modern culture are the rhetoric and the substance of economic individualism. This remains so even after a century or more in which many of the core premises of free-

dom of contract have been challenged and forced to yield to the
imperatives of wide-ranging regulatory and welfare policies. Thus
the advertising slogan of a prominent consulting company that one
can see today in business magazines sounds the following warning:
"In business, you don't get what you deserve; you get what you negotiate." This slogan summarizes pithily the core idea of private
contract; and it reminds us of the continuing importance of the
private sector—the realm of private transactions in which the institution of contract permits individuals or corporations in effect to
make law for themselves. They do so by means of the agreements
in contract—the formal extensions of promises—in which they
commit themselves to give over property, provide labor or services,
or desist from doing something. Commitments are made (except in
the case of gifts, which are a special form of contract) in exchange
for some specified quid pro quo, money or otherwise. The terms of
the promises are meant to be enforceable by the courts. The institution of contract has become in modern society the principal instrument for organizing the private marketplace; indeed, it is coex-
tensive with the market in its scope. Contract is indispensable to
the functioning of markets in which commerce and industry require a legal mechanism for arm's-length transactions that can
build into the dynamics of exchange the certainty of expectations
upon which individuals and firms rely.

The institution of contract has not always been so central to the
law in this sense, however, having occupied the dominant and expanding place that it has enjoyed in both Anglo-American and continental European jurisprudence only since the nineteenth century.
Before that time, as A. W. B. Simpson shows in chapter 1, in key
aspects of the development of English law from the fourteenth to
the nineteenth century it was the institution of *property* that
dominated the legal system. Simpson takes as a point of reference
one of the most famous passages in the literature of the law, from
William Blackstone's *Commentaries on the Laws of England*, published in the late 1760s, in which Blackstone extolled the right of
property as "that sole and despotic dominion which one man
claims and exercises over the external things of the world in total
exclusion of the right of any other individual in the universe."
Simpson analyzes the way in which alienability of land, separation
of property interests from the imperatives of family relationships,

the freedom to make gifts or establish trusts, and similar developments in the law were accomplished as the result both of the statutes passed by Parliament (that is, by innovations in public law) and of the process by which judges established rules and principles through the accumulation of precedent (that is, the judge-made "common law"). In these ways, a system once fixed and rigid in how it constrained property owners was transformed in the terms that were—albeit with some serious exaggeration—described in Blackstone's depiction of the law.

A sub-theme running through Simpson's analysis is how the institutions of property law and also of emerging contract law must be understood in terms of the larger framework of legal principle by which courts interpreted private promises and obligations. That framework consisted in part of the strictures of the common law as set down by the courts over time—for example, the concept of private nuisance, which forbade a property owner from using his property in a way that damaged the enjoyment of their property by others; or the more comprehensive (and perhaps more malleable, and certainly in the long run highly significant) concept of public nuisance, that is, uses of property that were harmful to the public at large, or to the interests of the state. The framework also consisted, however, of interventions by the legislature, for as Simpson shows the most significant abridgments of private rights in the eighteenth and nineteenth centuries were produced by the special acts of Parliament. Known as "local and personal acts," these laws authorized groups of landowners to engage in enclosures in order to modernize and rationalize agriculture in the countryside, displacing laborers and small tenants in the process; and authorized canal, road, dock bridge, railroad, and other public utility companies to take land from private owners in order to expedite the construction of their facilities. Evidence, as Simpson argues, supporting the view "that rapid economic development is not compatible with too strong respect for the individual autonomy of the landowner," this granting of special rights to entrepreneurs represented a major departure in law as it did in public policy. It was not long before demands would come from other quarters in the society for breaching the concept of "despotic dominion" and freedom of contract for another, very different, purpose: to restrict freedom of employers and property owners in the interests of protecting society against the ills of social and economic inequality that attended the growth of the modern industrial economy.

In chapter 2, by John Orth, our attention turns to the institution of contract itself in the history of English law. Orth recalls that contract law has consisted historically of the law of employment relations, as was true even in the golden age of contract in the nineteenth century. (Indeed, when the "liberty of contract" doctrine was given definitive form by the U.S. Supreme Court in 1905, it was in a labor case, *Lochner v. New York*, concerned with the effort of New York State to regulate the hours of bakers.) Orth's analysis of the development of contract offers a story that runs in counterpoint with Simpson's interpretation of the historic changes in the English law of property; and he shows how many of the functions of law performed through contract doctrine in later times were undertaken within the framework of property law. Here again, both judge-made law and public law in the form of parliamentary interventions worked their effects, for example, by determining the changing status of labor and specifying the degree of freedom that workers might enjoy. Beginning in the fourteenth century, Parliament established a labor regime in which workers were required to give service where it was needed, and in which, later, wages were set by the justices of the peace. "Labor," Orth writes, "remained more a matter of status than of contract," and the worker "belonged in a sense to the master." Later Parliament also imposed discipline on the labor force through "combination acts," which criminalized agreements for joint action by workers.

Not until the mid-eighteenth century did Parliament recognize, as Orth writes, that "private contracts could be an acceptable means of organizing economic activity." This recognition, in England, was the dawn of modern concepts of economic liberty—preceding in time, and soon merging with, the celebration of individualism and economic freedom that would be sounded in 1776 by Adam Smith in his *Wealth of Nations* and then reinforced by the political economists and by the utilitarian philosophers. Blackstone's encomium to "despotic dominion" encapsulated the ideal—though there is abundant evidence that it can hardly be taken as literally accurate even for the reality of his own day—of private property. Similarly, the founder of utilitarianism, Jeremy Bentham, would be invoked endlessly in later days by proponents of freedom of contract for his epitomization, in his *Defence of Usury* (1796), of the contract ideal: "that no man of ripe years and of sound mind, acting freely, and with his eyes open, ought to be hindered, with a view to his advantage, from making such bargain, in the way of obtaining money, as he thinks fit; nor (what is a necessary consequence) any body hindered from supplying him, upon any terms he thinks proper to accede to." How both English and American courts and legislatures confronted this kind of doctrine, first resisting and then accommodating labor combinations and collective action by workers, and how the legal system tested the creative potential of contract as a weapon for social organization, are delineated in the last section of this chapter. The themes are taken up again from different perspectives in chapter 6, by Charles McCurdy, and chapter 7, by Arthur McEvoy.

One of the transforming forces in the advent of contract, as it "began to emerge from the shadow of property," Orth writes, was a "new way of thinking about legal relations." This was the so-called "will theory"—the idea that the intentions of the parties ought to be taken by courts as a test of validity in regard to enforceability of agreements, that contractual obligations should reflect the will of the parties acting deliberately and purposefully in making promises rather than being an application of general principles governing what might legitimately be done and what was proscribed.

In chapter 3, a study in intellectual history of legal principles and their absorption into the law, James Gordley provides a different perspective on the genesis of will theory and its relationship to ideas of economic liberty. Rejecting the idea (elements of which are explicitly stated or else implicit in other chapters of this book) that the will theory of contract gained dominance as a reflexive reaction to the needs of commercial society, or else that it won favor because it was consistent with popular eighteenth- and nineteenth-century political philosophies, Gordley contends that the explanation lies in the internal history of legal thought. In particular, he ascribes the jurists' acceptance of will theory to the discrediting of Aristotelian thought, which rested on assumptions about human nature and the natural order that had lost their force as the result of the large intellectual movements of the Enlightenment period. With natural law, together with the constraints on human action (and legal instruments for effecting it) associated with natural law doctrines, now in eclipse, Gordley argues, the courts found it acceptable to rest contract law on will of the parties instead of judging the legitimacy and enforceability of contracts according to notions of fairness and social objectives. Looking ahead to the great political confrontations of modern industrial society, in both Europe and America, Gordley contends that the basic premises of will theory would influence the reformers no less than the defenders of the status quo—again a theme taken up and elaborated in chapters 6 and 7. Gordley's analysis includes a recapitulation of the continuing vitality of Roman law and natural law on the Continent, in the fields of both property and contract law. It needs to be kept in mind that elements of continental law, as he describes them, would reappear in the debates over economic liberty in Britain and in America during the early nineteenth century.

A striking reappraisal of how some of the leading figures in British jurisprudence, from Blackstone's time to the mid-nineteenth century, thought about contract is the subject of David Lieberman's discussion in chapter 4. He finds abundant evidence of the vigor with which traditional restraints on contractual freedom persisted after the great transformation marked by the broader general acceptance of will theory. He also provides striking evidence of the ways in which even the great intellectual foundation tracts—including the writings of Adam Smith—in jurisprudence and in political economy incorporated notions of justice, the public good, and collective or community values, variously expressed in constructs that owed much to the natural law jurisprudential heritage that Gordley has described. Thus the durability of "customary structures and practices," even in the commercial sector that was the driving force for the acceptance and spread of contract theory, was remarkable. (How the heritage of natural law as it classified obligations and rights was incorporated into a modern theory attuned to the realities of a commercial era, in concert with recognition of the new importance of contract and its separation from property law, is illustrated in Lieberman's closing discussion of the contributions of William Paley, an important but sometimes forgotten contemporary of Smith and Bentham.) Lieberman also examines the significance of legislative interventions in the eighteenth century, further elaborating the discussions of changing impacts of public law that were offered by Orth and by Simpson in regard to the Combination Acts and the special and local acts.

Chapter 5 shifts the focus of attention to the American side of the water, in an overview and analysis of economic liberty and state power. First, this chapter considers how, in the founding of the new republic after the Revolution, the American political leadership—having overthrown a mercantilist order directed from London—adopted a set of policies that were themselves neo-mercantilist and to a considerable degree interventionist. Second, the problem of how republicanism as a controlling political theory in the new nation related to the question of economic liberty is given attention. And finally, the competing concepts of economic individualism as they were expressed in law and policy, and the constitutional dimension of this problem, are considered for the nineteenth century and the modern era. To an extent that is not always given due recognition, perhaps because so much of American historical writing is premised on the idea of American exceptionalism, there were important parallels with emerging debates of the "industrial question" involving social conflict and dislocations accompanying economic growth and change in Britain.

Chapter 6 comes directly to the issue of "liberty of contract" in constitutional discourse and adjudication, and in the larger arena of American politics. Charles McCurdy offers an analysis of the principles that found full expression in the Lochner case and of the lines of continuity from the earlier political debates in which the ideal of free labor was made a central theme in rhetoric of the industrial-labor confrontations of the turn of the century. McCurdy deals with the process by which concepts of "neutrality" were advanced in legal discourse. He is especially interested in how these concepts were worked out in the several aspects of labor law (including industrial accident law), impelled by a commitment to individualism in the political credo that worked against interventions by courts that might be based on a recognition of inequality of bargaining power. The contributions to the debate over the legitimacy of intervention and abridgment of freedom-of-contract legal doctrines by progressive reform writers, including most notably Richard Ely, Roscoe Pound, and Ernst Freund, are given close analysis; and McCurdy offers a searching appraisal of the work of

Henry Farnham, a Yale professor of political economy whose role in the debate of law and social policy has previously been largely overlooked. Throughout, McCurdy pursues further the differences, as they appeared in these debates, between concepts of positive and of negative liberty—and what their respective premises indicated as a prescription for the law of labor relations and for social legislation—on the lines also set forth in the discussion in chapter 5. Finally, he provides an analysis of the Supreme Court's reversal of course in the 1930s, and rejection of the *Lochner* doctrinal heritage, underlining the Court's unwillingness to do more (doctrinally) than extend the terms of the police power, even when explicitly recognizing inequality of bargaining power as a marketplace reality. The Court did not accept the arguments for founding a doctrine of rights upon evidence of inequality, instead first pursuing an accommodationist course and then, finally, altogether "bow[ing] out of the controversy over freedom of contract and the state," leaving the issue of police power largely to the discretion of the legislature.

In chapter 7, Arthur McEvoy interweaves the history of American labor law, in relation to concepts of economic liberty, with the materials in John Orth's analysis of English development and with McCurdy's analysis of the debates that finally centered on the Lochner doctrine and its heritage. How far, McEvoy asks, did the realm of contract as an instrument for ordering employment relations actually extend in the course of American history? He sharpens and focuses the inquiry by identifying three spheres, or "social spaces," in which state power was exercised. One was "the public realm," the labor market in which wage relationships prevailed and which was the arena for collective labor action and the drama of industrial conflict. A second was the workplace itself, a separate realm, in which law operated on a continuing basis built on the initial contractual agreement; and the third was "the private realm of families, slave plantations, and other relationships," in which law operated on different premises. In the third, McEvoy argues, hierarchy, often oppressive and disempowering, was given broad discretion. The ideology of free labor and the paradox of unequal bargaining power are here too central themes. McCurdy stresses in his analysis the failure to assert or maintain a controlling judicial role in dealing with problems of inequality; McEvoy places the principal emphasis upon the difficulties that flowed from the voluntarist tactics adopted by the labor unions at a critical juncture in the history of industrial relations.

Although the relations of capital and labor in American economic and legal development hold the front-stage position when freedom of contract history is considered in the narrower sense, in the larger history of economic liberty in America there is no subject more significant than the question of natural resources and how they have been used. In chapter 8, Donald Pisani offers an interpretation of how public policy, including both privatization of resources and their regulation and conservation, reflects the ideology of individualism and the competing demands of collective rights and needs. "The state and the legal system worked hard to transform nature into marketable property," he argues; but just as the proponents of a notion of "social justice," challenging unfettered economic individualism, launched an attack on freedom of contract ideology in labor relations, so did proponents of resource conservation and a rationalized governmental control of resources challenge the ideals of privatism in the area of resource policy—and, by extension, launch a broadside attack on the "sacredness" of property rights. Here again, we find that the evidences of inequality of market power as a social reality were strikingly at odds with the premises of law and policy; but reform demands ran up against the rigidities of inherited doctrine and attitudes. A significant element in Pisani's depiction of the historical dynamics of policy debate regarding economic-development goals and collective values—an element that is not found so prominently in other areas of law, at least as considered in this book, but which is of vital importance to the confrontations over how to dispose of or otherwise manage resources—is the role of science.

More recently, as is shown in the final section of the chapter, there has also entered into the debates over environmental policy a philosophical controversy that centers on the claims of the ecosystem itself. These claims for ecosystem protection are posed against legal doctrines of resource use that are anthropocentric in their character, expressive of an individualism (aggressive or otherwise) that values economic uses and utilitarian ends. The problem, as Pisani poses it for the modern legal system in dealing with resources, is, thus, the novelty of the demands that "individual rights, public rights, and the rights of nature" all be accommodated—a vastly different challenge to the law than, for example, the accommodation of will theory in the nineteenth century or the confrontation of social welfare values and freedom of contract.

In our closing chapter, Martin Shapiro carries forward into the contemporary period many of the historical themes in the previous chapters. The "globalization" of business that has weakened both national sovereignty and the effectiveness of domestic regulatory laws in the industrial countries—as first the multinational corporations and then, with accelerating speed, the succession of innovations in electronic communication have transformed the basic conditions of business relationships—means that contract must be reconsidered in the new institutional context. Referring to the continuing tension in contract law history, "between a norm of contract as signifying the free will of the parties and a norm of contract as achieving a just, fair or equitable exchange"—the central subject of Gordley's discussion in chapter 3—Shapiro argues that this tension is evident in the new globalization context as well. There is multiplication and complexity, as various international conventions, model codes, and the like offer varied options to national governments in restructuring the substance of contract law to meet emerging necessities.

Shapiro rests much of his analysis, however, on how lawyers actually function, arguing that American practice and forms are coming to a position of dominance. He asserts an argument from the stance of Legal Realism, contending that "whatever the law written by legislatures, judges, and lawyers, actual business practices will be the principal source of contract law." One of the most interesting features of emergent contract law in the international arena is the regulatory thrust, which, as Shapiro argues, belies the rhetoric of deregulation. "There is more global freedom to contract in the sense of practices, rules, and institutions to facilitate contracting," he writes, for many barriers have come down, as government extends freedom by sufferance; but international business is also "constrained by a global growth in regulation." With probes in depth as to how contractual freedom has been manifest in particular sectors, for example the intellectual property area, Shapiro illustrates a remarkable degree of flux with respect to both institutions and rules.

Clearly in the world markets of the present day we are witnessing a sea change in social and economic organization at least as great as what was experienced when freedom of contract emerged in its classic form in the nineteenth century. Will the ideological and political confrontations that followed when freedom of contract ideals became entrenched, and the source of resistance to reformist ideas for ameliorating social ills based on inequality, in some form be repeated in the wake of the new globalization? That is a question well worth pondering in the light of the historic development of economic liberty as explored in the pages that follow.

< 1 >

Land Ownership and Economic Freedom

A. W. B. SIMPSON

THE SUBJECT OF THIS CHAPTER—the common law of landholding and its relationship to the idea of economic freedom—is a
very large one. Inevitably therefore I shall have to be very selective
as to subject matter, to gloss over various matters which are controversial, and to indulge in some fairly broad generalizations. I
shall not have much to say about its migration to the United
States, and to various other parts of the globe—Canada, Australia,
New Zealand, for example. Instead I propose to concentrate my attention on the common law as it developed in England.[1] It was
there that its basic conceptual structure was developed; and because land was the principal form of wealth and source of power,
this conceptual structure developed early. Much of the modern
language of property law would be immediately intelligible to
Thomas Littleton,[2] whose treatise on the subject, known as *The
New Tenures*, was written in about 1460 or so, and first printed in
about 1482.[3] Few of the categories and conceptions in use today are
later in origin than the seventeenth century, and virtually none
later than the early nineteenth. So it is that in the United States a
modern law school course on property law will involve discussion
of the effect of the Statute of *Quia Emptores Terrarum* of 1290, and
of the effect of the Statute of Uses of 1536.[4]

< I >

The Complexity of the Categories of the Land Law

The common law of property is both very complex and very malleable. A body of law which evolved in the medieval and early modern period has been able to work reasonably satisfactorily in modern industrial and postindustrial societies, as well as in agricultural

worlds where conditions more closely resemble those in which its basic ideas were evolved. It speaks in the language of the medieval world; it is used to respond to contemporary needs and pressures. Indeed no branch of the law better illustrates Holmes's claim that "The substance of the law at any given time pretty nearly corresponds, as far as it goes, with what is then understood to be convenient; but its form and machinery, and the degree to which it is able to work out desired results, depend very much upon its past."[5] Its complexity derives from two of its most striking features. One is its elaborate calculus of estates and future interests, and the other is its association with an institutionalized division between legal and equitable interests, which makes possible the trust. Its malleability is in its turn the consequence of the elaborate doctrine of estates and the recognition of the trust.

The simplest and most immediately intelligible conception of ownership in Western thought starts from the picture of one single person owning one single thing—"This is my book" or whatever.[6] The significance of such a statement does not differ very much if made in France, or Greece, or the United States. The owner will be treated by the law as having a special relationship with the thing which entails, or may even be thought to consist in, certain legal consequences. One will be a general right to exclude other persons from the physical control over the thing. This right, which has the consequence of maximizing the freedom of choice of the owner, may be protected with various intensities by civil law remedies and criminal procedures, as well as being generally accepted in the morality of the society.[7]

In the common law system it came to be recognized that ownership of land could be split up or divided between a number of different persons. Such division could be, for example, the result of two or more people in some way sharing ownership—husband and wife could be co-owners of a farm. Further to this the common law came to permit ownership to be split up so that a number of persons acquired rights to possession of the property successively. Thus a farm might be entitled to one person for his life, then to his widow for her life if there was a widow, and then to someone else absolutely. In situations of successive or split ownership of this kind it is somewhat puzzling to relate the situation to the paradigm of individual ownership. A familiar contemporary example is a commercial seven-year lease of shop property; shall we say the landlord owns the shop, or the tenant? Or is it more intelligible to say that neither owns? Or that the landlord owns the freehold, and the tenant the lease?

The common lawyers developed an elaborate analysis of successive split ownership. They classified the interests created by reference to their possible duration in time, and called them "estates." As it was put in *Walsingham's Case* (1573), "An estate in the land is a time on the land, or land for a time."[8] The biggest interest, the "fee simple," could last forever, for it was inheritable by both lineal and collateral heirs, and nobody dies without one or the other.[9] The next largest was the entailed interest, which descended only to lineal heirs, and so could end if the blood line failed.[10] Lesser still was the life estate.[11] One parcel of land might merely be owned by a fee simple owner; one person owning one thing. Or ownership could be split between a number of life tenants ("to A for life, then to B for life, then to C for life"), followed by as many entails as you wished (to my eldest son in tail, then to my second son in tail, and so on), with a fee simple owner at the end of the line in case all the entails ran out ("then to X in fee simple").

These interests, the "estates," were viewed as co-existing in the one piece of land, with a ranked order in which they gave a right to possession. Further complexities arose when the law came to recognize estates which might come into existence only in the future—to A in fee simple, but if A marries, to B in fee simple. The very elaborate doctrines regulating how successive split ownership interests could be created, transferred, and manipulated made it possible for property owners to establish elaborate regimes to govern the future enjoyment of property. They could, by using the complexity of the law, construct legal regimes whose existence would have been impossible in a more simple system. Today the most obvious illustration of the utility of split ownership is the landlord-tenant relationship. The elaborate doctrine of estates enhanced the dispositive power of landowners.

In the late medieval period the practice arose of transferring ownership in landed property to persons we would now call trustees,[12] who were instructed to hold the property for the benefit of someone else. A simple example would be the transfer of a landed estate by a landowner to three friends, on the understanding that they were to manage the property during the infancy of the land-owner's eldest son, and then perhaps transfer it to him absolutely when he attained majority. What was involved was a deliberate separation of powers of management and control, which were enjoyed by the trustees, to whom the legal ownership had been given, from the right to enjoy the benefit of the property—to live on it, or enjoy the income from it. In the common law system the rights of the trustees were protected in the courts of the common law.[13] A distinct institution, the Court of Chancery, protected the rights of the beneficiaries by imposing sanctions on trustees who did not perform their trust. The institution of the trust involves another form of split ownership—ownership which in the simplest case is united in one person, is split between trustees and beneficiaries. Lawyers say that the trustees have the "legal" ownership, and the beneficiaries the "equitable" ownership, because the jurisprudence of the Court of Chancery came to be called "equity."

The continued popularity of the trust, an invention of the late fourteenth and fifteenth centuries, reflects the flexibility it confers upon owners of property. In combination with the doctrine of estates it facilitates, for example, elaborate schemes for the dedication of property to public and charitable purposes, or to family maintenance and support. So far as the world of commerce and the market is concerned the primary interests traded are, and always were, the fee simple and the lease. The complexities of the doctrine of estates, and those of the trust, belong not to the world of buying and selling, but to the world of giving and receiving. Nobody buys, or ever has bought, life estates or entails except in very peculiar circumstances, nor are trusts in general the product of the market. It is true that family interests and trusts associated with family arrangements could be the product of the bargaining which preceded aristocratic marriages, but to assimilate such bargains to those of the commercial market involves a perverse refusal to attend to the wholly distinct social significance of different forms of exchange and reciprocity. This point seems to have been conclusively demonstrated by J. Davis.[14]

≺ II ≻

Blackstone's Despotic Dominion

Given the complex land law which I have outlined we need to have some basic notion of what would count as an ideal state of economic freedom in relation to landownership. I doubt if one could do better than start from a well-known passage from the mid-eighteenth century *Commentaries* of Sir William Blackstone: "There is nothing which so generally strikes the imagination, and engages the affections of mankind, as the right of property; or that sole and despotic dominion which one man claims and exercises over the external things of the world in total exclusion of the right of any other individual in the universe."[15] That certainly does sound like an account of total economic freedom in relation to landownership. For Blackstone it is clear that the paradigm case of despotic dominion is of one individual owning one thing. He is thinking of the central case which is analyzed in Honoré's discussion of ownership "the person who has the greatest interest in a thing admitted by a mature legal system."[16]

In technical legal terms he is talking about the legal position of the "tenant in fee simple absolute in possession." Economic freedom consists in being able to do exactly as you like with your own. Blackstone's conception of property is intensely individualistic, and the picture he presents is of a world in which most possible objects of property are owned by somebody or other. He acknowledged, however, that "there are some few things, which notwithstanding the general introduction and continuance of property, must still unavoidably remain in common." The examples he gave were light, air and water, and wild animals.[17] He also said that there were "other things, in which a permanent property *may* subsist, not only as to the temporary use, but also the solid substance; and which yet would be frequently found without a proprietor, had not the wisdom of the law provided a remedy to obviate this inconvenience." The remedy was to vest property in the sovereign, or his representative, and the examples given are forests and waste grounds,[18] wrecks,[19] estrays,[20] and game.[21] But in Blackstone's scheme of thought these are exceptional cases.

Systems of property law can exist in which individual ownership of land is simply not a possibility. Land, as a Nigerian chief said early this century when describing the basic assumption of his system of customary law, can even be owned by "a vast family of which many are dead, few are living, and countless numbers are yet unborn."[22] In West Africa in Ashanti customary law land is owned by the dead.[23] But for Blackstone the paradigm case of despotic dominion is that of one individual, not that of a number of individuals, or of a group or community, owning one thing. Indeed apart from cases of co-ownership by individuals, his statement that some things might remain "in common" is not a reference to communal ownership at all; it means no more than that they are not owned by anybody.

The dominance of this paradigm in common law legal thought, and indeed Western legal thought generally, is in some ways somewhat surprising. Feudal society involved complex structures of tenure. At the bottom of the structure there would typically be a peasant farmer, Pybus, holding property from the lord of the manor, Robert, in return for agricultural services or some form of quit rent; Robert in his turn might hold from a superior, Hugo, in return for military service, perhaps the provision of a knight; and Hugo in turn might hold from one of the great tenants in chief, Rannulf, who held directly of the Crown, owing the service of a number of knights. The picture can easily become much more complex if some of these persons hold mere life interests or entails; a very large number of individuals commonly possessed rights of one kind or another in the same land. The idea of attributing ownership to them as a group could well have emerged in legal thought. Instead the situation was analyzed in terms of persons all having individual interests in different individual things. The law of tenure described the intricate relations between the lords and the tenants, and the law of estates the various property interests enjoyed either in the land itself, or in the lordship over it. The subject of ownership could be in a straightforward way land itself, or it might be an abstract entity, a seignory or lordship.

Again the manorial economy with its scattered landholdings, cooperative system of agriculture, communally exercised rights over uncultivated or fallow lands, and even shared farm stock, together with its elaborate structure of customary mutual obligation, could only be fitted to a paradigm of individual ownership by the exercise of considerable ingenuity.[24] Equally striking is the treatment of family rights in land. In the landowning classes family lands were, in a moral sense, conceived of as being the patrimony of the family, ideally at least a permanent institution. From the seventeenth century until recent times much family land was held for successive interests under elaborate settlements. The current patriarch had a life estate in the property; his eldest son and other children were given successive entails. The aim was to pass the complete estate as a unit down the family line, ideally to a succession of males. The settlement would also make provision for the maintenance of the patriarch's widow, if his wife survived him, and for the payment of capital sums of money to younger children who were never going to succeed to the family estate itself. Thus the family land was employed as a patrimony for the whole family, in which individuals performed distinct roles. Such settlements were commonly recreated each generation, with the consequence that the property passed down a succession of life tenants. In substance what was involved was family ownership with limited management control in the current male head of the family. But the legal analysis of the arrangements made to endow and perpetuate families always contrived to describe them in terms of individual family members, some existing, some unborn, as each entitled to own discrete things—life estates, contingent remainders, entails, or whatever.[25] Indeed much of the complexity of the conceptual structure of the land law is a product of the difficulty in expressing forms of communal enjoyment in terms of a paradigm of individual ownership.

Blackstone's despotic dominion is, if you like, not simply an individualistic, but also in a sense a selfish one; it does not lay any emphasis upon the relations between individuals in society, or upon a scheme of mutual obligation directed towards the furtherance of public welfare. Not surprisingly its origin was thought to be found in the right of occupancy: "every man seising to his own continued use such spots of ground as he found most agreeable to his own convenience, provided he found them unoccupied by any one else."[26] In terms of the technical categories of the land law Blackstone, as we have seen, had in mind the position enjoyed by the central case of a land owner in the common law—the tenant in fee simple. Such a person enjoys the largest interest in land which the common law legal system recognizes as capable of existence.

As Littleton put it back in the fifteenth century: "Tenant in fee simple is he that hath lands and tenements to hold to him and his heirs for ever. And note, that a man cannot have a more large or great estate than fee simple."[27] In the passage in which he discusses the law relating to the fee simple, which comes later than the celebrated passage on despotic dominion, Blackstone lays no particular emphasis on the powers of enjoyment of the tenant in fee simple, but only upon its permanence in time, which was its defining legal characteristic.[28] I suspect this was because he simply took it for granted that a fee simple owner had so extensive a right over his property. Furthermore he had, in his discussion of the absolute right of property, stated that it consisted in "the free use, enjoyment and disposal of all his acquisitions."[29] Technically the wide power of a tenant in fee simple derived from the fact that such tenants were not liable, as were holders of life estates or lesser interests, for waste; in economic terms absence of liability for waste amounts to the same thing as being entitled to the capital value of the land, in contrast to the mere income.[30] They had therefore a largely unfettered right to exploit the capital value of the land, even if this dramatically reduced its future value—for example they could open and work out mines.

< III >

Feudalism, the Fee Simple, and the Right of Alienation

The preeminent legal position of such a tenant in fee simple was the product of a long process of legal development; the details of the process are somewhat controversial.[31] The common law of landholding originated back in the eleventh and twelfth centuries as the law of an aristocratic military elite, established in England after the Norman conquest of 1066. The system of social organization which underlay it has come to be called feudalism.[32]

A simple account of feudalism goes something like this— though it must come with the warning that the correspondence between ideal pictures of feudal society, and untidy reality, is problematical. In feudal society landholding was an aspect of a personal relationship between lord and vassal. Under this the vassal owed fidelity and service to his lord, and the lord in his turn owed protection to his vassal. The relationship originated in contract, and although it came in the end to acquire a permanent character, the rights and obligations of lord and vassal becoming heritable, it was long the case that renewal was required when one or the other party died. Grants of land provided the vassal with an economic competence which enabled the vassal both to perform the service and to enjoy a tolerable standard of living once the cost of providing the service was deducted. Thus a military tenant might owe the service of providing five knights to his lord; given the price of armor and war horses he needed considerable wealth to enable the service to be performed. But his landholding would be ample to cover the cost and leave wealth over. It was all very like Chicago in the days of Al Capone, when Capone's henchmen were installed in various profitable enterprises in return for an obligation to rub out rivals whenever instructed to do so. In return Al Capone provided them with various forms of protection—bribing the police, organizing the extermination of rivals, and resolving disputes over territories and the like.

Given this simple model of the basic feudal relationship, the whole of the landholding of society is organized in an elaborate pyramidical structure. At the top is the king as supreme lord. Below him are his great supporters, his tenants-in-chief. At the bottom are the peasants, and in between there is a complex hierarchy of lords and tenants. Wealth, ultimately derived from agriculture, passes upward to be consumed. At the higher levels the great lords, the tenants-in-chief of the king, are left with abundant wealth after performance of their services; at the bottom the miserable peasants keep just enough to live on. Essentially a parasitic system, it conforms to the rule that parasites must never destroy their hosts, and here the hosts are the working peasants.

In this world, particularly at the higher levels, the relationship between lord and vassal is no mere formality. It is sealed by the solemn ceremony of homage, and entitlement to hold land was originally thought to endure only so long as this relationship subsists. The rights of a landowner may also have been conceived of as rights against his lord and his lord's other tenants, rather than rights against the world generally, which is how we now regard property rights. Early feudal holdings were probably for life only, though there could well have been customary expectations that sons should succeed fathers, and that the successor to a lord would renew existing relationships. But fairly soon, probably during the twelfth century, this changed, and the vassals' rights increased at the expense of their lords.[33] Well before 1290, the date of the Statute of *Quia Emptores Terrarum* (because purchasers of land), which in effect merely recognized changes which had already occurred, what may be called the standard feudal holding, the "fee simple" or "fee pure," had come to be inheritable as of right. The scheme of inheritance allowed both lineal heirs and, in the absence of lineal heirs, collateral heirs to succeed. There were no limits to the remoteness of relationship which could found a claim. In consequence the fee was of indefinite and potentially unending duration. In terms of the analysis of interests in land by time it was the greatest interest.

The fee simple had also become freely alienable. Insofar as the early feudal world resembled Al Capone's Chicago, alienation, if it involved substituting one henchman for another, would obviously require Capone's consent. When landholding involves important mutual social relationships between lord and tenant there cannot be a free right in a tenant to substitute a new tenant without his lord's consent. But *Quia Emptores Terrarum* permitted and indeed required such substitution, and deprived lords of any power to prevent it.[34] So the Statute reflects a movement from a world of personal relationship related to landholding to a world of landownership in which such personal relationships no longer predominate. Lords, as a class, have lost power in favor of tenants.

Freedom of alienation also transferred power away from family and kin. For freedom to alienate the fee simple meant that a landowner could, by alienation, prevent those who might otherwise have inherited from ever coming into possession of the land. Freedom of alienation sacrifices family to the individual power of the current head of the family, normally a male.[35] Originally the power of alienation was only exercisable *inter vivos* (between the living). But in the later medieval period a power to dispose of land by will was evolved, though this testamentary power only came to be fully recognized in the seventeenth century.[36] Certain family limitations over the effects of free alienation, in particular the widow's right to dower, came to be easily bypassed, and by Blackstone's time the tenant in fee simple enjoyed a virtually uncontrolled power of free disposition, exercisable either by conveyance *inter vivos*, or by will. This freedom of alienating the fee simple was bolstered by a variety of technical doctrines—for example attempts to attach provisions in restraint of the alienation of a fee simple were legally void.

When Blackstone wrote his lyrical account of "despotic dominion" the right of free alienation was an important aspect of that dominion. In economic terms the fee simple was freely marketable and, because of its indefinite duration, it could be marketed for the full economic value of the land, the present price of which would embody capitalization of the future income stream ad infinitum. Powers of feudal superiors to control alienation had long since vanished, but the claims of family and kin remained very powerful. As a matter of law these claims carried no weight, and thus imposed no restriction at all on marketability. A tenant in fee simple could sell his land, spend the money in drink and dissipation, leave what was left to his mistress, and die in the knowledge that his children would be penniless. His power was indeed despotic. But the claims of family and kin had by no means passed away; they were preserved on a different plane as moral and social claims, exercising a powerful influence upon the ways in which despotic dominion was in practice exercised. The moral obligations to family and kin were dischargeable by gifts; gifts are of course often compulsory, but the compulsion is not legal.

One other development had significantly affected the economic position of the tenant in fee simple. In the early medieval world land was held by freemen (and freewomen) in return for services of one kind or another—military, spiritual, or agricultural in nature.[37] They performed services appropriate for free persons—their tenures were called freehold tenures. These services might be nominal, or onerous and substantial, and over the course of time they had tended to decline in significance, as a world ordered by contract replaced a world ordered by tenure. Many services were commuted into quit rents, which with inflation ceased to be worth collecting, or became impracticable to collect because of the complexities produced by subinfeudation and problems of proof.

Another product of the tenurial system was the liability of the tenant to occasional payments, called incidents. Feudalism thus, as we have seen, involved a form of parasitism in which wealth derived from the exploitation of land passed up a hierarchy to pay for war, the Church, and various forms of conspicuous expenditure by the upper orders. By Blackstone's time services and most incidents of tenure, so far as they had affected freeholders—Blackstone calls them "feodal clogs"—had long gone. Blackstone portrays their original imposition as an aspect of the oppressive violation of the old constitution of Anglo-Saxon British liberty imposed by the Normans, and progressively lightened so as to restore that liberty.[38] The more important feudal impositions had been done away with in the seventeenth century with the end of the military tenures, finally achieved by the Statute of Tenures of 1660. In the case of freeholders feudal obligations had ceased to expropriate wealth in favor of feudal lords, so that a freehold tenant in fee simple was entitled to the whole economic value of the property except insofar as some part of this was taken from him by Parliament-controlled taxation. The only consequence of freehold tenure, occasional survivals apart, was conceptual.

Blackstone continued to maintain, in a tortured passage, that even the tenant in fee simple did not enjoy the "ultimate property," but only a "feodal or qualified" property. "It is a man's demesne, *dominicum*, or property, since it belongs to him and his heirs for ever: yet this *dominicum*, property, or demesne, is strictly not absolute or allodial, but qualified or feodal: it is his demesne, *as of fee*; that is, it is not purely or simply his own, since it is held of a superior lord, in whom the ultimate property resides."[39] Considerable quantities of land in Blackstone's time were held, however, not by freehold tenure but by copyhold tenure. Copyhold was the name which had become attached to what had once been the tenure of unfree peasants—villeins. Although the unfree status had long vanished, and copyholders were fully protected landholders, economically significant rights still remained in the manorial lords from whom such tenants held. In the course of the eighteenth and nineteenth centuries copyhold tenure was progressively abolished, and what little was left went finally in 1926, though some of the lord's rights were preserved, for example sporting rights.[40] Though the tenure has gone, some such "feodal clogs" remain in England and Wales to this day; except in very rare instances no such clogs exist in overseas jurisdictions which have received the common law of landholding.

<< IV >>

Despotic Dominion, the Public Interest, and
the Protection of Neighbors

The fact that the landowner was legally entitled to alienate, either commercially, or by way of gift, without regard for family or kin, was one aspect of Blackstone's "despotic dominion." In the passage I have quoted he stressed a second aspect—the right of the land-owner to neglect the claims of the public interest in an entirely selfish way in his choice of land use. The example Blackstone gives is this:

> So great moreover is the regard of the law for private property, that it will not authorize the least violation of it; no, not for the general good of the whole community. If a new road, for instance, were to be made through the grounds of a private person, it might be extensively beneficial to the public; but the law permits no man, or set of men, to do this without the consent of the owner of the land. In vain may it be urged that the good of the individual ought to yield to that of the community; for it would be dangerous to allow any private person, or even any public tribunal, to be the judge of this common good, and to decide whether it be expedient or not.[41]

Blackstone, writing before the invention of the hidden hand, goes on, in a somewhat desperate passage, to argue that in the long run there is really no conflict between the view taken by the law and the promotion of the public interest: "Besides, the public good is in nothing more essentially interested, than in the protection of every individual's private rights, as modelled by the municipal law." He does not in this part of his *Commentaries* discuss either the regulatory controls which existed in his time, particularly in cities, though they amounted to little, nor the restraints imposed through the law of both public and private nuisance. Both regulatory law and the law of nuisance imposed curbs on the despotic dominion of the landowner. But nuisance law in Blackstone's time was not very developed, and even in the nineteenth century, when attempts were made from time to time to make use of it in egregious cases, it had little practical significance.[42] In any event its existence could be reconciled with the individual's "despotic dominion" as essentially protective of it. The rights of landowners as a class to do as they wished with their own property could be maintained only if the law took a firm line in restricting the degree to which the effects of the activities of individual landowners could be allowed to cross boundaries and impede the activities pursued by neighbors. Where a person or physical object crossed a boundary there was liability in the tort of trespass; where the problem was smell or noise there was a remedy in nuisance. Nuisance law was rationalized around the maxim *sic utere tuo ut alienam non laedas* (so use your own that you do not harm another), and despotic dominion was not, in general, thought to entail the right to use property to cause harm to neighbors.[43]

Blackstone's account of the law of private nuisance does not present the law as being restrictive of the rights of landowners at all; the law instead is treated as protecting landowners against invasion of their rights. This is brought out in his account of interference with light:

If a man builds a house so close to mine that his roof overhangs my roof, and throws the water off his roof onto mine, this is a nuisance, for which an action will lie. Likewise to erect a house or other building so near to mine, that it stops up my antient lights and windows, is a nuisance of a similar nature. But in this case it is necessary that the windows be *antient*, that is, have subsisted time out of mind; otherwise there is no injury done. For he hath as much right to build a new edifice upon his ground, as I have upon mine; since every man may do as he pleases upon the upright or perpendicular of his own soil; and it was his folly to build so near another's ground.[44]

The miscellaneous forms of public or common nuisances which Blackstone lists illustrate the general conception, which is that "*Common nusances* are a species of offences against the public order and oecenommical regime of the state; being either the doing of a thing to the annoyance of all the king's subjects, or the neglecting to do a thing which the common good requires."[45] They are again not presented as restrictive of property rights, any more than are other criminal offences.

The broad reality of the matter was that in Blackstone's time law imposed very little restraint on the economic freedom of a fee simple landowner to develop or not develop his land exactly as he wished, or to use it at pleasure. The principal restrictions were imposed by other property rights—for example by the existence of easements or profits, or by a very limited number of public rights of one kind or another.

≺ V ≻

Social Cost in Nineteenth-Century Law

This continued to be the state of affairs in the nineteenth century, though there was a progressive increase in regulatory control, mainly associated with the problems generated by urbanization.[46] There was, however, a school of thought in legal circles which played with the idea that the rights of landowners ought, to some extent at least, to be curbed by the common law itself in the public interest.[47] It was possible to point to situations where this was indeed the established position. Thus there existed a prerogative power to enter land for purposes of national defense.[48] Another curious example concerns lighthouses:

The King, being entrusted with the safety of navigation, possesses also by the common law, the prerogative right of erecting beacons and lighthouses . . . this right is considered so important to the public weal, that it will justify his Majesty in erecting a beacon on the land of a subject without his consent.[49]

The issue arose in a curious way in the great case of *Tipping v. St. Helen's Smelting Co.*, decided finally by the House of Lords in 1865.[50] Did a landowner simply have to tolerate, in the interests of economic development, serious industrial pollution from an enterprise located in an industrial area, and managed in the normal way for such an enterprise; or could he sue for damages or seek an injunction to abate the nuisance? This case arose because a copper smelting plant, situated in the heavily polluted industrial area of St. Helen's, was causing serious damage to a gentleman's residence and its associated farm lands, which lay just outside the expanding industrial areas. At this time there was no commercially practicable way of smelting copper ore on a large scale without causing serious pollution. The courts were presented with a clear opportunity to say that the "despotic dominion" of the landowner—here protected by a suit for nuisance—must give way to the needs of the community, which were furthered by industry. They refused to do so.

Later in the nineteenth century there arose in litigation a further opportunity for the courts to express a view as to whether there was a power to police the economic freedom of landowners on ethical grounds. The issue, which was perhaps more of theoretical than practical interest, was the problem posed by the malicious exercise of legal rights by a property owner. It excited the attention of legal scholars on both sides of the Atlantic. Holmes discussed it in his *The Common Law* (1881)[51] and again in a later article in the *Harvard Law Review* in 1894,[52] and Sir Frederic Pollock featured the issue in his treatise on the law of torts.[53] J. B. Ames also found the matter fascinating.[54] How far would the courts go in upholding the freedom of the landowner to do what he wished with his property even if he was acting entirely with a malicious motive? The standard example is that of the landowner who builds a spite fence with no other motive except that of spoiling his neighbor's view. The old case which possibly dealt with the matter was *Keeble v. Hickeringill* (1707),[55] but it was never very clear what this case, which involved interference with a duck decoy, actually did decide.

The issue could arise in various contexts—for example in connection with the abstraction of underground water, and this is how it arose in the case of *Mayor of Bradford v. Pickles*, which eventually reached the House of Lords in 1895.[56] The Bradford Waterworks Company had built a reservoir, known as the Hewenden Reservoir, west of the city. The supply of water to this reservoir came partly from two streams, and partly from a spring on the lands of the company. This spring derived its supply from underground sources under land to the west of the reservoir, the water accumulating underground between two fault lines. These lands were owned by Mr. Pickles. He engaged in an expensive and elaborate scheme for draining this water from beneath his land, and returning it to the valley below the reservoir, where it was of no use as a source for the water company. He engaged engineers and miners to construct a five-hundred-yard underground drainage tunnel. His story was that his only aim was to rid his land of subterranean water so that he could more easily excavate stone from under his land. Nobody believed this story. The Mayor and Corporation of Bradford, which had succeeded to the rights of the water company, sought an injunction to stop him from engaging in what they regarded as a form of blackmail, intended to force them to buy his land at a grossly inflated price. One argument used was that in setting out to drain the water, and deprive the Corporation of it, Mr.

Pickles was acting "maliciously." He was malicious because he was not seeking the benefit of dry land for himself, but merely seeking to threaten harm to the Corporation, and thereby coerce them to buy his land at an excessive price.

The decision of the House of Lords and the lower courts treated the question of motive as wholly irrelevant. All that was involved was a matter of property rights. It was settled law that a landowner was entitled to abstract subterranean water and to do whatever he wished with it. The Corporation had no right to the water until it emerged on their land; a landowner under English law had no right to receive the flow of underground water unless it was within a defined channel.[57] Even if Mr. Pickles was in some sense acting with a malicious motive—and it was not clear that he was malicious in trying to enhance the value of his land—this was wholly irrelevant.

In Blackstone's time, and to an increasing degree in the late eighteenth and early nineteenth centuries, another development to which he did not call attention greatly enhanced the individual power of landowners. This was the enclosure movement.[58] Enclosures abolished the communal system of agriculture which had long existed in much of lowland Britain; they reorganized scattered landholdings into discrete individual farms and enclosed and allocated former common land. This process of enclosures hugely reduced the significance of the elaborate structure of customary and prescriptive obligations which had survived from a time when agriculture had been essentially a group activity. It is true that many servitudes and customary rights and obligations survived in village communities; and in some parts of the country, for example the Lake District, the economic exploitation of marginal unenclosed land through sheep farming remains important. But in general, given the new organization of the farming world, the individual landowner was able to go his own way to a much greater degree than was possible under earlier arrangements. Individual decision replaced group decision. Each fee simple landowner became monarch of his own distinct territory, and within very loose bounds could do exactly what he wanted with his own.

≺ VI ≻

Sacrificing Property Rights for Economic Development

The autonomy of individual property owners inevitably causes problems in situations in which economic development can only take place through cooperation between a number of owners. The simplest illustration is the construction of a lengthy railway; the line can be changed to accommodate some cases of holdout, but in a practical sense a single landowner can either prevent the railway being built at all, or hugely increase the costs.

The reaction to this problem was the one really significant restriction upon the despotic dominion of landowners which was imposed by law in Blackstone's time. By what were known as Local and Personal Acts of Parliament, groups of landowners, or entrepreneurs, could come together and devise a scheme for land enclosure, canal or railway building, or whatever, and seek parliamentary approval for the scheme, embodied in legislation. Huge numbers of these acts were passed in the eighteenth and nineteenth centuries; they were the typical legal instrument of both the agricultural and industrial revolutions.[59] They were used for schemes to build tramways; tunnels; water, gas, and later electrical utilities; docks and harbors; burial grounds; turnpike roads; and improvements in the navigability of rivers. Local and Personal Acts were not simply used by private individuals. In the nineteenth century in particular they were also widely used by public bodies, such as municipal councils, to authorize schemes of town improvement, such as relocation of roads, or the provision of modern sewerage. Their force depended upon the doctrine of parliamentary sovereignty, according to which there were, in Blackstone's time and thereafter, no limits whatsoever of an enforceable legal character upon the powers of Parliament.

Much economic development could of course take place simply by the exercise of the landowner's right to do as he wished with his own property. Building a factory, for example, did not require the acquisition of special powers; the entrepreneur simply bought a site and built a factory. Where operation through the private market was difficult the use of a special act was the norm. I have given the example of a railway, but for the eighteenth century the typical example would be a scheme of agricultural enclosure; such

schemes tended to be attractive to the larger landowners and unat-
tractive to smaller proprietors, so that agreement was commonly
very difficult to achieve.

Special acts had two principal attractions. One was that they
overrode private property rights—for example, in the case of railways, by securing powers of entry on land for survey, and powers of
compulsory acquisition of land for construction. The other was
that they enabled entrepreneurs to secure conditions of partial monopoly, together with what amounted to powers of taxation. The
price paid in return was normally some degree of regulation of the
enterprise imposed in the public interest. For example a railway
might be bound to accept custom from the public, or a water utility
have its water rates regulated.

Blackstone was of course very familiar with the use of such acts
and makes the point that it was the settled practice to compensate
landowners for consequential loss of their rights. In discussing absolute right of property he went on:

> the legislature alone can, and frequently does, interpose, and compel the
> individual to acquiesce. But how does it interpose and compel? Not by ab-
> solutely stripping the subject of his property in an arbitrary manner; but
> by giving him full indemnification and equivalent for the injury thereby
> sustained. The public is now considered as an individual, treating with an
> individual for an exchange. All that the legislature does is to oblige the
> owner to alienate his possessions for a reasonable price; and even this is
> an exertion of power, which the legislature indulges with caution, and
> which nothing but the legislature can perform.[60]

In enclosure schemes the compensation took the form of the provision of land, supposedly the equivalent for land, and land rights,
lost; in fact some such newly enclosed land was of such poor quality that it degenerated into waste again; examples can still be seen,
for example in the villages around Otmoor near Oxford, where an
enclosure scheme produced serious rural rioting. Otherwise, for
projects other than enclosures, compensation was in money, and
often on a generous scale.[61] And insofar as the scheme caused loss
to persons outside the scope of the right to compensation, this was
rationalized by the theory that they, as members of the public, received implicit compensation.

Where do such Local and Personal Acts fit into a view of landownership and economic freedom? Their use, which as I have said

was very extensive, seems to me at least to reflect the belief that rapid economic development is not compatible with too strong respect for the individual autonomy of the landowner. The same point may be put slightly differently by saying that the public good which, it is hoped, will be generated by the construction of railways, lighthouses, or whatever, is unlikely to be produced in all situations by leaving matters to private property rights, the market, and individual self-interest. The hidden hand seems here to need a little help from the State.

I suppose another way of looking at the use of Local and Personal Acts is to see them as a mechanism whereby the profit motive was harnessed to the production of public goods. The Stockton and Darlington Railway was a notable product of the entrepreneurial spirit, for it was the first railway to be open to public use. In public nuisance litigation concerning it (*R. v. Pease*, 1832), the lawyer J. F. Pollock said: "The enterprise in this case is private: but it is one in which the public are largely interested. Like Waterloo Bridge, or the London Docks, it has a mixed object; profit for the adventurers, and public benefit."[62] In a sense the legal system enhanced the positive economic freedom of entrepreneurs at the cost of diminishing the negative freedom of individual property owners.

≺ VII ≻

The Fee Simple and the Land Market

In the common law world, land has been being bought and sold for a very long time, and in this sense there has always been a land market. But we need to be cautious in applying the conception of a market to land. In its simplest form a market is a place to which persons regularly resort, though perhaps only at certain times, to buy and sell a commodity, or a range of commodities. A market in this sense is an institution, or a set of institutional arrangements, whose function it is to facilitate exchange, which it does by reducing the costs of individual transactions. Today there are in Britain institutional arrangements which put buyers and potential sellers of landed property in touch with each other, and some of these operate at a national level. Thus if you want to buy a large country house you purchase the journal *Country Life*, in which such properties are regularly advertised. You can thereby establish contact, simply and cheaply, with potential sellers, through one of the estate agents who handle property of this character. There is no place where country houses are regularly sold, but there are arrangements which make it relatively simple to locate a suitable property and discover information about it.

In earlier centuries institutional arrangements for the purchase and sale of interests in land were much less developed, and more local in character; indeed in the early medieval world it perhaps makes little sense to talk of a land market at all. There is a chicken and egg question as to whether markets develop in response to demand, or themselves generate demand. So far as the purchase and sale of land is concerned the fee simple offered an appropriate and marketable interest, but the world in which it originated was one in which the motives for treating land as a marketable commodity were not as strong as they are today. Land was something one kept; perhaps in consequence land markets were not so highly developed. The ownership of land was closely associated with the acquisition of locally based political and social power; in such a world the purchase and sale of land as a mechanism for geographical mobility, one reason for buying and selling land, was less powerful. There were certainly other forms of wealth in which to invest in past centuries, but the choices were by no means as extensive as they are today.

By Blackstone's time market transactions of exchange, of purchase and sale, certainly took place on a very considerable scale as individuals moved in and out of the landowning elite, or bought and sold land as their landownership increased or diminished, or bought and sold to reorganize or rationalize their holdings. There were buyings and sellings of land to raise cash for expenditure on, for example, building. And there were also extensive land sales which were the product of over expenditure and consequential debt.[63]

≺ VIII ≻

Freedom of Alienation and Gifts

Yet the economic significance of freedom of alienation was not simply that land was marketable by way of sale or exchange, in

which case wealth would return to the landowner by way of *quid pro quo*. It also gave the landowner a free power to make gifts of land. Hence freedom of alienation does not simply mean the power to place property in the commercial market. The power of disposition by will, virtually unrestricted by legal constraints, also belongs to this world of gifts, and not to that of the market. This power of testamentary disposition enhances the economic freedom of the landowner by allowing him to postpone the exercise of his generosity until after his death. It thereby maximizes a landowner's freedom during his life. Landowners can both enjoy the use of property until death, and then dispose of it by gifts which, since they are dead when they take effect, impose no costs upon the donor. Insofar as they can be viewed as imposing costs, they impose them on those who would otherwise have hoped to succeed. In a strict sense, however, a hope of succession is not an entitlement to property, so that it is problematic to suppose that anybody loses when such a gift is made, which seems paradoxical. Gifts by will cost nobody anything. Blackstone was somewhat puzzled as to how to analyze the transmission of property rights on death and the fact that a deceased person's property was not available to the first occupant: "For, naturally speaking, the instant a person ceases to be, he ceases to have any dominion . . . All property must therefore cease upon death."[64] But as he points out, all Western systems of law in his time permitted such transmission.

It is easy to forget the very great significance of gifts in modern society as a mechanism for the transfer of wealth; it appears to be a somewhat neglected subject except among anthropologists.[65] Thus it is commonly said that freedom to alienate property is conducive to the maximization of wealth. The argument is that property tends to end up in the possession of those who value it most, so long, of course, as they have the wherewithal to buy. It may be simply a consequence of unfamiliarity with the literature outside my own field, but I do not know of any similar theory about the economic consequences of the power to make gifts. Perhaps we could say that there is a tendency for property to end up in the hands of persons whose benefactor thinks they will value it more, or in the hands of those who have the capacity to make their benefactor feel most guilty—ingenuity will suggest other possibilities.

In some situations gifts do of course function as a form of ex-

change, as where siblings give each other birthday presents, or social invitations are returned. In property law, however, gifts are, to
a considerable extent, one-way transactions, as where a parent
leave property by will to a child.

In the past much landed property was given in the context of
upper-class marriage arrangements. Here, commonly, wealth was
brought into the marriage from the bride's side of the family—a
sort of dowry. Income provided for the wife during the marriage
and during widowhood was financed from this dowry. Wealth,
commonly in the form of landed property, was put into the marriage from the bridegroom's side of the marriage. During the husband's life he usually had control over this property, though there
could be arrangements whereby the wife had separate property, not
under her husband's control. If the property with which the marriage was endowed was settled, with the husband having merely a
life estate, then the settlement served in part at least to protect the
wife and her children, and therefore the interests of her family,
from an unsatisfactory husband.[66] The typical legal arrangements
cannot be viewed as a sale of the wife, nor indeed as an exchange
transaction of any kind. It involved rather a cooperation in endow-
ing a new family, in which both sides to the transaction put wealth
into the new family and were, in return, offered a degree of protection.

So we distort understanding of the common law of landownership if recognition of freedom of alienation is related simply to
market transactions. In the landowning class of the aristocracy and
gentry the typical land transfer was the gift, either the gift *inter vivos* or the gift by will, rather than the sale. Gifts of property, then
as now, were usually made to discharge obligations of one sort or
another, but not obligations which were legally binding. Death and
marriage were thus the occasions on which very many transfers of
landed property took place; transfers at birth normally arose as a
product of contingent gifts created on marriage or at death. Gifts of
land could be made in fee simple, but many such gifts involved the
creation of limited interests in landed property, which did not
transfer to the donee a free power of alienation.

Hence although it is right to view the fee simple of the land law
as the marketable interest, the interest which could readily be
bought and sold as a commodity, it is important to be clear that

one use to which it was commonly put was to create interests which, although they no doubt possessed a market value, were not adapted to the land market. They expressed the idea that in the landowning world land was not an individually owned commodity to be traded in the market. Rather, it was an endowment belonging to a family, albeit under the control of the current patriarch, to be employed to maintain and enhance its status and power into the indefinite future.

≺ IX ≻

Limited Interests in Land

Limited heritable interests—what Blackstone calls "such estates of inheritance as are clogged and confined with conditions"[67]—were the product of gifts, not of market transactions. The typical limited interest was the entail, which is found in one form or other throughout western Europe; its purpose was to take land out of commerce.[68] The ideal function of the entail was to preserve a family landowning territory as a single block, and pass it down the male line of a family ad infinitum. Entails could have other characteristics—immunity from liability for debt, immunity from forfeiture for treason—and the management powers of the tenant in possession might be limited. Entails were also, ideally, not alienable, though the tenant might create interests for his own life. The history is complicated, but when the peculiar characteristics of the medieval entail were lost, its function was transferred to an institution known as the strict settlement, which came in to use in the mid-seventeenth century. Other forms of settlement, involving life estates and entails, had been in use well before this; the characteristic of the strict settlement, and what made it "strict," was the fact that the current head of the family could not, on his own, break the settlement, a result achieved by the use of a device known as limitation to trustees to preserve contingent remainders. The strict settlement relied on a manipulative use of life estates, another form of freehold limited interest, of entails, and of future contingent interests. If the labels are taken off, the strict settlement was simply a form of entail under a new name.

However, because of restrictions imposed by a complex body of law known as the rule against perpetuities, this new form of entail provided an opportunity, each generation, for the father of the family, in cooperation in the typical case with the heir apparent, commonly his eldest son, to break the settlement and secure a power of disposition over the fee simple. The rule against perpetuities essentially permitted arrangements of family lands to be set up under which a free power of disposition might not become available for a life time and a further period of twenty-one years, though in practice it usually became available in a very much shorter period.

The rule against perpetuities and associated doctrines came in relatively modern times to be regarded as economically desirable, in that their effect was to limit the degree to which land could be tied up in family settlements, and thus kept out of the market, and to prevent settlers from arranging to keep family lands off the market indefinitely. But when the rule against perpetuities was invented, back in the seventeenth and eighteenth centuries, it had nothing whatever to do with free-market economics.[69] In the world of the dynastic landholding family it was natural enough for the current patriarch to wish to make provision for his family, the family being viewed as a permanent institution, though perpetually at risk through the ravages of death, infertility, and individual folly. Yet if one patriarch was allowed to tie the lands up forever, later patriarchs would be unable to review the arrangements and modify them in the light of new circumstances. No patriarch could foresee the whole future, and the law should not allow patriarchs to behave as if they were gods. So a sort of compromise was reached, which limited the power of one patriarch to providing for contingencies within his own knowledge and foresight. He was not allowed to provide for contingencies which were too remote in time. So the function of the rule was to regulate a system of gift giving whose primary function was ensuring that the family retained a permanent endowment, and to permit that endowment to be preserved from the risk that any single individual would place it on the market.

The intermittent freedom to dispose of the fee simple which the system conferred was indeed usually not employed to place the family lands on the market, but merely to resettle them as seemed appropriate and tie them up for another generation. This was indeed the value served by the rule against perpetuities. Within the basic framework of the settlement, provision could be made for the support of widows and the provision of capital sums of money to younger children, who were not going to inherit the family land-holding.

Settlements, and the practice of resettlement each generation, gave expression to social and moral ideas of proper behavior among the landowning class. They were in a legal sense voluntary; as we have seen, family and kin had no enforceable legal rights against a landowner who held land in fee simple. But social pressures and the form of the settlement encouraged the perpetuation of the practice. Where it prevailed the consequence was that landed estates were passed down a series of life tenants, who enjoyed limited powers of management over the family lands. Provisions in settlements for the payment of capital sums to younger children (which in effect required the life tenant to find these sums) could impose heavy burdens of debt on life tenants. And for obvious reasons the system could discourage land improvement, partly because of the inability of the life tenant to tap the capital value of the land to pay for improvements, and partly perhaps because he could not expect to reap the benefits himself. Many of the disadvantages of settlements could be obviated by conferring on the life tenant enlarged powers, but there was no obligation on settlers to do this.

In the late eighteenth and the nineteenth centuries entails came under attack on three distinct though related grounds.[70] One was ideological. Radical liberals, influenced by the views of Adam Smith and the political economists, favored free trade in land, just as they favored free trade in most other commodities. In consequence they advocated the abolition both of entails and of settlements, which were plainly an impediment to such free trade; and they also favored schemes to reduce the very considerable costs of land transfer, so that land could be cheaply traded. The second was more political. Settlements, entails, and the optional system of primogeniture embodied in the system of settlement and resettlement were all associated with the power of the landowning class; those who wanted a more egalitarian society consequently wanted these legal trappings of the landed interest to be abolished. Debate centered upon the institution of primogeniture, which possessed a symbolic significance as central to the idea of an aristocracy.

The third was pragmatic. The impoverished condition of Ireland, and the grave problems to which it gave rise, was in part associated with the existence of run-down and unmanageable settled estates; a solution was to tackle such problems seriatim. In Ireland this produced legislation in 1849 under which a special court could authorize the sale of encumbered estates with the purchaser taking free of the third party rights which made such estates unmarketable.[71] In England a series of acts enhanced the management powers of tenants for life; the process produced in the end the Settled Land Acts of 1882 and 1925 which in general gave tenants for life of settled estates the management powers of a tenant in fee simple, while preserving the beneficial interests behind a trust. Curiously enough the legislation of 1882 was passed in the interests of the landowning classes, and what used to be called "the land question" has faded more or less entirely from the political scene. In this century several factors, one being the law of taxation, have combined to make the old entails and settlements obsolete, though of course gift transactions in the form of trusts established *inter vivos* or by will remain commonplace. And although no doubt entails and settlements significantly reduced the amount of land available on the market for development there is no evidence, so far as I am aware, that it did so to the extent of imposing some serious restraint on economic development. Where there were real difficulties the Local and Personal Act could always be employed, albeit at considerable cost, to deal with the problem.

≺ X ≻

Peasants and Farmers

The modern common law system of landholding, which has both survived in the country of its birth and been transplanted overseas, originated as the law of an aristocratic elite, and did so in a world very different from the world in which it operates today. Many of its basic concepts were in existence when Europeans first came to America, and long before they settled in such places as Australia and New Zealand. In the medieval period wealth was predominantly, but not of course exclusively, the product of agriculture. As anyone who has tried to grow his own vegetables knows, agriculture is a grim battle between man and nature; and in the past, before the rise of the agro-chemical industry, nature was always on the brink of winning. Hence in the medieval world the life of the peasantry was one of unrelenting toil.

Dependent upon the wealth created by the unrelenting toil of the peasantry were two principal elites—a secular elite associated with war and a variety of leisure activities closely associated with it, such as hunting; and a spiritual elite devoted to the massive service industry of mediating the relationships between mankind and God. These elites had to be paid for; today there are no free lunches and in the medieval world there were no free battles, and not many free masses. The hierarchical structure of the land law, its elaborate structure of dependent tenure, with villein tenants and socage tenants at the bottom and knights and castles and cathedrals at the top, was moderated in part by ethical conceptions of obligation, in part by the necessity for cooperation in local communities, and in part by the fact that the peasants at the end of the day were vital to the entire system.

Over the centuries there have been very important changes in the legal position of those at the bottom of this structure, or low down it. The feudal tenurial obligations have more or less all gone, so that medieval tenure as a system for transmission of wealth upward from producers to consumers has lost its significance. The unfree villeins, bound to the soil, have simply disappeared by a process which was more or less complete by 1600. Free tenants in villeinage became transmuted into copyholders, whose landholding was, by about the same time, fully protected at common law. Over the course of the next three centuries copyhold tenure itself declined in importance, and eventually it was wholly abolished. So far as freeholders are concerned, the significance of tenure largely disappeared in the seventeenth century. Only occasional relics of feudal tenure survive to amuse antiquarians. Medieval dependent tenure as a mechanism for organizing the world of landholding thus passed out of use.

One might suppose that we should be left with a system of individual proprietorship, at least in the agricultural world. Indeed by the time we reach the nineteenth century a considerable acreage of land has come to be owned by farmer proprietors, who enjoy the economic freedom of the holder in fee simple. Farming remained labor intensive, though progressively less so, but this labor was no longer provided by dependent tenure. Instead, insofar as it was not provided by family members, it was performed either by live-in "servants in husbandry" who became part of the farmer's family, or more usually by laborers hired by the day or week or month, who might live in cottages tied to their employment, for which they might or might not pay rent. The replacement of tenurial arrangements to provide agricultural labor by wage earning of one kind or another conforms to Henry Maine's picture of a society evolving from status to contract. There is a large literature on the history of the agricultural laborer, and on the effect of the enclosure movement on the poorest members of the village communities. If, as seems correct, what happened was the replacement of poor villagers who nevertheless possessed some property rights in land with laborers who possessed no such rights, the process cannot have enhanced the economic freedom of such persons. However they were in another sense more free than they had been in the past; they could, and many did, move to the growing cities of industrial England in which conditions, though no doubt grim, were perhaps no more grim than was life in the countryside, which we today tend to romanticize. In passing it is important to note that the free labor of the agricultural world remained well into the nineteenth century subject to criminal procedures for breach of contract.

Where land was not farmed by its proprietor, the legal arrangement which replaced feudal tenure was the farming lease for years, an essentially contractual institution. The farm tenant would, like the farm proprietor, again employ farm laborers under contracts of employment. Where land was held under settlement, or owned primarily as a rent-producing investment by such institutions as Oxford and Cambridge colleges, farms were in general not operated through managers. Rather, they were leased on a renewable basis for customary periods, for example on seven or fourteen or twenty-one-year leases, or sometimes by way of leases for the survivor of three lives.

Agricultural leases, like the earlier feudal tenure, served to pass wealth up the system from producers to consumers. They involved a division of function between landlord and tenant in which both were capitalists; the landlord provided the fixed capital, the tenant the working capital. The system of financing farming in this way still persists in Britain on a very considerable scale. Until fairly modern times the terms upon which land was leased was unregu-

lated by general law and left to freedom of contract and local custom. British society remained intensely hierarchical until very recent times, with the countryside dominated by wealthy landowning families, whose country house style of living was supported by
the rental income of their farms. What was critical to the relationship at common law was the absence of any right, independent of
contract, for the tenant to be compensated for improvements: and,
even more importantly, the absence of security of tenure beyond
the term of the lease which had been agreed. Furthermore rights in
the tenant to assign a lease were left to be regulated by private contract.

These features of leasehold arrangements inevitably placed tenants in a relatively weak economic position, weaker indeed than
the peasants of medieval England; in modern times they have been
radically altered by legislation which in effect converts agricultural
tenants into life tenants. The relatively short-term lease for years,
accompanied by no secured right to renewal, is not a powerful instrument of economic or any other sort of freedom. In the nineteenth century and even later the power of landlords could be associated with a hierarchical world in which there existed mutual obligations not unlike those which we tend to associate with medieval feudalism. It was at its worst in Ireland, where there was absen-
tee landlordism on a large scale, and where the landlord class and
the poorer tenants were separated by religion and nationality.
There the relationship between landlord and tenant became a political issue of considerable significance. So the institution of the
lease may be seen as having long preserved a sort of second-class
form of landownership, which departs to some degree from the
greater economic freedom associated with Blackstone's despotic
dominion, enjoyed to the full only by the owner in fee simple.

That such despotic dominion enhances the freedom of the for-
tunate individual who enjoys it hardly needs argument; the problem with the liberal institution of private property is that insofar as
property is unequally distributed, freedom and power are unequally
distributed as well, and one has only to look around the world to
see that the market does not correct this inequality. The desperate
attempts to establish some sort of moral foundation for the institution constitute a response to this uncomfortable fact. So do the attempts by writers to find some sort of utilitarian rationale in terms

of the social desirability of internalization, the supposed inefficiency of alternative regimes, and the assumption that somehow or
other everyone is better off, what is good for Henry Ford being good
for America. But these are matters I shall leave to wiser heads to
settle.

Contract and the Common Law

JOHN V. ORTH

CONTRACT IS SO PREVALENT a concept today, and the contract of employment so obviously a species of contract, that it is natural to assume the same has always been true; to assume, in other words, that contract has for centuries played a major role in ordering social relationships, among them the relationship of employment. But that would be a serious misunderstanding. In fact, the common law was a mature legal system with a well-developed property law long before contract law was more than merely rudimentary. Contract law as we know it today began to take shape only in the eighteenth century, and the modern law of contract developed only in the nineteenth century. The contract of employment, rather than being a mere application of general contract principles to the specific case of labor—one among many—instead played a major role in the emergence of modern contract law.

In one sense, the intimate connection between labor and contract, particularly in the application of the famous doctrine of freedom of contract, has long been obvious. In A. V. Dicey's widely read *Lectures on the Relation between Law and Public Opinion in England during the Nineteenth Century*, first published in 1905, "zeal for freedom of contract" appeared as an index of society's commitment to individualism, which Dicey inaccurately equated with Benthamism.[1] As Dicey expressly acknowledged, the succeeding legal regimes concerning labor largely determined his influential periodization of nineteenth-century English legal history into successive ages of Old Toryism (1800–1830), Benthamism (1825–1870), and Collectivism (1865–1900).[2] Dicey portrayed the emergence of freedom of contract in labor relations as the single most important progressive development in nineteenth-century England. Its threatened curtailment in the interest of collectivism darkened

his vision of the dawning twentieth century.[3] In America, too, freedom of contract, elevated to the status of constitutional dogma,
was developed by state and federal courts largely in cases concerning legislative attempts to restrict the terms of the labor contract,
most famously in *Lochner v. New York*,[4] also in 1905.

The obviousness of the tie between labor and contract early in
the twentieth century did not, however, translate into contemporary understanding of the historic role that developments in labor
law had played in the emergence of modern contract law. That role
was obscured by the abstraction with which the law of contract
was characteristically stated. Drained of all specifics, modern contract theory seemed to apply impartially to a wide range of legal relations, of which the employment relation was only one. To redis-
cover the historic interaction between labor and contract, one must
first recognize the gradual emergence of contract law from the
shadow of property law. From a system that was still largely dominated by concepts of property through the mid-eighteenth century,
the common law moved dramatically in the succeeding hundred
years in the direction of contract. Once the historic shift from
property to contract was accomplished, it was difficult to recognize
the diminished place that contract had previously occupied. Within
the shift from property to contract, new thinking about labor
played a crucial role. The "contractualization" of labor not only
brought to contract a vast and contentious new subject; it also
forced the pace of development of the general law of contracts.

< I >

From Property to Contract

The common law was made by lawyers with property on their
minds, so the deeper one goes in English legal history, the more
property one finds. In the time of feudalism, when property and office were confused, there was a tendency to reify all rights, to see
property everywhere, even where today we would plainly see contract.[5] For instance, a medieval man might purchase a corody, a
commitment by an abbey to provide him with room, board, and
care in his old age (an early form of nursing home insurance), but
his remedy in case the required services were not rendered was by

the assize of novel disseisin,[6] the identical remedy he would use if he were deprived of his estate in land. The right to care created by the corody was thought of as a thing, literally an incorporeal or bodiless thing, not a mere promise to provide services; nonperformance meant immediate material loss, not merely defeated expectation. Today, it is difficult even to describe the case without the use of contract words like "promise" and "breach," but medieval lawyers thought in terms more akin to "property" and "taking." (Actually, the demandant in the assize of novel disseisin averred that he had been disseised of his "free tenement.")[7] Pollock and Maitland, the classic expositors of common law history, believed that "a better example of medieval realism could hardly be given."[8]

Property subsumed all the ordinary and pervasive arrangements in what remained largely a landed society, even those extending over time like the lease, the mortgage, and the real estate contract. The lease of land had been conceptualized since at least the time of Sir Edward Coke in the early seventeenth century as a conveyance, not a contract. The wonderful oxymoron "chattel real," still occasionally used to describe the lease, encapsulates both its origin as personal (or chattel) property and its eventual qualification as real property.[9] In any event, the lease at common law—unlike in Roman law or the civil law systems derived from it[10]—was property, not contract. The tenant acquired an estate in land, albeit one qualified for historical reasons as a non-freehold estate; property brought with it status, security, and substantial procedural advantages.

The promissory element in leases had to be handled by so-called covenants, which were for centuries scrupulously held to be independent, in consequence of which the breach of a covenant by one party did not excuse nonperformance of another covenant by the other party.[11] Without mutually dependent covenants, no contract could be recognized, only an aggregation of dissociated promises. Seemingly the only exception to the rule of independent covenants in leases was the exchange of possession for rent, since failure of one excused denial of the other.[12] But the apparent exception only illustrates the difficulty lawyers had after the shift from property to contract in understanding the traditional law of leases. The so-called covenant to pay rent was not originally a promise at all. Rent was an interest in the land reserved in the lease by the land-

lord, not created by the promise of the tenant. As Pollock and
Maitland expressed it, the tenant did not in a sense even pay the
rent; "the land pays it through his hand."[13] The rent issued from
the land like timber or growing crops, which is why to this day in
case of a tenant's assignment, the assignee in possession of the
land is liable for the rent.

The mortgage, the Middle Ages' preeminent financing device,
was cast originally as a conditional conveyance, not a contract of
indebtedness. The mortgagor (the borrower) transferred property to
the mortgagee (the lender), on condition that the transfer would
become ineffective if the mortgagor paid the mortgagee a sum of
money by a certain date.[14] The conveyance, not the debt and promise of repayment, was the centerpiece.[15] The long history of the law
of mortgages is the story of the slow recasting of the transaction, in
legal effect if not in form, as a debt with property pledged as security for repayment.

Even the contract for the sale of land was treated more like a
conveyance than a contract. It is as if the common law—or the
common lawyers, rather—could not stand the thought of so important a contract remaining in executory limbo. The court of equity,
the Chancery Court, early established the rule that contracts for
the sale of land would be specifically enforced; that is, in case one
party refused to perform, the court would presume that money
damages (as for breach of contract) would be an inadequate remedy
and would order the party to perform as promised.

Because the contract for the sale of land was specifically enforceable in equity, it was held to create *ex proprio vigore* an equitable title in the purchaser,[16] a doctrine somewhat misleadingly labeled "equitable conversion" because the contract right was converted in equity into a property title. In consequence, the contract
was itself a conveyance. If by accident the real estate was damaged
while the contract remained executory, that is, before the deed was
delivered, the loss nonetheless fell on the purchaser. If the seller
was without fault unable to deliver a good title at the time for performance, the remedy in damages was limited by the so-called rule
in *Flureau v. Thornhill*[17] to restitution, that is, the return of any
downpayment and the reimbursement of necessary expenses, rather than expectation damages ("the benefit of the bargain"), which
became the usual remedy for breach of contract.[18]

Once contract-thinking displaced property-thinking, traditional doctrine came increasingly under attack; or, more accurately, became increasingly unintelligible. Although the lease continued to be regarded primarily as a conveyance until the middle of the twentieth century, it thereafter rapidly lost that character, at least with respect to residential leases. The modern "rental agreement," as the old lease is now more descriptively called, is today often treated "like any other contract."[19] To the amusement of contract lawyers, it has at last been solemnly announced that covenants in leases are "mutually dependent."[20] So rapid and complete has been the overthrow of traditional doctrine that late in the twentieth century a *Restatement of the Law of Property—Second*, devoted solely to the law of landlord and tenant, was required.

The mortgage, too, is now widely interpreted in terms of its intention, not its form. In America the distinction still persists between states adhering to the old "title theory," that a mortgage gives the mortgagee some sort of legal title to the land; and the newer "lien theory," that a mortgage creates only a lien on the property to secure repayment. The title theory is clearly beleaguered, however, supported more by precedent than reason, and of relatively little practical significance.[21]

The real estate contract, too, is increasingly that: a contract, not a conveyance. The doctrine of equitable conversion, long the target of academic criticism, is receding.[22] England abandoned it by statute in 1925.[23] In America, as always, the process is messier. A uniform act adopted in a dozen states deals with part of the problem,[24] and even courts that continue to adhere to the doctrine do so with an apology.[25] The rule in *Flureau v. Thornhill*, that restitution rather than expectation is the proper measure of damages for a seller's breach without fault, is also steadily eroding in America in favor of treating such contracts "like any other."[26]

What was missing from the common law before modern times was a robust notion of contract. This is not to say that the elements of modern contract law were altogether absent from the earlier common law: John Baker has pointed out that they were present as early as the sixteenth century.[27] But it is to say that contract-thinking was rare; the exception, not the rule. Common lawyers did not think often or easily about contracts, particularly long-term executory contracts.[28] Contracts were instead seen as the hand-maidens of property, a useful means of transferring title from one person to another. Referring to Book 2 of Blackstone's *Commentaries*, on the so-called "rights of things" (the law of property), A. W. B. Simpson has pointed out: "Contracts are here conceived of as a sort of conveyance."[29] In this limited sense, contract has always been "property in motion": the contract of sale, whether of land or chattels, moved title at the moment of effectiveness. The only question was when title passed, and there were key differences between contracts for realty and personalty because of the doctrine of equitable conversion.[30]

Starting about the middle of the eighteenth century, contract began to emerge from the shadow of property. The so-called "will theory" of contract, described by James Gordley, entered the common law tradition. Here was literally a new way of thinking about legal relations, emphasizing intention rather than possession, voluntarism rather than vestedness. Suddenly, at least in terms of the long history of the common law, legal thinkers began to reconceptualize many long-standing legal arrangements. Precedents were seen in a new light; old information placed in a new framework. To use a metaphor that has proved useful in the history of science, another body of organized knowledge, it was like "picking up the stick by the other end."[31] If contracts looked to Blackstone like "a sort of conveyance," conveyances soon thereafter looked to many lawyers like a sort of contract. As Lawrence Friedman discovered in his examination of nineteenth-century American case law, deeds were often equated with contracts, not vice versa.[32] Clearing the legal mind on the subject was not simple. The primordial system of writs dispersed related problems into the disparate categories of debt, covenant, and assumpsit. Maitland once memorably called trespass the "fertile mother of actions."[33] With contract the life-giving process was consolidation, not proliferation; and until debt, covenant, and assumpsit came together as a more or less unified law of obligations, contract could not be thought about, let alone "freed." The process was not a purely intellectual one. Real-world events, most notably the perennial problem of labor, drove the law to recognize a new and leading role for contract.

≺ II ≻

Labor and Contract

In the secular shift from property to contract, the development of labor law played an important role—one unanticipated, even unnoticed, by contemporaries, who did not normally think about labor in terms of contract. For centuries labor had been thought of primarily as a status to which rights and duties were attached rather than as the performance of an executory agreement. Wages were a matter of public policy, not private contract. The legal history of labor was succinctly summarized by Adam Smith in *The Wealth of Nations*: "[T]hough anciently it was usual to rate wages, first by general laws extending over the whole kingdom, and afterwards by particular orders of the justices of the peace in every particular county, both these practices have now gone entirely into disuse . . . Particular acts of parliament, however, still attempt sometimes to regulate wages in particular trades and in particular places."[34] Smith recognized, in other words, two phases in the history of wage regulation: an early phase, actually medieval, in which national wage rates were set by statute; and a later phase, early-modern, in which the power to set local wage rates was devolved to the justices of the peace.

By Smith's day, in the late eighteenth century, wage-setting by the justices of the peace had just about petered out. What took its place had, of course (with the inevitability conferred by hindsight), to be contract. But to those involved the route to the modern labor contract was neither simple nor obvious. Parliament tried for a century to regulate wages by combination acts applying, as Smith said, to "particular trades in particular places." Although ultimately failing in the endeavor to master the necessary economic details, it managed in the process to discover a new role for contract.

The earliest legal memory of labor in England dates to the aftermath of the Black Death in 1348. That terrible winnowing of human life resulted in a drastic shortage of labor. Long before Adam Smith demonstrated how supply and demand set prices, the powers-that-be felt the pinch caused by a straitened labor market. Criminal law first registered the response of England's rulers. The Statute of Laborers (1350), among the earliest entries in the English statute book, compelled work at wages that had prevailed before the catastrophe.[35] All men and women under the age of 60 and without land or a trade sufficient for self-support had to serve whoever required their labor, although lords had the first right to the service of their tenants. Contract obviously had no place in this scheme of things.

The next great legislative impulse came two centuries later, in the Tudor period. The Elizabethan Statute of Artificers (1563), which replaced the medieval Statute of Laborers, set the framework for labor law until well into the eighteenth century.[36] Under the act of Elizabeth, the justices of the peace in each county were required to set annual wages. Concomitant with wage regulation went a legal code of behavior for workmen, including a prohibition on leaving work unfinished. Labor was compulsory, not voluntary, so the role of contract—the word was not actually used in the statute—was limited to connecting masters with eligible servants; such, for example, as had not wrongfully departed their prior service. Further clauses of the Statute of Artificers, giving rise to the misnomer the Statute of Apprentices, regulated the training of skilled labor. Before practicing any craft, a workman had to serve an apprenticeship of at least seven years. Thereafter he became a journeyman, qualified to work for a master and eligible, if he could assemble the necessary capital, to graduate into a master himself.

Two hundred years later, at the time of Sir William Blackstone's *Commentaries on the Laws of England (1765–69)*, the wage regulation provisions of the Statute of Artificers, although unrepealed, were in practice a dead letter,[37] but labor still remained more a matter of status than contract. Contract itself, as earlier remarked, had yet to emerge from the shadow of property. Blackstone had next to nothing to say about contract.[38] In the entire four-volume *Commentaries*, extending over two thousand printed pages, labor law (such as it is) occupies ten pages in Book 1, on the "rights of persons." A chapter on "master and servant" leads off a series of chapters on what Blackstone calls the "great relations in private life,"[39] including, in addition to the employment relationship, familial relationships such as "husband and wife" and "parent and child" and the substituted family of "guardian and ward."

As Blackstone described it, the employment relationship, like the marital relationship, begins with a contract; but he spent many more pages commenting on the contractual aspect of marriage than on the contractual aspect of labor. The law treats marriage, according to Blackstone, "as it does all other contracts."[40] The ensuing discussion is arranged under still familiar headings in the law of contracts. There must be agreement ("the meeting of the minds") and capacity to contract. Then follows a short list of disabilities, some peculiar to the marriage context, such as prior marriage, but others generally applicable, such as nonage and mental incompetence. Finally, there must be compliance with formal requirements.

The contract of marriage carries the parties, as it were, to the threshold of their new status, but not beyond. After marriage, the law of husband and wife governs the new relationship; for instance, the notorious law depriving a married woman of the right to hold property in her own name. Not a product of the marriage contract, the rule was consequently unalterable by agreement between the parties. To escape it, in cases in which enough foresight, counsel, and money was involved, one shifted to another, more sophisticated, property regime: a trust for her sole and separate use.[41]

The contract of marriage resembles the contract for the sale of land in that once executed, it creates a new relationship that is governed by its own body of law, the law of property, not by the agreement of the parties.[42] For example, a contract for deed, or even a deed itself, that purports to convey a fee simple estate but restricts the new owner's power to re-convey falls foul of the common law policy against restraints on alienation.[43] Marriage, like the fee simple, comes in one shape and size: Take it or leave it. It is not happenstance that the traditional marriage ritual recalls the wording of an old deed, including the memorable words *habendum et tenendum*, "to have and to hold."

The relation of master and servant also begins with a contract, one that "arises upon the hiring,"[44] although Blackstone forbore to repeat the contract learning he applied to matrimony: agreement, capacity, disabilities, and formalities. As befit an Oxford professor, he also had little to say about the actual terms of employment, assuming they would be filled in by custom or law. With respect to duration, the law—based, he said, on a "principle of natural equity"—construes a general hiring of domestic servants without particular term to be for one year.[45] As to laborers, the Statute of Artificers sets their hours summer and winter and empowers the justices of the peace "to settle their wages."[46] The truth is that Blackstone knew nothing about a contract of employment, only a contract of hiring. Like the contract of marriage or the contract of sale, the contract of hiring was a portal to a new relationship or status: husband and wife, purchaser and vendor, master and servant.[47]

When property-thinking predominated, a servant, once hired, belonged in a sense to the master. Blackstone referred to "the property that every man has in the service of his domestics; acquired by the contract of hiring, and purchased by giving them wages."[48] If another enticed away his servant, the master had a remedy in the ancient writ *per quod servitium amisit* (whereby he lost his services), dating to the Statute of Laborers. A century later, when the law of strikes was being forged, the issue would be whether a trade union could lawfully induce workmen to withdraw their labor. By then contract had supplanted property, so the hoary law of enticement became interference with contract.[49] The law of master and servant, the legal code of behavior for workmen, forbade leaving work unfinished. So long as labor was viewed as a status and wages were regulated, this simply spelled out one of the workman's duties. When wage regulation faltered and labor was reconceptualized in terms of contract, the law of master and servant survived as an increasingly anomalous criminal law punishing breach of contract, appearing now in the iniquitous guise of state support for capital against labor.[50] Apprenticeship, too, at first an orderly educational arrangement to assure quality, came to be regarded—as labor was reconceptualized as a commodity—as a throttle on the supply of skilled workmen.[51]

≺ III ≻

The New Statutory Regime

Behind the logical structure of Blackstone's *Commentaries*, as behind the grand Palladian facades of the great country houses, much of interest was going on out of sight. When wage-setting by the justices of the peace had just about run its course, Parliament began to legislate specially for particular trades in particular places.[52] The first of a series of eighteenth-century combination acts was aimed at the journeymen tailors of London,[53] who staged an early work stoppage to protest beggary in the trade after the South Sea Bubble burst—the same financial catastrophe, incidentally, that induced John Gay to write *The Beggar's Opera*, the beggar in question being the author. Ironically, in light of the use to which freedom of contract was later put, the contracts that troubled the lawmakers in 1721 were not those *between* the journeymen and their masters. Rather, they were those supposedly entered into by the journeymen *among themselves* to concert their demands for higher wages and shorter hours, the contracts (so to speak) that constituted the journeymen tailors' nascent trade union.[54] The "contracts" the legislators had in mind seem to have been simple agreements to abide by the union rules or pay a fine to the union treasury. These agreements were voided; indeed, they were criminalized. Parliament exercised its grand magistracy and itself settled wages and hours in the trade.[55]

A few years later, in 1726, unrest in the venerable woolen industry provoked another statute prohibiting journeymen's contracts to orchestrate their demands concerning wages and hours.[56] As a sort of *quid pro quo* for denying the right to organize, the weavers' combination act outlawed the truck system in the trade, by which masters paid for work in goods rather than money.[57] When experience over three decades proved the ban on truck ineffective, a second act was passed in 1756, doubling the penalty and strengthening the procedures for enforcement.[58] In addition, the new act directed the justices of the peace to set wages, by setting the prices masters had to pay for each yard of woolen cloth.

At the first exercise of this power, the masters objected that the order was impossible to obey because of the various shapes in which cloth was made.[59] The wage regulation section was repealed the next year,[60] a fact that led Sidney and Beatrice Webb to claim that Parliament was exchanging "its policy of medieval protection for one of 'Administrative Nihilism'"[61]—hyperbolic in both directions, but accurate enough in signposting that a watershed was being crossed. For present purposes, the amendment to the second weavers' act is significant for what it substituted for wage regulation by the justices of the peace: contracts between the parties. The 1757 act explicitly authorized wage agreements between masters and journeymen, declaring them "good, valid and effectual, to all intents and purposes," any law or custom concerning wage setting to the contrary notwithstanding[62]—the first statutory recognition of labor contracts, part of the dawning parliamentary recognition that private contracts could be an acceptable means of organizing economic activity.

Almost half a century was to pass before the example of the weavers' act was generalized. In the meantime, Parliament continued to legislate for particular trades, as its attention was drawn to one or another: the London tailors (again) in 1768,[63] the Spitalfields silk weavers in 1773 and 1792,[64] the hatters in 1777,[65] the papermakers in 1796.[66] In the process, the legislators received an education in the complexities of modern industrial production. The second tailors' combination act established a new schedule of journeymen's wages and hours, registering apparent improvement since 1721.[67] A constant wage rate was recognized as unrealistic, and an exception was created for periods of general mourning, when a death in the royal family sent London's elite hastening to their tailors for a new black wardrobe.[68] A time of such high demand caused a rise of more than double in the rate, leading one modern historian to wonder wryly "how many church-going tailors . . . prayed with all their hearts for the health of the royal family."[69] In other industrial sectors, the economic balance was altered by restricting the supply of skilled labor: master silk weavers in Spitalfields were limited to two apprentices each,[70] while master hatters were required to employ one journeyman for each apprentice.[71]

In the papermakers' combination act in 1796 Parliament descended into even greater detail. This time, hours of labor were regulated, but in terms comprehensible only to initiates in the trade: "vat men" were to spend half an hour on each "post," while "dry workers" were to labor twelve hours a day,[72] a provision undoubtedly opaque to most of the members of Parliament who voted for it. The attempt to legislate the terms of employment in all the myriad industrial occupations was doomed to failure. A government of gentlemen, even well-meaning and hard-working gentlemen, could not possibly master all the necessary details—quite apart from the fact that parliamentary attention was distracted at the time by foreign affairs, notably the wars sparked by the French Revolution. The accelerating pace of technological change soon made even the most fully informed legislation outmoded; in papermaking, for example, mechanization represented by patents beginning in 1801 eliminated vat men, posts, and dry workers altogether.[73]

<< IV >>

Conspiracy Law

F. W. Maitland once aptly styled the eighteenth century "the century of *privilegia*": "It seems afraid," he said, "to rise to the dignity of a general proposition."[74] Parliament in the eighteenth century legislated, when it had to, for particular trades in particular places. By contrast, the judges, the keepers of the common law, were more inclined to seek for principle. In 1721 some journeymen tailors in Cambridge, probably caught up in the same maelstrom of prices surrounding the bursting of the South Sea Bubble that led to the first tailors' combination act, were convicted of "a conspiracy amongst themselves to raise their wages."[75] Outside London and therefore beyond the reach of the tailors' combination act, the Cambridge journeymen had allegedly agreed to concert their demand for higher wages—under the statute (had it applied), an illegal contract; at common law (as applied in this case), a criminal conspiracy. Common law crimes like conspiracy were not dependent on statute but were recognized by the judges in their decisions of individual cases. Contract and conspiracy, both rooted in agreement, underwent rapid doctrinal development in the eighteenth and nineteenth centuries, and in both cases the force that drove the development was the imperative need to deal with labor.

Conspiracy law had traveled a long and circuitous route before it came to be invoked against the journeymen tailors of Cambridge in 1721. First defined by statute in 1304, conspiracy was originally a malicious agreement to cause a false indictment of an innocent person.[76] For Sir Edward Coke in the early seventeenth century, it remained recognizable as concerted misuse of the legal process: "a consultation and agreement between two or more, to appeal, or indict an innocent falsely, and maliciously of felony,"[77] although Coke characteristically dismissed the medieval statute as merely declaratory of the pre-existing common law.[78] Even so late as the mid-eighteenth century, Blackstone, conservative legal scholar that he was, still ranked criminal conspiracy as simply one among many "offenses against public justice."[79] By the early eighteenth century, conspiracy had in fact slipped its original moorings. Serjeant Hawkins in his influential treatise on criminal law, which saw seven editions spanning the entire eighteenth century, defined the crime expansively: "all confederacies whatsoever, wrongfully to prejudice a third person."[80] It was this generic version of conspiracy, an agreement to prejudice another, that was applied in the case of the journeymen tailors of Cambridge.

It is, perhaps, useful to dwell for a moment on what came to be seen, after the triumph of contract, as the paradox of conspiracy law: it made certain concerted actions illegal, although the same actions, if done without concert, would have been legal. As the judges explicitly recognized in the journeymen tailors' case: "[I]t is not for the refusing to work, but for conspiring, that they are indicted, and a conspiracy of any kind is illegal, although the matter about which they conspired might have been lawful for them, or any of them, to do, if they had not conspired to do it."[81] The gist of the offense at common law, in other words, was agreement,[82] just as the gist of the various statutory offenses was contract. Common law and statute law advanced in tandem, the judges and legislators mutually supporting and encouraging one another. Nonetheless, the extension of common law conspiracy along the lines of the tailors' combination act did entail one momentous consequence. Under the statute and others like it, wages and hours (or regulations concerning payment in truck, the number of apprentices or journeymen, even the operations of vat men and dry workers) were set by law; whereas common law conspiracy was only a prohibition. As a matter of institutional competence, the judges could punish certain agreements; unlike Parliament or quarter sessions, they could not even attempt to manage the daily details of labor.

In 1783 another dispute in the tailoring trade, this time in Liverpool, again outside the scope of the tailors' acts, came before the common law judges. The case required a restatement of the law of conspiracy, and Lord Mansfield obliged with a by-then routine formula: "[T]he offense does not consist in doing the acts by which the mischief is effected, for they may be perfectly indifferent, but in conspiring with a view to effect the intended mischief by any means."[83] It is his lordship's next thought that is significant for present purposes: "every man may work at what price he pleases."[84] As a statement of current law, then still officially committed in general to wage regulation by the justices of the peace (or by Parliament), this was more than questionable. As a recognition of where the law was headed, of the general proposition to which it aspired, however, it is evidence of Mansfield's farsightedness. There can be no doubt that the majority of judges a century later would have agreed, and that the U.S. Supreme Court would have said the same thing *mutatis mutandis* in 1905 in *Lochner v. New York.*

≺ V ≻

The Regime of Contract

Only at the very end of the eighteenth century did Parliament hazard a general proposition, one largely in keeping with Mansfield's dictum. Ironically, the precipitating event was an invitation to continue with business as usual, legislating for a particular trade. In 1799 the master millwrights of London presented Parliament with a petition requesting a statute "for the better preventing of unlawful combinations of workmen employed in the millwright business, and for regulating the wages of such workmen."[85] When the committee to which the petition was referred reported in favor of a bill,[86] William Wilberforce, the celebrated campaigner against African slavery, objected that combinations were "a general disease" for which "the remedy should be general."[87] In response, Prime Minister William Pitt proposed legislation modeled on the papermakers' act but applicable to all workmen.[88] In any general proposition concerning labor, the regulation of wages would raise immense administrative difficulties, but the choice of the papermakers' act as a model made not thinking about them much easier. That particular act regulated hours rather than wages and in terms specific to one industry; vat men and dry workers had obviously no place in a general regulatory statute.

Drawing on lessons learned over the course of a century in legislating for particular trades, Parliament was able to produce its first general combination act in short order. No regulatory provisions were included, and the putative contract constituting a labor organization was voided and made criminal in the most sweeping terms.[89] When a little reflection led to amendments a year later, the description of an illegal contract was clarified. Formal legal equality was achieved by also outlawing contracts among masters to lower wages or increase hours, the reciprocal of the banned contracts among journeymen.[90] And by the addition of parenthetical matter, it was made clear that a contract between a master and one workman concerning the work of that individual was not voided: "(save and except any contract made or to be made between any master and his journeyman or manufacturer, for or on account of the work or service of such journeyman or manufacturer with whom such contract may be made)."[91] Some such exception was necessary since on a literal reading the 1799 act had outlawed even the contract between master and journeyman. No longer merely a contract of hiring as in Blackstone's day, the agreement was becoming an employment contract, executory for the duration of the service, creating and defining the rights and duties of persons soon to be called employer and employee.

Because of its fear of men in groups, particularly angry, discontented men at a time of pan-European disturbances, Parliament in 1799–1800 banned group action. The contract that was the new basis of employment was limited to governing "the work or service of such journeyman or manufacturer with whom such contract may be made." There was to be no collective agreement, with an employer on one side and a trade union on the other. The rule was "every man for himself," which (to the extent it could be enforced) would disadvantage the individual workman bargaining with his employer.

A quarter century later, in 1824–25, in an early installment of reform the door was finally opened to limited collective action, attributable in part at least to the machinations of a Benthamite clique.[92] A new statute permitted workmen to coordinate their bargaining for wages and hours.[93] All the old Combination Acts were repealed[94] and because of the way the judges had applied conspiracy law to labor, a special exemption from common law prosecution was also created.[95] By this time, contract no longer seemed the right word to describe what held voluntary associations like labor organizations together; it had become instead the nexus of economic relations. Thereafter, attention in labor law, narrowly considered, shifted to permitted techniques of strikes and, eventually, picketing.[96] More broadly, labor law began to include statutory controls on working conditions (in the form of factory acts), payment of wages (truck acts), and hours (the Ten Hours Act). "Medieval protection," such as it was, was no sooner abandoned than modern protection, such as it is, began. In historic terms, the Age of Administrative Nihilism was brief, more an ideal than a reality.[97] The remaining question, of course, concerned the line between the regime of contract and the regime of regulation. Believers in freedom of contract like A. V. Dicey would have it drawn in one place, the so-called English socialists in another.

In America the story was broadly similar—with, of course, the significant exception of the slave labor system in which property atavistically triumphed over contract. With respect to free labor, the Philadelphia cordwainers' case[98] of 1806 embodied exactly the same idea, deriving all rights from the individual contract, as the English Combination Act of 1800. And the 1842 decision of Massachusetts Chief Justice Lemuel Shaw in *Commonwealth v. Hunt*[99] generalized the principle in the English Combination Laws Repeal Act of 1825 that collective agreements by labor are permissible.[100]

In both countries, the rethinking of labor in terms of contract, the invention (so to speak) of the contract of employment, seemed to solve many problems. Only a few weeks before deciding *Commonwealth v. Hunt* in favor of labor, Chief Justice Shaw had used contract-thinking to limit employer liability for employee injuries. The contract of employment had, he held, already allocated the risk of injury to the employee.[101] In due course, the House of Lords agreed in *Bartonshill Coal Co. v. Reid*.[102] Duration of service, too, seemed to be determined by the contract. Whereas Blackstone had taught that the law generally set the term of the relationship and that "natural equity" had something to do with it, the new view was that duration was simply one of many terms in the contract. In England the Blackstonian rule was swallowed by exceptions, while in America judges and jurists more candidly avowed the doctrine of employment at will.[103] Whether wages could be made payable in truck seemed to some judges best left to contract: "He may sell his labor for what he thinks best, whether money or goods," intoned the Pennsylvania Supreme Court in *Godcharles v. Wigeman*,[104] an early case on freedom of contract.[105] And, famously, in *Lochner v.*

New York the contractual hours of labor were declared constitutionally protected.[106]

Emphasis on the contractual aspect of employment offered certain benefits to labor. Formal legal equality, treating each party to the contract, employer and employee, as presumptively equal, seemed to recognize the dignity of labor.[107] As a practical matter, workers may have been at least as well off looking after their own interests as they were under a regimen of wage regulation. The state never was (and never will be) wholly disinterested in economic matters; and, as Adam Smith astutely warned two centuries ago, "Whenever the legislature attempts to regulate the differences between masters and their workmen, its counsellors are always the masters."[108] In the rough and tumble labor market, employment at will meant that strikes could be called at short order without fear of penalty for inducing breach of contract.[109] Also, gains won by collective action strengthened the collectivity, specifically the labor organization, and encouraged loyalty and discipline, albeit at the expense often of the unorganized masses.[110]

On the other hand, emphasis on contract magnified the effects of employer market power. Although workers were free to form labor organizations, they were also free to contract away their freedom. The yellow dog contract known in England as "the document," became widespread in certain industries.[111] In America the question inevitably arose whether a legislature could, consistent with the Constitution, prohibit the yellow dog contract. The answer, given in the *Lochner* era, was predictably negative: freedom of contract protected even the freedom to agree not to associate with others.[112] The use of the employment contract to preclude the associational "contract" presents the curious spectacle of history seemingly running in a circle. Contract had first appeared in labor law in the 1721 tailors' Combination Act as the means that united journeymen against their masters. Outlawed at first by statute and common law, workmen's contracts of combination later gradually gained acceptance. In the meantime, the contract of employment supplanted the old-fashioned contract of hiring. Finally, the employment contract developed the potential to do by agreement, for those with sufficient market power, what had once been done by statute.

Lochner-era freedom of contract in America was about contract and the Constitution, but above all it was about labor—a fact commonly obscured by scholars intent on demonstrating the erroneousness of the constitutional analysis. Similarly, early English labor law, primarily intended to suppress labor organizations, was about contract—again a fact commonly obscured by scholars eager to denounce the policy-makers' class bias. Read as a single narrative, the legal history of labor and contract reveals important lessons about both, and about the common law.

When wage-setting by the justices of the peace faltered and Parliament proved unable to manage the minutiae of economic regulation, a new legal mechanism for determining wages and hours was required: contract was chosen by default. Ready to hand because of its use to define labor combinations when they were outlawed, contract entered upon its new career of defining the employment relation. Blackstone's contract of hiring, the gateway to the status of master and servant, yielded to the contract of employment, an executory contract comprehensively defining the rights and duties of the parties, including not only compensation but also allocation of risk, duration of service, payment in truck, and hours of labor. The contract of labor, perhaps the single most important contract in the lives of ordinary people, powerfully demonstrated the role that contract could play in organizing social relations.

≺ VI ≻

Freedom of Contract and the Modern Legal Order

The reconceptualization of labor in terms of contract, which began in the mid-eighteenth century and was complete by the mid-nineteenth century, was a major factor in the re-orientation of the common law as a whole in the direction of contract. Although ultimately justified as increasing the role of individual volition in social affairs, the move toward contract in labor relations was in fact pragmatic, only grudgingly accepted. The initial preference of policymakers was to remain in control of economic life. As the Elizabethan system of wage regulation by the justices of the peace decayed, Parliament attempted to direct the economy, but that required mastery of the details of life in many individual trades: the London tailors, the woolen weavers, the Spitalfields silk weavers, the hatters, the papermakers, the London millwrights. Surrender of control was reluctant, at first confined to the special case of the woolen weavers in 1757. Experience with the complexity of the issues, ever increasing as technology developed, and the pressing nature of other demands, notably foreign affairs in the age of revolutions, eventually forced a devolution of power to the parties themselves. Without the necessary administrative apparatus and with no political possibility of creating it, Parliament chose this course in extremity and by default. Legislation recognized the legal efficacy of individual will in structuring employment: starting in 1800 the individual employment contract and in 1825 the collective labor agreement.

Contract's first appearance in labor relations, other than as the innocuous contract of hiring, had been threatening. The labor contract that had originally attracted legislative attention was the contract that bound workmen together in pursuit of their own ends and in defiance of authority: the combination of journeymen tailors in London in 1721, thereafter combinations in assorted trades and places throughout the eighteenth century. The threatening aspect of contract, its power to mobilize forces for harmful purposes, also elicited a judicial response: the rapid redeployment of conspiracy law. So long as government attempted to maintain control of economic life, contract appeared as a weapon in the hands of the opposition.

Only when control was relaxed and private ordering accepted, could contract assume a benign appearance. Displacing contract from its locus *among* workmen and relocating it *between* employers and employees made possible the perception of contract's positive and creative potential. "Picking up the stick at the other end," legal thinkers discovered contract as a powerful instrument of social organization. What had begun as an expedient became a virtue. Contract, it appeared, particularly in the newly fashionable form of the will theory then sweeping European legal circles, exactly suited the institutions of the nineteenth-century state. Little was required except a judicial system to enforce agreements freely entered into.

Nor was small government the only benefit. Enlargement of the scope of private contract also suited the ideology of individualism. When in his maturer years A. V. Dicey looked back at the nineteenth century, he saw its golden age as a time when reform "swept away restraints on individual energy."[113] Students of American legal history will recognize the phrase from the influential work of Willard Hurst: "the dominant value" of nineteenth-century America was, Hurst wrote, "the release of individual creative energy."[114] Contract permitted individuals to make their own enforceable legal rules, tailor-made to their unique situations, just as voters made general laws through representative democracy.

The evolution of the employment contract demonstrated that contract was a practical device for ordering economic relations. The necessary interests of the state could be safeguarded without the need to intervene in every economic decision. Defanged and domesticated, contract could be safely relied upon to define labor relations; indeed, it could be generalized as the preferred form of social organization. By 1875 Sir George Jessel, master of the rolls, announced with supreme assurance: "if there is one thing more than another which public policy requires, it is that men of full age and competent understanding shall have the utmost liberty of contracting"; "freedom of contract" was, he said, "paramount public policy."[115] Fifty years later, Benjamin Cardozo in *Lochner*-era America respectfully recalled Jessel's "often quoted judgment."[116] The problem by then had become keeping the legislature in line.

Familiarity with the executory contract at the crucial junction of capital and labor helped spread the notion of the executory contract as the defining element in all durational arrangements. Great emphasis came to be placed on the agreement by which social relations were created; a diligent search of the contract was undertaken to find terms, express or implied, to govern all aspects of the relationship over time. Not only was labor reconceptualized, but much of the common law was recast in terms of contract. Property, the historic centerpiece, was displaced, many of its most characteristic arrangements rethought. The lease, the mortgage, the contract for the sale of land, even the deed itself began to assume the appearance of contracts rather than conveyances. Property rights in general have been progressively relabeled—under the influence of contract-thinking—"expectations," specifically "investment-backed expectations."[117] Even the contract of marriage, which Blackstone thought of solely as effectuating the transition from the single to the marital state, is beginning to resemble the executory contract. Going beyond the old marriage settlement, essentially a property arrangement, the new prenuptial agreement shows signs of governing the rights and duties of the spouses throughout their marriage.[118]

No revolution solves all its problems. The primacy of contract was no sooner established than it began to be subtly undermined; both in England and America, statutes created an ever lengthening list of implied terms, read by law into many of the most common contracts, including the contract of employment.[119] Taking the long view, the medievalist S. F. C. Milsom predicts that "a legal historian of the future" will look back and see "how many rights and duties of the parties today do not flow from the contract of employment, how far we have moved back from contract towards status."[120] Finally, the emphasis on intention—the heart of contract, as possession is the heart of property—is posing its own troubling question: Why regard the intention at the moment of contracting (what in another context is called the "original intention") as superior to intention at all later times? Intention unconfined can undermine contract. Patrick Atiyah, at least in his theoretical writings, has even called for the end of enforcement of fully executory contracts.[121] Lately, scholars have proposed a new concept, the "relational contract," to cover contracts that are not mere transactions or conveyances, but long-term relationships, for which an initial moment of agreement on all essential terms is unrealistic.[122] The contract of employment is offered as typological, suggesting that once again law and labor may be interacting to drive legal development.

Contract, Property, and the Will—
The Civil Law and Common Law Tradition

JAMES GORDLEY

IN THE NINETEENTH CENTURY, arguments about justice focused as never before on the role of the state with regard to private contracts and private property. Some thought the state should not interfere with them. Others thought the state should interfere to curtail the advantages which, in their view, some citizens were obtaining at the expense of others. Although the arguments took different forms in Europe and the United States, everywhere they turned on the significance of private rights of contract and property.

In understanding the significance of these rights in that century, it is helpful, as David Lieberman suggests, to distinguish the social and economic relations subject to the institutions of contract and property, the law that defined and shaped these institutions, and the larger theories of society in which these private rights figured.[1]

Other chapters of this book are concerned with the first and third of these phenomena and suggest that the story to be told about them is less simple than many historians have assumed. Historians have often described the nineteenth century as a transition from a pre-capitalist economy subject to traditional restraints to a capitalist economy in which labor and physical resources are commodities to be freely bought and sold. But Donald Pisani describes the abundance of land in the United States as creating conditions that were neither pre-capitalist nor capitalist. Historians have often assumed that nineteenth-century liberal theories of freedom of contract were rooted in the work of earlier thinkers such as Adam Smith, Jeremy Bentham, and Immanuel Kant. Yet David Lieberman argues that these theories cannot be read backward into Smith and Bentham. If that is so, it would be surprising if they could be read into Kant.

This chapter concerns the second phenomenon—the law of contract and property itself—and its relation to the other two. It primarily concerns the way the law of contract and property was understood by lawyers themselves. In the nineteenth century, throughout Europe and the United States, jurists developed so-called "will theories." Contract was defined in terms of the will of the parties. Property was defined in terms of the power of the owner to do as he chose with his own. The will of the contracting parties or of the owner was then used as a first principle to explain as many legal rules as possible.

Historians have often thought that the will theories arose because of the first or third phenomenon just mentioned. According to some historians, most of them English or American, they emerged because the social and economic relations governed by contract and property law were changing. According to other historians, most of them from continental Europe, they emerged because liberal philosophical, political, and economic theories arose in which contract, property, and the individual will played a major role. We will see, however, that the jurists who developed the will theories were not responding to nineteenth-century social and economic conditions or theories of society but to an intellectual crisis within their own discipline. Natural law theories of property and contract that had dominated law for at least three centuries were breaking down, and something had to be found to replace them. We will also see, however, that even though the will theories were not the product of nineteenth-century economic conditions or social theories, once they emerged, they played an important role in the controversy over how the state should respond to the new economic conditions of industrial society. They exacerbated the tendency to think that whenever the state regulates contract and property in the interests of justice, it must necessarily abridge the contract and property rights of private parties.

≺ I ≻

The Innovation of the Will Theorists

Our first task will be to identify the features characteristic of nineteenth-century will theories. It is important not to confuse these theories with two earlier events in legal history: the recognition of the right to make contracts and dispose of property by expressing the will to do so; and the flourishing of other theories of property and contract that also made use of the concept of will.

Before the will theories emerged, both common law and civil law systems had recognized a person's right to make contracts and dispose of property by expressing the will to do so. The phrase "common law" refers to a system of judge-made rules that had grown up in England and later spread to the United States and the British Commonwealth. Until the nineteenth century, the common law was not organized in terms of contract, property, or tort but in terms of writs. Different writs authorized the royal courts to hear different types of cases, and each writ had its own rules. By the early seventeenth century, English courts were using a writ called "assumpsit" to enforce what lawyers now call an informal executory contract.[2] "Informal" means that no special procedure was used to make the contract, and "executory" means that neither party has yet made the performance the contract calls for. It is true that in the nineteenth century, contract law became more important in the eyes of lawyers, and that a systematic body of contract doctrine developed for the first time. Nevertheless, for a long time previously, English courts had enforced informal executory contracts.

In "civil law" countries, courts had traditionally decided cases by applying ancient Roman texts collected by the Emperor Justinian in the sixth century A.D. in a work later known as the *Corpus Iuris Civilis*. Since the rediscovery of Roman law in the twelfth century, generations of law professors had adapted its texts pragmatically and with considerable ingenuity to the problems of the societies in which they lived. One adaptation was the recognition that informal executory contracts were enforceable. By the seventeenth and eighteenth centuries, French and German courts enforced them even though, according to their Roman texts, only certain contracts such as sale, lease, partnership, and agency (*mandatum*) were binding merely upon consent.[3]

Before the nineteenth century, then, both common and civil law systems enforced contracts because the parties expressed the will to be bound to them. In certain exceptional cases such as gifts, more than a mere expression of will was required in both common and civil law, but these exceptions remained in the nineteenth century. As we shall see, the change that occurred with the rise of the will theories was not that jurists recognized that the parties could normally bind themselves by an expression of their will. It was that jurists thought of a contract as merely an expression of their will. Limits to what the parties could legitimately will became puzzling.

Similarly, before the coming of the will theories, common law and civil law courts allowed even supposedly feudal interests in property to be alienated at will by the owner. As A. W. B. Simpson notes, the fee simple had been freely alienable since the late thirteenth century and freely disposable by testament since at least the seventeenth century. Feudal services and incidents had disappeared for practical purposes by the seventeenth century.[4] Similarly, in France, feudal property had been freely alienable and freely transmissible by testament since the later Middle Ages. By the eighteenth century, feudal duties of military service had long since died out,[5] and feudal rents had been commuted to cash payments that had largely lost their significance due to centuries of inflation.[6] It is striking that in the eighteenth century, when Blackstone in England said that an owner had a "sole and despotic dominion,"[7] and when Pothier in France said he had "the right to dispose of a thing at his pleasure,"[8] both of them were speaking of an owner who was technically a feudal tenant.

Again, the rise of the will theories did not mean a recognition of the principle that one could use or alienate property according to one's will. As we will see, it meant that limits to what an owner might will became puzzling.

We can see these changes clearly if we compare the will theories to those that preceded them. In civil law countries, from the sixteenth to the eighteenth century, jurists had subscribed to natural law theories of contract and property. These theories also used the concept of will. The common lawyers, in contrast, were not engaged in building theories until the nineteenth century. Indeed, before then, the common law was not usually taught in universities, and there were hardly any treatises and little systematic doctrine. The circumstance that the will theories were the first common law theories of any kind has confused some English and American historians about what made them new and different. Some have thought that abstraction in dealing with the law of contract[9] or property[10] was a nineteenth-century innovation. Patrick Atiyah has claimed that the idea of will was new. "[T]raditionally," he said, "a contract was primarily conceived of as a relationship involving mutual rights and obligations; there was not necessarily an implication that the relationship was created by a conscious and deliberate act of will."[11] Similarly, he believes that property law changed as people began to think of themselves as owners with a right to dispose of their property as they chose.[12]

But the natural law theories of contract and property which had flourished for centuries on the Continent were also abstract and also used the concept of will. To understand what was new about the will theories, we must examine what these pre-nineteenth-century theories were like.

The basic features that were to characterize the natural law theories first appeared in the work of a group of sixteenth-century jurists centered in Spain and known to historians as the late scholastics or Spanish natural law school.[13] Their members included Domingo de Soto, Luis de Molina, and Leonard Lessius. They explained the Roman texts with principles taken from their intellectual heroes, Aristotle and Thomas Aquinas. They were the first school of jurists to build theories of any kind. Neither the ancient Romans nor the medieval civilians had been given to theorizing. The Romans had clarified legal concepts, not by defining them or tracing them to higher principles, but by testing them against a myriad of hypothetical situations. The medieval jurists had solved their problems by juxtaposing Roman texts.

In the seventeenth and eighteenth centuries, the authority of Aristotelian philosophy waned. Yet, paradoxically, many of the ideas of the late scholastics that had been founded on Aristotelian principles were borrowed and disseminated widely by the northern natural law school founded by Hugo Grotius and Samuel Pufendorf. Indeed, the theories of the northern natural lawyers shared the same basic features. When we compare the natural law theories of the late scholastics and the northern natural lawyers with the will theories, we can see that the nineteenth-century innovation was not to use the concept of the will. It was to use that concept exclusively, without introducing any other concept that could limit what legitimately could be willed. In contrast, in the natural law theories of the late scholastics and northern natural lawyers, such limits were built into the institutions of contract and property. Whether this change in theory led to any significant change in the law in force is another question to which we will turn shortly. But first we must see what kind of theoretical innovation the will theories represented.

At the core of the contract theories of the late scholastics and the northern natural lawyers was the idea that, although a party made a contract by expressing his will to be bound, he might legitimately enter into either of two basic types of arrangements: a gratuitous contract in which he enriched the other party at his own expense, or an onerous contract in which he exchanged his own performance for one of equivalent value.[14] Grotius and Pufendorf devised elaborate schemes of classification to show how the contracts familiar in Roman law can be fitted into these two grand categories.[15] The French jurists Domat and Pothier, who were deeply influenced by the natural lawyers, described these as the two *causes* or reasons for making a binding promise.[16]

For the late scholastics and northern natural lawyers, this classification meant more than the tautology that a party either does or does not receive back something in return for what he gives. In a gratuitous contract, the donor must actually intend to benefit the other party, and if he does not, the contract is not a gratuitous contract whatever the document to which the parties subscribed may say.[17] In an onerous contract, a party must receive, not simply a counterperformance, but one of equivalent value.[18] They also used this principle of equivalence to explain the implied terms that the law would read into a contract absent express consent of the parties. An example is the civil law rule that a seller must warrant his goods against defects. The reason, they explained, is that otherwise the buyer would have paid more than the goods were worth.[19] According to Domat, the seller could expressly disclaim this warranty, but only if he reduced the price so that equality was preserved.[20]

The late scholastics and the northern natural lawyers did not think of the requirement of equality in exchange as an interference with the choices the parties might legitimately make.[21] A party chose a type of contract that corresponded to a legitimate purpose he had in mind: either to enrich another, or merely to exchange. In the latter case, each party must receive an equivalent because each merely wished to exchange and not to enrich the other party at his own expense. If the parties wrote into the contract that any excess over the just price should be considered a gift, Grotius wanted the court to ask whether the party disadvantaged by the contract had actually intended to confer a gratuitous benefit on the other.[22]

Similarly, in the natural law theories of property, the right of the owner to deal with his property as he pleased had been limited by its place in a larger theory about the legitimacy of private property. Typically, the late scholastics and the northern natural lawyers said that by nature or originally, all things belong to everyone. They described private ownership as instituted to overcome the disadvantages of common ownership: for example, people might quarrel more easily, or refuse to work.[23] Accordingly, they all said that the rights of a private owner are qualified rights that must yield in certain cases to the needs of another. The standard example is necessity. A person in urgent need is entitled to use the property of another.[24] Grotius also suggested that there is a right of innocent use: one person can use another's property if he can do so without causing any loss or inconvenience.[25]

In contrast, in the nineteenth century, in both civil and common law countries, the will theorists defined contract in terms of the will or consent or agreement of the parties without any attempt to delimit what could legitimately be willed.[26] They did not explain why the law should enforce contracts or why the expressed will of the parties should be respected. As Valérie Ranouil observed in her study of the French will theories, they took the binding force of contract for granted rather than demonstrating it.[27] She quotes Gounot's characterization of their view: "The contract is obligatory simply because it is the contract."[28]

Having defined the contract solely in terms of will, the will theorists regarded the will as the source of all the terms of the contract. They no longer claimed that these terms rested on the principle of equality or the nature of the parties' agreement. As we will see, they regarded any attempt to interfere with the express terms of the contract in the interests of justice as paternalistic. Indeed, they identified no source other than the will of the parties for the implied terms that the law read into the agreement when the parties failed to specify terms expressly. Some said vaguely that will was the source of all the parties' obligations.[29] Laurent thought that the provisions of the French Civil Code governing various types of contracts were merely those the parties would have thought of themselves. The Code listed them "to dispense the parties from writing them into their instruments."[30] Some jurists suggested that even though the parties would not have thought of these terms, they willed their obligations to be those the law would read into their contract. At the turn of the century, one critic caricatured: "Question, what does the law will? Answer: what the parties will. What do the parties will? What the law wills!"[31]

Similarly, the will theorists defined property as the power of the owner to dispose of what belonged to him according to his will.[32] They did not explain why the owner should have this power or why society should recognize the institution of property. Thus, as in the case of contract, they had no principle to look to other than the will of the owner to explain the rules of property law. As we will see, they found limits that the law placed on what the owner could do to be theoretically inexplicable.

In the case of both contract and property, then, the innovation of the will theorists was not to use the concept of will but to use it to the exclusion of any other principle by which the will could be limited. Having identified this innovation, we can now ask whether it was due, as many historians think, either to the social and economic changes in the nineteenth century, or to the emergence of some new and distinctively modern concept of choice.

< II >

The Will Theories and Social and Economic Change

According to some historians, the will theories arose to remove some obstacle to social and economic change. The trouble is that it is difficult to associate the rise of the will theories with any change in the rules of contract or property law that were actually in force. One might compare the spread of the will theories among jurists to the acceptance of some fashionable modern ethical theory. Its spread may be an important intellectual event which may, in the end, have practical consequences. But we cannot assume without

evidence that those who espouse a particular ethical theory are actually living their lives differently than those who do not.

Again, a source of confusion for common law historians is the
fact that England and the United States were developing systematic
doctrines of contract and property at the same time that they were
adopting will theories. Before the nineteenth century, the common
law had been organized, not by doctrines, but by writs. Even thinking in terms of "contract" rather than "assumpsit" was an innovation. And, as John Orth observes, contract law was comparatively
less important to legal thinking than property law, which had always been the staple of the common law courts.[33]

To a great extent, the common lawyers were repeating the experience of the civil lawyers. Once, civil law had also been unsystematic; but it had been arranged into doctrines by the late scholastics and the natural lawyers. In the *Corpus iuris civilis*, no general
principles had been laid down to govern contract formation, texts
about mistake had appeared haphazardly in a chapter on the law of
sales, rules on duress and fraud in chapters on the actions *quod
metus causa* and *de dolo*, and so forth. The late scholastics and the
natural lawyers tried to formulate general principles about contract
formation and about the influence of mistake, fraud, and duress on
the will. Similarly, before the nineteenth century, the English approach to assumpsit had been unsystematic. Courts had required
there be a promise and consideration without defining either promise or consideration. In the nineteenth century, common lawyers
defined promise as an expression of the will and discussed how
mistake, fraud, and duress affected the will—much as the civil
lawyers had done for centuries—mining the case law for English
examples. They tried for the first time to define consideration, initially equating it with what Pothier and Domat called the *causa* of
an onerous contract.[34] As Simpson and I have shown, the common
lawyers systematized their law by borrowing massively from the
civil lawyers.[35]

It is no wonder that common law historians, seeing English and
American writers move from a few pages on contract in Blackstone
to systematic treatises on contract law, have often thought phenomena to be closely related that are really quite distinct. These
include the attention given contract law, which was a feature of
ancient Roman and medieval civil law but was new to the com-

mon law; the development of systematic contract doctrine, which was a feature of civil law since the time of the late scholastics but was new to the common law; and the rise of the will theories, which was a new phenomenon among civil and common lawyers in the nineteenth century. One cannot assume that any of these changes affected the way cases were actually decided as distinguished from the way in which decisions were explained or rationalized. But in any case, the will theories cannot have been responsible for changes that occurred when the common lawyers borrowed doctrines to which civil lawyers had subscribed before the rise of the will theories.

If we ask what changes in the rules in force the will theories themselves might have caused, we discover, surprisingly enough, that the changes one would expect did not in fact occur. Consequently, it is hard to believe these theories arose to remove some obstacle that these rules presented to social and economic change. The principal difference between the natural law theories and the will theories was that the will theories had no room for limits placed on the will. In contract law, the jurists could not explain the relief that courts gave from an unfair bargain. Many of them concluded that such relief should not be given. But, surprisingly enough, no great change occurred in the relief that courts actually gave. In England and America, courts of equity continued to give relief. As I have shown elsewhere, American equity courts did so rather freely.[36] The change in the nineteenth century, as Simpson has shown, was that jurists said (implausibly) that relief was given, not because a transaction was one-sided, but because its one-sidedness was evidence of fraud.[37] Similarly, common law courts— as distinguished from courts of equity—never examined the adequacy of consideration. The change was that jurists in the nineteenth century said that to do so would interfere with the will of the parties and entail mystical notions of value.[38]

Similarly, the French Civil Code had preserved a traditional remedy, modeled on a Roman text, for a person who sold land at less than half its just price.[39] By the early twentieth century, statutes had given remedies to other victims of unfair bargains.[40] Jurists were puzzled. Some of them said that the remedy was really given for fraud, mistake, or duress, rather than unfairness.[41] Others said that it had no justification at all.[42] But the remedies remained.

In Germany, in the areas in which Roman law was in force, the courts interpreted the Roman text just mentioned expansively, as most continental courts had done since the Middle Ages, to afford a remedy not just for sales of land but wherever there was *laesio enormis*, a deviation by more than half from fair value. In some areas, this remedy was abolished by statute.[43] Yet the courts consistently refused the invitation of the jurists to interpret the text narrowly to apply only to sellers of land.[44] Again, the important change was that the remedy had become puzzling to the jurists. They now said that relief for *laesio enormis* was an exception to the basic principles of contract law.[45]

Similarly, in property law, the principal change in theory was that the jurists were now puzzled by limits the law placed on the owner's will. An example is the law of nuisance and its civil law analogues. The law had always limited the extent to which an owner could use land in ways that interfered with his neighbors, for example, by making noise or smoke. The law continued to do so in the nineteenth century. Both before and after the rise of the will theories, jurists found it difficult to formulate a clear rule. Sometimes, they said that an owner's rights depended on how much his use interfered with others and on whether that use was appropriate to the area. These two factors had been mentioned by common law courts[46] and by Blackstone.[47] They had been mentioned by civilians as early as Bartolus in the fourteenth century[48] and as late as Domat[49] and Pothier in the seventeenth and eighteenth centuries.[50] In the nineteenth century, these factors continued to be mentioned in England,[51] the United States,[52] France,[53] and Germany,[54] although it is still hard to see a clear rule consistently applied.

The nineteenth-century jurists could not explain these limits. But they did not wish to abolish them. The change was that limits on the will had become puzzling. Although the natural lawyers had never really integrated rules about conflicting land use into their theories of property law, nevertheless it did not trouble them that the owner's rights had some limits. In the nineteenth century, however, American[55] and French[56] jurists were caught in the paradox that the owner, who by definition had an absolute right to the use of his property, could not use it any way he chose. So were the Germans. In a famous article the German critic of will theories,

Rudolf von Ihering, showed that one can escape the paradox only by abandoning the idea that the owner has such an absolute right.[57] Ihering took it for granted that his opponents' idea of property rights was so absolute it could tolerate no limits at all.

The change, then, was not in the law in force so much as in the aspects of the law in force that troubled theoretically minded jurists. Paradoxically, more aspects of the law in force in the nineteenth century were puzzling after the rise of the will theories. It therefore seems implausible that the will theories arose to remove obstacles to social or economic change presented by the law in force.

Even if there were no such obstacles, social and economic changes might still explain the rise of the will theories if these changes discredited the natural law theories by producing phenomena that the natural law theories could not explain. While Anglo-American historians have not looked closely at the natural law theories, they have identified social and economic conditions that supposedly conflicted with traditional ideas and led to the rise of the will theories. The trouble is that the conditions they mention are as old as urban civilization: for example, prices fluctuate, merchants profit, and land uses sometimes conflict. The natural law theorists were aware of these phenomena. Moreover, even if these conditions had been altogether new, one cannot say the will theories arose because of them without the aid of a minor premise that only a will theorist would find congenial: that will theories provide the best or at least the most obvious explanation for them. Indeed, the very historians who are the least sympathetic to the will theories seem to rely on this minor premise implicitly.

Horwitz and Atiyah, for example, think that traditional ideas about just prices were undermined when people noticed that market prices fluctuate and merchants profit by buying low and selling high.[58] In small villages in the non-commercial societies that anthropologists study, people do, in fact, conceive of a fair price that way: ideally or invariably so much of one commodity should be exchanged for so much of another.[59] The very fact that a party has bought low and sold high shows that he has broken the rules. The reason seems to be that where markets are thin or non-existent, people protect themselves against lack of information and sudden scarcity by exchanging at fixed rates with regular trading partners.[60]

But these conditions have not existed in the European cities since the commercial revival of the eleventh and twelfth centuries. Moreover jurists, from the Middle Ages onward, described the just price as the price for which an object could be sold commonly,[61] an amount that would differ from day to day and region to region.[62] One could legitimately buy at one price and sell at another.[63]

The problem may be that the historians, like the will theorists, think that no one could believe in a just price after noticing that prices fluctuate and merchants profit. Atiyah claims that Thomas Aquinas must have been thinking, not of "the world of trade," but of "the largely closed medieval village community."[64] It must be so, according to Atiyah, because in the world of trade, merchants profit.[65] But Thomas was thinking of merchants.[66] Atiyah confuses his own conviction that Thomas was wrong with an historical explanation of the rise of will theories.

Similarly, Horwitz suggests that before the nineteenth century, jurists did not notice that land uses conflict. He believes that an owner was entitled to use his property as he chose, whatever the interference with others, and that such a situation was tolerated because "the low level of economic activity made conflict over land use extremely rare."[67] But people have noticed that land uses conflict ever since they began living near each other. The early common law cases force pig sties[68] and breweries[69] out of villages. When the medieval jurist Bartolus discussed conflicting uses of land, he was interpreting a Roman text which prohibited a cheese shop from discharging smoke that bothered people living upstairs.[70]

The problem may be that Horwitz, like the will theorists, imagines that as soon as one notices that land uses conflict, one will be puzzled, as the will theorists were, that the owner's use is restricted even though his property rights are as complete or absolute as property rights can be. Blackstone defined property as a "sole and despotic dominion . . . in total exclusion of the right of any other individual."[71] Horwitz assumes that Blackstone must have believed an owner's rights were absolute in the nineteenth century sense, so that they were not limited in any way. He concludes that Blackstone must have thought an owner could use his property as he chose however much his use might interfere with that of others.[72] Therefore, land use conflicts could not have been frequent enough in Blackstone's day for him to see the difficulties of this position.[73] In fact, however, Blackstone described the law of land use conflicts with a banal statement that would not have been out of place in Bartolus's or our own time: if one person's use interferes with another, "it is incumbent on him to find some other place to do that act, where it will be less offensive."[74]

A final difficulty with social and economic explanations for the rise of the will theories is the timetable. Industrialization began in England in the late eighteenth and early nineteenth centuries, and spread to the mill towns of the northern United States in the 1820s. It came quite late—after mid-century—in France and Germany. But the will theories appeared and passed into mainstream opinion at roughly the same time in all these countries: from about 1820 to 1860. And if we ask how seriously the jurists took them, and how elaborately they worked out the details, the timetable is still worse. In Germany, fairly rigorous theories were developed by Savigny and Puchta in the 1840s, and the most complete version by Windscheid in the 1860s. For French law, the most serious and consistent theories were developed in the 1860s and 1870s by Demolombe, Larombière, and Laurent, though none of them was as rigorous and complete as the German theories. In the common law world, a genuinely dogmatic will theory did not appear, perhaps, until Langdell, and the best worked out version was developed by Pollock under German influence in the 1880s.

≺ III ≻

The Will Theories and Changes in Ideas

We turn, then, to the explanation for the rise of the will theories favored by many continental historians: that the jurists were borrowing from then fashionable philosophical, political, and economic theories in which the individual will played a major role.

On even a cursory view, however, the will theories seem different from other intellectual movements that stressed individual choice. The views of philosophers, economists, and political liberals were the subject of endless disputes, no single view winning out. The will theories, in contrast, enjoyed an easy and universal acceptance. They were espoused by both liberal and tradition-minded jurists.

Moreover, participants in the other intellectual movements that stressed individual choice discussed at great length what choice is and why it is important. Their views as to the nature of choice were as different as the views of Bentham and Kant. In contrast, the will theorists defined contract and property in terms of will without explaining what the will is or why it matters.

In England and the United States, it is hard to see the influence of any fashionable nineteenth-century school of thought. Sir Frederick Pollock, who built the most elaborate will theory, explained that jurists should leave alone "topics which . . . may be philosophical, or ethical, or political, but are distinctly outside the province of jurisprudence."[75] The "business" of jurists is simply "to learn and know . . . what rules the State does undertake to enforce and administer, whatever the real or professed reasons for those rules may be."[76]

Similarly, Ranouil observes in her study of the French will theorists that they seem hostile to philosophy, that they never cite Kant, and that, until the end of the nineteenth century, they never even speak of the autonomy of the will.[77] She concludes, nevertheless, that the will theorists must have been using the concept of autonomy of the will "as Monsieur Jourdan used prose—without perceiving it."[78] It would be more reasonable to conclude that the will theorists were not drawing on the ideas of Kant or any other philosophical, economic, or political explanation of why the will was important.

In Germany, Savigny, who was one of the principal architects of the will theories, was also one of the most philosophical of German jurists. He gave an account of law that owed a good deal to Kant and Hegel. Law existed to protect freedom,[79] and its source was the *Volksgeist*—the unconscious mind or spirit of a particular people.[80] But neither he nor his followers rested their theories on a specifically Kantian or Hegelian conception of will. Indeed, Savigny sharply distinguished the legal concept of will from any philosophical conception: "We in the area of law are not at all occupied with the speculative difficulties of the concept of freedom. For us, freedom is based simply on the appearance, that is, on the capacity, of making a choice among several alternatives."[81]

Instead of identifying some distinctively modern idea of will in the works of the jurists, historians have simply concluded that because the jurists used the concept of will they must have been inspired by or in league with some other intellectual movement in the nineteenth century.[82] But seventeenth- and eighteenth-century natural lawyers used the concept of will. Increasingly, continental historians have met that objection by claiming that the natural lawyers must also have held a modern, individualistic theory of property or contract.[83] In this modified account, the nineteenth-century philosophers, economists, and political thinkers are no longer the parents of the will theorists but siblings. They do not directly inspire the will theorists; rather they and the will theorists bring to full expression in the nineteenth century ideas that the natural lawyers pioneered.

But, as we have seen, the natural lawyers took the basic features of their theories from the late scholastics of sixteenth-century Spain. Some historians have concluded that therefore the late scholastics were the pioneers of modern ideas of contract and property.[84] And yet one can trace the same ideas back even further. The late scholastics built their theory, self-consciously and expressly, on ideas taken from their intellectual hero, Thomas Aquinas. And Thomas had taken them, partly from Roman and Canon law, but principally from Aristotle. Aristotle had distinguished distributive justice, which gives each citizen a fair share of wealth, from commutative justice, which preserves the share of each. According to Aristotle, exchange was an act of voluntary commutative justice which required equality so that each party's share of wealth could be preserved.[85] Thomas concluded that when a person transferred goods to another, he was performing either an act of commutative justice or an act of another Aristotelian virtue, liberality.[86] He used the requirement of equality to explain the doctrine of *laesio enormis*[87] and the rule that a seller must warrant against defects.[88]

Similarly, Aristotle, arguing against Plato's view that all property should be common, had agreed that external things existed to serve the needs of everyone but pointed out the disadvantages of common ownership: there would be perpetual quarrels, and those who labor much and get little will complain of those who labor little and get much.[89] Thomas concluded that while in principle, external things should be common, private property was instituted to remedy these disadvantages of common ownership.[90] These ideas gave the late scholastics the ground plan on which they built. I suppose someone could claim that Thomas Aquinas and Aristotle were the true pioneers of modern ideas about contract and property, but at that point, I begin to lose track of what medieval or ancient ideas are supposed to look like.

It would be better to concentrate, not on the idea of will, which was common to all of these theories, but on the limitations to what one can legitimately will, which we find in Aristotle, Thomas Aquinas, the late scholastics, and the northern natural lawyers, but not in the will theories. If we ask why these limitations disappeared, the simplest answer is that they were based on an Aristotelian philosophical tradition that had lost its authority. The natural law theories of contract had been built on Aristotle's idea of equality in exchange which was founded in turn upon Aristotle's distinction between distributive and commutative justice. The natural law theories of property had been built on Aristotle's idea that private rights were instituted to remedy the disadvantages of common ownership. These ideas rested in turn on a concept of human nature in which need was different than desire, in which human needs differed in their importance, and in which human society existed to ensure that the most important needs were met. In the seventeenth and eighteenth centuries, jurists had gone on using such ideas implicitly long after modern philosophers had attacked them. But they could not do so forever. Sooner or later, they would either have had to rehabilitate these concepts—difficult as the job might be in a post-Aristotelian intellectual climate—or junk them. The real surprise is that seventeenth- and eighteenth-century jurists had continued to use these concepts uncritically while professing allegiance to modern anti-Aristotelian philosophers.

If I am right, then, the central intellectual event that produced the will theories is not the rise of modern notions of choice—as expressed in the philosophical, economic, and political writings popular in the nineteenth century—but the fall of the Aristotelian philosophical tradition, an event that caught up with the lawyers a bit later than with everyone else. These events are related since modern philosophy, economics, and political theory also began with a break from the Aristotelian tradition. But the will theories are less like offspring or siblings and more like second cousins.

Because they originated in a rejection of distinctively Aristote-

lian ideas rather than in an acceptance of any positive philosophical, economic, or political justification, the will theories caught on
easily and universally. None of the jurists objected to jettisoning
older ideas that seemed problematic. Few if any of them would
have found a notion like commutative justice intelligible, and to
use such an idea to explain law would have been to venture into
philosophical realms where few if any were equipped to go. Moreover, none of the jurists objected to retaining a concept of the will
so amorphous that it seemed unobjectionable. In contrast, contemporary philosophical, economic, and political theories were controversial because they were developed around some definite ideas
about choice.

≺ IV ≻

The Impact of the Will Theories

Thus far, we have seen that the will theories arose neither in response to a change in social and economic conditions nor in response to the new individualistic theories fashionable in the nineteenth century. Once in place, however, they interacted with these
theories and so affected people's understanding and response to the
new social and economic conditions which they confronted.

With the rise of the will theories, jurists, for the first time,
claimed that a coherent theory of contract and property could rest
on the idea of the will alone and need not take account of the substantive fairness of a transaction, the needs of non-owners, or the
fairness of the distribution of wealth. When the jurists made this
claim almost unanimously, non-jurists tended to assume that they
were right.

One consequence was that the new individualistic theories
seemed more credible. Because the jurists' idea of will was so
amorphous, anyone—indeed, everyone—with a philosophical, political, and economic theory that stressed freedom or choice could
regard the jurists as allies. In the eighteenth century, in contrast,
the jurists had seemed to be an obstacle to such theories. Bentham
had to argue that Blackstone was talking nonsense. Kant said he
had to emancipate himself from the teachings of the natural lawyer, Christian Wolff.

A more significant consequence was that the will theorists'
conceptions of property and contract seemed plausible even to
those who opposed the individualistic theories of the time or were
concerned about the consequences of industrialization. They, too,
concluded that contract and property meant enforcing the expressed will of the parties or the owner, and that in these realms,
questions of fairness and human need did not legally matter. Consequently, they, like their adversaries, imagined that legal rules
that went beyond enforcing the will of parties or owners must necessarily be interferences by the state with the normal operation of
contract and property law. But they were in favor of interferences.

This tendency to conceive of state intervention as an interference with the normal operation of contract and property law was
characteristic of reform efforts in continental Europe. Typically, reformers did not claim that the institutions of private property and
contract presupposed a fair distribution of wealth and a substantively fair contract. They did not expect judges to ask whether substantive fairness in an employment contract required, for example,
that the employer be liable for industrial accidents or provide security of employment. Reform efforts led in two quite different directions. One was the enactment of so-called "social legislation," beginning in France, with a statute imposing liability on employers
for industrial accidents,[91] and in Germany, with the industrial accident and social security legislation of Bismarck. This legislation
was never thought to cohere with the provisions on contract and
property of the continental civil codes. Even today, civil lawyers
are inclined to see legislation prescribing the terms of contracts or
limiting the use of property as a matter of "public law," as an interference by the state, however justifiable, with an autonomous and
internally coherent body of private law. The second reform effort
was the formation of socialist parties. Again, a sharp line was
drawn between private contract and property and state action, but
this time the goal was to replace contract by state administration
and private property by state ownership.

In the United States, the enactment of comprehensive social
legislation lagged (and still lags) behind Europe, and strong socialist
parties never formed. Yet one can see the same tendency among reformers to distinguish the normal operation of contract and property law from intervention by the state, and to make the case for

state intervention by criticizing the institutions of contract and property. Charles McCurdy points to Richard Ely's *Studies in the Evolution of Industrial Society* in 1903 as typical of the reform literature of the time.[92] Assume that people are equal, Ely argued, and "each one can guard his own interests individually, providing only the hampering fetters of law should make way for a reign of liberty." But instead, "back of the contract lies inequality in strength of those who form the contract . . . Wealth and poverty, plenty and hunger, nakedness and warm clothing, ignorance and learning, face each other in contract, and find expression in and through contract."[93] These arguments were tracked by Roscoe Pound in his famous essay in 1909, "Liberty of Contract."[94] For both Ely and Pound, they explained why there had to be less contract and more state intervention.

Their critique of contract law was constructed on the very premises of the will theorists. If contract merely expressed the will of the parties, then any concern by court for the fairness of a contract would, indeed, be an interference with the determinations of the parties. When the American will theories were initially being constructed, Joseph Story had explained:

[E]very person who is not from his peculiar condition under disability is entitled to dispose of his property as he chooses; and whether his bargains are wise and discreet or profitable or unprofitable or otherwise are considerations not for courts of justice but for the party himself to deliberate upon.[95]

In effect, Pound and Ely went one step farther: if contract left the parties to protect their own interests, contract must mirror disparities in the ability to protect them. The idea that the standards of fairness belong to the very institution of contract—an idea that jurists had defended for centuries—seems to have vanished from the face of the earth. The result, for reformers such as Ely and Pound, was that contract, taken in itself, was inherently impossible to reform. The terms of a contract must necessarily reflect, not justice, but power. Therefore, the state must intervene to protect people from contract.

In Europe and the United States, then, though responses to industrialization differed, the rise of the will theories encouraged non-jurists as well as jurists, and reformers as well as partisans of laissez-faire, to think of contract and property in terms of individ-

ual will. Once that step was taken, the case for reform could not be
made by appeal to norms intrinsic to the institutions of contract
and property. Indeed, it became difficult to call for reform without
conjuring the specter of state interference with contract whenever
the bargaining strength of the parties was unequal, which is to say,
nearly always.

In the United States, the rise of these theories also set the stage
for the great constitutional battle over freedom of contract which is
described in other chapters of this volume. There was no real parallel to this battle in Europe where courts lacked the power to declare legislation unconstitutional.

From 1905, when it decided *Lochner v. New York*,[96] until 1937,
when it retreated in *West Coast Hotel v. Parrish*,[97] the American
Supreme Court struck down legislation prescribing the terms on
which parties must contract unless it could be justified by the
promotion of public health and safety. As the Court explained in
Lochner, the state could require a ten-hour day for railway engineers because safety depended on their alertness, but it could not
do so for bakers since the wholesomeness of their bread did not depend upon how long they worked.[98] The New York bakeshop law
that attempted to do so was therefore an unconstitutional infringement of the parties' contractual rights.

In his famous dissent, Oliver Wendell Holmes objected that
"The Fourteenth Amendment does not enact Mr. Herbert Spencer's
Social Statics."[99] We miss the point of his remark unless we realize
that the majority of the Court would have denied it was deciding
the case on the theories of Herbert Spencer or anyone else. The
majority claimed its view rested, not on social theory, but on law.
It could do so because the rise of the will theories had provided the
Court with the minor premise of its argument. The major premise
was that the United States Constitution protected contract rights.
The minor premise might have been taken from Joseph Story, who
had said that as a matter of contract law, "every person . . . is entitled to dispose of his property as he chooses." Judge Peckham,
speaking for the Court in *Lochner*, affirmed "the general right of an
individual to be free in his person and in his power to contract."[100]

A similar result was narrowly averted when the Supreme Court
ruled on state regulation of the use of property. In 1926, in *Village
of Euclid v. Amber Realty Co.*,[101] the Court considered the consti-

tutionality of state zoning laws. Four justices considered them to be an unconstitutional infringement of the right to property. Here, as in *Lochner*, the minor premise of their argument was provided by the will theories. As we have seen, for the will theorists, the law of property protected the right of the owner to do as he chooses just as the law of contract protected the right of the parties to agree as they choose. Nevertheless, in *Village of Euclid*, the legislation was upheld when Justice Sutherland broke ranks.

Sutherland upheld the legislation by drawing an analogy to the law of nuisance. From our earlier discussion, we can see why this analogy was still available. As we saw, the law of nuisance was as troublesome to will theories of property as rules requiring fairness had been to will theories of contract. Both imposed limits on a will that was in theory unlimited. Nevertheless, Anglo-American will theorists had reacted differently. They admitted that the law of nuisance puzzled them, but they did not try to abolish it or pretend it was not there. In contrast, they did pretend that courts never gave relief for the unfairness of contractual terms. They claimed that courts of equity gave relief for unconscionability only to prevent fraud and not because of unfairness. Decades later, the case against government regulation of land use did not appear to Sutherland as clear cut as the case against government regulation of contract terms.

It may be, of course, that the majority in *Lochner* and the dissent in *Village of Euclid* were influenced by the individualistic theories of the time, as Holmes suspected; or by class bias; or by any number of other factors. The will theories, however, allowed them to move to their conclusion seemingly by deductive logic and seemingly without straying outside the province of law itself. And we have no reason to doubt that the judges themselves sincerely believed they had done so.

We can appreciate their sincerity more easily if we look at the difficulties that had been created for them by the rise of the will theories and the acceptance of the premises of these theories even by their adversaries. It is all very well to say that their conception of freedom was "formal." But what Ely and Pound offered as a corrective was intervention by the state to redress inequalities in bargaining power. But according to them, the terms of all contracts are determined by relative bargaining power as surely as the motions of particles are determined by the vectors of opposing forces. They proposed no standard for determining, any more than one could with the motion of particles, whether the exercise of this power or its results were just or unjust. Consequently, they proposed no standard for determining when the state could justly intervene.

It is no wonder that in the opinion of the *Lochner* majority, this approach meant turning those with political power loose to interfere with people's rights whenever they chose. As Charles McCurdy describes in chapter 6, Oliver Wendell Holmes proposed to say in one of his opinions that "to suppose that every other force may exercise its compulsion at will but that the government has no authority to counteract the pressure with its own is absurd." He backed down when his colleagues objected. Indeed, McCurdy has shown that even the reformed Supreme Court was afraid of where ideas like this would leave private rights.

It might have helped to distinguish, as jurists had once done, among state interventions that distribute resources more justly, that prevent one party to a contract from exploiting the other by diminishing his share of resources, and that merely take resources from one person who lacks political power and give them to another person who has it. Intellectual clarity, of course, does not by itself prevent injustice. Resources were often badly distributed and people were often exploited in the centuries when educated people believed in distributive justice and commutative justice. But clarity may prevent the tragic conflict that takes place among sincere people who defend extreme and simplistic principles because they can see no middle ground.

Contract Before "Freedom of Contract"

DAVID LIEBERMAN

EIGHTEENTH-CENTURY ENGLAND witnessed few dramatic changes in the common law and equity courts' treatment of contract
disputes.[1] Nevertheless, this was an era which has been thought
crucial to the history of freedom of contract. From the final quarter
of the century onwards, distinctive bodies of social speculation—notably Adam Smith's political economy and Jeremy Bentham's utilitarian jurisprudence—entered public currency, and these proved decisive in shaping the individualistic intellectual orthodoxy that facilitated the rise of contractual freedom and the defeat of earlier, paternalistic approaches to market exchange. This was the historical
narrative A. V. Dicey confidently published in his 1905 *Law and
Public Opinion in England during the Nineteenth Century*,[2] and (as
we shall see) key features of this treatment survive in current legal
histories.

The aim of this chapter is to revisit and qualify this long-lived
interpretation. It seems correct to suppose, with Dicey and others,
that the rise of freedom of contract implicated the reforming doctrines of the eighteenth century in important ways. But, as I shall
seek to show, the lines of influence and connection are much less
firm and self-evident than is suggested in standard legal histories.
And, in particular, the period preceding the rise of freedom of contract needs to be characterized with far greater care and precision
than has been done by the historians of nineteenth-century English
law.

≺ I ≻

The Rise of Contract and Its Themes

The scene, in thematic terms, can be set by invoking two deservedly famous productions of academic legal studies in England. The

first was, quite literally, the original instance of university-based common law scholarship: Sir William Blackstone's *Commentaries on the Laws of England*. Presented as a course of lectures at Oxford University in 1753 and published in four volumes 1765–69, Blackstone's *Commentaries* aimed to furnish "a general map of the law" in England, "marking out the shape of the country, its connections and boundaries, its greater divisions and principal cities."[3] And, as numerous modern readers have noted, it was a map in which contract law nearly vanished from the landscape. In part the vanishing act was the product of Blackstone's isolating into discreet and established legal topics material that succeeding English jurists would unify under the law of contract. Thus, mortgage was treated as one of the several "estates upon condition" known at common law, while leases were placed within the discussion of "title by deed."[4] The law regulating employers and employees was handled within the traditional category of "master and servant," which Blackstone located (along with the laws of "husband and wife," "parent and child," "guardian and ward") under the larger unit of "private oeconomical [that is, household] relations."[5] The field of contractual remedies was organized according to the technical structure of common law writs into "three distinct species": debt, covenant, and assumpsit.[6]

In a work of over 1,800 pages, Blackstone's most concentrated engagement with contract was confined to a 30-page survey of the modes of acquiring title to personal property by "gift, grant, and contract."[7] "Blackstone's treatment of contract," A. W. B. Simpson reports of this discussion, "is unsatisfactory";[8] and this judgment echoes those of Blackstone's contemporary admirers who noted the *Commentaries*' more pervasive failure in treating areas of the law governing commercial enterprise and exchange. Thus, Sir William Jones justified his 1781 treatise on the law of bailments by observing that "our excellent Blackstone, who of all men was best able to throw the clearest light on this, as on every other subject, has comprised the whole doctrine in three paragraphs, which, without affecting the merit of his incomparable work, we may safely pronounce the least satisfactory part of it."[9]

The treatment of contract in the second academic law-book supplies a conveniently sharp point of contrast. The work in question—Henry Maine's 1861 *Ancient Law*—appeared roughly a century after the first edition of the *Commentaries*. The most famous statement contained in Maine's most famous book was, of course, the summary theme of Maine's historical and comparative jurisprudence: that as far as such developments manifest themselves in legal materials, "we may say that the movement of the progressive societies has hitherto been a movement *from Status to Contract*."[10] Not only did contract in this manner give shape to the nature and direction of previously experienced societal progress; modern society itself could be distinguished in terms of the pervasiveness of this legal relationship. As Maine confidently reported in introducing his later chapter on "the early history of contract":

There are few general propositions concerning the age to which we belong which seem at first sight likely to be received with readier concurrence than the assertion that the society of our day is mainly distinguished from that of preceding generations by the largeness of the sphere which is occupied in it by Contract. Some of the phenomena on which this proposition rests are among those most frequently singled out for notice, for comment, and for eulogy. Not many of us are so unobservant as not to perceive that in the innumerable cases where the old law fixed a man's social position irreversibly at his birth, modern law allows him to create it for himself by convention.[11]

The dramatic juristic space between Blackstone's mid-eighteenth-century neglect of contract and Maine's mid-nineteenth-century celebration has deservedly attracted sustained historical attention. While the legal literature on the relevant English history is less voluminous than the corresponding American consideration of the routes to and from *Lochner*, the "Rise of Freedom of Contract" remains a well-studied and well-contested theme. In approaching this scholarship now, it is useful to distinguish three distinct, though admittedly nested, themes that are frequently at issue in these historical treatments.

The first theme might be classified as the economic and social history of freedom of contract. This concerns the (now) familiar process of social change by which areas of economic activity, hitherto organized under a range of regulatory regimes, came to be assimilated to the category of contract. For commentators of Maine's era, perhaps the leading instance of this form of the rise of freedom of contract appeared in the area of work and labor.[12] Relations of employment, previously governed by customary right, municipal and craft regulations, the medieval statutes of laborers, and the

Elizabethan Statute of Artificers, were now determined by free contracts between employer and employee. The prior legal category of "master and servant" had been replaced by "contract"; and by extension more generally, the rise of freedom of contract referred to the manner in which the law of contract came to do more legal work than in earlier eras. In Maine's words, what was observed so strikingly was "the largeness of the sphere occupied by contract."

A second major theme of the history of freedom of contract can be placed under the rubric of doctrinal legal history. Here the object of attention is the process by which a certain version of contract law and theory came to attain authority in the nineteenth century. The juristic delineation of this "will theory" (or "classical" or "consensual" version of contract, or the "wholly executory" contractual form) has received intense scholarly consideration in recent years.[13] The (now) familiar classical conception—that "a contract is primarily an agreement based on the intention of the parties, and that it is their will which creates the legal obligation"[14]—involved a critical set of jurisprudential reorientations. "The emergence of the general principles of contract law," P. S. Atiyah explains of the leading doctrinal changes, "saw the shift in emphasis from property law to contract; and within the realm of contract . . . the shift from particular relationships, or particular types of contract, to general principles of contract, and the shift from executed to executory contracts."[15]

For the themes pursued in this chapter, the contributions by J. H. Baker and A. W. B. Simpson to recent historical scholarship are especially instructive.[16] Both have stressed the combination of institutional and intellectual developments which facilitated the formation of a general law of contract in the nineteenth century. At the institutional level, the development of a general *law* of contract (as opposed to the mere resolution of contract disputes at common law) required procedural changes concerning the distribution of responsibility between judge and jury. Intellectually, the exposition of highly generalized and systematic principles of contract law in treatise form involved a common law assimilation of continental legal literature; a process of appropriation that Philip Hamburger has shown to be well under way by the late seventeenth century.[17] These studies warn us against regarding the doctrinal dimensions of the rise of freedom of contract in terms of the substitution of a "modern" set of contract rules for a prior legal regime in which contract was routinely sacrificed to theories of just price or a paternalist hostility to market mechanisms.[18] Instead, the nineteenth-century "will theory" of contract rested on a selective and novel ordering of legal materials that were already well established in English law. As J. H. Baker succinctly puts it, "all the features of contract theory" associated with the period after 1770, "were present in the law long before."[19]

There is, additionally, a third dimension to the history of freedom of contract, which can be usefully distinguished from the more purely doctrinal story scrutinized in legal history. This concerns the way in which contract came in the nineteenth century to be presented as the centerpiece of the legal order itself. Not only was contract doing more work, not only was there a distinctive way of conceptualizing the nature of contract which unified a range of previously discrete legal relationships; beyond all this contractual association was now the juristic construction for the basic ordering of modern social affairs. Discussing what he termed the "general principles of legislation" in his 1891 *Elements of Politics*, Henry Sidgwick explained:

Withdraw contract—suppose that no one can count upon any one else fulfilling an engagement—and the members of a human community are atoms that cannot effectively combine; the complex cooperation and division of employments that are the essential characteristics of modern industry cannot be introduced among such beings. Suppose contracts freely made and effectively sanctioned, and the most elaborate social organization becomes possible, at least in a society of such human beings as the individualistic theory contemplates—gifted with mature reason, and governed by enlightened self-interest.[20]

Sidgwick, in these remarks, was avowedly summarizing what he recognized as a reigning orthodoxy of late nineteenth-century political speculation (though there was much in this orthodoxy he was eager to qualify and revise). And, as he went on to explain, the precise rendering of this orthodoxy had profound implications for the then-current political contest between "individualism" and "collectivism," and the political clash over the proper sphere of the state's legislative interventions. It was in terms of this late nineteenth-century debate that many of the most robust rehearsals of freedom of contract came to be advanced; and it was in terms of these categories of debate that Dicey formulated his long-influential history of modern English law.[21]

Sidgwick's characterization of the "general principles of legislation" implicated the nineteenth-century "will theory" in two critical respects. First and most famously, it explicitly incorporated the idea of individual choice and self-determination which the "will theory" emphasized, and thereby attributed the moral value of personal freedom to a society based on contractual association. And second, and less explicitly, it presumed the unity of those relationships assimilated by law to the category of contract. Precisely because so many kinds of relationships were particular instances of contract, the fundamental, organizing terms of social intercourse could be captured by this single, expansive category of law. Accordingly, we might think of this version of freedom of contract as operating at the intersections of the legal history and political sociology of nineteenth-century society. Its presence serves as a useful reminder that in examining contract before the era of "freedom of contract"—as I am seeking to do here—we can usefully consider ideas both about contract itself and about the place and significance of contract in the more general operations of the legal order.

≺ II ≻

Smith, Bentham, and Contract

One way to begin is to examine in greater detail the manner in which eighteenth-century materials have commonly figured in previous histories of the rise of freedom of contract. In recent years, the most ambitious and sophisticated of such surveys has been supplied by P. S. Atiyah in his massive 1979 study, *The Rise and Fall of Freedom of Contract*. It is tempting to compare Atiyah's work to that of Dicey. Atiyah—confining himself more narrowly to contract law, yet drawing on a far more extensive body of source materials—follows Dicey in seeking a legal history that relates legal change to broader transformations in economy and political culture. And Atiyah frequently is at pains to insulate his own account of law and public opinion in nineteenth-century England from the criticisms leveled against Dicey's earlier history of legal transformations. Thus, for Atiyah, the juristic elaboration of freedom of contract is indeed to be linked to doctrines of laissez-faire individualism. It would be wrong, however, to imagine that laissez-faire ever monopolized specific phases of nineteenth-century reform; or to ignore the several settings, such as temperance agitation and educational improvement, where the defenders of individualism looked to government to increase the scale of its legal involvement.[22]

Where Atiyah remains most faithful to Dicey is in his general intellectual history. For both, "Individualism" figured as the critical organizing category of social and political reflection to England's "Age of Freedom of Contract"; and for both, the influential, theoretical construction of this "individualism" was the handiwork of the famous firm of "Smith and Bentham." "The intellectual background to the legal developments" of the period 1770–1870, Atiyah explains, "was dominated by two bodies of thought. The first, associated with Adam Smith and his successors, were the economic theories . . . known in their time as 'political economy'. And the second was the body of thought, known . . . as utilitarianism, associated, inevitably with Jeremy Bentham, and his coterie."[23] The two bodies of thought "were closely associated" and "mutually reinforcing"; they enjoyed extensive influence; and "the concept of freedom of contract" lay "at the very heart" of Smithian economics.[24]

Even allowing for the kind of distortion that inevitably occurs as a result of Atiyah's concern to survey the cultural landscape from the perspective of mid-nineteenth-century contract doctrine, this is a woefully selective reading of the relevant "intellectual background" to nineteenth-century law reform. It dramatically abbreviates the legacies of Smith and Bentham, whose teachings often proved ambiguous or marginal to later generations. Thus, the *Wealth of Nations* was relatively silent on matters such as poor relief and the bullion question, which dominated economic debate in the post-Napoleonic era; and, as Biancamaria Fontana reports of economic theorizing in the first quarter of the nineteenth century, "Smith's views had never attained an unchallenged dominance, even within the restricted world of the Scottish universities."[25] The question of Bentham's influence remains fiercely contested and easily exaggerated, even if we resist the claims of those historians who insist that "had Bentham never lived, most of the reforms popularly ascribed to his influence would probably have come about."[26] But most important, Atiyah's emphasis on Smith and Bentham serves to obscure the range of cultural sources for nineteenth-century individualism and its accompanying critiques of paternalistic economic policy. In a series of important studies, Boyd Hilton, for example, has elaborated the essential theological orientation of the economic program of liberal Toryism, finding in moderate Evangelicalism the most potent sources for "free trade individualism." The economic writings of "an avowedly moralistic and specifically Christian standpoint," Hilton reports, "provide the most vivid insight into the 'official mind' of the period, and it is they—more than the 'classical economists'—who throw light on the ideological elements . . . behind the policies of Free Trade and the Gold Standard."[27]

These historical researches point to the difficulty of scrutinizing nineteenth-century legal change in terms of any simple dichotomy between "older paternalistic traditions" and a "newer individualist morality."[28] The problems this perspective produces for the history of contract can be highlighted by exploring more directly the doctrines of the putative intellectual heroes of Atiyah's account: Smith and Bentham. Atiyah, himself, recognizes a striking paradox in this regard. Notwithstanding the influence on contractual freedom ascribed to Smith and Bentham, and notwithstanding the centrality of freedom of contract ascribed to each of their speculative systems, the awkward fact is that neither Smith nor Bentham actually ever had all that much to say about freedom of contract. "We now come," Atiyah observes, "to a curious point in the history of these various intellectual movements. Despite the constant association of freedom of contract with the ideals of classical political economy and of utilitarianism, no real thought was ever devoted to the law of contract and its relationship to the outer framework of law."[29] Atiyah, in this passage, chiefly refers to the absence of discussion concerning the state's function in enforcing contracts. But the observation invites a more general question concerning the extent to which "contract" or "freedom of contract" functioned as organizing elements in Smith's and Bentham's conceptualizations of the legal order and programs of reform.

Of Smithian political economy, the claim is that "the concept of freedom of contract was at the very heart" of the system.[30] Of

Smith, himself, the idea more accurately should be stated: the virtue of justice was at the center of his moral speculations, from *The Theory of Moral Sentiments*, through to the (unpublished) *Lectures on Jurisprudence*, and finally in the scrutiny of commercial society in *An Inquiry into the Nature and Causes of the Wealth of Nations*. Like other eighteenth-century Scottish moralists, notably David Hume, Smith was struck by the exceptional character of justice in the canon of moral virtues. Violations of most virtues stimulated disapproval on the part of those who learned of the misdeed. Violations of justice, in contrast, properly led "to resentment and consequently to punishment." Justice, moreover, was unique in comprising "upon most occasions but a negative virtue."

The man who barely abstains from violating either the person, or the estate, or the reputation of his neighbors, has surely very little positive merit. He fulfills, however, all the rules of what is peculiarly called justice . . . We may often fulfill all the rules of justice by sitting still and doing nothing.[31]

Yet, notwithstanding this "negative" character, justice was the sole indispensable virtue for effective social existence. "Society cannot subsist," Smith explained, "unless the laws of justice are tolerably observed, as no social intercourse can take place among men who do not generally abstain from injuring one another."[32]

Finally, because the requirements of justice could be specified with an exactitude and detail not appropriate to the discussion of other virtues, it was possible to delineate "the particular rules of justice" and to evaluate systems of positive law according to the standard established by such "systems of the rules of natural justice." This kind of juristic project Smith believed to have been inaugurated by Grotius, whose "treatise on the laws of war and peace" Smith celebrated as perhaps the most complete "system of those principles which ought to run through and be the foundation of the laws of all nations."[33]

In the *Lectures on Jurisprudence*, which he delivered as part of his teaching duties as Professor of Moral Philosophy at Glasgow University and long promised for publication, Smith presented his own version of a Grotian system on natural jurisprudence.[34] This setting gave him the opportunity to elaborate the conception of justice introduced in his *Theory of Moral Sentiments*. The virtue, again, was specified "negatively": justice was fulfilled by not inflicting "any injury or hurt without cause"; and the bulk of Smith's discussion comprised an account of the system of "rights" possessed by an individual—either as a man, or as a member of a family, or as a member of a state—whose violation constituted acts of injustice.[35] As in other systems of natural law produced by Grotius and his successors, property rights received lavish attention. Contract figured as part of a not particularly highlighted section on the personal rights an individual could attain to the performance of another's service.[36] Smith grounded contractual obligation upon "the expectation and dependence which was excited in him to whom the contract was made," distinguishing this account from rival treatments which based the obligation on the idea of willing or on the duty to truthfulness.[37] Finally, Smith set out a summary history of the enforcement of contracts in English law and equity.

Most of the structure and categories of Smith's jurisprudence were conventional, including his positioning of contractual obligations late in the discussion of property rights. If we adopt the contrasting conceptions of contract used to distinguish the modern will theory from its predecessors, Smith's treatment is traditional: there is no readily discernible "shift in emphasis from property law to contract."[38] What was more distinctive and innovative was the amount of attention Smith gave to the historical development of property rights, according to the changing pattern of subsistence that attended society's progress from rudeness to refinement. Smith, in first explaining the idea of a natural jurisprudence in his *Theory of the Moral Sentiments*, had stressed no system of human law would ever "coincide exactly, in every case, with the rules of which the natural sense of justice would dictate."[39] In most social settings, political abuses or social conditions might easily subvert the legal order's capacity to do justice. In the *Lectures on Jurisprudence*, Smith exemplified the theme frequently, pointing to legal rules which presupposed particular levels and forms of societal development, and property rules which unduly restricted the network of rights specified by natural justice.[40]

An Inquiry into the Nature and Causes of the Wealth of Nations is not typically regarded as a book about the virtue of justice.[41] Nonetheless, the themes of Smith's earlier reflections on the virtue form a basic, connective thread through the Smithian system of political economy. Where this is most readily perceived is in the discussion in book 5, in which Smith examined "the Expence of Justice" and the duty of the sovereign to establish "an exact administration of justice." There he simply reproduced much of the analysis of the virtue of justice that had been developed in his earlier moral and legal philosophy.[42] But an equally important and suggestive section of the text appeared in book 3 (on "the different progress of opulence in different nations") where Smith continued the historical reflections first elaborated in his jurisprudence. It was here that Smith presented the complex moral case for commercial society by delineating the connections among commerce, liberty, and justice. The social revolution in early-modern Europe produced by "commerce and manufactures," Smith maintained, had introduced "order and good government, and with them, the liberty and security of individuals." The feudal nobility had bartered its "power and authority" in order to purchase the luxuries supplied by trade and commerce. In the transition from feudalism to commercial society, the laboring poor, previously situated in a condition "of servile dependency upon their superiors," found themselves instead dependent on an impersonal market. By subduing the personal power of the nobles, commerce had enabled more ordered and settled forms of government, and with them less partial institutions of justice. Commercial society thereby created opportunities for liberty and security and for relations of justice, which had simply been absent in earlier eras. This transformation, Smith concluded, was "the least observed," but "by far the most important of all [the] effects" of commerce and manufactures.[43]

Through such arguments, Smith valorized the achievement of commercial society beyond its capacity to produce wealth and comfort. Following this historical reconstruction, he next (and more famously) pursued the discussion of commerce and liberty in book 4's trenchant critique of physiocracy and mercantilism, and of the prevailing structure of economic protectionism. Smith's strictures against the current system of bounties, tariffs, colonies, and labor restraints were twofold: such measures undermined prosperity and they violated the principles of justice and natural liberty.[44] Having already achieved in Britain the institutions of regular government and the impartial administration of justice, what generally was required was the removal of those economic regulations which frustrated the accumulation of wealth and sacri-

ficed the rights of most of the community to the sectional interests
of others. "All systems either of preference or of restraint . . . being
thus taken away, the obvious and simple system of natural liberty
establishes itself of its own accord. Every man, as long as he does
not violate the laws of justice, is left perfectly free to pursue his
own interests in his own way."[45]

As Atiyah properly recognizes, Smith's system of "natural liberty" did not amount to a program of laissez-faire (though it is
doubtful whether Atiyah or other historians of contract have taken
the full measure of this insight).[46] The virtue of justice, and its
connection with the benefits of liberty and security, was central to
the Smithian science of commercial society and market exchange.
Of course, to display in this way Smith's concern with justice
throughout all of his moral philosophy is, in some sense, also to
show his concern with the institution of contract; since contractual rights featured squarely in the bundle of personal rights which
Smith, as was common, placed in the system of natural justice.
But, to make this point, as Atiyah does, by claiming that "freedom
of contract" was "at the heart" of Smithian political economy is to
draw a thin and rather misleading return on a substantial body of
intellectual capital.

In fact, this inflating of the importance of freedom of contract
appears chiefly the result of a selective reading of Smith's controversial case for freedom of trade.[47] The liberalizing case for free
trade presented in the *Wealth of Nations* was avowedly radical: to
expect its full implementation in Great Britain, Smith conceded,
"is as absurd as to expect that an Oceana or Utopia should ever be
established in it."[48] Smith strictly qualified his reforming program:
he identified considerations, such as national defense, where free
trade was appropriately sacrificed, and advocated a gradualist approach to the repeal of the prevailing system of bounties and impositions. Moreover, the case for international free trade went along
with a defense of various kinds of restraints on domestic exchanges, such as the regulation of interest rates or the credit practices of banks.[49] Nonetheless, these qualifications were easily neglected in the specific settings in which Smith's teaching was first
received and contested. The corn law debates of the late eighteenth
century provided one such formative setting, and on this issue
Smithian political economy most readily (though misleadingly)

could be summarized in terms of the complete removal of legal restraints on private markets.[50] Equally significant for Smith's legacy may have been the readiness of his admirers to make the Smithian case against legal restraints even in those areas of economic activity where Smith, himself, defended a regime of regulation.

It is at this juncture that Benthamite utilitarianism can be reintroduced into the discussion, initially through the vehicle of Bentham's own 1787 tract in *Defence of Usury*. The *Defence of Usury*, one of Bentham's few eighteenth-century publications to receive any sustained public notice, embraced the Smithian case against economic paternalism to repudiate the prevailing arguments in support of laws against usury, including the arguments advanced in the *Wealth of Nations*. The deployment of political economy in the work is quite revealing, not least because much of Bentham's polemic against the usury statutes did not involve any doctrines concerning the nature and causes of the wealth of nations. Thus, in later years, he described the work as an applied exercise in the principles of critical legal classification, in this instance exposing a penal law which lacked the required justification in public utility.[51] And one of the tract's organizing claims derived from Bentham's developing theory of language, where he sought to show how the value-laden associations of the term "usury" frustrated any objective evaluation of the legal restraints on interest rates.[52] Nonetheless, it was "Dr. Smith" and Smithian political economy that Bentham chose to highlight. The case for freedom of trade in monetary bargains, Bentham emphasized, utilized "weapons" which Bentham had been taught "to wield" by the *Wealth of Nations*.[53]

The *Defence of Usury*'s arguments against legal restraints upon market exchange figured prominently in several of Bentham's economic writings, which likewise displayed their Smithian credentials prominently. "Dr. Smith," he reported, was "a writer of great and distinguished merit"; and any attempt to consider implications of the science of political economy for legislative policy naturally began with *The Wealth of Nations*.[54] In the section of *The Theory of Legislation* devoted to the "Principles of the Civil Code"—the setting for his most extensive treatment of property rights and obligations—Bentham continued the campaign against economic paternalism and in favor of free exchange. Thus, for example, in treating the welter of regulations historically attached to the conditions of "master and servant," Bentham insisted that "competition" (and not law) would "best regulate the price of these mutual services." Conditions of service were "a matter of contract. It belongs to the parties interested to arrange them according to their own convenience."[55] In other areas and more generally, it likewise was the policy of the civil law to facilitate voluntary exchange. "The total advantage of useful exchanges," Bentham observed in his treatment of "title by consent," "is far more than equivalent to the total disadvantage of such as are unfavourable. The gains of commerce are greater than the losses . . . Alienations in general ought, then, to be maintained."[56]

Nonetheless, on closer inspection, Bentham proves to be an even more recalcitrant hero of nineteenth-century freedom of contract than Adam Smith.[57] With regard to matters of doctrinal perspectives, Bentham (like Smith and others) approached contract in terms of the mechanisms for acquiring property title and not in terms of promise-keeping. And (like Smith again), he explained the rules of contract in terms of the need to secure expectations, repudiating rival natural law treatments which supposed that "the contract" required some "original and independent reason" for its enforcement other than the general utilitarian justification of private property law.[58] Even more important, freedom of contract never figured as an organizing unit or privileged value in Bentham's account of how the state related to market activity through the vehicle of law. In large part, this was the product of Bentham's acute concern in his jurisprudence to make clear the general relationship between law and freedom. The rights and freedoms enjoyed through the operation of law all existed because of the logically prior imposition of legal duties. "It is not possible to create a right in favour of one, except by creating a corresponding obligation imposed upon another"; and by "creating obligations" the law necessarily "trenches upon liberty."[59] Thus, although the security of rights was absolutely fundamental to the effective operation of a legal system, and although Bentham believed that the application of his utilitarian principles would most often serve (as in the case of usury) to liberalize existing legal arrangements by eliminating misguided restraints, all this benefit still required that the law create duties and thereby restrict liberty. To suppose that the law's

CONTRACT BEFORE "FREEDOM OF CONTRACT"

primary operation was to promote freedom—contractual freedom or any other freedom—in a manner that did not presuppose the imposition of restraint was to invite dangerous and even anarchical intellectual confusion.[60]

Accordingly, Bentham did not posit freedom or liberty as the organizing value of his principles of civil law. Rather, he identified four basic goals whose achievement ensured the promotion of public happiness: security, subsistence, abundance, and happiness. Of these, security enjoined a special primacy: it was the "principle object of law," and its maintenance was "entirely the work of law."[61] In many situations, Bentham explained, the legal preservation of security (along with the derivative goal of preventing frustrated expectations) also served the goals of subsistence and abundance, and less directly served the goal of equality. Thus Bentham's principles of property law were largely a system of techniques for enhancing security and coordinating the other ends; and in most cases, this system involved rules which would facilitate and liberalize alienation and exchange. But the value of these property rights was always conditional on their tendency to promote public happiness, which meant there was no inconsistency in laws which simply prohibited certain instances of voluntary exchange (such as the sale of poisons) or certain forms of property (such as chattel slavery) on account of the manifest disutility of such practices.[62]

Moreover, it was entirely consistent to recognize certain, less typical circumstances in which rules preserving the security of property actually worked to frustrate the other purposes of the civil law, especially the goal of subsistence. And when such circumstances obtained, it was legitimate—indeed necessary—for government to intervene and constrain private exchange. Thus, in his 1801 *Defence of a Maximum*, composed in response to conditions of wartime dearth, Bentham advocated the legal regulation of the price of corn, resisting the arguments for freedom of contract he earlier embraced in his *Defence of Usury*. The point, he stressed, was that the case for market freedom, just like the case for legal regulation, had to be reckoned according to the promotion of general happiness:

I have not, I never had, nor ever shall have, any horror, sentimental or anarchical, of the hand of government . . . The interference of government, as often as in my humble view of the matter any the smallest balance on the side of advantage is the result, is an event I witness with altogether as much satisfaction as I should its forbearance, and with much more than I should its negligence.[63]

≺ III ≻

Liberty, Property, and Commercial Society

To display (as I have been endeavoring to do thus far) the relatively modest role contract law occupied in the thought of Smith and Bentham is to call into question one long-favored rendering of the intellectual background to nineteenth-century freedom of contract. Certainly this intellectual background was shaped by theories of liberal individualism; and certainly the testimony of Smith and Bentham was readily (if selectively) pressed into service to support the removal of legal restraints upon contractual exchange. But from this it does not follow that the ideology of freedom of contract emerged full-blown from the pages of the *Wealth of Nations* or the *Theory of Legislation;* nor that Smith and Bentham were anything like as decisive in creating the intellectual orthodoxies legal scholars standardly associate with them. As far as the nineteenth-century history of contract is concerned, the routes from "public opinion" to the "rise of freedom of contract" have yet to be mapped effectively.

These same considerations also suggest the benefit of exploring alternative approaches to the eighteenth-century intellectual pre-history in Britain of freedom of contract. In past scholarship, the failure of eighteenth-century jurists to give contract its thematic due has been explained in terms of "conservative" biases or "old fashioned" opinions.[64] But such assessments appear much less compelling in the instances of such self-conscious innovators as Smith and Bentham. Why, even for the self-conscious moderns, should the notion of freedom of contract not have been pressed into greater conceptual service?

The answer to this question demands giving much greater specificity and content to the relations among jurisprudence, government, and economic change in eighteenth-century Britain. Legal historians, in presenting the "economic background" to freedom of contract, standardly invoke the societal transformations as-

sociated with the most cataclysmic versions of capitalist industrialization.[65] These treatments not only neglect those studies which
emphasize the relatively late, localized, and gradualist nature of
British industrialization.[66] They also fail to attend to the explana-
tory categories favored before the mid-nineteenth century. When
eighteenth-century commentators regarded their society and economic change, they spoke of "commerce" rather than "capitalism"
or "industrialization." The standard linkages were to what Burke
described as "our commerce and our empire" or to Blackstone's
characterization of a "polite and commercial people."[67] Early in the
Wealth of Nations, Smith supplied a characteristically forthright
version of a commonplace term:

When the division of labour has been once thoroughly established, it is
but a very small part of a man's wants which the produce of his own labour can supply. He supplies the far greater part of them by exchanging
that surplus part of the produce of his own labour . . . for such parts of the
produce of other men's labour as he has occasion for. Every man thus lives
by exchanging, or becomes in some measure a merchant, and the society
itself grows to be what is properly a commercial society.[68]

As Smith's definition reveals, "exchange" was a constitutive
feature of "commercial society"; and there was much else in the
speculative orthodoxies of the era likewise to direct attention towards exchange and contract. The prestigious natural law theories
of Grotius, Pufendorf, and their eighteenth-century popularizers
maintained that the foundations and structure of human authority
and political power should be conceptualized as the results of an
open-ended process of negotiation and exchange among rights-
bearing individuals.[69] Recent research on political theory in the period after 1688 has suggested that English whiggism was less fix-
ated on the idea of an historical "original compact" between monarch and people than had long been supposed.[70] Nonetheless, natural rights and hypothetical contracts pervaded the contemporary
literature on ethics and jurisprudence; and the contractual logic
regularly used to clarify the relationship between subjects and sov-
ereigns could be deployed more widely to elucidate more mundane
features of the legal order.

The "same principle" of "an implied original contract to submit
to the rules of the community whereof we are members," Blackstone proposed, explained the individual's liabilities to "a forfeiture

imposed by the by-laws and private ordinances of a corporation" or
"an amercement set in a court-leet or court-baron."[71] Sir Robert
Chambers, the successor to Blackstone's Oxford professorship, argued similarly in his own lectures on English law. Discussing the
property claims founded "*quasi ex contractu*," Chambers explained
that just as in "all political institutions it is supposed that protection and obedience are reciprocal," so in "the greatest part of the
dealings between man and man" the law frequently supposed "implicit contract without direct or positive stipulation." Such obligations were especially "copious and frequent" in a "commercial and
busy country": "The stranger that enters an inn knows that the host
does not exercise gratuitous hospitality and therefore by the mere
act of calling for meat and wine obliges himself to payment."[72]

Accompanying the pervasiveness of exchange, real and hypothetical, was a regularly rehearsed and (now) frequently noted preoccupation with the rights of property. "The respect which attended property was a striking feature of the mental landscape of
the eighteenth century," Paul Langford rightfully stresses in an
important recent study.[73] The contemporary understanding of the
primary function of public law in securing personal liberty centered on the defense of property. English law was above all to be
praised for its devotion to civil liberty; and nowhere was this better
manifest than in the lavish system of legal remedies it elaborated
for the protection of property. The Lockean dictum that "the great
and chief end" of political society was "the preservation of . . .
property" referred in its original formulation to the public defense
of far more than the stability of private possession.[74] Later echoes of
the Lockean formula, however, became more pointed and restricting. "Civil government, so far as it is instituted for the security of
property," observed Smith, "is in reality instituted for the defence
of the rich against the poor."[75] Moreover, the property in question
tended more and more to be modeled theoretically on the individualized right of private owner. To cite Blackstone once more (in one
of his much quoted moments of effusion):

There is nothing which so generally strikes the imagination and engages
the affections of mankind, as the right of property; or that sole and despotic dominion which one man claims and exercises over the external
things of the world, in total exclusion of the right of any other individual
in the universe.[76]

Historians have been quick to note that there were few forms of valuable possession in Blackstone's era that came close to conforming to this abstract model of "property in general."[77] Nonetheless, a prominent line of legal development saw the delineation of private rights from what previously had been less individualized networks of use-right and wealth. Paul Langford has exemplified the pattern in a telling manner. The Church of England, for instance, in principle constituted "a propertied institution" quite distinct in form from the property of the laymen. In practice, church wealth supplied a brisk traffic in leases, advowsons, presentations, pew rents, and chaplaincies. Copyright, the object of parliamentary statute and famous litigation, furnished but one of the settings in which property was newly asserted "in the products of mind itself." Common use-rights fell to parliamentary enclosure and the game laws.[78] "Thus our legislature," concluded the *Encyclopaedia Britannica*, "has universally promoted the grand ends of civil society . . . by steadily pursuing that wise and orderly maxim of assigning to every thing capable of ownership a legal and determinate owner."[79]

To the extent that eighteenth-century England featured private ownership and market exchange, it scarcely differed from earlier periods. What was more distinctive of commercial society was the velocity of property's circulation, the extent of the market's domestic and overseas reach, and the intensity of material appropriation. Historians now chronicle England's "consumer revolution," noting the remarkable inventiveness of entrepreneurial retailing and advertising, and the ready evidence of the growing variety and numbers of household goods, particularly in the homes of the urban "middling ranks."[80] "What was distinctive about consumer behaviour . . . was that those who had possessed little bought more, those who had inherited ample possessions bought new ones, and those born to superfluity seemed eager to add to the excess with every passing fashion."[81] These findings echo the commonplace speculations of contemporary observers who felt, with Dr. Johnson, that there simply was no other age "in which trade so much engaged the attention . . . or commercial gain was sought with such general emulation."[82]

Commerce was also transformative. "But nothing hath wrought such an alteration in this order of people," Henry Fielding insisted, "as the introduction of trade. This hath indeed given a new face to the whole nation . . . and hath almost totally changed the manners, customs, and habits of the people."[83] Through trade and empire, Britain had become opulent and powerful. Through the expedients of public finance and wartime debt, its constitutional balance had been restructured. Under the impact of material bounty and material appetite, moral pieties and social hierarchies had been challenged. Along with its other potent impacts, commerce and commercial life had plainly transformed the kingdom's law. Lord Chancellor Hardwicke at mid-century noted the "new discoveries and inventions of commerce" which had so inflated the business of Chancery.[84] And Blackstone recorded in his catalogue of the "chief alterations" in the "administration of private justice" since 1688, such innovations as "the introduction and establishment of paper credit," "the erection of courts of conscience for recovering small debts," and "the great system of marine jurisprudence, of which the foundations have been laid."[85]

Such testimonies to appetitive zeal and institutional novelty might be easily and helpfully multiplied. But to do so risks creating an all-too-modern image of commercial society, whereby eighteenth-century England comprises little more than an inventory of "pre-conditions" for capitalist industrialization. Instead, the challenge is to grasp commercial society *at the same time* in terms of those elements which only later came to appear as the relics of an earlier order. English agriculture was market driven, and in many areas increasingly capitalized into larger units of production. But in moments of agrarian crisis, market producers invoked the norms of moral economy and magistrates intervened to set wages and prices. Urban growth and prosperity stimulated greater levels of middling-rank confidence and self-consciousness, but middle-class protest spoke the language of landed independence and manipulated the traditional institutions of the common law. British trade furnished opportunity for the creation of some spectacular and lavishly publicized merchant fortunes, but political power still rested securely on landed wealth. Addison celebrated the Bank of England as the embodiment of modern cosmopolitanism and religious toleration, but England was no less the place of church establishment and the Test and Corporations Act. "There is little point in debating whether eighteenth-century Britain . . . was essentially a landed society or a commercial society," Linda Colley observes of a familiar historiographic dichotomy. "It is the *relationship* between land and trade that is the important issue."[86]

It is in terms of commercial society's distinctive mixing of inherited and more novel institutional forms that we need to approach the perceived relationships among economy, law, and contract in the eighteenth century. Consider, for example, some standard accounts of commerce's emergence and progress in earlymodern England. The origins of England's mercantile prosperity were most often located in the Tudor period and linked to a specific series of public measures. The Crown's campaign against the power of the feudal nobility served to promote the interests and wealth of the commons, a process that was further encouraged by the dissolution and distribution of church property at the time of the Reformation. In its foreign policy and chartering of monopolies, the Crown moved to advance the kingdom's merchants and traders. The monarch "raised and pushed to the highest degree," Bolingbroke reported of an enlightened Elizabethan foreign policy, "a spirit of discovering new countries, making new settlements and opening new veins of trade."[87] In the *Commentaries*, Blackstone produced a legalistic version of this chronology and process. Here the enterprises of the common law judges paralleled the policies of the monarchs. The "gradual influence of foreign trade and domestic tranquillity" undermined "the spirit" of the kingdom's "military tenures." The "judges quickly perceived" that "the old feudal actions" ill served the "more simple and commercial mode of property" that succeeded feudalism. Through a series of "fictions and circuities," the writ of ejectment was adopted "to facilitate exchange and alienation." "We inherit," Blackstone concluded, "an old Gothic castle, erected in the days of chivalry, but fitted up for a modern inhabitant."[88]

The *Commentaries'* rhapsody on "the modern method of prosecuting a writ of ejectment" and the proposed image of English law as a refurbished "gothic castle" have often been taken as classic indicators of Blackstone's complacency and antiquated orientation. And certainly we seem to be eras away from those historians of modern contract doctrine who assume that the legal history to be placed at the center of the story "is the law which the Industrial Revolution left in its wake."[89] But Blackstone's centering of com-

mercial society on the changes in the law of real property was by
no means eccentric. It was in the treatment of real property that
common lawyers were often moved to their most robust declarations on the legal transformations wrought by commerce and exchange. "It is a universal notion," Mr. Justice Willes intoned from
King's Bench, "that in a commercial country all property should be
freed from every clog which may hinder its circulation," and then
went on to rule in a case concerning contingent remainders.[90]

Nor was the linking of real property and commerce a piece of
narrow, lawyerly provincialism. Adam Smith likewise gave commercial modernity a long ancestry in associating its origins with
the deteriorating position of the feudal nobility. And he too invoked the "writ of ejectment" in emphasizing the extent to which
commercial prosperity in England was a function of the common
law's protection of the rights of tenants and proprietors. There was,
of course, much in Smith's history of commercial society that subverted common law orthodoxies. English liberties were modern,
not ancient. The Crown had not subdued the power of the barons;
the barons had bartered away their social power by purchasing the
superfluities peddled by merchants and artificers. And most important, the mercantilist regime of economic protection hindered
rather than promoted national wealth. But ironically, these momentous revisions in the historical narrative tended to enhance the
significance of those changes in real property which figured so
prominently in common law scholarship. "Those laws and customs so favourable to the yeomanry," Smith noted, "have perhaps
contributed more to the present grandeur of England than all their
boasted regulations of commerce together."[91]

The history of commercial society was not only protracted and
gradual as well as transformative; England's commerce, since its
rise in the Tudor period, was throughout extensively shaped by the
action of law and government (even when, as for Smith, such state
policy was unjust and counterproductive). More recent eighteenth-
century experience confirmed the presumption that government intervention pervaded commercial activity and promoted prosperity.
Where this experience was at its most conspicuous, of course, was
in the imperial project and system of protective duties. As Montes-
quieu observed of English foreign policy, "England has always made
its political interests give way to the interests of its commerce."[92]

But the program of commercial empire was only one element in an extensive mix of polity and economy. The eighteenth-century economy was chronically short of specie, especially of small denomination, which meant that even quite modest enterprises functioned on debt and the web of paper credit. As a result, the political stability of the state and its foreign relations became of direct business concern, since war and political crisis immediately affected interest rates and grain markets.[93] The regular revisions to the schedule of commodities affected by the excise stimulated business interests into organizing themselves as parliamentary lobbies, so that they could be the effective advocates of their trades and influential sources of fiscal information.[94] The provisions of the 1720 Bubble Act required that joint-stock companies be sanctioned by specific acts of Parliament, which rendered large capital investment legally risky in the absence of parliamentary endorsement. Accordingly, private acts of Parliament, which so bloated the eighteenth-century statute book, came to serve as the great facilitative instrument of those countless turnpike trusts, canal projects, and agrarian enclosures which have long figured as the convenient index of England's eighteenth-century economic expansion.[95]

Excepting matters of war and finance, eighteenth-century parliamentary legislation was notoriously localized in character and particular in its reference. In a vast range of cases—private estate bills, urban "Improvement Acts," laws authorizing the repair of streets and construction of bridges—Parliament created law by responding to local initiatives and authorizing proposals that had been generated by those parties directly benefiting from the measures in question. Instances of more generalized forms of legislation tended to consolidate the accumulated product of earlier and more particularized statute-making. "Blackstone's omnipotent Parliament," Langford observes, "resembled nothing so much as a gigantic rubber stamp, confirming local and private enterprise, but rarely undertaking initiatives of its own."[96]

Quite weighty examples of public policy, moreover, conformed to this pattern of particularistic law-making. The Combination Acts of 1799 and 1800, for example, have since the late nineteenth century figured prominently in British labor historiography, often being treated as major legal milestones in the capitalist transformation of employment relations. Yet, as John Orth has documented,

these two general Combination Acts functioned to unify and extend nationally an episodic series of eighteenth-century combination statutes which, more characteristically, were enacted in response to local labor disturbances and which were limited in legal
scope to particular trades in particular regions.[97] Even the great system of protective tariffs and bounties, which Smith in the *Wealth
of Nations* conceptually synthesized into a comprehensive system
of mercantilism, had its origins in particular and ad hoc parliamentary law-making. England's tariff system was transformed in the
fifteen years following the 1688 Glorious Revolution less through
the adoption of a general program of protectionism than through a
set of piecemeal and often originally temporary fiscal measures,
stimulated by the crushing burden of war finance. It was only decades later under Walpole that these expedients came to be routi-
nized and consolidated as a system of protective trade policy.[98]

This kind of legislative practice disclosed a distinctive and insufficiently noted logic for relating private enterprise and the state.
Under the later (and now more familiar) regime of freedom of contract, individuals (in theory) were left to make their own bargains
and the law (in theory) interposed only retrospectively if and when
the private parties to the bargains failed to keep their promises.
"Public policy requires," as it was declared from the bench in 1875,
"that men of full age and competent understanding shall have the
utmost liberty of contracting and that their contracts . . . shall be
held sacred."[99] Under the forms of eighteenth-century law-making,
individuals likewise made their own bargains for themselves, and
there was no more expectation than in the succeeding era of freedom of contract that the state would initiate those economic projects left to private enterprise. But in this setting, the state interposed at the outset, supplying legal authorization for these private
initiatives through the vehicle of particularized parliamentary
statute.[100] In contrast to "freedom of contract," the eighteenth-
century regime of "liberty and property" thus depended on the
more immediate and easily visible mobilization of public power.

In addition to its legislative particularity, eighteenth-century
statute most often innovated in a manner that *preserved* established structures of law and governance. The turnpike trusts supplemented rather than abolished the traditional system of parish-
based "statute labour" for maintaining highways. The administra-

tive institutions created in urban "Improvement Acts" operated alongside the existing system of local government. Poor Law "Incorporations" maintained the parish basis of poverty relief by authorizing particular groups of parishes to consolidate their administrative capacities. The mass of capital statutes which constituted England's infamous "Bloody Code" did their legal work in a manner that sustained the established categories of "clergyable" and "non-clergyable" felonies. .

The same structure of conserving innovation could be found in areas of law less influenced by parliamentary law-making. Recent scholarship warns us against presuming that the advance of contractual ideas necessarily or uniformly tended in the direction of nineteenth-century conceptualizations of freedom of contract. In his study of employment law in early-modern England and America, Robert Steinfeld finds that "neither the new arguments about the superiority of free labor nor the significant intensification of market activity" in eighteenth-century England served to undermine the traditional legal restraints upon the mobility of labor.[101] In the context of labor service, the appeal to contract served as often to justify customary status conditions as it did to transform them. "The restrictions on liberty contained in traditional law were entirely compatible with an active system of bargaining between masters and workers over the terms of service."[102] Susan Staves, in her work on married women's separate property, observes a trend in eighteenth-century cases concerning separate maintenance contracts whereby an "older view of the marital relation in which the husband's authority has a religious and hierarchical justification" was displaced "by a newer view more dependent on the rhetoric and logic of contract." But the shift from status to contract in this specific area proved ephemeral, as late in the century the common law courts came to resist "the relevance of this logic in domestic cases and repudiated some of the earlier decisions."[103] Philip Hamburger, in examining the utilization of the civilian "consensus theory" of contract in the period before 1800, rightly stresses that the "consensus theory was more clearly affiliated with legal arguments for paternalism than freedom in contract law."[104]

Even in those areas of law most closely associated with what Lord Chancellor Hardwicke termed "the inventions of commerce,"[105] where contemporary observers frequently detected quite rapid phases of legal change, innovation did not necessarily subvert customary structures and practices. By the late eighteenth century, it was commonplace to regard the very most recent episode in the common law's centuries-long adjustment to trade and commerce as the personal achievement of Lord Chief Justice Mansfield, who presided over the court of King's Bench between 1756 and 1788.[106] Mansfield's admirers hailed "the founder of the commercial law of this country" and celebrated the "system of mercantile jurisprudence" he skillfully elaborated from the bench.[107] Mansfield's law reform enterprises did not lack for critics; and in several important areas his efforts at legal modernization seemed to threaten settled common law doctrines. His controversial attempt to re-examine some of the settled, technical rules of real property law was reversed during his own chief justiceship; and in the decades after he left King's Bench, his judicial successors moved to counter what they saw as his failure fully to honor the institutional division of law and equity.[108]

But, significantly, in those areas where Mansfield received his most lavish praise, and where his labors appeared immediately connected to the kingdom's distinctive commercial conditions, legal improvement did not take the form of replacing an antiquated set of legal rules with more modern and socially apposite alternatives. Rather—in such paradigmatic areas of "mercantile jurisprudence" as the law of negotiable instruments and marine insurances—legal modernization involved the judicial elaboration and refinement of legal rules governing discrete forms of commercial instruments and transactions, which served to supplement rather than reverse established common law jurisprudence.[109]

The dynamics of commerce produced its more direct challenge to England's customary law in the area of procedure and proof. The Arbitration Act of 1698, sponsored by John Locke and the recently established Board of Trade, strengthened the procedures for the out-of-court arbitration of mercantile disputes; by the 1770s, as the statute intended, private arbitration emerged as an important alternative to the common law for the resolution of causes among merchants and traders.[110] Far more disturbing for common lawyers such as Blackstone was Parliament's enactment of a network of "court of requests" for the recovery of small debts, which settled disputes without trial by jury and dispensed with the costly, time-consuming intricacies of common law process. Characteristically, the legislature created this new institutional structure by increments, enacting statutes to create a single local court at a time and leaving in place the common law tribunals that otherwise heard such causes.[111]

<< IV >>

Property, Liberty, and Contract

The distinctive experience of law and governance in eighteenth-century England goes some way towards understanding the absence of freedom of contract as a discrete or vital unit of conceptual analysis. Of course, there was much in that experience which, in hindsight, reasonably seems to have more than prepared the ground for nineteenth-century intellectual orientations. Private property was celebrated as the first object of law's attention; market exchange was acknowledged as the source of beneficent social progress; commercial greatness equipped the nation against its continental rivals and transformed the character of its inhabitants. "Every country and every age has dominant terms, which seem to obsess men's thoughts," observed Lewis Namier. "Those of eighteenth-century England were property, contract, trade and profits."[112]

But the obsession with "property, contract, trade and profits"—which Namier in any case tended to exaggerate—did not of itself generate an ordering of the social world in terms of freedom of contract (even in the case of reformers such as Smith and Bentham, who championed the social benefits of contractual exchange and pressed the case for contract freedom in critique of customary restraints). Commerce had extensively altered the legal, no less than the social and economic, landscape. But the process did not need to be described in the terms familiar in nineteenth-century orthodoxies. It was the intervention of law and government, as much as the removal of legal restraints, that facilitated economic innovation. Legal change was gradual rather than epochal. Traditional common law remedies and categories had been adjusted, supplemented, and supplanted, but not repealed or destroyed.

In the more ambitious and systematic reflections on the rela-

tions between law and the social order, promise-keeping and contract tended to remain important but secondary features of the
more central categories of property and justice. David Hume, observing organized society's paramount task to provide for the administration of justice, conjectured that "the vast apparatus of our
government" could be thought to have "ultimately no other object
or purpose" but "the support of the twelve judges. Kings and par-
liaments, fleets and armies, officers of the court and revenue, am-
bassadors, ministers, and privy counselors, are all subordinate in
their end to this part of administration."[113] And the virtue of justice, whose maintenance dwarfed so much else in public life,
clearly dictated the enforcement of contractual obligations. But for
Hume, the analysis of justice began with the "stability of possession"; and the major part of the explication of this virtue concerned
the issue "of the rules which determine property." The further and
more contractual elements of justice—"the transference of property by consent" and "the obligation of promises"—were dis-
patched with far greater economy.[114] In Hume's moral theory, as
more generally in eighteenth-century speculation, the category of
contract was overshadowed by the category of property. "Freedom
of contract," in this sense, was preempted by "liberty and property."

If eighteenth-century moral speculation limited contract by
treating it within more general and central units of analysis, eighteenth-century legal speculation frequently scattered contract
across a range of discrete legal conditions. As we have seen, later
constructions of freedom of contract in the nineteenth century
placed intense pressure on the idea of the unity of contract law and
of the range of social relationships that could be unified under the
category of contract. "The law of contract grew fat with the spoils
of other fields," as Lawrence Friedman explains of nineteenth-
century U.S. legal history. The general law of contract, Grant Gilmore noted, in theory supplied the same set of rules for major
business enterprises as it did for "charitable subscriptions, ante-
nuptual agreements, and promises to convey the family farm provided the children will support the old people for life."[115] This nineteenth-century theory of contract, as numerous critics in this century have stressed, was a highly selective and controversial con-

struction: it obscured an important range of unfreedoms and inequalities that attended contract-making; and it neglected a significant range of doctrinal discontinuities that attended contract-
enforcement.[116] These criticisms, in turn, perhaps make it easier to
appreciate the situation in the period before the age of "freedom of
contract" when such a tendentious ordering of legal materials had
yet to be embraced.

Blackstone's *Commentaries* has proved a favorite text in accounts of the pre-history of freedom of contract—a focus which
makes obvious sense given the scale and prestige of Blackstone's
survey and the general lack of attention directed at contract itself.
But the meaning of this example is easily mistaken. The tendency
has been to attribute the relative absence of contract in the *Commentaries* to Blackstone's conservatism and antiquated sentiments. Blackstone, in important respects, was indeed a conservative jurist;[117] and there is little reason for departing from A. W. B.
Simpson's judgment that in the *Commentaries*'s coverage of personal property, "the law is the law of the country, not Cheap-
side."[118]

But rather than stress Blackstone's "neglect" of contract, we
might better emphasize his simple decision to maintain the unity
of certain social relationships (such as the extended domestic
household) at the expense of others (such as contracts of employment).[119] Like all legal arrangements, Blackstone's *Commentaries*
was a highly technical and selective exercise, with its distinctive
priorities and limitations. Contemporary readers of the *Commentaries* were well aware of the tentativeness and inadequacy of
Blackstone's treatment of important topics in contract and commercial law. But the shortcomings were not imputed to Blackstone's choices concerning matters of typology and classification.
In 1803, William David Evans, the future translator of *Pothier on
Obligations*, published a two-volume *General View of the Decisions of Lord Mansfield*, a survey which unsurprisingly praised the
chief justice's achievement as "the founder of the commercial law
of this country" and devoted ample space to his efforts at legal
modernization in such areas as the law of marine insurances and
negotiable instruments. But in choosing a scheme for presenting
Mansfield's decisions, Evans explicitly embraced "the arrange-

ment" of "the valuable *Commentaries,*" notwithstanding the frequent contrast between Mansfield's sophistication and Blackstone's blundering on matters of mercantile jurisprudence.[120]

Blackstone, as the first professor of English law at an English
university, faced special challenges in composing a general "map"
of the legal order.[121] But although his *Commentaries* came to over-
shadow all its rivals, Blackstone was not alone in attempting a syn-
thetic exposition of English law. Nor was he alone in devoting
such relatively scant attention to the category of contract. Given
the structure of the common law writs, the power of settled legal
categories, and the sheer amount of English jurisprudence that
concerned the law of tenures and estates, there was perhaps ample
reason for contract to remain a peripheral landmark in these eighteenth-century legal mappings—whether the cartographer was the
celebrated Blackstone or the uncelebrated Thomas Wood, Francis
Sullivan, Robert Chambers, or Richard Wooddeson.[122]

If common law thus proved an unfruitful setting for the conceptual unification of contract law, a more promising candidate legal
order might be found in the fashionable and better established jurisprudence of the eighteenth-century universities: the "law of nature and nations." After all, the law of nature and nations (notwithstanding its presumptions to a cosmopolitan universality)
drew extensively on classical Roman materials, where contract occupied a prominent position in book 3 of the *Institutes*. And the
early continental contract treatises, such as Pothier's, which were
to have such a profound influence on the nineteenth-century
common law theory of contract, themselves developed in conscious reflection on the jurisprudence of Grotius and Pufendorf.[123]
Yet even here the situation is not without its ambiguities and
complexities.

To return briefly to the example examined earlier, Adam Smith
identified the discussion in his *Lectures on Jurisprudence* with the
Grotian project, and there adopted a conventional classification of
the legal order in terms of a threefold distribution of personal
rights. In this arrangement, the broader category of "property"
thoroughly eclipsed the category of "contract." Smith's reliance on
this particular organizing scheme no doubt reflected the operation
of institutional restraints. Grotian jurisprudence had been introduced into the Scottish curriculum earlier in the century; it was

adopted by Smith's revered teacher, Francis Hutcheson; and there was no reason for Smith, in inheriting the teaching of moral philosophy at Glasgow in 1751, to deviate from the recently established pedagogy. Still, there is no ground to suppose that Smith found this ordering of legal materials in any way limiting or antiquated. Indeed, given his own intellectual route from the *Lectures on Jurisprudence* to the *Wealth of Nations*, it is striking how effectively Smith utilized this ordering of legal rights in order to disclose and analyze the distinctive features of modern, commercial society. What the Smithian example here reveals is the relative ease with which one could recognize the pervasiveness of exchange for the functioning of commercial society without requiring an understanding of the legal order that centered on the category of contract.

The accounts of the "laws of nature and nations" developed by Grotius and his successors provided moralists and jurists with a very broad and general classification of the legal order, and some of the longevity of the Grotian structure must be attributed to flexibility with which it could be modified and revised. It remained entirely possible for the arrangement of legal rights to be developed in a manner that gave contract greater notice and centrality. This possibility can be explored by considering the work of another rough contemporary of Smith and Bentham, the Anglican divine and moralist William Paley, whose long-influential *Principles of Moral and Political Philosophy* has received at best glancing notice in histories of the rise of freedom of contract.[124]

The Principles of Moral and Political Philosophy, which set out a systematic utilitarian analysis of private morality and public institutions, enjoyed extensive currency in the half century following its 1785 publication. The treatise was based on Paley's Cambridge lectures of the 1760s and 1770s; and like most of the university-based ethical pedagogy of the period, Paley approached his subject in terms of the leading models set out in the "writings of Grotius and the larger work of Puffendorff." His moral teaching retained many of the elements of Grotian theory, but he emphasized his concern to shift attention away from much of the arcane technical detail of natural law jurisprudence, and instead focus on those subjects "which arise in the life of an inhabitant of this country in these times."[125] In practicing these precepts, Paley produced a treatise whose originality most often owed less to the content of its ethical instruction than to decisions about which subjects to abbreviate and which to expand.

In the case of contract, much of the account was scarcely novel. Contract figured as a part of the exposition of the system of "relative"—that is, not absolute—and "determinate" rights and duties which facilitated organized social relations. The key institutional embodiment of such rights and duties was property; and as in so many other eighteenth-century treatments, the rules of contract were reached through an analysis of the rights and duties of property. And although a lengthy chapter on "promises" formed the link between the discussion of property and the discussion of contract, contractual obligation, according to Paley, centered on the law's general concern with the security of title and expectations, rather than on any specific devotion to the sanctity of promises or the idea of contractual freedom.[126]

If this general approach to contract—as well as the more detailed treatment of such matters as the grounds of contractual obligation, the conditions of contractual liability, the effects of mistakes in bargains—was conventional, much less predictable was the distribution of coverage in this part of the treatise. In contrast to most contemporary discussions, Paley honored "contract" with twice as many chapters as he gave to "property." To do so, he ruthlessly truncated the standard elaboration of property rights, barely noticing several contested questions which had acquired lavish juridical coverage in the literature on natural law. He dismissed most of the controversy over the moral title by which common property was replaced by individual appropriation, and he spent but two paragraphs considering the historical development of property rights.[127] At the same time, the treatment of contract expanded to include several topics which other jurists accommodated elsewhere. Many of the rights and duties concerning corporate structures were treated in separate chapters on "contracts of labour regarding offices" and "contracts of labour regarding partnership." The law of "master and servant" vanished as a discrete legal category, and its contents were accommodated within a chapter on "contracts of labour regarding service."[128]

The accumulated result of this ordering of legal materials was to grant contract a prominence and range absent in other eighteenth-century discussions. Rather than contract appearing as an epilogue to the rights of property, property appeared as a preface to contract. Given the points of reference with which the history of modern contract is conventionally written, it is tempting to think we here observe a significant moment in the creation of a new conceptualization of contract. At the same time, however, it is worth noting how much of the new orientation was the result of the drastic abbreviation of the treatment of property. Intellectual innovation, in this case as elsewhere, owed perhaps more to what was discarded than to the novelty of what was introduced.

Economic Liberty and the Modern State

HARRY N. SCHEIBER

THE RELATIONSHIP OF economic liberty to the law—and especially to the legal or constitutional norms that give legitimacy
to state interventions which trench on the asserted rights of private
property and enterprise—has been an important element in the experience of all the modern democracies. In the course of the developments through which freedom has become established in the
modern Western world, the claims associated with the ideal of
economic liberty have been connected to the vital issue of how individual and group rights are to be defined. These claims also have
come into play in policy debates addressing a broad range of important social and economic policy contexts. The issue thus has been
confronted in a variety of historic contexts: in ordinary political
and legislative controversies, in some principled and critical confrontations over basic constitutional doctrines, and, at several notorious historical junctures, in the course of profound political upheaval and revolution. In this chapter, I will deal with the history
of economic liberty as an ideology, as a formal construct in law,
and as an element of legal culture in American history. The analysis is intended to illustrate the social and economic functions of
law in shaping both the dynamics of economic change and the
character of economic institutions in relation to the modern state.

≺ I ≻

Liberty and the Legal Culture

This inquiry necessarily involves some consideration of the common aspects of legal culture that are shared between Great Britain
and America; for one needs to keep in mind that the common law
heritage is distinctive in important ways from the legal traditions

and historic patterns of class politics, social conflict, and revolution in continental Europe.[1] As is evident from the perdurable strength of civil law and of European commitments to a "social contract" approach to employment rights and welfare rights, the distinctiveness of the Continent's legal and political culture persists to this day. It is a culture, however, subject increasingly to the new convergences evident in economy, society, and policy as a result of "globalization" of markets and the internationalization of contract and regulatory norms.[2]

In the context of the exceptionalism of Anglo-American law, the concept of freedom of contract—the notion that owners of property are entitled to enjoy maximum freedom to manage and dispose of what is "their own"—has continued to play a central role in the relationship of state power to the market economy throughout the entire span of modern economic development. Its importance has been manifested in two distinctive ways. First has been the concept's influential technical function as a rule of judgment in the law. In this regard it reflects a social commitment to reliance upon voluntary contractual relations and the private market in the ordering of social and economic life.[3] Second has been the way in which the concept has been deployed (though not without challenge, to be sure) in American legal and policy discourse, as a metaphor for economic liberty in its much more comprehensive sense.

Both defenders of economic individualism in a free marketplace, on the one side, and those who have argued for various interventionist social and economic programs, on the other, have sought to mobilize for their respective purposes the ideals of economic liberty and (no matter how incongruously, at times) the logic and rhetoric of freedom of contract. In historic debates of law and policy, the moral and legal imperatives of economic liberty therefore have been invoked, first, in the cause of "negative liberty," by which private interests—small and powerful alike—have protested against state interference with their private dealings.[4] But second, these same imperatives have been invoked in a different, assertive mode that seeks to advance a conception of "positive liberty." This latter notion justifies interventions by the state on grounds that public investments, regulatory regimes, and explicitly redistributive social programs are necessary instruments for bringing social realities into line with the theoretical premises upon which the economic liberty ideal and freedom of contract were originally formulated. In this latter enterprise, those who demand intervention typically have not sought to jettison the conceptual apparatus or normative content of "contract thinking." On the contrary, they have often cast their interventionist proposals in a way clearly designed to claim intellectual lineage from freedom of contract ideas—not least by stressing the imperatives of individualism that are at the very core of those ideas. Thus they have framed their appeals for innovation in law and policy in a way that portrays interventionist objectives as a return to original principles, rather than as a repudiation of the freedom of contract ideal or of traditional justifications of economic liberty. This was true, for example, of the political rhetoric in which artisans in the early Republic developed an explicitly republican view of individualism. Their ideology called for regulatory interventions to govern the terms of labor contracts as a way of achieving the goal of sustaining a regime of personal economic autonomy.[5]

The same paradox was evident in the late nineteenth-century antitrust movement, when systematic governmental oversight and regulation of corporate activities in the market were demanded in the name of assuring an authentically *competitive* economic order. Thus Attorney General Richard Olney's oft-quoted rationale when in 1894 he demanded a breakup of two giant corporations that had become dominant in their respective industries and markets, the Standard Oil and American Tobacco trusts. He first voiced the mantra "Competition is the Life of Trade," and then justified the prosecution of the two trusts on grounds that the law must assure "fair play, justice, and equality of opportunity and treatment." These values were invoked to override the results that market behavior and market forces had produced, but Olney used the very same rhetorical terms as those in which reformers and commercial interests in an earlier era had demanded liberation of entrepreneurs from the constraints of governmental regulation.[6] The massive interventions of the New Deal era and later reform episodes in modern American history that have produced the phenomenon of giant government were similarly championed on the grounds that they are necessary instruments for correcting institutional and market imperfections. By correcting those imperfections, it is asserted, the new reforms will restore the structure of opportunity for individualism, creativity, and release of energy that had once been seen as attainable largely through the medium of free and unfettered markets.[7]

In nineteenth-century England the same contradictions and perplexities of a competitive marketplace inspired successive generations of Liberal Party reformers to reconsider and reformulate their individualistic ideology so as to justify massive ameliorative social and economic interventions by government—all the while professing that they retained their devotion to the core beliefs of classic liberal philosophy, and resisting democratic-socialist alternatives. The great British debate over compulsory public education, for example, was impelled by such reformist Liberals. This group of reformers, invoking the ideals of individualism in a new context, similarly gave its support to educational reform and to the Factory Acts, utilities regulation, and social programs that assured minimum income and public health standards as each of those causes came to center stage in British politics.[8]

What has made a resort to the individualistic, freedom-of-contract tradition an effective tool for those seeking to influence policy in the United States has been the extent to which the ideals associated with economic liberty have been absorbed into the legal culture since the late eighteenth century, and even to the present, as part of the "shared values" of the society.[9] The wide acceptance of these ideals has been evident historically in America in the popular ideas and attitudes about law that constitute what is generally termed the "general legal culture" of the society, and to no less a degree in the "high legal culture" of academic legal scholarship and the formal discourse of jurisprudence.[10] Thus, throughout this chapter, references to the larger political and legal culture will be frequent and often of central importance to the interpretations of historical change that are set forth.

The United States has witnessed deep partisan and ideological cleavage, as for, example, over the questions of slavery prior to the Civil War, of segregation and discrimination from the 1860s to our own day, of women's rights, or of exploitation, deprivation, and dependency in an industrial society. Whatever the gravity of complaints about exploitation and other evils of the industrial system—and however much some analysts might regret that Ameri-

cans did not share more widely class or race or gender consciousness, and were not more militantly radical or more determined to
resist economic trends—the evidence is clear that there was a
"substantial consensus" (as Willard Hurst has written) regarding
the desirability of material growth and expansion. This was an
"impatiently opportunistic society," busy with the activities of the
"expectant capitalists" who were the object of commentary for virtually every foreign observer before and after Tocqueville. And this
substantial—not complete, and certainly not necessarily "just" or
"fair"—consensus reflected "the values of the striving, business-
oriented middle class."[11] Moreover, the view that prevailed in the
shaping of public policy, nurtured by an elite leadership but (again)
seldom successfully challenged by the electorate at large, was that
there must be "substantial autonomy for free will in the market"
and "large play for individuality."[12] Herein lies the compelling
force of Hurst's influential interpretation of nineteenth-century
American law—cited by several other authors in this book—as a
system that sought to encourage creativity of individuals and organizations in both the profit and voluntary sectors to achieve a
"release of energy," to realize their full potentiality, and to advance
both economic productivity and general economic well-being of
the population.[13]

A key element of the nineteenth-century legal culture that valued economic liberty so highly was its commitment to the institution of private property—a commitment that, at least on the surface, has been extraordinarily persistent into our day.[14] Even among
the people in the wagon trains that made their way across the
plains and mountains on the Oregon Trail, the behavior that was
recorded in the emigrants' diaries and letters indicates, as John
Reid has argued, that "all understood and a vast majority respected
the legal principles vesting in the individual exclusively enjoyment
of property lawfully possessed." The patterns of personal behavior
mirrored the formal requirements of the established legal order
concerning respect for private property rights. When disputes or
emergencies arose, or people wanted to transfer their rights in
goods or to purchase services, Reid contends, they acted upon

mutual expectations concerning duties and rights [that] may as accurately
be labeled "legal" behavior as may behavior dictated by fear of police enforcement. What their words and conduct tell us is that for 19th century

Americans the definition of binding "law," vesting rights and obligations, was not limited to a command or set of commands from the "sovereign" backed by threats or by force. Nor was "law" some abstraction discovered or justified by appealing to "natural" or universal rules of deportment. Law was the taught, learned, accepted customs of a people.[15]

Veneration of property rights was incorporated, too, into the formal constitutional jurisprudence of the new Republic very early in its history. And it persisted robustly as a coherent doctrine well into the twentieth century, evidenced at no time more emphatically than in the *Lochner* era of constitutional law. One of the greatest modern commentators on the Constitution, Edward S. Corwin, termed the doctrine of "vested rights" in property nothing less than "the basic doctrine of American constitutional law" and centered his entire interpretation of constitutional history around the concept.[16]

Americans' reverence for private property rights could take truly grotesque and caricatured forms, whether or not expressive of sincere beliefs. For example, industrialists and landowners have opposed as violative of their alleged "inalienable rights" even rudimentary governmental regulations such as air or water pollution rules, or the most basic worker safety regulations such as those sought in the long and troubled history of efforts to secure the safety of miners underground.[17] The obverse side of such extreme invocation of "market values" may be seen in the theoretical position staked out by some of the more zealous free-market economists and libertarian philosophers, arguing that any form of governmental intervention that reduces a citizen's wealth or property values—zoning regulations, environmental laws, even taxation, which one such critic has termed a form of "theft"—should be viewed as a "taking," no different from eminent domain takings, hence constitutionally requiring compensations to make "injured" parties whole again.[18] Such proposals are put forth with the justification that they accord with formal legal precedent and with the basic principles of law that were intended by the 1787 constitution's framers, who—according to Richard Epstein, for example—incorporated tacitly and in some respects explicitly the English common law rules on property as they had then recently been codified by Blackstone.[19]

This appeal to constitutional "original principles" and the

Founders' "intent" distorts the framers' views; and it also completely misrepresents the larger legal and constitutional tradition
of the nineteenth century. For even at the height of *Lochner*-era
conservatism, the principal figures in American legal theory and
constitutional jurisprudence—even the treatise writer and judge
Thomas Cooley, or Justice Stephen Field, exemplar of freedom-of-
contract constitutionalism—approvingly acknowledged the legitimacy of an equally robust tradition in our law of "public rights"
and regulatory principles.[20] In evaluating the authority of individualistic property-rights doctrines and notions of economic liberty in
American legal culture, we need to keep in mind that no matter
how much American society cherished the axiom that "private
property ought to remain secure from the government," it was intervention that represented arbitrariness and caprice that was at issue. For American society also supported innovations in policy that
recognized the need for government to deploy its power to defend
and advance the public interest. Common good (the "common
weal" in the vocabulary of eighteenth- and nineteenth-century
American law) required the assertion of what American courts produced as a fully developed doctrine of "rights of the public." Under
this doctrine, not only taxation and eminent-domain takings of
private property, but also a panoply of regulatory measures covering all manner of social and economic activities, were seen as a legitimate expression of government's—or, in republican terms, "the
people's"—sovereignty.

As will be argued in remaining sections of this chapter, American law has been dominated entirely neither by the vested rights
doctrine nor by a pragmatic legal ethic that made productivity and
growth—that is, the imperatives of material development—the sole
standard for the validation of government interventions and their
limits. Rather, in constant tension with these other validating can-
ons, the competing doctrine of public rights was given primacy at
critical junctures of legal and economic development; and it was
often of controlling importance in determining how far public
authority might be permitted to go in regulating economic institutions and social relations.

Even in the jurisprudence of property and contract law, there
was intellectual tension reflecting powerful contending forces in
the society. Hurst went to the root of that tension when he empha-

sized, in his analysis, on the one hand the respect accorded by American law to static, established "vested rights" that were articulated to sustain property as an institution "merely of security"; and, on the other, the way in which the law honored the claims of "dynamic property . . . [as] an institution of growth" in the form of new business ventures and initiatives to apply new technologies.[21] In general there was a preference for dynamic property—for property as an engine of entrepreneurial innovation and economic expansion. This preference became manifest in the ways in which legislatures and courts set priorities, often to the disadvantage of established interests (large or small) so as to provide opportunities and support for specific kinds of activities or for specific firms.[22] This legal process was often closely linked to the jurisprudence of public rights, because once legislatures had allocated specific priorities in extending privileges, immunities, and resource-access advantages to one kind of enterprise over another (for example, to miners over agriculturists), the courts often would rule that these legislative policies themselves served to define the "public interest," common good, and public rights. In this way the courts validated actions that diminished the value of the expectations, not only the existing uses of their property, for those who were the losers in this kind of competition for legislative favor.

≺ II ≻

Property Rights and Economic Liberty:
A Dualistic Heritage

The security of property rights was a major ideological as well as practical political concern of the American Republic's founding generation, and this concern found abundant expression in both the political rhetoric and the legal and constitutional debates of the constitutional founding period. There is nothing in the record of the early Republic to indicate that either elites or the society at large showed even the slightest interest in undermining the essential capitalist character of social and economic relations. In a capitalist system, of course, it was essential that the law provide a system of rules that would offer property owners protection of their ownership rights and stability in the legal context within which they could use their property (or transfer it through contractual agreements) to advance their own purposes.

Many of the early state constitutions included provisions that protected property rights from seizure by the state through exercise of the eminent domain power, requiring that such takings be for a "public use" or "public purpose" and specifying that a property owner who suffered such a loss must be made whole by compensation from the state.[23] Moreover, when the framers met in Philadelphia in 1787 to write a new national constitution, one of their greatest concerns was the protection of property rights. They had been frightened by the prospect of "anarchy," a word that appears often in the correspondence of these men during 1786–87, because of an uprising in Massachusetts (Shays's Rebellion) against collection of debts and because of "stay laws" and other legislation in several states that gave legal relief to debtors.[24] And they regarded the prospect of tyrannous majorities slashing away at the structure of private rights as a danger to the survival of the nation exceeded only by the inability of the existing national government to deal effectively with England and other hostile foreign nations in the arena of international relations.[25]

In the convention debates at Philadelphia in 1787, and in the ratification debates that followed, virtually all the champions of the new constitution reaffirmed constantly their belief that the rights of property would be well secured by the adoption of the new system. This would be true, they argued, first, because of structural protections—in the division of powers between the central government and the states, and in the separation of powers as between executive, judicial, and legislative branches. Second, they could point to the inclusion of the Contract Clause in Article I, Section 10 of the Constitution which prohibited the states from "impair-(ing) the Obligation of Contracts," thus providing, as Madison wrote, "a constitutional bulwark in favor of personal security and private rights."[26]

That "property must be secured, or liberty cannot exist," as John Adams would write in 1790, just after the new government went into operation, was an axiom thoroughly accepted by both the Constitution's proponents and their anti-federalist opposition.[27] The same kind of evident consensus among the electorate and the party leadership prevailed across partisan lines in the 1790s, when

Madison and Jefferson led their followers into an organized opposition. Differences of view came to a focus mainly on how strong a centralization was necessary, and whether the surrender of state powers to the national government would not itself become a threat to the security of vested rights and an invitation to an undermining of the republic polity by privileged interests.[28]

In a case decided only a few years after the new government was instituted, Justice Patterson would declare: "The preservation of property . . . is a primary object of the social compact . . . The rights of acquiring and possessing property and having it protected is one of the nature, inherent, and inalienable rights of man."[29] He did not finish with that classic affirmation of the rights of property, however, for he followed immediately with a qualification indicating the public obligations and the common weal must be given consideration. Thus he referred to the power of eminent domain as a "despotic power . . . that exists in every government," one that the state might mobilize to meet its necessities and before which private claims (though they must be compensated) had no choice but to yield.[30] As David Lieberman points out in chapter 4, in the writings of both Adam Smith and Jeremy Bentham there was similarly an acknowledgment that with the rights of property also came obligations. The same was true in the leading American constitutional treatises by James Kent and Joseph Story, both of them conservatives—but both explicitly granting that there must be ample room for state action that trenched on private rights when the health, welfare, safety, and public morality of the community required regulation.[31]

On the bench, Kent was faithful to this view of public rights, for example ruling in 1805 that private actions that interfered with public use of navigable river could be abated by an injunction through equity action.[32] A little more than a decade later, Kent handed down a landmark decision on the tort liability of state canal officials who, in pursuit of their duties, entered private property as authorized by the legislature to run surveys or take materials for construction. The Erie Canal was a "great public object," Kent declared, "calculated to intimidate by its novelty, its expense, and its magnitude," and should not be hampered in its execution by excessive solicitude for the private rights of individual property owners. Hence, Kent ruled, no charge of trespass could stand against the canal authorities as they pursued their duties; and so he set the American doctrine of sovereign tort immunity upon a foundation that would hold firm to the modern day.[33] Following on this precedent, when the State of Ohio similarly undertook canal construction in the 1830s, the supreme court in that state ruled that "the power to construct [a state] canal is a high attribute of sovereignty, and in the thousand subordinate operations attending the execution of so vast a work, there is a necessity for the exercise of large discretionary powers."[34]

We have been focusing mainly on the ways in which American lawmakers and courts treated the legal defenses of property—that is, on the law as it was conceived in regard to the "negative" aspect of economic liberty and its mandates. In addition to asserting property rights as fundamental, the earliest state constitutions also gave expression to a positive conception of economic liberty, of "property in motion." Its ambit extended well beyond the defensive problem of protecting vested rights—in short what Hurst, as we have already noted, termed the dynamic aspect of property and its function in the "release of energy." Thus in the first Pennsylvania constitution "acquiring, possessing, and protecting property, and pursuing and obtaining happiness and safety" were included among the "natural, inherent, and inalienable rights" to which all men, "born equally free and independent," were entitled. The document also guaranteed the right of all persons to "emigrate from one state to another that will receive them, or to form a new state in vacant countries," an affirmation of freedom of movement that had its counterpart in liberal naturalization laws of the day.[35]

The Virginia Declaration of Rights earlier had similarly identified as inherent rights "the enjoyment of life, liberty, with the means of acquiring and possessing property, and pursuing and obtaining happiness and safety."[36] These phrases bespoke something much more than defense of vested rights in property and quiet possession, instead conveying a commitment to protecting the dynamic uses of property and of private energies and talents more generally. (Such language was incorporated into the constitutions of many of the western states, as the nation expanded and they came into the federal Union throughout the nineteenth century.)

These concerns with acquisition and free use of property indicated the extent to which the founding generation regarded open economic opportunity as a vital element of "the pursuit of happiness" and of "the blessings of liberty." The public values that were embodied in the constitutional documents of the period reflected the contentions of Thomas Paine in *The Rights of Man* (1792), to the effect that Americans had made the invaluable discovery that "true happiness" was produced when every citizen enjoyed the right to "pursue his occupation, and enjoy the fruits of his labors, and the product of this property, in peace and safety, and with the least possible expense."[37]

A distinctive aspect of the early state constitutions and their assertions of inalienable rights, reinforcing other evidence of America's commitment in the founding era to economic liberty, was the occasional assertion of the general rights of all citizens to have access to common resources. This was an important variant of the theme of "public rights." For example, the Pennsylvania document of 1776 specifically reserved to the citizens of the commonwealth "liberty to fowl and hunt in seasonable times on . . . lands . . . not enclosed; and in like manner to fish in all boatable waters, and others not private property."[38] Similarly, in South Carolina in the early nineteenth century the common people of the interior repeatedly went to the legislature and to the courts to demand relief from mill dam construction projects that blocked passage of fish and thus threatened both established commercial fishing operations and important sources of subsistence. They made these demands, as the historian Harry Watson has recently written, in a mode that spoke to their republican ideology and sense of entitlement to common resources. Thus they referred in one petition to "the free passage of boats and fish as . . . our natural Rights the free gift of God[,] and we as free men natural born citizens and Republicans in spirit and principle plead for our natural Rights as both are profitable and Desirable."[39]

The specification of such public rights was a declaration, in effect, of property claims—claims that were communal in their character, rather than strictly private. It constituted a highly significant variant of the ideals of economic liberty embodied in the law—not only in Pennsylvania but also in other states whose courts would need to adjudicate disputes involving such communal claims, based on both common law and constitutional writ.

Even when courts in that era denied such claims, it was often by introducing a distinction, usually based on navigability—between "public" rivers and those deemed strictly private property—a distinction drawn from a seventeenth-century treatise on common law which established that the public enjoyed access "by common right" to the larger streams. Thus the streams were "under the servitude of the public interest" even where private ownership could be claimed along the shore or in the streambed.[40] This doctrine, formulated by Lord Hale Matthew and perpetuated and elaborated through precedent over the entire course of the nineteenth century, became the doctrinal centerpiece for the regulatory state. It justified, for example, regulation of railroads and grain elevators in the 1870s because they were deemed under "servitude of the public interest," or "affected with a public interest."[41]

≺ III ≻

An Active (Republican) Government: American Neo-Mercantilism

We come now to the question of how the American commitment to rights of private property was connected to the question of positive state intervention in economic affairs. One of the main results of the American Revolution—and, as nearly all historians will argue, certainly also one of the objectives of the Revolutionary leaders in organizing the resistance that became the War of Independence—was the winning of freedom from British mercantilism and the overthrowing of controls that it had imposed upon the colonial economy. The immediate issues that triggered the conflict stemmed from the British government's enforcement of its rule in brutal violation of what the colonial leaders regarded as inalienable political and civil rights, but the constraints that mercantilist regulation had placed on the American economy had long been a subject on their own terms of intense resentment and increasing colonial resistance. Throwing off the burdens of British mercantilism was one of their great achievements, as the leadership of the new nation thought, giving the republican experiment a better chance to survive and thrive in a hostile world.[42]

That achievement was celebrated in political discourse of the day, in terms that bespoke a powerful commitment to the idea of security of private property rights, including the need to honor legitimate "expectations" of those property owners who risked their resources and their energies in commerce, land speculation and development, and agriculture. British policies, which as the Americans believed had been arbitrarily framed and imposed, had systematically defeated important expectations in all these areas of economic activity. But did it follow, because the Revolution had defeated the British mercantilist leviathan, that the Americans would themselves renounce mercantilist principles and once in charge of their own government shift to a policy of laissez-faire, giving maximum free play to private entrepreneurs in pursuit of their self-interest in the marketplace?

Especially in light of the pervasive evidence that the freedom of contract ideal and security of property rights had been incorporated into the very root and branch of political thought and constitutionalism in the new republic, and in light of the more comprehensive commitment to limited government that was embodied in the constitutional settlement (including the adoption of the Bill of Rights amendments), a principled move to enshrine laissez-faire ideals would not have seemed terribly incongruous or surprising. Far from moving in that direction, however, the new nation's leaders opted for a system of intervention—mainly geared to promote rather than confine economic activity, to be sure, but an interventionist program nonetheless. The emerging political parties, the Federalists and the Jeffersonian Republicans, despite powerful differences of view on some specific policy issues of great moment, occupied an important measure of common ground with respect to political economy.

This commonality was reflected in the shared conviction that a robust economic nationalism—not duplicating but certainly drawing heavily upon the British model, adapted to the interests of American merchants, farmers, and manufacturers—was essential to the successful launching of the new republic under the 1787 constitution. Contrary to the impression conveyed by historians and legal scholars who recently have attributed to the Founders a faith in "civic humanism" and "republican virtue" that was linked with a pervasive distrust of economic individualism and competi-

tive market values, the new nation's leaders on all sides actually
were much concerned to advance material growth and to support
American enterprises. There were constant reiterations of the way
in which expansion of commerce would contribute to the "sociability" (in that wonderful phrase of the Scottish philosophers) of relations among the citizenry, offsetting and checking the dangerous
tendencies of competitive individualism and pursuit of self-interest. In these was evident the influence of Adam Smith's thesis that
the rise of commerce had been a principal force behind the achievement of rule of law.[43]

Laissez-faire precepts—either in their raw and unvarnished
form, or on the more complex and nuanced model that had been
set forth by Smith—were never taken as a serious option by a significant faction of either the Federalist or the Republican party.
Only later, in the crucible of rising partisanship and sectionalism,
did a principled antagonism to guidance and channeling of economic activity through intervention appear. It came first in modest
form during the Republican ascendancy and then in much more
doctrinaire form during the Jacksonian era—but even in those later
days the very champions of laissez-faire were often those who most
adamantly demanded active intervention by government as needed
to protect the system of slavery in the South.[44]

Questions of political economy were at the very heart of the
Washington administration's policy concerns from the moment
that the new government was formed. Indeed, the economic policy
issues were, in a sense, the real unfinished business of the debate
over the Constitution and its ratification during 1787–89. From the
earliest hours of the first Congress, once the Bill of Rights amendments were hammered out and a judiciary act written—complet-
ing, in a sense, the full measure of *constitutional* reformation that
the Constitutional Convention had set in motion—the leading issues before the lawmakers were economic. As Fisher Ames declared in the House debates in 1789, "the fond hopes entertained
by our constituents" for the new government were founded on the
notion that it "would ensure their rights"—and it speaks elo-
quently of the importance of economic policy in the hierarchy of
concerns that when Fisher Ames said "their rights" he referred in
particular to the protection of their economic interests.[45] The patri-

ots' complaints of their "rights" being violated, which often as not centered on Britain's assaults on what colonial society regarded as vested economic interests, thus had their echoes in talk about rights in this first Federalist congress.

The economic ideas of those who engaged in the debate of economic policy in the 1790s were subject to testing by the standard of various contemporary views of representation of interests in a republican polity, and of the demarcation—in law and policy—of that delicate line which Hamilton termed "the salutary boundary between POWER and PRIVILEGE."[46] But the assumption on which these debates were premised was a common one—that it was the duty of government, in the public interest, to pursue the job of defining that boundary. The assertion of demands by concrete economic and social interests in that process was an accepted element of the political discourse. Mobilization of governmental power and public resources for the advancement of a common interest, as part of the process that included boundary-drawing and the accommodation of interest-group pressures, was accepted by Federalists and Republicans as essential to the foundations of the new government and as an integral function of a republic no less than of other polities. In fact, their own thirteen small republics had pursued interventionism with a fair degree of vigor in the 1780s, under the Confederation government. Indeed, these very economic policies had been the concern that had motivated the Annapolis Convention movement and were among the leading objects of reform when the framers gathered at Philadelphia in 1787.[47]

What the Federalists had condemned in the polices of the new state governments, under the Articles of Confederation, was not the efforts of individual state governments to promote or to regulate economic interest—though to be sure, they vigorously deplored stay and tender laws, or any government-sanctioned abrogation of contract. Instead, what the Federalists found objectionable was the disunity and weakness to which the dynamics of thirteen separate economic policies had contributed. The Federalists wanted to substitute in place of such autarchy a strong and unified national policy, a single set of rules—and in some respects, a single set of controlling institutions—with respect to the core objectives of the classical mercantilist programs of the eighteenth-century states and European powers. "The regulation of these various and interfering interests," as Madison wrote, "forms the principal task of modern Legislation."[48]

What were these standard mercantilist objectives? First was a policy for the periphery (in the European case, for colonies; in the American, for the West and the territories that would be created there, in the context of rising concern that the western area must enjoy free access to the Gulf of Mexico outlet and be linked eventually by improved east-west transportation to the Atlantic Coast ports).[49] Of equal priority among mercantilist-style objectives was, second, "an adequate provision for the support of the public credit"—which, as an early congressional document, dated September 1789, declared, was "a matter of high importance to the national honor and prosperity."[50] Third, however, a mercantilist system must have as its centerpiece acts of trade and navigation, designed to pursue the right "balance," through prohibitions and limits as well as through subsidies, discriminations, and duties; and nothing was so explicitly accepted, in the earliest days of the Federalist era, as the need for such legislation.[51]

"The advancement of agriculture, commerce, and manufacturing, by all proper means," as Washington declared in his first annual message, was so vital a task of government that it did not require more than mention to be recommended to Congress.[52] The Senate promptly responded formally to the message, assuring the President that "all proper means in our power" would be used in this cause.[53] James Madison called upon Congress in its early months "to consider the means of encouraging agriculture; which I think may be very justly styled the great staple of the United States."[54] Note Madison's use of the word "encouraging," an active role for government; and how agriculture, in this context, far from being the idealized realm of Jefferson's "chosen people of God" was very simply a "staple," the most important of the country.[55]

Even Jefferson, however, also became a staunch advocate of carefully targeted intervention, authoring a report on the Atlantic fisheries which was presented to Congress along with his recommendations that a vigorous federal program of subsidy for the marine fishery and the whaling industries be inaugurated and sustained with national revenues.[56] It was little wonder, then, that Hamilton himself, in evaluating the policy conflicts over political economy in the 1790s, should have commented of his principal critic, Madison, that "he has the same end in view as I have"— except on the issue of how Anglo-American commercial relations should be ordered.[57] Even for those who, like Madison, yearned for the day when free trade principles could prevail altogether in the commercial policies of the nation, "In order to overcome mercantilism, it was first necessary to play the mercantilist game and exploit trade as a police weapon."[58]

Pursuit of a common end through the instrument of an American neo-mercantilism did not mean, however, that the Federalists and the opposition agreed upon how economic individualism and the self-interested pursuits of an enterprising people ought to be regarded in a large philosophical perspective. On the one side, speaking forthrightly in terms of needing to harness the most powerful and the most wealthy to the new government, Hamilton went so far as to argue explicitly that corrupt instincts and ambitions might be best curbed if the interests in question were aligned and intertwined with that of the governmental establishment. On the other side, there was, again, Madison in his pragmatic vein, as when he argued that while the "old maxim" was right, that "trade is best left to regulate itself," still "circumstances may and do occur to require legislative interference."[59] (It must be said, however, that Madison saw the dangers of privilege, monopoly, and a crushing of legitimate private enterprisers as the likely result of Hamilton's approach to such questions as the Bank issue; rather than harnessing private ambition to the government, he pursued a vision of the government as arbiter and balancer.) Recommending the model of British mercantilism to his Virginia compatriots in 1783, Madison had said the doctrinaire preferences that regulatory intervention be minimized, with which he personally agreed, must be set aside in the circumstances of the new nation: "Nor ought the example of old and intelligent nations be too far or too hastily condemned by an infant and inexperienced one." He declared "that Great Britain is in the science of commerce particularly worthy of our attention." Whatever the direction that Madison's views would take later in his life, while engaged in the business of establishing the new republic's foundational economic policies, he was above all a realist seeking to assure that the economy was placed on a strong footing for future growth.[60]

On a broader canvas, a South Carolina Federalist representative,
William Smith, amidst the debate on the tonnage bill, portrayed
the political landscape as one in which the states stood expectantly
by waiting for Congressional succor. He reminded the House that
when the states had accepted the new Constitution they had done
so expecting protection, solicitude for their interests, even the favor of largesse when the "fostering hand of government," as Madison and others were wont to say, was clearly required for a highly
important national purpose: "the manufacturing States wished the
encouragement of manufacturing," he declared; "the maritime
states the encouragement of shipbuilding, and the agricultural
states the encouragement of agriculture." There was no suggestion,
in Smith's speech, that this was a deplorable betrayal of republican
ideals, no hint here that there had been a departure from legitimate
republicanism: it was part of the realm of politics, an essential part
in a mercantilist age.[61] And what polity would require a coherent
mercantilism and its vigorous administration more than a young,
small one such as the newly independent republic clinging to the
Atlantic seaboard and struggling to establish credibility with foreign antagonists in an uncertain world?

One should not conclude from any of the foregoing that either
the Federalists or the Republican opposition leaders had kicked
over concern for the public interest in favor of "the private pursuit
of happiness,"[62] divorced from the classical ideal—or for that matter, divorced or even clearly distinguishable from the venerable
common law rule of *salus populi*, or even from the more modern
idea of an organic general interest that was expressed positively in
the general will and the sovereignty of a republican people. Some
profoundly serious differences emerged over how to define that interest in specific terms, but these were not differences of opinion
over the necessity for some kind of governmental program on mercantilist lines. In this sense, what emerged in the specific Federalist policies of the 1790s, I think represented a well-developed
eighteenth-century view of how government ought to organize
economic interests, establish priorities, and articulate and balance
interests. Indeed, the very idea of "balance" had been a quintessen-
tial part of the mercantilist view, no less than it would be incorporated in Aristotelian rhetorical terms into neoclassical republican
thought.

Thus the views of the "speculative-entrepreneurial wing" of the Republican party—a group that championed high tariffs, skeptical of the pro-British policies pursued by Hamilton, at the same time enthusiastically supportive of the Federalist tonnage laws and mildly protectionist tariffs—have been characterized appropriately as a program designed in quest of a "balanced and independent national economy."[63] Virtually the same words, however—expressing the wish to advance the cause of a "balanced and independent national economy"—can be invoked without serious challenge in describing the intentions of virtually every other faction and important leader in the debates of the 1790s over economic policy. Some of them believed that the "balance" might be tipped in favor of the agricultural interests, or should reveal a particular solicitude for expansion and settlement of western lands; for others, it was better to tip the balance in favor of household manufacturing, agricultural processing industries, or commerce. A few favored outright subsidizing of the factory-based industries.

But what all the factions in that era held in common was a robust faith in the tried and established instruments of governmental intervention, inherited from the eighteenth century. These instruments, they believed, ought to be applied in support of the new nation, triumphant in winning independence yet still only precariously holding on in a world of hostile and powerful states, with its economy just beginning to produce surplus capital enough to sustain commercial banking, investment in new manufacturing ventures, and (as yet only a well-formed hope in most of the states[64]) investment in the transportation facilities that were understood to be a vital prerequisite to initiating a pattern of vigorous economic growth and material expansion. And the legislative program of Congress in the era of Federalist ascendancy during the 1790s—the tariff and navigation acts, the measures to fund state debts and establish the public credit, establishment of the first Bank of the United States, and special subsidy bills—reflected that understanding of the positive, interventionist role that could be legitimately asked of government.[65]

In the period of Republican ascendancy in national politics that followed, from the election of 1800 to the 1820s, the Jeffersonian leaders took an increasingly rigid ideological view that favored decentralized government. They were suspicious of excessive power at the center, in the national government, and supportive of a concept of federal governance that left major areas of policy with the individual states. Conveniently congruous with the interests of the South in protecting the slave system, the states' rights view did not stand in the way, however, of the Republicans' accepting the chartering of a second Bank of the United States, or supporting significant national programs of aid for transportation improvement, or in 1816 enacting a protective tariff to foster infant industries. Still, what the Jeffersonians bequeathed to the successor movement led by Andrew Jackson, elected to the presidency in 1828, was a shift toward increasingly ideological commitment to limited government at the center; and continuing emphasis upon the dangers of special privilege as a corrupting factor in republican government, couched in the rhetoric of equal rights as well as of economic liberty.

These preoccupations broadened into a concern that constitutional doctrines that took a generous view of congressional powers under the general welfare and commerce clauses of the Constitution were establishing a legal foundation for "consolidation" of all significant power in the national government, which in turn would set the stage for capture of control over all significant policies by the rich and powerful interests in the society.[66] Hence President Jackson's veto message, sounding his opposition to a re-chartering and continuation of the Bank of the United States:

In the full enjoyment of the gifts of Heaven and the fruits of superior industry, economy, and virtue, every man is equally entitled to protection by law; but when the laws undertake to add to these natural and just advantages artificial distinction, to grant titles, gratuities, and exclusive privileges, to make the rich richer and the potent more powerful, the humble members of society . . . have a right to complain of the injustice of their Government. . . Many of our rich men have not been content with equal protection and equal benefits, but have besought us to make them richer by act of Congress. By attempting to gratify their desires we have in the results of our legislation arrayed section against section, interest against interest, and man against man, in a fearful commotion which threatens to shake the foundations of our Union.[67]

Jackson's crusade against privilege went another step forward as he dealt with internal improvements policies, again seeking to rectify the "fearful commotion" of special-interest pressures that he saw crowding on Congress in the form of demands for national financial aid to transportation projects. (These projects were seen by the Whig opposition, of course, as vital infrastructure for a developing economy, parallel to the contributions to the economy of the national bank that they championed against Jackson's assault.) In his 1831 Maysville Road veto message, Jackson denounced the policy of extending any form of aid—whether use of the Army Engineers to run surveys; or the appropriation of cash subsidies, land grants, or federal investments in "local" projects, as he called them—and declared an end to the national government's leadership in transport planning and expansion.[68] In the period from 1837, when Martin Van Buren succeeded Jackson—and took an even more rigid line in molding the new Democratic party's limited-government ideas, merged with a pro-slavery constitutional defense, into a party orthodoxy—until the Civil War, the economic policy agenda and most of the responsibility for intervention shifted decisively to the state level and away from the national legislature.

In one other respect, the Democrats achieved a decisive break with the neo-mercantilist framework that had been inherited from the Federalist era. This was in the adoption of the tariff of 1846, embodying the so-called "revenue-only" principle (though in fact steep duties were retained on all luxury goods as well as some items in the non-luxury category) and renouncing the protectionist approach. Adopted in the very year when the English Corn Laws were repealed, bringing British policy into a principled free-trade mode, this new tariff approach was maintained until 1857, when another set of reductions brought United States trade policy as close to free trade as it had ever been or would be for another century's time. The tariff policy, like the limited-government initiatives of the Democrats in that period, was put forward as part of a program to root out privilege and subsidy that ran against the principle of equal rights and equal access to the market—elements of an ideology of economic liberty on the individualist model.[69]

≺ IV ≻

Enterprise and the Active State

Although the national government was thus curtailed in its interventionist role, there was no comparable general diminution in

Americans' commitment to the active use of public power to provide a favorable framework within which private-sector interests could pursue their activities. The focus simply had shifted to the states. Active promotion of their economies brought the states into large-scale public transport enterprises, beginning with the Erie Canal project in New York State in 1817 and emulated widely elsewhere in the ensuing decades. The policy debates over canal and other transport investment in the state legislatures evoked an explicit concern for rationalized planning for construction priorities, and also for maximizing the natural advantages of substate regions and localities. The pressure of interests, however, often undermined planning efforts. Local demands were often couched in formal egalitarian terms that can be termed "the doctrine of equal benefits," expressing the notion that when a republican government allocated its largesse it was the ideal that all must share in it as equally as possible.[70]

Another side of the same egalitarian thrust in the antebellum era was the opposition to legislation granting special charters for individual corporations. Given the preference for dispersion of power, the pragmatic advantages of corporate form for mobilization of capital investment, and the obvious usefulness of corporate structure in entrepreneurial ventures, there was little sustained opposition on principle to granting corporations such advantages as limited liability. Nor was there objection to legislatures' authorizing a high degree of freedom to corporate stockholders in ordering their firms' internal allocations of authority.[71] What egalitarian and individualistic concepts did impel was a spreading movement for a policy that companies should be given the privileges and immunities or incorporation only through general laws by which all qualifying firms could incorporate. This movement was an attack on privilege, expressing in its own way the imperatives of a popular legal culture that valued economic liberty. Similarly, various regulations were adopted that would apply to all corporations equally, indicative of a determination to maintain a balance between giving private interests wide play in the marketplace and the assertion of public interests. The Marshall Court's interpretation of the Contract Clause as including protection for corporations, and not only for individuals, against what it found to be arbitrary governmental actions, established the ground rules for governmental supervision.[72]

"A consensus appears from the face of the legislation, which was substantially the same in all states," Hurst has concluded, "that businessmen properly should enjoy the utility of the corporate form, but under some restrictions designed to keep corporate business within limits consistent with maintaining a free market."[73] Popular support for corporations as a practical instrument was not inconsistent with the free labor ideology that was an important element in freedom of contract ideas both then and later in America, despite the obvious paradox that inheres in these corporations representing concentrated power rather than reflecting the image of the sturdy and independent yeoman farmer or artisan worker.[74]

In sum, the general pattern in the states was that government intervened in ways that were receptive to enterprise, that expedited short-term profitability of exploitation of resources, and that responded to popular demands for wide sharing of largess and of access to the advantages of public works such as canals and roads. Moreover, the system of decentralized power meant that there was wide room for competitiveness among the states in the quest for capital, for immigrants, and for enterprise. The dynamic of economic policies that structured the market in which private interests bargained and dealt through contract was, therefore, one that may usefully be described as a pattern of "rivalistic state mercantilism."[75]

Promotion was not the whole story, however, for within the pattern of intervention there also was a continuing exercise of public power by the state and local governments for traditional regulatory purposes—measures imposed with the specific purpose of setting limits upon private contractual agreements and uses of economic power and property in the marketplace. As has been noted here already, the courts validated such interventions across a broad range through the application of a doctrine of "public rights."[76] The regulatory legislation that came up for judicial review was wide in its scope, indicating that bargaining in the marketplace and liberty in uses of private property came under important constraints. The states imposed what in the law were called "duties to serve" upon inns, private transport companies, bridge companies, and other kinds of enterprise that were found to come under the old common law category of property that was private in ownership but public in use—the principle of *publici juris*.[77] The statute books of many states contained laws that imposed rules of navigation, fishing, and other uses of public rivers and streams; prohibited private owners on river and coastal shores from building structures that interfered with navigability; and mandated the drainage of wetlands or the development of harbors and basins. Others required those selling produce to conform with public market rules and standards; and licensed a variety of trades, including auctioneers, innkeepers, distillers, and even general merchants and retailers.[78]

In passing on the constitutionality of this great panoply of regulation, the courts invoked criteria that were found not only in the common law tradition but also in the jurisprudence of the civil law of continental Europe.[79] Thus in the leading state case on the police power, in the Massachusetts Court in 1851, Chief Justice Lemuel Shaw upheld the state's regulation of the navigable shoreline waters against obstruction by private wharves, founding the power to regulate such waters "for the best interest of the public" upon categories first systematized as common law rules by Lord Hale two centuries earlier. But he also mobilized maxims from English law: *sic utere uo ut alienum non laedas* (use your own property in such manner as not to injure that of another) in an analogy with regulation through public law. Thus Shaw declared that

every holder of property, however absolute and unqualified may be his title, holds it under the implied liability that his use of it may be so regulated, that it shall not be injurious to the equal enjoyment of others having an equal right to the enjoyment of their property, nor [shall it be] injurious to the rights of the community.[80]

From the civilian writers came declarations that inherent in the basic concept of sovereignty was the power to legislate for the common good, overriding private claims. The most influential of the cases in this line was that of the Charles River bridge decided by the Taney Court in 1837. In it the court turned back the claims of an old private bridge company against the Massachusetts legislature's decision to build a competing bridge, declaring that "the community also have rights, and that the happiness and well-being of every citizen depends on their faithful preservation."[81] A decade later, in a case dealing with the power of the states to require licenses, Chief Justice Taney declared the broad doctrine that the police (regulatory) power was "nothing more or less than the powers of government inherent in every sovereignty to the extent of its dominions."[82] In a broad sense, this was the obverse side of Chief Justice Marshall's invocation of natural rights, founded in continental law, as a barrier to arbitrary state action derogatory of vested claims to property and to the legitimate expectations of economic liberty.[83]

When we speak, then, of the nineteenth century in America as the "age of contract," when a small-scale and limited government left many vital areas of economic and social ordering to the market, it must be in terms that recognize the myriad ways in which free bargaining and uses of property in that market went forward in a dualistic framework with both promotional and regulatory functions. It was a legal regime different, however, from the one that would emerge as the response to post–Civil War and twentieth-century industrialization. The jurisprudential heritage of the early nineteenth century afforded an ample doctrinal basis for powerful regulatory responses by government in the new industrial order. That heritage fell far short, however, of providing unquestioned endorsement of giantism in government, extensive bureaucratization, and the resort to explicitly redistributive types of intervention and social policies that would become the staple of modern political economy.

Modern reform efforts needed to overcome hostility to "class legislation" as a barrier to acceptance of much more pervasive kinds of state intervention than had been known before. They also needed to assault inherited popular and juristic concepts of economic liberty as associated with privatism and individualism, with the other side of that heritage—the function of a traditional regulatory framework for advancement of the common good—seen as something separate and entirely distinguishable from economic liberty. Both in England and in the United States, therefore, a major thrust of reform movements was to recapture in the law and to re-awaken in the political culture the idea that intervention itself could be liberating by giving protection to the processes through which the creativity and autonomy of the individual might be protected and nurtured.[84]

≺ V ≻

Individualism and Classical Contract

If the rules that governed nineteenth-century private contract existed within the framework of promotional and regulatory law generated by the legislatures, still the common law continued to coexist and develop alongside public law. There was a dualism in the jurisprudence bearing on freedom of contract in this respect as well. The antebellum American judges tended to give deference to the legislature's judgments of what constituted the public interest and the common good, albeit while also articulating a standard that denied arbitrary or capricious interference with private rights. Yet these same judges operated in what amounted to virtually a separate legal universe when it came to the interpretation and enforcement of private contract. The regime over which they presided, constituting the domain of private law including contract, tort, and property relationships, was not a static one either before or after the Civil War. Elaborations of doctrine were instituted continuously by the courts, in the tradition of the common law process as the rules were adjusted to new technologies and market conditions. But the domain of the common law was at its core a domain that protected economic individualism and a rigorous respect for market values.

The theoretical model has been described many times in the terms used by the historian Leonard Levy in characterizing how in the day of Chief Justice Shaw the Massachusetts high court defined the rights of parties in private contractual relationships. The common law was harsh and unyielding, Levy writes, and tended towards abstraction of private parties at the bar. So long as the controversies at issue were not explicitly regulated by positive statutory legislation, the courts' role was to apply universal principles to the particular case:

The common law knew society only as so many John Does and Richard Roes, which is to say that it had scant regard for society collectively. Social and economic problems were reflected in the common law merely as conflicts of personal interest between contending parties. They might possess an unequal status and power; their case might involve great and grave social interests. But to the common law, indifferently neutral . . . the parties were theoretically interchangeable personalities to be dealt with on equal terms and with scant regard for others.[85]

The parties to contract were assumed to be rational actors, capable of (and responsible for) looking out for their own interests, making agreements to which they should be held rigidly unless fraud, duress, or some other recognized special reason militated against courts' strictly construing their obligations freely entered into. On the whole, it was a legal regime that was premised on self-reliant, free-willed men and women who must guard their own interests. The courts were responsible for seeing that agreements were kept. To interfere for reasons extraneous to the private arrangements in question (except, as noted, where the evolution of common law had produced a rationale for judicial interference such as proof that fraud or coercion had prevailed) was regarded as a pernicious fact of judicial paternalism.[86]

The ethos of individual responsibility and economic liberty was most dramatically evident in commercial sales transactions. To what extreme the doctrine of *caveat emptor* (buyer beware) could run was illustrated by the South Carolina court in a land sale case in 1843. When the buyer of a property discovered, after a sale was concluded, that there was some defect in the property which a forthcoming seller would have disclosed beforehand, it was the buyer's problem; and no remedy would be afforded him by the court. The buyer, declared Judge F. H. Wardlaw, is one who has "the means of forming his own judgment," and so a "prudent man would have discovered" the defects that formed the cause of his petition for the court to overturn the contract. The bargaining process itself was a "contest of puffing and cheating," the court said rather cavalierly, and as such constituted a test of individual judgment. The seller took care of his side of things "and left the other to the buyer," who was out of luck and must absorb the costs of his misfortune.[87]

Although this kind of rhetoric departed from the more detached and systematic philosophical style in which jurists more typically couched the harsh doctrinal realities of common law of sales, the substance of the decision was not exceptional. Countless numbers of hard bargains, the results of "puffing and cheating," or simply subtle and shrewd misrepresentation, doubtless never went to court precisely because the potential plaintiffs who had suffered loss knew very well how slender would be their chances of redress. Contract jurisprudence favored the private individual will, ex-

pressed in the presumption of legality for all contracts, and reinforced by the notion that it was the courts' role to operate "as detached umpires or referees." Courts do not, it was said, make contracts for the parties.[88]

The facade of judicial neutrality did not mean, of course, that
judges did not engage in adaptation, adjustment, and innovation in
the process of building, reconsidering, and applying relevant precedent doctrine. At some moments of high drama, the courts had to
settle truly fundamental questions such as whether tradesmen's
organizations constituted per se conspiracies in American law.[89] At
times, also, the courts were required to reconsider inherited general
rules in light of concrete changes in economic conditions and relationships. Such an area was the old common law rules of bargains
made in restraint of trade—the anti-monopoly and anti-engrossing
doctrine—which American state courts applied continuously
throughout the nineteenth century, before and after enactment of
the first federal antitrust law, the Sherman Act of 1890, diverging
in some important respects in the last decades of the century from
how the English courts were developing their own doctrine in judging the enforceability of contracts that constrained competition.[90]
Such significant changes as came from the courts were often scarcely
visible; they were incremental and subtle, as indicative of judicial
ingenuity in creating legal fictions as expressive of an overt concern for doctrinal reform with meaningful consequences. Thus the
law of common carriers evolved, with a gradual shift towards
judges' requiring express companies and other transport firms to
take responsibility for the safety and timely delivery of cargoes.

Technical doctrinal adjustments of many kinds were instituted
by the courts in order to advance the cause of regularity, predict-
ability, and certainty that was so important to a society in which
the volume and complexity of commercial dealings were so much
on the rise. Interaction and borrowing of doctrinal ideas as between
England and America were evident in court decisions that dealt in
evolving terms with such issues as the remoteness of damages, the
instructions that should be given to juries with respect to disputed
questions of fact, the nature of implied warranties of quality at
time of sale, and the like.[91]

The decisions did not all run in a single direction. Most of the
refinements and innovations served the purpose of clarifying the

terms so as to hold parties to an agreement strictly to its terms. This function of adjudication was given new impetus with the academic movement after 1900 to formalize a general theory of contract law, an effort led by Christopher Langdell and Samuel Williston.[92] Founders of what became known as the twentieth-century "classical school of contract," which dominated academic and juridical discourse until the 1950s, they contended for a theory based on explicit postulates. The central one was the bargain theory of consideration, under which agreements must be seen in objective terms, so that the courts would only ask what the parties did and what words were used, rather than inquire into intention. Exemplifying this theory was the statement of one of America's most respected federal judges, Learned Hand, in a contract case decided in 1911 and later upheld by the Supreme Court, that:

a contract, strictly speaking, has nothing to do with the personal, or individual, intent of the parties. A contract is an obligation attached by the mere force of law to certain acts of the parties, usually words, which ordinarily accompany and represent a known intent. If, however, it were proved by twenty bishops that either party, when he used the words, intended something else than the usual meaning which the law imposes on them, he would still be held [responsible for the obligation], unless there were some mutual mistake, or something of the sort.[93]

Withal, the classical school offered "a system of standardized and vigorously objective axioms that seem to have reflected implicit exemplary cases involving anonymous transactions [by rational persons] in perfectly competitive markets"[94]—an intellectual system that had remained faithful to its lineage in the harsh and rigid regime of late nineteenth-century contract jurisprudence.

It would misrepresent the realities of the law, however, if we failed to recognize also that the American courts sometimes ingeniously redefined realities in the construction of formalized but fictional constructs. They did so to soften the sharp edge of contract law when it worked terrible hardships on individuals, or obviously ran against the entire thrust of public policy as expressed in relevant legislative acts; or when facts could be teased out of the bargaining history that suggested some kind of coercion or fraud or the equivalent. Formalism, in other words, could be used to bring justice back into the contract law; it was not only a "sycophant of commerce, [which] paid homage to the free market and the right of

the individual to be free to contract and own property without government interference."[95] Professor Friedman, the leading historian
of the subject, believes that decisions based on equitable principles,
smuggled in under the rhetoric of classic theory, were handed
down fairly frequently in the workaday functioning of American
courts.[96]

Moreover, the legislatures did not stay out altogether. There
was a movement for adoption of civil codes of procedure that abolished the tedious and arcane "forms of action" that for centuries
had complicated and frustrated the efforts of litigants. The codes
also merged equity and law so as to simplify adjudication and provide a single undisputed judicial forum for parties at the bar. New
York led the way in 1848 with adoption of the code written by
David Dudley Field, with other states following in considerable
numbers; and in 1852 and 1854 the Procedure Acts adopted by Parliament similarly reformed key aspects of the common law courts'
rules for considering private law claims.

Other reforms adopted by the state legislatures dealt with such
issues as a homestead immunity for the debtor who had invested in
a home on land that was lost through debt action; abolition of imprisonment for debt; and extension to married women of rights to
hold property and to undertake contractual obligations. Friedman
argues that these legislative interventions were probably more important, on balance, than almost anything done in the way of doctrinal innovations by the judges themselves.[97] The procedural reforms were also a major opportunity for judges to increase their
discretionary power; for, as Kevin Teeven has shown, when the legislatures abolished the complex ancient forms of pleading it left
the door wide open for the courts "to fill in by developing general
principles." Although the new principles they put forward were
generally consistent with the freedom of contract and individualist
ideal, some courts also seized the chance to reintroduce standards
of equitable dealing and public policy, for example developing a
doctrine of unconscionability that could override the strictures of
caveat emptor in sales transactions.[98]

In the field of employment relations and related tort liability
law, however, the courts generally adhered to a harsh standard of
personal responsibility that worked to the entire advantage of owners and management, and against the interests of workers who suf-

fered in accidents—issues that are discussed fully in chapters 6 and 7. It is ironic that the sustained concern of nineteenth-century American courts to challenge regulatory legislation that might be construed as "class legislation" never led to judicial recognition that in the field of industrial accident law and (later on) application of antitrust laws to crush union activities, the courts were themselves engaged in precisely the deployment of power that they were wont to deny to legislatures.[99]

With adoption of the Fourteenth Amendment in 1868, the way was opened for federal and state judges alike to apply the new constitutional terms, that no state might "deprive any person of life, liberty, or property without due process of law; nor deny to any person within its jurisdiction the equal protection of the laws," in a manner that would lead to overturning of various social and economic regulatory laws. This process reached its high point in the *Lochner* decision of 1905 and the subsequent elaboration of the *Lochner* doctrine by a business-minded Supreme Court. Alongside the development of a jurisprudence that set new limitations on regulatory intervention, however, the political movements for an expanded interventionist role along a broad front registered major victories. They began with the first national law for transport rate regulation, in the Interstate Commerce Act of 1887, and went on to embrace antitrust regulation (by the Sherman Act in 1890), and the pure food and drug, banking, and railroad and maritime labor legislation of the Progressive era. Despite repeated constitutional challenges, mainly by reference to Fourteenth Amendment guarantees but also by invocation of Commerce Clause interpretations, nearly all of this legislation either emerged untouched in its original form or else (as with antitrust) survived in basic form permitting later amendments and restructuring for effective regulation.[100]

What is most important for us to recognize, in terms of how the framework of economic liberty has been affected by reform efforts and constitutional adjudication of its legislative product, is that large chunks of social and legal ordering have been taken over wholesale as the province of positive legislation. Hence areas of contract formerly left to the private law regime, developed almost exclusively by the courts, were now moved over into the aegis of public law. The important story, for the twentieth-century history of contract, is that "developments in public policy . . . systemati-

cally robbed contract of its subject matter."[101] In part this development has been narrow and has intruded on the technical doctrinal
aspects of contract, most notably adoption of the Uniform Commercial Code which in the last 60 years has invaded what had been
the nearly exclusive preserve of the courts in rules making for
commerce.

In other respects, however, the expansion of public law at the
expense of the classic contract regime in the common law courts
has been broad, involving a comprehensive set of regulations and
procedures in such areas as employment relations, environmental
protection, public health, and social security. Although private parties still engage in the making of agreements, the realistic meaning
of "bargaining" not only is curtailed by unequal economic power of
the contracting parties, but also is given a new constraining
framework as the result of the standardization of detailed terms of
contracts in areas of law such as insurance, stockholder-manage-
ment relationships, employment relations, and even government
entitlements.

Even to the present day, however, how to square the desiderata
of economic liberty with the expectation that courts will do justice
and acknowledge important social interests continues to be a question that agitates scholars and jurists in the field of contract law.
The courts have not withdrawn from the field. On occasion they
serve as innovators—for example, in decisions that have imposed
tort liabilities on commercial dealings and created an entire departure from earlier doctrine in the rules of strict liability and industrial liability; or in doctrines of enforceability that rest on a conception of equality of bargaining power that will invalidate obscure
contract terms or take cognizance of the consumer's lack of information, skill, or market leverage. They may also reassert on new
terms in federal courts the old strictures of Contract Clause limitations on the power of legislatures to interfere in what is deemed an
arbitrary way with autonomous private transactions.[102] The traditions of public rights and sovereign regulatory authority, on the
one side, and the jurisprudential heritage of freedom of contract in
the individualist mode, on the other, still coexist in American law
today—though in a very different balance than in earlier historical
eras.

≺ VI ≻

Individualism, the New Property, and
the Claims of "Positive Liberty"

A profoundly important debate on how concepts of "positive liberty" must be re-conceptualized in an era of giant corporations, social dislocation, unemployment, and widening income gaps opened up in England in the late nineteenth century. The terms of the discussion centered on the contentions of reform Liberals such as T. H. Green and Lord Acton, that inequalities of bargaining power must be realistically appraised; and that only through state intervention in fields such as public education and factory employment regulation could true liberty, defined as the sustaining of individual autonomy and opportunity, be honored. On the one hand, the reformers acknowledged the importance of unequal bargaining power as a reflection of the larger political problem of wealth in industrial society. "If there is a free contract," wrote Lord Acton in 1881,

in open market, between capital and labour, it cannot be right that one of the two contracting parties should have the making of the laws, the management of the conditions, the keeping of the peace, the administration of justice, the distribution of taxes, the control of expenditure, in its own hands exclusively . . . Justice required that property should—not abdicate, but—share its political supremacy. Without this partition, free contract was . . . illusory.[103]

Hence T. H. Green's famous lecture on "Liberal Legislation or Freedom of Contract," delivered at Leicester in 1881, in which the Oxford philosopher and prominent contributor to the debate over liberalism contended that "freedom in the positive sense" must become the legitimating standard for intervention by the state. By this he meant "the liberation of the powers of all men equally for contributions to a common good."[104] Sir Henry Maine believed that the progress of humankind was represented in the transition from Status to Contract. Lord Acton, on the premise that liberty "is itself the highest political end," and not only a means, contended that on the other hand "to be real it [liberty] must be circumscribed"; and that "advancing civilisation invests the State with increased rights and duties, and imposes increased burdens and constraint on the subject." Thus "compulsory obligations," which at an earlier stage of society's development might have been "thought unbearable," are now to be accepted because they are for the general good in a complex modern industrial society.[105]

From this debate in England came the shift of the Liberal party towards sponsorship of social reform legislation. It bespoke what a leading analyst of that era's reform thought called "the emergence of the concept of community in liberal thought, not as an appendage forced on it by circumstances, but as a logical development of liberal fundamentals when confronted with the changing needs of society."[106]

The terms of the great debate over liberalism and social policy in England also came to dominate—albeit in the special context of American constitutional discourse—an emerging academic and legal debate in America. The debate was over the legitimacy of class legislation and of explicitly redistributive policies that were being proposed to address the gap between egalitarian ideals and social realities, and, withal, over the need to centralize the formation and implementation of social and regulatory policies against the perdurable imperatives of an old-style dual federalism.[107] The basic intellectual charter of the post–World War II welfare state, the Beveridge Report, was published in England at a time when on the American side of the Atlantic both political leaders and jurists were addressing the question of personal rights, social needs, and constitutional legitimacy of welfare-state and regulatory-state interventions in the new terms that had been set down by the New Deal Court in the late 1930s.

In two cases in 1934 the Supreme Court had laid to rest staple doctrinal instruments that long had served property-minded conservatives well in their resistance to state regulation. One such doctrine that the court set aside was the old "affectation with a public purpose" doctrine, which had served to immunize specified categories of enterprise from comprehensive regulation. The other was the traditional view, dating from the Marshall Court, of the Contract Clause as a barrier to laws that suspended mortgage or other debt payment obligations.[108] Following this came the decision in *U.S. v. Carolene Products* (1938), in which the Court announced a hierarchy of freedoms, the "preferred freedoms" being the basic political guarantees concerning speech, press, and assembly; at a lower level, warranting less searching judicial scrutiny, were private rights of property.[109]

Subsequently, the Commerce Clause collapsed dramatically, in the Court's hands, as an obstacle to congressional exercise of virtually plenary police power in economic affairs, extending even to the private consumption of a farmer's production in his own home. In a decision considered at length in chapter 6, the Court finally came to grips with the objections to "class legislation," upholding the authority of the national government to exercise its power to regulate wages and hours at the legal nexus of the employment relationship.[110] In a broader perspective, the autonomy of private contracting was drastically curtailed because of the imposition of command-and-control regimes over planned sectors (agriculture and transport), and the vast expansion of administrative law governing transactions in banking, commerce, transportation, and telephone communications and radio.[111]

Contemplating the high court's disconnecting of personal from property rights, Learned Hand, the judge who would have resisted the testimony of twenty bishops, was led to remark: "Just why property itself was not a 'personal right' no one took the trouble to explain."[112] Did the vicissitudes of modern industrial society and the Depression emergency justify an expansion of constitutional warrant for regulatory action that would trump, as it seemed, concerns for economic liberty in an individualist mode that were part of the political legacy from Madison, Paine, and Lincoln?

The short answer to Judge Hand's remark was that, although the narrowly constitutional dimension of economic liberty had undergone a drastic alteration, a commitment to the individualism associated with economic activity remained fully alive in the legal and political culture. The English Liberal reformers had justified in terms of fulfilling human potential and providing men and women with meaningful liberty their reform measures for public education, the factory acts, and, in later days, the full spectrum of modern welfare-state measures in medical care, housing, unemployment insurance, and the like.[113] So now did America's progressive liberals, after World War II, defend the record of the 1930s New Deal programs in individualist and economic-liberty terms, as, for example, with respect to the emergency employment programs, the

Social Security system, the public housing and other legislative in-novations of the Depression period.

Indeed, not only in the GI Bill of Rights just after the war, and new entitlement programs—including a vast expansion of the So-cial Security system's coverage and introduction of new anti-poverty measures in the 1960s—but also in the support of civil rights, school desegregation, and equal economic opportunity for minority citizens, American public policy expressed a strong, ex-plicit concern for positive liberty. But laissez-faire conservatives, hoping to restore the pre–New Deal constitutional order, were then (as now) unconvinced by what they saw as disingenuous rationali-zations for a damaging kind of legal and social paternalism.[114] Par-ticularly offensive to the conservative mind was the kind of think-ing that would state, in the words of a leading liberal constitutional scholar, that, "in a very real sense, the true liberty of the individual may be promoted by restrictions that the society imposes upon him in his own interests"![115]

Economic liberty and the ideals once closely associated with freedom of contract have been worked out to a remarkable extent, in recent decades, in terms of a complex fusion of political and psychological concepts of individuality, personal independence, and personhood. The lumping together of these concerns in consti-tutional texts today under the rubric, typically, of "Rights of Indi-vidual Autonomy," reflects a body of case law precedents, elabo-rated by new theories of property rights and economic entitlements first advanced by Professor Charles Reich under the banner of "the New Property," and also strikingly derivative from Warren Court jurisprudence and its agenda.[116]

No less distressed than anti–New Deal liberal conservatives by the specter of a smothering kind of paternalism in modern govern-ance, Reich wrote in the 1960s a series of articles contending that the legal system ought to bestow entitlements on a constitution-ally guaranteed basis instead of making government contracts, oc-cupational licenses, welfare and Social Security benefits, and the like subject to the discretion of administrators. Such entitlements would serve the same function as property in an earlier era of eco-nomic development and in a simpler social order: they would pro-vide the basis for true autonomy, give palpable meaning to the idea of a zone of privacy. In Reich's view, "property affords day-to-day protection in the ordinary affairs of life."[117]

In 1969 the Supreme Court heard a case in which a state's residency requirement for eligibility to receive welfare assistance was challenged. Speaking for the court's majority, Justice Brennan declared that "our constitutional concepts of personal liberty" merged with the dictates of federalism to require that all citizens have freedom to travel. He portrayed the process of a needy person's migration as part of a quest to "resettle, find a new job, and start a new life;" it was not the prospect of a dole but the vision of economic opportunity that was placed at the center of Brennan's picture.[118] A year later, in a decision upholding welfare clients' rights to a hearing before benefits were terminated, Brennan wrote for the court that "Public assistance . . . is not mere charity, but a means to 'promote the general Welfare, and secure the Blessings of Liberty to ourselves and our Posterity.'"[119]

Although the Court has subsequently retreated from this high water mark of concern for guaranteeing entitlements as a basis of economic liberty, a similar association of individualism with a jurisprudence of newly fashioned specific rights can be found in many features of contemporary constitutional decisions in the state courts, to the present day.[120] On the other hand, in the "Contract with America" of the Republican congressional candidates in the 1994 election, and of course in the radical retrenchment and reaction that was embodied in the "welfare reform" bill of 1996, the rhetoric of freedom of contract was voiced loudly in terms of "individual responsibility" and a radical curtailment of any governmental responsibility for minimum levels of living—a reversion to the *Lochner*-era version of economic liberty and its imperatives.

Neo-conservatives have launched a well-articulated and in many ways highly successful counterattack against "paternalism," as they denote it, in contending that governmental interventions generally work against efficiency and often are indistinguishable from outright confiscation. As Donald Pisani indicates in chapter 8, there has been a new so-called "property rights" movement which denies the legitimacy of the entire public rights tradition in American law. This movement operates on essential anti-historical terms, resolutely ignoring the regulatory content of American constitutional traditions and the inherited legal culture. These terms have not, however, detracted overmuch from the force it has exerted in pushing public policy in the direction of principled anti-governmentalism, at least with regard to social welfare and regulatory policy. Ironically, some of the same elements in neo-conservative politics who invoke individualist ideals in the defense of property against taxes and regulation are associated with a new renascent communitarian movement that rejects the ideals of individual autonomy and privacy associated with traditional individualism. They contend instead for the need to impose social conformity through control of school curricula, tearing down of much of the church-state separation in modern constitutional law.[121]

Fittingly enough, neo-conservative proposals for legal reform and policy initiatives have also come to a narrow focus on freedom of contract—again revealing profound differences in the ways in which "freedom," in the contract context, can be defined and pursued. Among the principal targets of neo-conservative reform proposals are industrial product liability, as, for example, in the cigarette death cases; and tort claims associated with private contractual relationships—product warranty, professional malpractice, and the like.

On a broader canvas, critics of the modern system of legal ordering in economic relationships attack the entire style of "legal adversarialism," by which American courts are the arena for intensive litigation associated with contract claims but also associated, in prominent instances, with the efforts of public interest groups to influence regulatory policies and their implementation, for example in environmental regulation.[122] Hence we are witnessing an extraordinary reversal of the political alignments of an earlier day over jurisprudence of contract. Balancing of "economic liberty" values with claims of the community, and weighing the legitimacy of private claims against the egalitarian warrant for "economic opportunity," thus remain, even today, at the heart not only of constitutional dialogue but of contract ideology itself.[123]

The "Liberty of Contract" Regime
in American Law

CHARLES W. MCCURDY

A T THE CLOSE OF THE nineteenth century, two stories about
freedom of contract and the state got recited time and again in
the United States. The first, told primarily by renowned lawyers,
was grounded in American exceptionalism. David Dudley Field's
address at the Columbia Exposition in 1893, "American Progress in
Jurisprudence," may be taken as a representative example. "We began," he said, "with asserting the sovereignty of the people," pro-
claiming "certain rights . . . inherent in every human being," and
establishing a frame of government "purely American, without
precedent in the past and ready for development in the future."
Field understood "development in the future" as a progressive elaboration of the timeless founding principles. Above all, it involved
the eradication of legal forms inherited from the Old World that denied the blessings of liberty to some classes in favor of others. Field
reported that great progress had been made. Primogeniture and the
remedy of distress for unpaid rent had been abolished. The chartering of business corporations by special act of the legislature had
ceased. So had improvident grants of monopoly in the ordinary
avocations of life. "We have emancipated woman from the thrall-
dom of her husband," Field exclaimed; "we have freed the honest
debtor from the possibility of passing his life in prison." But the
abolition of slavery constituted the nation's greatest "act of deliv-
erance." It established for all "the right to labor when, where, and
for such reward as the laborer and his employer may agree to between themselves." Freedom of contract thus fulfilled the founding
ideal. Once it had been achieved, Field contended, any derogation
meant a corruption of America's promise and destiny as the land of
the free.[1]

The second conventional story, told primarily by the profes-
sionalizing social scientists, was grounded on German historicism.
Richard T. Ely's *Studies in the Evolution of Industrial Society*,
published in 1903, may be taken as a representative example. Ely
claimed that society must be understood as a product of continuous historical change from which even America could not escape.
Industrialization, the driving force of the modern age, worked
changes in social relations that made a mockery of the "negative
liberty" celebrated by lawyers like Field. They assumed, Ely wrote,
that "inasmuch as men are essentially equal, each one can best
guard his own interests individually, providing only the hampering
fetters of the law should make way for a reign of liberty." But the
assumption was wrong. The principal threat to liberty in modern
society came from private coercion, not from public law. "The coercion of economic forces," Ely explained, "is largely due to the
unequal strength of those who make a contract, for back of the
contract lies inequality in strength of those who form the contract
... Wealth and poverty, plenty and hunger, nakedness and warm
clothing, ignorance and learning, face each other in contract, and
find expression in and through contract." For Ely, then, the modern
conception of liberty had to be positive rather than negative. "True
liberty," he asserted, "means the expression of the positive powers
of the individual." It could be achieved only by vigorous state action that "modifies and qualifies nominally free contract."[2]

A new concept, "social legislation," lurked beneath the rival
stories about freedom of contract and the state. It also figured in
the constitutional doctrine of "liberty of contract," a major focus of
acrimonious exchanges between the likes of Field and Ely at the
turn of the century. "Social legislation" was a European construct.
"The term came from Germany and there originated about the beginning of the eighties," Ernst Freund explained in *Standards of
American Legislation*. "By the term social legislation we understand those measures which are intended for the relief and elevation of the less favored classes of the community; it would thus be
held to include factory laws, but hardly legislation for the safety of
passengers on railroads." American progressives talked incessantly
about the enactment of "social legislation" to protect the weak and
poor from exploitation, to provide some security for those unable
to obtain it themselves, and to effect a modest redistribution of

wealth and opportunity. "Social legislation" did not become a jurisprudential category, however, until 1940. The Supreme Court
never used the term before then; appellate judges in the several
states used it only three times—in 1914, 1916, and 1923. This
should come as no surprise. In the "liberty of contract" era, consi-
titutional challenges to "social legislation" turned on the scope of
the police power rather than on the type of statute at issue. But the
distinctive languages of courts and progressive reformers did not
conceal the tension between them. Courts always regarded
"legislation for the safety of passengers on railroads," to invoke
Freund's example, as legitimate exercises of government's acknowledged power to curtail freedom of contract in the interests of
health, safety, and public order. Statutes "intended for the relief
and elevation of the less favored classes of the community" stood
on a different footing. Absent a clear public justification for disturbing freedom of contract, such laws were by definition unconstitutional.[3]

The classic expression of the distinction Freund made so effort-
lessly came in *Lochner v. New York*, where the Supreme Court
held in 1905 that a ten-hour law for bakery workers infringed "the
general right" to make contracts secured by the Fourteenth
Amendment. Justice Rufus Peckham, speaking for the five-four
majority, described the Court's standard of review as follows:

The mere assertion that the subject relates though but in a remote degree
to the public health does not necessarily render the enactment valid. The
act must have a more direct relation, as a means to an end, and the end itself must be appropriate and legitimate, before an act can be held to be
valid which interferes with the general right of an individual to be free in
his person and in his power to contract in relation to his own labor.

Ten-hour laws for railway engineers met this standard because the
traveling public had a palpable safety interest in alert engineers.
But "clean and wholesome bread," Peckham remarked, "does not
depend upon whether the baker works but ten hours per day or
only sixty hours a week." Nor did bakery work seem to endanger
the health of bakery workers. It followed that the statute could be
understood only as an attempt to confer benefits on one class of
persons at the expense of others. This, said Peckham, the Constitution forbade. "The question whether this act is valid as a labor law,
pure and simple, may be dismissed in a few words," he declared.

"There is no reasonable ground for . . . [assuming] that bakers as a class are not equal in intelligence and capacity to men in other trades or manual occupations, or that they are not able to assert their rights and care for themselves without the protecting arm of the State, interfering with their independence of judgment and action. They are in no sense wards of the State."[4]

People devoted to Field's story about freedom of contract and the state were quick to hail *Lochner* and its precursors. Fans of Ely's story denounced such decisions. Striking down "social legislation," they said, implicated courts in one unforgivable sin after another. Courts relied on a formal conception of equality that did not fit the facts of modern industrial society. Courts chose to protect a counterfeit "negative liberty" rather than permitting the luxuriation of "positive liberty." And courts achieved these deplorable things by usurping the legislative department's authority to define public purposes. Roscoe Pound, who anchored his "sociological jurisprudence" on the work of Ely and his associates in the new social sciences, elaborated all three arguments in a famous article published in 1909. Not surprisingly, Pound treated the "liberty of contract" question as an irrepressible conflict between opposing versions of history, liberty, and the judicial function. He took it for granted that one version would endure, the other would perish. So did fellow warriors on both sides of the controversy between 1890 and 1910.[5]

This chapter breaks away from the terms of debate that prevailed at the turn of the century. Doing so is not to discount the sense of Field and Ely, Peckham and Pound, that they stood at a great divide in American history. All of them had reason to believe what they believed. But their perspectives obscure both the origins of the "liberty of contract" regime and its most significant effects. Another perspective is developed in the pages that follow. In them, I first consider the origins of the "liberty of contract" doctrine in American constitutional law and try to explain why it emerged in the form it did when it did. I then consider the effects of the doctrine's form on progressive thought; I attempt to explain why "social legislation" meant something different in 1940 than in 1900, why the term "positive liberty" all but disappeared from the American vocabulary, and why "sociological jurisprudence" became a theory of legislation rather than a guide for constitutional adjudication. My principal claim is that the "liberty of contract" doctrine generated a process of accommodation that gradually eviscerated both *fin de siècle* stories about freedom of contract and the state. What materialized by degrees was a new regime, a new synthesis, a New Deal order that fused Field's American exceptionalism with Ely's industrial imperative in ways that neither could have anticipated or approved.

≺ I ≻

Rethinking the Origins of the "Liberty of Contract" Regime

In recent years, legal historians have linked *Lochner*-era police power jurisprudence with a "principle of neutrality" in constitutional adjudication. The "principle of neutrality," the argument goes, was rooted in the Madisonian aspiration of a faction-free politics and the Jacksonian revulsion with special privilege; it inclined courts to insist that legislation conferring special benefits on any one group also provide benefits to the public generally. Statutes that contained "naked preferences" for favored groups or classes, then, were denounced as "class legislation." Studies of the "liberty of contract" regime that explain its rise and fall in terms of the "principle of neutrality" have greatly enhanced our understanding of an important era in American constitutional history.[6]

Yet no amount of thoughtful revisionism can erase the fact that the "principle of neutrality" did not have a uniform operation. As Willard Hurst once observed, the freedom of contract decisions handed down by American courts beginning in the 1880s showed "a definite bias of policy" against statutes favoring "the interest . . . of labor." Hurst pointed out that courts often sustained police regulations that conferred "a legal advantage" on "one set of business interests" relative to its competitors. When confronted with constitutional challenges to such statutes, courts tended to ignore the redistributive effects of government intervention and to compel "the challenger to show beyond a reasonable doubt that the legislature could not reasonably find that the act was an appropriate means to serve some public interest." But courts often proceeded differently in labor cases. "[W]here a statute apparently sought to offset the weak bargaining power of workers," Hurst wrote, "the fact that the statute would confer particular benefit on labor was taken as enough to show a lack of justifying public interest. Such was the Supreme Court's approach in *Lochner v. New York*."[7]

There is no gainsaying Hurst's observation. Consider *Godcharles v. Wigeman* and *Powell v. State*, two decisions handed down four months apart by the Pennsylvania Supreme Court. At issue in *Godcharles*, decided on October 4, 1886, was a statute requiring manufacturing and mining corporations to pay their workers in cash rather than company-store orders. Justice Isaac G. Gordon, speaking for the seven-judge panel, produced a brief opinion that shot from the hip. Without citing any provision of the Pennsylvania constitution, Gordon simply stated that the anti-truck law was "degrading and insulting" to the workers and that the legislature had attempted "to do what cannot be done; that is, [to] prevent persons who are *sui juris* from making their own contracts." The worker "may sell his labor for what he thinks best, whether money or goods," Gordon declared, "just as his employer may sell his iron or coal, and any or every law that proposes to prevent him from so doing is an infringement of his constitutional privileges, and consequently vicious and void." In *Godcharles*, the parent "liberty of contract" decision, the Pennsylvania court did not even consider why the state legislature might have deemed it necessary and legitimate to enact such a statute.[8]

Powell, decided on January 3, 1887, involved a statute prohibiting the manufacture and sale of oleomargarine. Although the Pennsylvania legislature called the statute a public health measure, it was an open secret that the law had been designed to protect the dairy industry against a new competitor. Justice James P. Sterrett spoke for the six-one majority that sustained the act; he produced a long opinion studded with quotations concerning the judicial department's duty to presume the constitutionality of police regulations. "We cannot say the Act in question is not a valid exercise of the police power of the State," Sterrett declared. The petitioner's offer of proof as to the wholesomeness of oleomargarine was immaterial. So was his claim that the public's interest in wholesome food might be protected with a less restrictive statute. "The legislature was doubtless satisfied that the manufacture and sale of the prohibited articles were prejudicial to the public good to such degree that a remedy was needed," Sterrett explained; "we have no right to say that a penal statute, less severe and sweeping in its terms would have afforded an effective remedy. That is a legislative and not a judicial question."[9]

The *Godcharles* and *Powell* opinions suggest two generalizations about the "liberty of contract" regime in American law. First, judges tended to assume that contracts of employment were somehow special; the very "specialness" of the labor contract inclined judges to suspend the presumption of constitutionality when legislatures intervened. Second, the disproportionate bargaining power of employers did not provide a legitimate ground for government intervention. This is, of course, simply another way of saying that "a definite bias of policy" against labor legislation permeated American constitutional law at the close of the nineteenth century and the beginning of the twentieth. Yet to underscore this characteristic of *Lochner*-era jurisprudence is not to explain it. What follows is an attempt to derive an explanation from the habits of thought, legislative practice, and common law adjudication that prevailed before courts began to enforce freedom of contract as a constitutional right in 1886.

≺ II ≻

The "Specialness" of the Labor Contract

The specialness of the labor contract in American law was the product of a "free labor" ideology that virtually all northerners— Republicans and Democrats, workers and employers—regarded as an expression of the North's distinctive social order from the 1840s through the 1870s. Underlying the "free labor" ideology was a negative image of the slave South, where most working people labored at the will and for the profit of others. Things were different in the North. "Free labor" ideologists held that things were different, first, in the formal sense that all northerners owned their own toil. Slavery had been abolished by a variety of mechanisms, indentured servitude had disappeared, courts of equity had ceased to mandate the specific performance of labor contracts, and "masters" had lost the right to beat refractory "servants." Adult males had freedom of contract.

A second, equally important component of the "free labor" ideology was grounded on the concept of economic independence. As Eric Foner has shown, northerners not only distinguished the North's "free labor" system from the South's slave labor system but also contrasted the dignity and vitality of the free white worker in the North with the laboring man's poverty, degradation, and lack of opportunity for advancement in the South. For northerners, free labor "meant labor with economic choices, with the opportunity to quit the wage-earning class." In the 1850s, the dynamic, expanding economy of the North, itself a product of the free labor system, was said to generate opportunities for the wage-earner's advancement of a sort that did not obtain in the South. "Advancement, improvement in condition—is the order of things in a society of equals," Abraham Lincoln remarked in 1859; he stridently assailed the proslavery theorists who argued that northern wage-earners were "fatally fixed in that condition for life." In 1862 Lincoln described the Civil War as "a people's contest . . . for maintaining in the world that form *and substance* of government whose leading object is to elevate the condition of man; to lift artificial weights from all shoulders; to clear the paths of laudable pursuit for all; to afford all men an unfettered start and a fair chance in the race of life."[10]

Free-labor ideas had a configurative effect on Reconstruction. As northerners imposed their conception of the good society on the South, they learned that their "free labor" ideology set outer limits on the range of policy options at their command. Congress enacted the Civil Rights Act of 1866 in response to the notorious black codes, and the first protected right Republican lawmakers enumerated was freedom of contract. Congress also kept the Freedmen's Bureau going until 1868; the chief function of that War Department agency was to provide a forum for the enforcement of labor contracts. Yet government agents neither prescribed standards for employment agreements nor chancered them when complaints about exploitative terms materialized, and land redistribution proposals evoked protests derived from free labor concepts that most northerners deemed persuasive. As a result, the abolition of slavery generated fundamental change in the legal relations between southern whites and southern blacks, but fostered very little change in class relations. By 1880 a maturing body of law defined sharecroppers as wage-earners paid in kind. White landowners who

"employed" black croppers could thus exercise complete managerial control—determining what would be grown and how, determining the hours and pace of work, determining when and at what
price to sell the croppers' shares. "If the legal changes supported a
clearly repressive society that fell far short of what the freedmen
and their northern supporters had envisioned following emancipation," writes Harold Woodman, "they did nevertheless support a
free labor system in the postwar South, a system that in its essential features replicated that of the North."[11]

The "free labor" ideology also shaped labor legislation in the
post–Civil War North. Beginning in 1865, a great many northerners
started to wonder whether there was not at least a grain of truth in
the antebellum southerners' claim that northern wage-earners were
just as dependent on their employers as slaves were on their masters. Moralists and labor reformers anxiously pointed out the dis-
sonance between the rhetoric of the free labor system and the
changing structure of the industrial economy. "One capitalist em-
ployes five men now where he employed one twenty years ago,"
remarked a writer in the *New-York Times* soon after the Confeder-
ate armed forces surrendered. This loss of independence, he said,
foreshadowed "a system of slavery as absolute if not as degrading
as that which lately prevailed at the South. The only difference is
that there agriculture was the field, landed proprietors were the
masters and negroes were the slaves, while in the North manufactures is the field, manufacturing capitalists threaten to become the
masters, and it is the white laborers who are to be slaves." If the
five-man workshop threatened the "free labor" ideal, the armies of
employees the factories already had begun to assemble provided
occasion for real alarm. "The next great step for American statesmanship," a Fanueil Hall mass meeting resolved on November 2,
1865, "is the adoption of measures" designed to maintain the
promise of independence for the northern wage-earner.[12]

Ira Steward, the Boston machinist who framed the resolution,
offered a political solution for the problem of wage slavery. "The
legislation necessary to secure," he said, was a "law making eight
hours a legal day's labor." The eight-hour day, Steward argued,
would allow the wage-earner more time for self-improvement, the
chief prerequisite for achieving economic independence. Nor was it
necessary, he explained, for the reduction in hours to be coupled

with a reduction in wages. The commonsense view of "less work, less pay" assumed that shorter hours would reduce the national product while the proportions of its division would remain constant, so that workers would end up with less. In Steward's view, however, this was nonsense rather than common sense. He claimed that the reduction in hours would expose wage-earners to new and more complex social relations which, in turn, would generate new tastes and increase demand for manufactured commodities. Enhanced demand would stimulate production, promote the use of machinery, and lower unit costs. Rising productivity could be expected to increase profits while hourly wages increased because of the eight-hour day.[13]

The ensuing attacks on Steward's economic theory need not concern us. The eight-hour idea caught on despite them. Eight-hour leagues sprang up all over the industrial North during the mid-1860s; the National Labor Union, a federation of state labor organizations established in 1867, made eight-hour legislation the centerpiece of its program for political action. What does concern us is how labor reformers and their allies in the several state legislatures proposed to institute the eight-hour system, thus salvaging the "free labor" ideology, without undermining the principle of free contract in the employment relation.

It was one thing to suggest that statutes ought to be enacted making eight hours a legal day's work; it was something quite different to prohibit industrious, ambitious wage-earners from working more than eight hours if they chose to do so. The relationship between wages and hours also posed problems. All the terms of the employment contract could not be prescribed by law, the *New York Evening Post* observed, for "to decree that a man should be compelled to pay any fixed amount for the eight specified hours of work would be the worst species of demagogic tyranny, making the masters and the employed in turn the veriest slaves." Thus the metaphor of slavery, which had earlier generated a broadly shared ideology celebrating the "free labor" system, cut two ways during the 1860s. As prospects for advancement appeared to diminish, wage-earners seemed to labor permanently and at the will and for the profit of others, making them mere wage slaves. Yet proposed legal interventions that threatened to restrict each worker's right to determine how long to work and on what terms evoked the *Eve-*

ning Post rejoinder: that, too, would make wage-earners "the veriest slaves."[14]

How the several state legislatures met this dilemma reflects the extraordinary durability of the "free labor" ideology. In 1867 six jurisdictions enacted statutes prescribing eight hours as a legal day's work; California and Pennsylvania enacted comparable statutes the following year. Yet none of them said anything about wages; all of them authorized wage-earners to contract out of the eight-hour system if they chose to do so. The Wisconsin law was typical. It provided that in "all engagements to labor in any mechanical or manufacturing business, when the contract is silent on the subject, or where there is not express contract to the contrary, a day's work shall consist of eight hours." It goes without saying that such laws were ineffective. But it is wrong to claim, as John R. Commons did early in this century, that the labor reformers were "easily befuddled by skillful politicians." Even Ira Steward called only for "a law making eight hours a legal day's labor in the absence of a written agreement" to the contrary. The labor reformers were befuddled not by the politicians but by the very "free labor" ideal they sought to salvage. As David Montgomery has shown, northern wage-earners "shared their employers' commitment to the ideology of the free-labor system, which the maturing industrial order already had rendered anachronistic. Also like their employers, workmen sought remedies for their problem from the machinery of state." Their employers succeeded because their call for tariff protection only necessitated rejection of laissez-faire ideas. Even the workers, however, were unprepared "to defile the *sanctum sanctorum* of free contract" in the employment relation. Given their ideological imprisonment, all labor reformers could request from the state was a declaration of community goals and sentiments. As New York labor leader Ezra Heywood remarked in 1867, the eight-hour law was valuable not "as an arbitrary standard, but as an enabling act to assist labor to make fair terms." As matters developed, the statutes proved useless even in that restricted capacity.[15]

One additional aspect of this episode in American labor history merits attention. Because nobody called for a compulsory eight-hour law, there was no call for a discussion of constitutional limitations on government's power to regulate the labor contract. Nevertheless, some commentators considered the question. Thurlow

Weed, editor of the *Albany Evening Journal,* sympathized with the
aims of labor reformers yet regarded the eight-hour measure enacted in New York as so much "buncumbe and bagatelle." "It ac-
complishes nothing for the labor interest," he said, "because it
makes no change in relations which already exist." But "on the
other hand," Weed added, "any attempt to prescribe by arbitrary
legislation the length of time for which one party shall pay and the
other contract to serve, would be liable to fatal constitutional objections." Three thousand miles away in California, James McClatchy, editor of the *Sacramento Bee* and a close friend of Henry
George, said much the same thing in a slightly different context.
The California statute not only proclaimed eight hours to be a legal
day's work "in all cases within this State, unless otherwise stipulated by the parties" but also dealt with the question of public
works. Section two of the act provided that "eight hours of labor
shall constitute a legal day's work . . . and a stipulation to that effect shall be made a part of all contracts to which the State or municipal governments . . . shall be a party." On public works, then,
employers could not require laborers to work more than eight
hours as a condition of employment; but, as the California Supreme Court later explained, wage-earners remained free to work
more than eight hours for extra pay if they chose to do so. When
the bill was first introduced in the state legislature, however, section two made it a crime for contractors on state work to permit
overtime labor. "Of course," McClatchy wrote in a lead editorial,
"the Judiciary Committee to whom it was referred, changed all
that, for men have a right to agree to labor as many hours as they
please. This is a Constitutional right granted by the Bill of Rights,
and any law to the contrary would not stand the test of Judicial investigation."[16]

Neither Weed nor McClatchy explained why compulsory eight-
hour laws would be unconstitutional. Weed simply stated that
such a statute "would be liable to fatal constitutional objections."
McClatchy asserted that freedom of contract had been "granted by
the Bill of Rights." It is possible that both were thinking in terms
of due process. It is more likely, however, that the "free labor" ideology was so pervasive that the precise constitutional basis for
freedom of contract never came consciously to mind. The Weed
and McClatchy editorials, in other words, foreshadowed the shoot-

from-the-hip style of the Pennsylvania judges who decided *God-charles v. Wigeman* two decades later. The assumptions that shaped the eight-hour movement of the 1860s also help to explain why courts constitutionalized the "liberty of contract" doctrine when they did. Beginning in the early 1880s, state legislatures enacted a new form of labor legislation. Maximum-hours laws, anti-truck laws, coal-weighing laws, and laws prohibiting wage deductions for imperfect work all provided criminal sanctions for violators, suggesting that the regulated parties could not "contract out" of the statutory scheme. Implicit in the new statutes was an unarticulated premise: legislatures might establish the terms and conditions of contracts if the parties had unequal bargaining power. Labor reformers and enough lawmakers to secure the enactment of such measures embraced this presumption. With few exceptions, courts did not.[17] For the roots of this second signal characteristic of *Lochner*-era constitutional law—judicial unwillingness to acknowledge disproportionate bargaining power as a justification for legislative regulation of employment contracts—it is instructive to examine another episode in the development of American labor law before 1886.

≺ III ≻

Workers, Employers, and the Scope of Public Interest

The fellow servant rule is perhaps the best known common law doctrine of the nineteenth century, and its implied contract premise is too familiar to require elaboration here. What is not always appreciated, however, is the fact that employers could have attained the same result with express contracts immunizing them from liability for injuries sustained by workers in the course of employment. Before the fellow servant rule was established in Pennsylvania jurisprudence, for example, the Pennsylvania Railroad Company required all of its employees to sign a standard agreement providing that "the regular compensation will cover all risk or liability, from any cause whatever, in the service of the company." In 1853 a Pennsylvania common pleas judge held that such a waiver was unquestionably valid. The fellow servant rule and the doctrine of contributory negligence eventually made the

formality of having workers expressly contract out of their right to
recover for job-related injuries rather superfluous; presumably the
Pennsylvania Railroad ceased to bother with the paperwork long
before 1860.[18] In some jurisdictions, however, the worker's capacity
to bargain away his right to sue his employer reemerged after the
Civil War and generated some fascinating case law. It also evoked a
very suggestive dialogue between judges who later embraced "liberty of contract" as a constitutional right and a thoughtful commentator who detested that epoch-making innovation.

The employers' liability laws enacted by Georgia in 1855, Iowa
in 1862, Wyoming Territory in 1869, and Kansas in 1874 gave employers new incentives to require their workers to waive their
rights at law as a condition of employment. The statutes applied
only to railroads and left the contributory negligence defense intact; but they abrogated the fellow servant rule and consequently
threatened to enlarge the companies' liability. The railroads apparently resorted to special contracts with workers limiting their liability as a matter of course.

The Georgia court was the first appellate tribunal to consider
the legality of such agreements. In *Western & Atlantic R.R. Co. v.
Bishop*, a wrongful death case decided in 1873, it assumed that the
employee's capacity to contract out of his rights under the statute
was unquestionable. The opinion bristled with "free labor" ideology. "It would be a dangerous interference with private rights to
undertake to fix by law the terms upon which the employer and
employee shall contract," the court's spokesman declared.

> For myself, I do not hesitate to say that I know of no right more precious,
> and one which laboring men ought to guard with more vigilance, than the
> right to fix by contract the terms upon which their labor shall be engaged.
> It looks very specious to say that the law will protect them from the con-
> sequences of their own folly, and make a contract for them wiser and bet-
> ter than their own. But they should remember that the same law-giver
> which claims to make a contract for them on one point, may claim to do
> so upon others, and thus, step by step, they cease to be free men.

Equally significant was the Georgia court's attempt to distinguish
the Supreme Court's landmark decision in *New York Central R.R.
v. Lockwood*, decided earlier in the same year.[19]

At issue in *Lockwood* was the enforceability of a contract in
which a shipper had waived his right to recover for any loss of live-

stock caused by the carrier's negligence. As Morton Horwitz has shown, the legality of such agreements troubled judges and commentators beginning in the 1830s. In some jurisdictions, including New York, "the dominant contractarian ideology" that generated the fellow servant rule also "seduced" appellate courts into sustaining contracts that limited liability for the carrier's own negligence. Since *Lockwood* was a diversity case with a commercial law context, the doctrine of *Swift v. Tyson* came into play. Counsel for the New York Central Railroad not only had to defend the New York decisions on point but also had to show that their underlying logic was so persuasive that the Supreme Court ought to adopt the New York rule as a matter of "general jurisprudence." And in the mind of counsel, the fellow servant rule provided a compelling analogy for the commercial contract practices of the New York Central Railroad. "The only objection [to the contract]," counsel contended, "is that it would violate public policy; but this objection would equally forbid the rule, now long established, that a servant . . . impliedly engages to bear the risk of injuries from fellow servants."[20]

Justice Joseph Bradley, speaking for the Court, was so unimpressed with the fellow servant analogy that he did not even allude to it. In the Court's view, moreover, the New York decisions involving a carrier's capacity to contract out of liability for negligence were just wrong. Bradley explained that such contracts were against public policy for two reasons. First, the common carrier's business was essentially a public one; the public, generally, had an interest in ensuring that railroad corporations paid attention to matters of safety and care in the operation of their enterprises. If carriers were permitted to contract out of liability for negligence, they would have no incentive to exercise the care on which the public depended. Second, the railroad corporation had far greater bargaining power than the shipper. "The carrier and his customer do not stand on a footing of equality," Bradley declared.

The latter is only one individual of a million. He cannot afford to higgle or stand out and seek redress in the courts. His business will not admit such a course. He prefers, rather, to accept any bill of lading, or sign any paper the carrier presents; often, indeed, without knowing what the one or the other contains. In most cases, he has no alternative but to do this, or abandon his business.

It followed, Bradley added, that "contracts of common carriers, like those of persons occupying a fiduciary character, giving them a position in which they can take undue advantage of the persons with whom they contract, must rest upon their fairness and reasonableness." The Court unanimously concluded that waivers of liability for negligence in situations involving carriers and shippers were neither fair nor reasonable.[21]

Just as counsel for the carrier in *Lockwood* assumed that the fellow servant rule was a compelling analogy in the shipper-carrier context, counsel for the deceased railroad worker in *Bishop* assumed that *Lockwood* was a compelling analogy in the employment context. But the Georgia court set a face of flint against any penetration of *Lockwood* into the law of employment. "None of [the Supreme Court's] reasoning applies to the case before us," the Georgia court explained. "This suit is not against the railroad company as a carrier" but against the railroad company as an employer. The deceased worker's "relation to the company was strictly a private one. His contract of service was a free one. He did not stand in the situation of a traveler, or a shipper of goods, 'who cannot stop to higgle'" because, in its capacity as an employer, "the railroad company has no monopoly of service. It is only one of a million of employers with whom the husband of the plaintiff might have sought employment. He deliberately, and for a consideration, undertook that he would not hold the company liable for the negligence of its servants, or even for the negligence of the company itself."[22]

With disarming candor, the Georgia court thus enunciated two closely related propositions that later infused the "liberty of contract" doctrine in American constitutional law. The labor contract was distinguishable from other types of agreements in which the public might have an interest. And the concept of unequal bargaining power, though it might be pertinent in some bargaining contexts, could not affect the law of employment because workers had "million[s]" of choices when they entered the labor market.

The Georgia court did not have the last word on this subject. By the mid-1880s scores of carriers had begun to require their employees to contract out of their rights at law in order to evade judgments not only under employers liability laws but also under new judge-made doctrines such as the safe-tool and vice-principal rules.

Bench and bar responded to these developments in two ways, fore-shadowing, in effect, the subsequent controversy over "Lochner-ism." In 1886 Seymour Thompson published a treatise on *The Law of Negligence* in which he strenuously argued that the contract of employment was no different than contracts between shippers and carriers. Like counsel for the deceased worker in the Georgia case, Thompson contended that the conceptualization in *Lockwood* ought to govern relations between the parties in both contexts. The Georgia judges who handed down *Bishop*, he complained, were wrong on two counts: "They ignore[d] the unequal situation of the laborer and his employer. They depart[ed] from the analogy of the rule of law which denies to carriers the right to enter into contracts with those whom they serve, stipulating against liability for their own negligence; and in so doing, they place[d] the life of a man upon a lower footing than the proprietary interest which a man may have in his chattel." Six years later, Thompson criticized the doctrine "liberty of contract" on the same grounds. For courts "to talk about freedom of contract" in cases like *Godcharles v. Wigeman* "is the veriest sham," he wrote. "It is not even truthful or sincere. No such freedom of contract exists. Every judge knows it; every other man knows it; and it is the duty of judges in framing their decisions to take judicial notice of what everybody knows."[23]

Thompson's critique of *Bishop* failed to catch on for the same reason that his critique of the "liberty of contract" doctrine failed to catch on. Judges were simply not prepared to use the concept of unequal bargaining power as a major premise in cases involving the employment relation. But in two cases decided in 1886, the courts of Ohio and Arkansas did reject the Georgia court's holding in *Bishop*. In each instance *Lockwood* figured prominently in oral argument and in each instance the court appropriated one but only one of Justice Bradley's justifications for declaring contracts that limited liability for negligence against public policy. The neglected justification, of course, was inequality in the bargaining relation.

In *Lake Shore & Michigan Southern Ry. v. Spangler* the Ohio court considered the case of a brakeman who had been seriously injured due to the negligence of the train's conductor. Since the Ohio court had previously adopted the vice-principal doctrine, the railroad company's liability ordinarily would have been unquestionable. But in the contract of employment the plaintiff had stipulated that "while the company will be responsible to me . . . for any neglect of its own, yet it will not be responsible to me for the consequences of my own fault or neglect, or that of any other employees of the company, whether they . . . are superior to me in authority, as conductor [or] foreman, or not." The contract, said a unanimous court, was against public policy; consequently plaintiff's right to recover under the vice-principal doctrine remained unimpaired. "Such liability is not created for the protection of the employees simply," the court explained, "but has its reason and foundation in a public necessity . . . which should not be asked to yield or surrender to mere private interests and agreements." For the Ohio court, the public interest in this particular type of labor contract was so "obvious" that no further elaboration of its potentially baneful effect on public safety seemed necessary.

The Arkansas court took a slightly different tack in *Little Rock & Fort Smith Ry. v. Eubanks*. "It is for the welfare of society," generally, it observed, that railroad companies "shall not be permitted under the guise of enforcing contract rights, to abdicate their duties" to prevent harm to the persons and property put into their care. If courts enforced such contracts, the "natural tendency would be to relax the employer's carefulness in those matters of which he has ordering and control . . . and thus increase the perils of occupations which are hazardous even when well managed. And the final outcome would be to fill the country with disabled men and paupers, whose support would become a charge upon the counties or upon public charity."[24]

The *Eubanks* and *Spangler* courts instinctively resisted the very idea of essentially unfree labor contracts in 1886. The Pennsylvania judges who decided *Godcharles* that same year did as well. Whether adjudicating a private law dispute or a challenge to a statute, judges took it for granted that alleged disparities of bargaining power could not provide a ground of decision. The "free labor" ideology made the contract of employment a special one; absent a palpable public health or safety interest in a labor agreement, freedom of contract prevailed. This is not to say that allusions to disproportionate bargaining power never penetrated judicial opinions between 1840 and 1910. Justice Henry Brown, speaking for the Supreme Court in *Holden v. Hardy*, said a few words about inequality in an 1898 opinion that sustained a ten-hour law for mine workers.

But the bulk of Brown's opinion emphasized the state legislature's competence to protect the mutual interest of workers in well-rested, alert associates during shifts of dangerous underground labor. Seven years later, Brown joined the majority in *Lochner v. New York*.[25]

Justices John Marshall Harlan, Edward D. White, and Rufus Day dissented in *Lochner* yet shared the majority's assumption that unequal bargaining strength, without more, could not justify government interference with freedom of contract. Their disagreement turned on the presumption of constitutionality maxim. In Harlan's view, with which White and Day concurred, the Court had no authority to reassess the state's claim that laboring more than ten hours daily endangered the health of bakery workers. If the proffered justification for a statute was within the scope of the police power, Harlan remarked, "we cannot say that the State has acted without reason nor ought we to proceed upon the theory that its action is a mere sham." When *Adair v. United States* came up in 1908, however, Harlan and Day and White joined their colleagues in the *Lochner* majority to strike down an act of Congress prohibiting contracts that made promises not to join a union a condition of employment. Harlan spoke for the Court; he insisted that no legitimate public purpose could be effected by the bar on "yellow-dog" contracts. Arguments concerning the inequality of individual workers in their dealings with railroad corporations did not move him. "The employer and the employee have equality of right," Harlan declared, "and any legislation that disturbs that equality is an arbitrary interference with the liberty of contract, which no government can legally justify in a free land."[26]

≺ IV ≻

Rethinking the Effects of "Liberty of Contract"

In 1908 all but one justice on the Supreme Court worked from the same "free labor" premise that shaped the response of state legislatures to the eight-hour campaign of the 1860s and the judicial response to special contracts limiting the liability of railroads for job-related deaths or injuries in the 1880s. The one justice who dissented in both *Lochner* and *Adair* was Oliver Wendell Holmes, Jr.

Holmes's dissents are legendary. On both occasions, he ignored traditional police power categories and refused to acknowledge "liberty of contract" as a constitutional right. Courts ought to refrain from declaring legislation unconstitutional, he said, "unless it can be said that a rational and fair man necessarily would admit that the statute proposed would infringe fundamental principles as they have been understood by the traditions of our people and our law." Holmes took the "rational and fair man" standard from his friend James Bradley Thayer, who had argued in 1893 that the duty of the appellate judge in reviewing an act of a legislature was essentially the same as the duty of the trial judge in reviewing the verdict of a civil jury. But Holmes's inclination to defer to the judgment of legislative majorities antedated Thayer's famous *Harvard Law Review* article. "The first requirement of a sound body of law," he wrote in 1880, "is, that it should correspond with the actual feelings and demands of the community, whether right or wrong." In *Lochner* and *Adair*, the Court had violated that maxim. "Men whom I certainly could not pronounce unreasonable," Holmes remarked in *Lochner*, "would uphold" the maximum hours law for bakeshop workers "as a first instalment of a general regulation of the hours of work. Whether in this latter aspect it would be open to the charge of inequality I think it unnecessary to discuss." He was equally forthright in defending the prohibition of "yellow-dog" contracts in *Adair*. "The question what and how much good labor unions do is one on which intelligent people may differ," he said. "I could not pronounce it unwarranted if Congress should decide that to foster a strong union was for the best interest, not only of the men, but of the railroads and the community at large."[27]

Progressives lionized Holmes. Richard T. Ely dedicated his *Studies in the Evolution of Industrial Society* to him "in appreciation of the enlightened philosophy so conspicuous in his opinions, which is laying a firm foundation for a superstructure of industrial liberty." But people committed to the defense of a constantly increasing stream of "social legislation" could not tailor litigation strategies to Holmes's sensibilities. He had only one vote. Instead, they had to work within his associates' insistence on a boundary between the police power and impermissible restraints on freedom of contract. The trick, of course, was to downplay inequality justifications for police regulations and to conjure up other public interests in the contractual relationships government attempted to regulate. Each victory in the Supreme Court would take some bite out of "the liberty of contract" doctrine. It would also supply a serviceable justification or analogy for the next effort. A succession of victories would result in the extraction of all the doctrine's teeth, leaving only a set of empty jaws.

Two lines of cases decided between 1909 and 1917 reinforced the progressive impulse to pursue such a strategy. The issues in both had figured prominently in the emergence of "liberty of contract" as a constitutional right. One involved statutes regulating company-store scrip and coal-weighing procedures. The other involved statutes prohibiting employers from "contracting out" of duties to employees which the state imposed but workers chose to waive. Both forms of "social legislation" not only passed judicial muster but also enabled progressives to envisage a gradual disintegration of the "liberty of contract" regime in American law. As they learned to work with their opponents' tools, progressive lawyers and scholars also reconstructed the conceptions of history, liberty, and the judicial function which Ely, Pound, and others had expounded at the turn of the century. They collapsed the distinction between twentieth-century "social legislation" and the emancipatory nineteenth-century statutes which David Dudley Field celebrated in 1893. They blurred the distinction between "positive liberty" and "negative liberty." And they qualified their opposition to vigorous judicial protection of individual rights. The process of accommodation, begun in the crucible of Supreme Court litigation, reshaped the liberal tradition in America.

≺ V ≻

The Supreme Court and the Process of Accommodation

Early in the twentieth century, the Supreme Court put its imprimatur on a variety of wage-payment statutes comparable to those which state courts had frequently overturned in the 1880s and 1890s. The Court upheld anti-truck laws requiring that company-store scrip and other evidences of indebtedness issued by employers in payment of wages be redeemable in cash on demand. It also upheld statutes directing that, where miners' wages were calcu-

lated by the amount of coal mined, the weighing had to take place
before company officials screened the coal. *McClean v. Arkansas*,
decided in 1909, was the leading case. Justice Day, speaking for the
seven-two majority, conceded that coal-weighing statutes and anti-
truck acts interfered with freedom of contract. But both could be
conceived as police regulations of a common sort. "Laws tending to
prevent fraud and to require honest weights and measures in the
transaction of business have frequently been sustained in the
courts," he explained, "although in compelling certain modes of
dealing they interfere with freedom of contract." Analogous police
regulations included statutes "requiring the sale of coal in quantities of 500 pounds or more . . . [and] that milk shall be sold in wine
measure." It followed that the Court could not hold that such laws
"had no reasonable relation to the protection of a large class of laborers in the receipt of their just dues."[28]

The Court's reliance in *McClean* and kindred cases on an "evidence of fraud" rationale, which the legislature was said to have
ascertained and the Court was "unable to say" had no merit, reso-
nated with contemporaneous conceptions of unconscionability in
the private law of contract. The unconscionability defense had all
but disappeared from American jurisprudence in 1824, when New
York's highest court renounced the "arbitrary power [of] interfering
with the contracts of individuals and sporting with their vested
rights." Courts continued to treat inadequacy of consideration as
possible evidence of fraud; but exploitative contract terms, unsupported by additional evidence of unfair dealing, did not trigger judicial relief. "The common law makes no pretence of being a social
reformer, and does not profess to reduce all persons to an absolutely equal position by eliminating natural advantages," Francis
Bohlen wrote in 1906, "but rather, recognizing society as it is, considers social inequalities as the natural inevitable tactical advantages of those lucky enough to possess them." As James Gordley
has shown, however, nineteenth-century courts often refused to
enforce hard bargains even though the evidence of fraud did not
amount to fraud in a conventional legal sense. This move permitted courts to maintain what amounted to an unconscionability defense without impairing the will theory of contracts. The Supreme
Court did much the same thing in cases like *McClean*. Its fraud
prevention rationale allowed the anti-truck and coal-weighing

statutes to stand without making inequality of bargaining strength a legitimate justification for legislative interposition between employer and employee.[29]

Viewed from this perspective, the Court's most revealing opinion in a wage-payment case was *Keokee Consolidated Coke Co. v. Taylor*, decided in 1915. There a unanimous Court rejected a "liberty of contract" challenge to a Virginia statute that forbade any person or corporation engaged in mining or manufacturing to pay wages in scrip redeemable only in company stores. Chief Justice White assigned the case to Holmes; as usual, his draft opinion went right to the heart of the matter. "It is now recognized by legislatures and courts as well as by everyone outside of them, that as a fact freedom may disappear on the one side or the other through the power of aggregated money or men," Holmes wrote.

[A]nd to suppose that every other force may exercise its compulsion at will but that government has no authority to counteract the pressure with its own is absurd. It is said that the power of duress has changed sides and now is with the United Mine Workers. But if it be admitted, as it certainly is established, that the legislature may interefere with theoretic [equality] in the interest of positive freedom, it would require a very clear case before a court could declare its judgment wrong and its enactment void.

None of this language survived to find its way into the opinion Holmes finally wrote for the Court. "This is highly suggestive," Justice Willis Van Devanter wrote in the margin next to this paragraph, "and calculated to breed all sorts of legislation on short notice." Justices Charles Evans Hughes, Horace Lurton, and Joseph McKenna also objected to it. Holmes eventually produced a very brief opinion that said nothing about the "fact" of private duress or "the interest of positive freedom." The opinion of the Court evoked no reaction at all, for Holmes's colleagues did not permit him to extend the police power justification for wage-payment acts beyond the ground Day had staked out in *McClean*.[30]

The Court's response to legislation barring "contracting out" was at once equally guarded and more susceptible to further development. Richard T. Ely, writing in 1903, called restrictions on the right of employers to subvert public policy in special contracts with workers an "absolute necessity." The adoption of social insurance schemes, generally, and workers' compensation laws, in particular, would come to nothing in an uncompromising "liberty

of contract" regime. "Let us suppose," Ely remarked, "it is determined to be public policy, as it has been determined in Germany
and in England, that accidents to employees . . . shall be regarded
as a part of the expenses of manufacturing plants and agencies of
transportation, to be paid for as any other costs of doing business,
out of the proceeds of the business. Unless it is rendered impossible for an employee to contract-out of the obligation, this wise provision in the interests of a large industrial liberty will be nullified
by private contracts." Ely and fellow advocates of "social legislation" had cause for concern. In the mid-1880s, corporation lawyers
devised a new and very effective contractual form for minimizing
the costs which employers liability laws imposed on business
firms.[31]

The new form of "contracting out" hinged on the creation of a
company welfare plan, called a "relief association," funded in part
by deductions from wages and in part by private insurance. Workers were then required to sign contracts in which they agreed to
make the acceptance of benefits from the "relief association," not
the contract itself, a bar to any action at law against their employer. Railroad corporations pioneered this form of "contracting
out" in the face of decisions like *Spangler*, which held that public
policy forbade the enforcement of any contract tending to impair
the public interest in the prevention of accidents. Beginning in
1888, a flurry of federal and state decisions sustained the legality of
"relief association" contracts. In each instance, courts distinguished contracts by an employer against his own negligence from
those at issue. "It is not the signing of the contract," the Pennsylvania court explained in 1894, "but the acceptance of benefits after
the accident that constitutes the release. The injured party, therefore, is not stipulating for the future, but settling for the past; he is
not agreeing to exempt the company for liability for negligence, but
accepting compensation for an injury already caused thereby."
Since "relief association" contracts did not implicate public interests in health or safety, courts saw no reason to interfere with the
freedom of contract enjoyed by workers and employers.[32]

Union officials and social scientists did see a reason for government interference, and state legislatures began to prohibit the
new form of "contracting out" in the 1890s. Congress adopted such
a prohibition in the Federal Employers Liability Act (FELA), passed

in 1908. Section five of the statute provided that "any contract, rule, regulation, or device whatsoever, the purpose or intent of which shall be to enable any common carrier to exempt itself from any liability created by this Act, shall to that extent be void." The framers made it clear that "relief association" contracts were included in the bar. A "proviso" to section five authorized carriers to "set off . . . any sum it has contributed or paid to any insurance, relief benefit, or indemnity" fund from which the injured party had drawn before filing suit under the statute. All of the worker's compensation acts adopted in the several states beginning in 1910 contained comparable provisions. Defending the policy of such measures was easy. In congressional hearings on the FELA, one witness after another described the company rules that required injured workers to report accidents before consulting attorneys and the haste with which company officials thrust "relief association" funds upon eligible families.[33]

Defending the constitutionality of such measures, however, was more difficult. Employers liability laws set standards for compensation, not for prevention. So too did those covering worker's compensation. Consequently the public interest in "relief association" contracts could not be described in the conventional police power terms of health and safety. Brandishing *Lochner* and *Adair*, corporation lawyers confidently claimed that the new prohibitions on "contracting out" would be declared unconstitutional. They were mistaken.

The Court's initial consideration of the new "contracting out" form came in *Chicago, Burlington & Quincy Railroad v. McGuire*, decided in 1911. The petitioner in the court below, having been injured in the course of employment, had accepted a check from the "relief association," and the railroad claimed that his prior contract of release barred him from obtaining a judgment under Iowa's employer liability law. An amendment to the Iowa statute that purported to nullify such waivers, counsel for the railroad argued, impaired the liberty of contract guaranteed by the Fourteenth Amendment. Justice Hughes's opinion for the unanimous Court was as circumspect as Day's in *McClean*. "The power to prohibit contracts, in any case where it exists," he said, "necessarily implies legislative control over the transaction, despite the action of the parties . . . If the legislature may prohibit the acceptance of the

promise as a substitution for the statutory liability, it should also
be able to prevent the like substitution of its performance." The
question begged in this analysis was, of course, the source of the
public interest in the performance of agreements between employers and employees after an accident had occurred. Hughes conceded that the Iowa legislature apparently had been animated by
the idea that the payment of "relief association" benefits, if permitted to result in a discharge of the carrier's liability, "would operate to transfer from the corporation to its employees a burden
which . . . the corporation should be compelled to bear." But the
intentions of the Iowa legislature, in the exercise of an acknowledged power, could not affect the Court's judgment. "The scope of
judicial inquiry in deciding the question of *power*," Hughes declared, "is not to be confused with the scope of legislative considerations in dealing with a matter of *policy*."[34]

The *McGuire* decision had a limited scope, but it saved the prohibitions on "contracting out" in the FELA and the worker's compensation laws. In the *Second Employers Liability Cases*, decided
the following year, the Court rejected the "liberty of contract" challenge to section five of the FELA with a single sentence. "If Congress possesses the power to impose . . . liability," Justice Van Devanter wrote for a unanimous Court, "it also possesses the power to
insure its efficacy by prohibiting any contract, rule, regulation or
device in evasion of it." Justice Mahlon Pitney not only invoked the
same rationale in *New York Central R.R. Co. v. White*, decided in
1917, but also tackled the question begged by Hughes's opinion in
McGuire. Pitney acknowledged that the New York worker's compensation law "does not concern itself with measures of prevention" and therefore could not be justified on the usual police power
grounds. "But the interest of the public is not confined to these,"
Pitney declared. "One of the grounds of its concern with the continued life and earning power of the individual is its interest in the prevention of pauperism, with its concomitants of vice and crime."[35]

Pitney was not the first American judge to identify a public interest of this sort. The same concerns shaped the Arkansas court's
decision in *Eubanks* 30 years earlier. Its emergence as a justification for the exercise of the police power in 1917, however, caused a
sensation. Here was a principle with the capacity for luxuriant
growth. Louis Brandeis once remarked that "but for Pitney, we

would have had no workmen's compensation laws."[36] Although the
conclusion is doubtful at best, Brandeis's enthusiasm for Pitney's
opinion in *White* is understandable. It provided his friends in the
National Consumers League and the American Association for Labor Legislation with a general principle, consistent with the
Court's reluctance to consider inequality as a justification for police regulations, on which to ground further advances in the field of
"social legislation." Minimum wage laws and unemployment
compensation laws could—and eventually would—be justified as
expressions of the public interest in the "prevention of pauperism."

The wage-payment and "contracting out" decisions of 1909–
1917 did more than map a path of least resistance for litigators
dedicated to the defense of "social legislation." *McClean, McGuire,*
and *White* subverted the "specialness" of the labor contract. In
each instance, the primary purpose of the challenged statute was to
mitigate the superior bargaining strength of employers relative to
workers. Yet in each instance, the Court identified a secondary
public purpose, commensurate with the police power, which the
challenged statute fulfilled. Consequently the Court ruled that the
acts at issue could not be disturbed without violating the judicial
department's duty to presume the constitutionality of legislation.
Edward S. Corwin, writing on *White* in 1917, proclaimed that the
Court had closed the gap between the "constitutional laxism" displayed in *Powell v. Pennsylvania* and the "constitutional rigorism"
displayed in *Lochner v. New York.* "Constitutional rigorism," he
reported, "is dead."[37] We now know that Corwin spoke too soon.
But other progressives shared Corwin's assumption and it prompted
some to reconsider their working premises about history, liberty,
and the judicial function in constitutional adjudication. The concept of "social legislation" cut across each domain of thought and
merits especially close attention.

≺ VI ≻

"Social Legislation" and Accommodation
in Progressive Scholarship

At the turn of the century, "social legislation" connoted a new
kind of statute—an unprecedented but necessary abridgment of free

contract to counteract the inequalities of wealth, power, and opportunity incident to modern industrial society. Richard T. Ely, for example, drew a sharp distinction between the "positive liberty" goals of such legislation and the "negative liberty" goals of the nineteenth-century statutes that abolished imprisonment for debt, distraint for rent, and the contractual disabilities of married women. The new "social legislation" effected social justice; the old emancipatory legislation effected equal justice. In 1910 the two conceptions of liberty and justice, anchored on the same premise about the history of American legislation, seemed to be at war with one another. In 1917 they no longer did. The Court's wage-payment and "contracting out" decisions showed that social justice might be effected without impairing the principle of equal justice, that "positive liberty" might be achieved without sapping the vitality of "negative liberty." Only two moves were required to give "social legislation" a new meaning, a new history that connected the progressive struggle for social security with the symbols and ideals of American exceptionalism. The first was to suggest that the nineteenth-century statutes securing equal justice had also redistributed wealth, power, and opportunity. It might said, for example, that both the abolition of coverture and the enactment of worker's compensation laws "indicated a conscious social policy, or an intention to influence social structure." The second move was to define any statute having these characteristics as "social legislation."[38]

Giving "social legislation" an American history consonant with the founding ideals was the brainchild of a remarkable economist named Henry W. Farnam. The idea that any statute designed "to influence social structure" should be regarded as "social legislation" provided just enough glue to hold together his *Chapters in the History of Social Legislation in the United States to 1860*, a work thirty years in the making. Farnam's history began with the social policies of John Winthrop, whose "City on a Hill" had been built with an innovative mix of land, labor, price-regulation, and licensing legislation that not only accommodated inherited ideals to a challenging new physical environment but also laid the foundations for a republican society dedicated to both individual rights and the common good. The book concluded with a series of chapters on the labor laws of the early national period. Farnam gave special attention to the advent of marine hospitals for sick and disabled seamen which Congress financed with a tax on wages beginning in 1798. Such legislation provided an historical pedigree for other forms of social insurance. On every intervening page, whether describing "the social ideals of the fundamental law of the republic" or accounting for the rise of the mechanic's lien, Farnam developed the same themes. Freedom of contract and "social legislation" were complementary, not opposites, and always had been. What made America exceptional was the people's readiness to employ law enacted by deliberative assemblies both to extend the blessings of liberty and to promote the general welfare. Some statutes established equal justice, others secured social justice; but a great many statutes fulfilled both purposes simultaneously. Political democracy and social democracy thus reinforced one another from the beginning of American history.[39]

Farnam was not always so upbeat about the possibility of forging an accommodation between freedom of contract and "social legislation." At the height of the *Lochner* era, the judicial decisions that shaped the thought of Ely and Pound outraged him as well. The idea that "the states are laboratories for social experiments" began its career in one of Farnam's books, *The Economic Utilization of History*, published in 1913. Like Brandeis, who repeated the phrase in a landmark Supreme Court opinion twenty years later, Farnham complained that the "power of our courts to nullify laws . . . constantly interrupted" the process of experimentation. "It is," he said, "as if a biologist were to suddenly find his laboratory invaded and wrecked by an over-zealous anti-vivisectionist." Throughout his life, the experiments that most interested Farnam were those which courts were most inclined to strike down. He was a cofounder of the American Association for Labor Legislation (AALL); he succeeded Ely as the association's president in 1908 and remained active in the drive for minimum wage laws, social insurance programs, and statutes abolishing "yellow-dog" contracts until his death in 1933.[40]

Ely and Farnam had a good deal in common. Both belonged to the group of early American university scholars trained in Germany, and both imbibed their commitment to schemes of social betterment while abroad. But Farnam was more resistant to socialism in the 1880s and less doctrinaire in the decades that followed.

The emotional appeals to inequality and brotherhood that figured so prominently in Ely's work had no place in Farnam's. His first publication in English (he published two monographs in German) after being appointed professor of political economy at Yale in 1880 was a justly famous review of Ely's *The Labor Movement in America.* "Dr. Ely says—and he certainly ought to know—that he is no socialist," Farnam wrote. "Yet much that he says sounds so much like what a good many of the socialists say, that he ought hardly to complain, if people occasionally mistake him for one. If a man should march in a socialistic procession, bearing a red flag with the inscription, 'I am no socialist,' he could hardly pick a quarrel with the newspapers for reporting him as a socialist."[41]

The use of historical analogy in defense of social reform was the distinguishing characteristic of Farnam's scholarship from beginning to end. His work went through two phases. As late as 1910, he believed that the history of money and banking supplied the most apt analogy for the making of modern labor law in the United States. "The general term labor legislation," he declared at the third annual meeting of the AALL, "embraces at the present day a heterogeneous mass of enactments which impinge upon the individual in very different ways, and which really fall into three quite distinct classes, if we group them with reference to their immediate bearing on economic processes."

Farnam called the first type "protective labor legislation." It included child-labor laws, maximum-hours laws, and statutes requiring the use of safety appliances on dangerous machinery. This sort of legislation, he insisted, had the same purpose and effect as legislation designed to curb the operation of Gresham's law on the money supply:

The buying and selling of labor did not cease. The demand and supply acted as before. But the conditions under which they acted were changed. A child of ten years was no longer legal tender in the labor market. A day of thirteen hours was no longer a legal standard of time wages. The government did for labor what it had done for money, by providing that certain kinds of service would be illegal as were certain kinds of money.

And the results of both forms of government intervention provided general benefits.[42]

Farnam called labor laws of the second type "distributive." Minimum wage laws and worker's compensation legislation, for

example, affected the terms of exchange rather than the standard of
exchange. But these schemes also had an analogy in the history of
monetary legislation. "Just as the monetary standard has sometimes been changed in order to benefit a certain class, especially to
bring about a redistribution of wealth between debtor and credi-
tor," he said, "so most of these laws endeavor to bring about a redistribution of wealth either between employer and employed, or
between present and future income." Farnam conceded that
"history has taught us the danger of changes which are made deliberately with the intention of helping one class at the expense of
another." But the "danger" had never been "great enough in all
cases to condemn it." Changes in the relative value of gold and sil-
ver required changes in the monetary standard during the administration of Andrew Jackson, and changes in the incidence of industrial accidents required changes in the structure of tort and contract law at the beginning of the twentieth century. Since courts
had sustained the one form of government intervention, Farnam
believed that they should sustain the other.[43]

"Permissive" legislation, enacted to encourage the formation of
new institutions, was Farnam's third type of government action.
He included in this category statutes that established collective-
bargaining units by majority preference of the affected workers and
provided for the creation of arbitration boards to resolve labor disputes. "Labor laws of the third class," Farnam contended, "also
find their analogy in monetary legislation." The national banking
acts of the 1860s provided for the chartering of banks, set standards
for the issue of notes, and linked the private interests of
"enterprising capitalists who desired to organize themselves under
the law" with the public interest in a convertible currency. Federal
taxation of rival institutions, the state banks of issue, acted as the
linchpin of the system. Thus the architects of national banking legislation used "protective" and "distributive" methods to encourage
the beneficial operation of private institutions created under "permissive" laws. In Farnam's judgment, government had a duty to facilitate collective bargaining through comparable mechanisms.[44]

The second phase of Farnam's work was less imaginative yet
had a greater impact. In 1902 the Carnegie Institution of Washington, founded to administer funds donated by Andrew Carnegie "to
encourage, in the broadest and most liberal manner, investigation,

research . . . and the application of knowledge to the improvement of mankind," asked Farnam and two eminent colleagues to prepare a plan for economic research. The first subject of inquiry on their list was "the social legislation of the States, which should be critically examined with reference to its results." This became Farnam's bailiwick; he directed the production of a great many monographs in the years that followed, first as a member of the Carnegie Institution's Department of Economics and Sociology and later, after the collapse of the Carnegie department in 1916, as chairman of the Board of Research Associates in American Economic History.

Farnam understood "social legislation" in the prevailing narrow sense until 1917. The initial published studies written under his direction included histories of factory legislation in Pennsylvania and New York, child labor legislation in New Jersey, and labor legislation of all sorts in Rhode Island, Connecticut, Iowa, and California.[45] Two things changed Farnam's focus and conceptualization in his major work in progress, *Chapters in the History of Social Legislation*. One was the Supreme Court's 1917 decision in *White*. The other was the publication of Ernst Freund's *Standards of American Legislation* later the same year.

Freund, a fellow laborer in the AALL, made two main points that struck Farnam as right and a third he thought was wrong. Both points on target involved the role of appellate courts in the "liberty of contract" regime. Freund claimed, first, that "any apprehension of a permanent hindrance on the part of courts to any phase of legislative progress is groundless." Time and again the Supreme Court, in particular, had framed its opinions in such a way as to maintain avenues of "honorable retreat" from the positions assumed in *Lochner*. "No constitutional right is asserted," Freund remarked, "without placing in convenient juxtaposition a saving on behalf of the public welfare." The *White* decision, which came down after *Standards of Legislation* went to press, clinched the point in Farnham's mind. Second, Freund claimed that a virtual surrender of the judicial veto, as Holmes had counseled in his *Lochner* dissent, would be unwise. Freedom of conscience, speech, and association—the latter an AALL rallying cry against "yellow-dog" contracts—required aggressive judicial protection. "Our main reliance for the perpetuation of ideals of individual liberty," Freund wrote, "must be in the continued exercise of the judicial preroga-

tive." For Freund, as for Farnam, the principal task of modern legislation was to reconcile established conceptions of liberty with intensified government intervention, not to overthrow the one to secure the other. Farnam approved both claims (as well as a number
of others) in a laudatory review for the *Nation*. In his judgment,
however, a third main point in the book gave aid and comfort to
extremists on both sides of the "liberty of contract" debate in
American public life. Freund's first chapter, "Historic Changes of
Policy and the Modern Concept of Social Legislation," maintained
the conventional distinction between nineteenth-century statutes
"wiping out personal differences in relation to legal rights" (laws
predicated on equal justice) and twentieth-century "social legislation" providing for "the relief and elevation of the less favored
class of the community" (laws predicated on social justice). Farnam
dedicated the rest of his life to the collapse of this distinction;
Clive Day, his longtime Yale associate, put *Chapters in the History
of Social Legislation* into final shape for the publisher in 1938.[46]

≺ VII ≻

The New Deal Synthesis

Farnam's revisionist history of "social legislation" appeared at a
crucial moment in Supreme Court history. One year earlier, the
Court took the path of "honorable retreat" and sustained a minimum wage law comparable to statutes which it had struck down in
1923 and 1936. Why the so-called "big switch" occurred is still a
matter of great controversy among lawyers, historians, and political scientists. One thing about *West Coast Hotel v. Parrish* can
nonetheless be said with confidence. Chief Justice Hughes's opinion for the five-four majority tried to reconcile minimum wage
regulation with the principle of neutrality in constitutional adjudication. Hughes did not deny that freedom of contract was a constitutional right. "But the liberty safeguarded," he said, "is liberty in
a social organization which requires the protection of law against
the evils which menace the health, safety, morals, and welfare of
the people." There were "many illustrations" of the legislative department's "power under the Constitution to restrict freedom of
contract." The wage-payment decisions provided one, the "con-

tracting out" decisions another. Hughes cited both lines of cases. Yet the principle of neutrality mandated a connection between the challenged statute and a legitimate public purpose; here the "prevention of pauperism" justification pioneered in *White v. New York Central R.R.* finally became decisive.[47]

"We may take judicial notice of the unparalleled demands for relief which arose during the recent period of depression and still continue," Hughes declared for the Court in *Parrish*.

> The exploitation of a class of workers who are in an unequal position with respect to bargaining power and are thus relatively defenseless against the denial of a living wage is not only detrimental to their health and well being but casts a direct burden upon the community. What these workers lose in wages the taxpayers are called upon to pay . . . The community is not bound to provide what is in effect a subsidy for unconscionable employers. The community may direct its law-making power to correct the abuse which springs from their selfish disregard of the public interest.

Hughes thus finessed the once vital distinction between (impermissible) legislation designed to redress inequalities in bargaining strength and (permissible) legislation designed to prevent pauperism. After *Parrish* the distinction no longer mattered. What the Court's 1937 decision firmly established was that in constitutional law, at least, the labor contract could not be regarded as a special one. The presumption of constitutionality applied to labor laws as well as to other police regulations that served some public interest while providing special benefits to a particular class or interest group. "Even if the wisdom of the policy be regarded as debatable and its effects uncertain," Hughes proclaimed for the Court, "still the legislature is entitled to its judgment."[48]

The collapse of the distinction between "pure and simple labor laws" and legitimate police regulations in 1937 encouraged the announcement of another distinction in *United States v. Carolene Products Co.*, decided the following year. There the Court, speaking through Justice Harlan Fiske Stone, deliberately abandoned the neutrality principle in constitutional adjudication. "Regulatory legislation affecting ordinary commercial transactions is not to be pronounced unconstitutional," Stone declared, "unless in the light of the facts made known or generally assumed it is of such a character as to preclude the assumption that it rests upon some rational basis within the knowledge and experience of the legislators." In a famous footnote, the Court suggested that "there may be narrower scope for operation of the presumption of constitutionality" if the challenged statute appeared "on its face" to trench on personal liberties specifically protected in the Bill of Rights; appeared to restrict "political processes which can ordinarily be expected to bring about the repeal of undesirable legislation"; or appeared to be "directed at particular religious, national or racial minorities." This is not the place to assess the coherence of a "double standard" in the review of legislation. But it is appropriate to suggest how the accommodation impulse in progressive scholarship, itself a product of the "liberty of contract" regime, shaped the formulation and implementation of the *Carolene Products* description of the judicial function.[49]

Consider first the matter of implementation. The bifurcated structure of review postulated in *Carolene Products* required a new jurisprudential category that distinguished statutes subject only to a "rational basis" test from those subject to heightened scrutiny. The resulting category was, of course, "social legislation." Since 1940 the Supreme Court has used the term on scores of occasions and the state courts have used it more than 800 times. Appellate judges have employed it as a descriptive term for statutes that, to invoke Farnam's taxonomy, are protective or distributive or permissive; they have employed it in cases involving government's eminent domain and taxing powers as well as the police power. For half a century "social legislation" has denoted any statute designed "to influence social structure," whether by imposing new duties on the strong to protect the weak or by curtailing legal rights held by some to enhance the liberty of others. A once threatening term imported from Germany has thus been thoroughly Americanized. In modern constitutional law, as in Winthrop's Boston, the common good and freedom of contract meet as equals in deliberative assemblies charged with ranking and balancing the two values in particular contexts.

The accommodation impulse shaped the formulation of the *Carolene Products* standard in a different way. What the New Deal Court did not say as it buried the principle of neutrality was as significant as what it did say. At no point did the Court suggest that contracts between parties with unequal bargaining strength were inherently coercive. At no point did it endorse the concept of "pos-

itive liberty." And at no point did it embrace the method of "sociological jurisprudence," which Pound described in 1909 as "the
movement for the adjustment of principles and doctrines to the
human conditions they are to govern rather than to assumed first
principles."

The New Deal Court's circumspection was no accident. Hughes
and Stone, in particular, had never been comfortable with the Ely-
Pound story about freedom of contract and the state. In 1915
Hughes helped suppress Holmes's talk about duress and "the interest of positive freedom" in the draft opinion for *Keokee Consolidated Coke.* Also in 1915 Stone contended that because "notions
of social justice may differ with the individual," courts had no
business invoking them. "The phrase 'social justice,'" he wrote in
Law and Its Administration, "as stating any definite legal conception, is meaningless." According to Stone, Pound's call for a "sociological jurisprudence" had been misdirected:

As a philosophy of legislation, our system affords a more or less satisfactory method of ascertaining and applying "social justice." The legislator is
elected to his office for a short term, after popular discussion, and usually
he stands as a candidate for office on a party platform promising a distinct
legislative program. If elected, his election carries with it the mandate of
the people to carry out that program. He is thus left in no uncertainty as
to the requirements of social justice, and in carrying his legislative program into effect . . . he experiences none of the embarrassment which a
judge must experience, if he overturns judicial precedents in order to formulate law harmonizing with his theories of social justice.

Stone acted on these propositions 25 years later. Once he decided
that, as a "legal conception," the boundary between freedom of
contract and the police power was no more definite than social justice, he framed a constitutional doctrine that put responsibility for
determining both in the hands of legislative majorities. For him, as
for Farnam, political democracy and social democracy were insepa-
rable. If the latter floundered because of restrictions on access to
political participation, the Court could invoke the representation-
reinforcing prong of the *Carolene Products* footnote to keep public
debate robust and wide open. American exceptionalism thus survived in a new wrapper.[50]

Yet unanticipated consequences arose from the New Deal
Court's reluctance to adopt the language of inequality, coercion,
and "positive liberty" as it brought an end to the "liberty of con-

tract" regime in American law. Alexis de Tocqueville once observed that "scarcely any political question arises in the United
States that is not resolved . . . into a judicial question." As a result,
"all parties are obliged to borrow, in their daily controversies, the
ideas, and even the language peculiar to judicial proceedings . . .
[and] the language of the law thus becomes, in some measure, a
vulgar tongue."[51] By retiring from the field without throwing its
weight behind either freedom of contract or social legislation, the
New Deal Court contributed nothing to the "vulgar tongue." It is
often said that modern American law provides less protection
against exploitation, illness, and unemployment than the laws of
other Western nations. Many factors—the structure of the American polity, the American devotion to market process, the underlying strength of American individualism—help to account for the
relative weakness of social-welfare liberalism in the United States.
But if "politically effective opinion" remains "stubbornly centrist"
on the question of inequality, as Willard Hurst has remarked,[52] at
least some of the responsibility should be attributed to the rise and
fall of the "liberty of contract" doctrine in American constitutional
law. First the courts repulsed arguments grounded on inequality,
then the courts encouraged counsel to develop accommodationist
tactics, and finally the courts simply bowed out of the controversy
over freedom of contract and the state. At no point during the five
decades in which its jurisdiction was paramount did the judiciary
say anything that assisted the cause of social-welfare reform. As
the "liberty of contract" regime fades further into the past, this
may turn out to be its most important legacy.

Freedom of Contract, Labor, and the Administrative State

ARTHUR F. MCEVOY

LABOR-LAW HISTORIANS generally divide the history of freedom of contract in America into three periods. Between 1800 and the 1880s the doctrine developed hand in hand with the industrializing economy; reformers upheld the "free labor" ideal as a model for republican citizenship in an increasingly commercial society. Between the 1880s and the 1930s free contract took a more defensive posture, as lawyers, judges, and treatise-writers used what they called "liberty of contract" to stave off challenges to employers' authority by workers and their allies. A third phase began during the New Deal, as lawmakers strove through overt government administration to balance employer prerogative with workers' demands for union recognition and collective bargaining. State power pervaded labor relations in each period, though it took different forms in each. Free contract remained a fundamental norm throughout, particularly as it bore on state authority to regulate the wage bargain itself.[1]

In each period, lawmakers used free contract ideology to guide labor relations in three distinct social spaces. Freedom of contract most forcefully controlled relations in what the law recognized as the "free" market for labor. Here, workers and employers met as ostensible equals to bargain out the terms of the employment contract: wages, hours, benefits, and the authority to act collectively. Inside the employment relation was the realm in which production actually took place: here, although free bargaining creates the relationship, employers have historically enjoyed great power to determine such matters as workplace organization, safety, and the terms on which workers could quit. The law has more or less immunized employer authority in this realm from state intervention by virtue of the putative freedom of the wage bargain. Outside the labor market, finally, was a third space in which production took place under no legally-recognized employment bargain and under more or less "unfree" conditions. Households, family farms, and slave plantations were "private" spaces, in which private authority reigned and the law governed imperfectly if at all. Freedom of contract marked out the boundaries between the labor market, workplaces, and households: in different ways that themselves changed over the course of the doctrine's history, it sustained complex balances of freedom and subordination in each.

Like any ideology, freedom of contract has a complex and unstable relationship with the social order it purports to explain.[2] Nowhere is this relationship more problematic than in the area of labor relations, where economic and technological change constantly disrupt settled arrangements between employers and workers. Because economic production is so important to social order, labor regulation is crucial to the interplay between law, society, and history; historically, labor has been a prime focus of fundamental conflicts over state power and social organization.[3] Most work, of course, goes on without direct reference to law; its organization is held in place by such extra-legal forces as deference to traditional hierarchy, overt oppression, and economic necessity. To that extent, free contract has little to do with the real-world experience of work.

Freedom of contract and labor regulation confront each other head-on, however, when extra-legal forces lose their grip on production: at that point lawyers and judges intervene to stabilize things according to legal principle.[4] One function that principle serves in this process is *descriptive*, as legal agencies bring contested work relations into line with their ideology's distilled knowledge of society as it is. Another function is *prescriptive*: ideology guides legal actors, to the extent they are able, in restructuring unstable labor relations as they ought to be. A third function of ideology, finally, is *hegemonic* or *disciplinary*: principled resolutions of legal conflicts aim to persuade workers and employers of the justice, rationality, even the inevitability of their situations as regulated by law. Freedom of contract has influenced the history of labor relations, then, not only by guiding the resolution of particular conflicts when they come to law but also by constraining people's expectations of what the law would do for them and even their ability to imagine alternatives to their situations.[5]

As powerful as the idea has been, freedom of contract has also been fraught with contradictions, both conceptual and historical.[6] Conceptually, the doctrine invokes both consent and coercion. Some measure of force lies at the root of every "voluntary" agreement, even if only to the extent that the threat of losing a desired bargain motivates each party to accept the other's terms. The more coercive the need that motivates the contract, therefore, the more "voluntary" is the consent to the terms.[7] Consent extracted by fear or necessity, however, is not real consent: nowhere does this contradiction operate more forcefully than when workers must agree to their employer's terms if they wish to work at all. Locke's social contract theory finessed this conundrum by ascribing existing inequalities of wealth and power to people's varying levels of talent and industry and by postulating a kind of "tacit consent" by which people joining society agreed to live with established hierarchies and inequalities.[8] Free contract thus promotes both individualism and paternalism, consent and coercion at the same time.[9]

The second source of the free contract doctrine's instability is historical. Eighteenth-century American republicanism revolved around the idea that the consent of the governed measured the legitimacy of all secular authority.[10] After 1815, when lawmakers shifted their attention from state formation to economic development, the market replaced politics as the main arena in which Americans worked out the balance between consent and coercion, self-determination and inequality. Lawmakers committed to free contract restructured one area of social relations after another, from commercial finance to workplaces and even families, so as to liberate individual capacities to pursue wealth and progress. The society that emerged from their efforts, however, generated new forms of power and inequality as the economy grew. An ideology committed to individual initiative thus helped to produce an increasingly interdependent economy in which ostensibly free workers found themselves bound up in new, unimaginably powerful systems of domination.

≺ I ≻

Free Labor, 1800–1880

Between 1800 and 1880 industrialization transformed the United States from a sparsely populated, agrarian nation into an economic colossus. Manufacturing replaced agriculture at the heart of the economy; wage labor under free contract replaced the traditional, patriarchal labor relations that prevailed in antebellum craft shops, family farms, and slave plantations.[11] Industrialization entailed a thoroughgoing transformation, not only in technology and markets but in social relations as well.[12] Lawmakers played a key role in the process, devising legislation and reworking the common law to promote the efficient use of labor, capital, and resources. Free contract was their ground norm: they understood society as a network of voluntary relationships between autonomous individuals and strove to limit the power of the state to interfere with private ordering. As Willard Hurst put it, the first three-quarters of the nineteenth century were "above all, the years of contract in our law."[13] The Revolution had redefined Locke's social contract in terms of choosing one's rulers rather than simply consenting to them. To its heirs, the ability to choose one's relationships was the essence of the inalienable right to liberty; "pursuit of happiness" meant exercising that liberty in the self-interested pursuit of wealth in the marketplace.

Citizens' freedom to labor where, for whom, and under what conditions they chose was crucial to the transformation. From the early efforts to end indentured servitude in the North to the abolition of slavery in the Thirteenth Amendment, reformers gradually removed legal restrictions on the freedom of workers to sell their labor on their own terms. Union victory in the Civil War purportedly represented the triumph of free labor and free contract over the last vestiges of the pre-industrial regime.[14] Legal equality in the labor market did not mean democracy in the workplace, however. At the same time courts freed workers to make their own wage bargains, they also ruled that the employment relation incorporated many of the traditional, hierarchical aspects of eighteenth-century master-servant law. Families, farms, and plantations, meanwhile, remained largely outside the legally-constituted free

market for labor, although contractarian ideology cast a strong
shadow over production in those areas, as well.

Revolutionary-era Americans most clearly articulated the theory of free contract in a political context, in which people's right to
choose their government became the organizing principle for politics and for social order in general. The ideological division between the "public," or political sphere and the "private," economic
one in which free contract ideas flowered came only with the
emergence of a market-oriented liberalism in the early nineteenth
century.[15] Free contract ideas, as shown in chapter 2, had been
making their way into the law of employment relations for some
time. In England the various types of work relationships had by
Blackstone's time more or less collapsed into the generic category
"master-servant," but a formally unregulated market for labor did
not come into being until the Poor Law reform of 1834.[16]

Common law restraints on workers generally did not apply to
wage-earners in eighteenth-century America, but bound labor remained the norm in the colonial period: indentured servitude and
apprenticeship in the North, slavery in the South.[17] Northern forms
of unfree labor withered rapidly after the Revolution, particularly
as journeymen proclaimed themselves the political equals of their
employers. To them, republican citizenship entailed the right to
self-government in the economic sphere as well as the political
one. Everything short of free labor bore the taint of slavery.[18] While
free labor ideas had been developing over the whole of the eighteenth century, then, they matured in the early nineteenth under
the combined influences of the Revolution's ideals and economic
development.

Theoretically, the challenge to early nineteenth century-law-
makers was to square the emerging economic order with the contractarian ideals of the Revolution. Revolutionary republicanism
portrayed work as the production by free citizens of useful goods
for the benefit of the community. According to the logic of the
emerging industrial economy, however, work was a market relation, not a political one: employment was a contract for the sale of
labor power between formally equal bargainers, each party maximizing its self-interest through the price mechanism.[19] Industrial-
ism, moreover, required that large numbers of workers operate together under a single authority. Who would possess that authority

and how it would work was the central issue of antebellum labor politics.

What emerged as the "free labor" ideology of the Republican party synthesized revolutionary ideals and the emerging economic order. Antebellum courts abandoned their traditional role in administering the substance of the wage bargain, as they did in contract law generally, leaving only the will of the parties as manifest in the bargain to control the relationship.[20] Free contract in the wage bargain made workers and employers equal before the law and allowed them to allocate the risks and rewards of work between them voluntarily. Because wages were the measure of the bargain, republican ideals of work gradually gave way over the antebellum period to a more market-oriented vision of work as the mere sale of labor power, at a price determined by the impersonal laws of supply and demand.[21] The political aspects of the employment relation—control over the work itself, duties of care and obedience between workers and employers, and so on—were subordinate to the contract relation and thus disappeared from legal view. For Locke the possession of land signified one's "tacit consent" to the established order of society.[22] In the same way, the free labor theory built on the wage bargain to imply the consent of workers, who generally owned only their labor, to increasingly powerful— but legally invisible—systems of power and subordination.

In practice, the legal constitution of the early nineteenth-century American labor market developed under the terms of the common law doctrine of conspiracy.[23] One of the first contests over labor in this period came in the *Philadelphia Cordwainers'* case of 1806. Journeymen shoemakers organized to set wage rates and regulate working conditions, and to pressure the master artisans who employed them to hire only union members. To the journeymen, citizenship in a free republic made them the equals of their employers and entitled them to self-government in their working lives. Prosecutors, on the other hand, maintained that legislating rules for the trade amounted to an effort to set up an illegitimate private government outside the democratically elected one. The court agreed, declaring the combination a criminal conspiracy: in the labor market, workers and employers would confront each other as individuals.[24]

The British Parliament immunized workers' organizations from

conspiracy prosecution in 1871.[25] Massachusetts Chief Justice
Lemuel Shaw reached the same result three decades earlier, in the
1842 case of *Commonwealth v. Hunt*.[26] Shaw dismissed an indictment against journeymen bootmakers in Boston who had pressured
an employer to fire a particular employee. A combination of workers, Shaw thought, was not per se a criminal conspiracy, and the
indictment had alleged no specific acts of organized coercion
against the employer. As Robert Rantoul, the bootmakers' lawyer,
put it, "the great question important to the defendants and to the
public" was

> whether workmen are guilty of a crime punishable by law, in disposing of
> them[selves] at what price, to whom and on what terms, that they may re-
> spectively think fit. Whatever any individual may lawfully do, several
> may agree together to do. If a laborer may prescribe whatever terms and
> conditions they [sic] think fit, any or all those in the same trade may agree
> to do the same thing.[27]

Hunt was only a limited victory for free labor principles: combinations that aimed actually to interfere with employers' control
over the job or to entice workers away from a particular job remained illegal, as they had traditionally been under the common
law. In any event, what few prosecutions for labor conspiracy there
were before the Civil War seem to have generated only minimal
penalties for defendant workers. Journeymen's associations were
powerful in local politics; judges and juries, meanwhile, frequently
disagreed on principle as to how far they were privileged to go.[28]
Economic dislocations, finally, may have dampened labor activism
between the Panic of 1837 and the Civil War era.[29]

Hunt guaranteed the journeymen's freedom to agree among
themselves on the terms under which they would enter an employment contract. As such, it was consistent with other pro-
market, growth-promoting decisions of the antebellum period.[30]
Once inside the employment relation, however, workers enjoyed
only limited power. The law seriously limited their freedom to
quit, for example. By 1880 only about half the states allowed workers to recover wages for work already performed when they left
their jobs before their contracts expired; until then, most followed
the traditional rule that the labor contract was "entire" and obli-
gated workers to remain on the job for the full term if they wished
to be paid at all.[31] Antebellum courts also presumed that the wage

bargain bound employees to obey their bosses' direction as to how the work would be done. "Outside of the service to be rendered," in the words of one Ohio judge, "the employer has no more control over the person he has employed . . . than he has over the person of any other individual."[32] Within the bounds of the service, however, the employer's command was absolute: workers fired for disobedience generally had no right to recover wages for work already performed.[33] Free contract thus entitled workers and employers to enter the wage bargain as equals, but courts universally implied into the bargain the workers' agreement to obey their masters "faithfully."

Nowhere did the legal device of implied contract do more to divide the free realm of the labor market from the hierarchical realm of the workplace itself than in the area of liability for industrial accidents. Here again, Chief Justice Shaw articulated the standard that most American courts followed until after the turn of the twentieth century, in the 1842 case of *Farwell v. Boston and Worcester Railroad*.[34] Engineer Farwell had lost his right hand when a careless co-worker had caused his locomotive to derail. For guidance in "an action of new impression in our courts," Shaw went straight to contract principles: "the general rule, resulting from considerations as well of justice as of policy," was that one who accepted a job at a bargained-for wage "takes upon himself the natural and ordinary risks and perils incident to the performance of such services, and in legal presumption, the compensation is adjusted accordingly."[35] These "natural and ordinary risks" included those of injury from the negligence of fellow servants. Workers were in the best position, Shaw reasoned, to observe their fellows' conduct, to "give notice of any misconduct, incapacity, or neglect of duty, and [to] leave the service" if the employer refused to take appropriate precautions. That being the case, "one sustaining an injury in the course of his own employment . . . must bear the loss himself, or seek his remedy, if he have any, against the actual wrong-doer."[36]

As the courts read them into the wage contract, the assumption-of-risk and fellow-servant doctrines, along with the doctrine of contributory negligence, insulated employers from nearly all liability for industrial injuries through the rest of the nineteenth century. Whether or not Shaw and other development-minded nine-

teenth-century judges designed the employers' defenses as a deliberate subsidy to developing industry is the subject of controversy
among legal historians.[37] What *is* certain is that the doctrines effectively insulated employers' practical control over workplace safety
from scrutiny under either the civil or the criminal law, even
though the free contract rhetoric of *Farwell* put workers in charge
of their own destinies.[38] One result was the large and growing toll
that accidents exacted from industrial workers as the nineteenth
century progressed. Investment in safety, whether in the form of
technology or of workplace organization, was the employer's le-
gally-guaranteed prerogative.

Economic necessity and the myth of the wage bargain justified
this manifest and deadly inequality in the workplace. As the Pennsylvania Supreme Court put it in 1854, workers and employers
were "equal before the law, and considered equally competent to
take care of themselves."[39] The law "would violate a law of nature
if it should provide an immunity to any one against the ordinary
dangers of his business, and it would be treating him as incapable
of taking care of himself."[40] Deviating from the *Farwell* rule
"would embarrass the conduct of all business, where any risk is to
be run."[41] As the law established formal equality in the labor market, then, it ratified the decidedly unequal power of employers to
expose their workers to injury and death on the job. Both *Farwell*
and *Hunt* rested on a social vision, part aspiration and part fantasy,
in which workers and employers were equal partners simply because the law said they were.

Free-labor principles did not apply to all workers. Despite its
claims to universality, early nineteenth-century doctrine recognized people's freedom of contract only to the extent that they
were *sui juris*, that is, legally entitled to participate in the market.
A great deal of productive work, however, took place outside the
realm of the wage bargain. Slaves, of course, were legally incapable
of contracting for the hire of their labor or for anything else: indeed, contrary to the *Farwell* case, injuries to hired slaves in the
South were the responsibility of those who hired them, not the
owners. Here, the free contract logic of northern employers' liability law did not apply.[42] Similarly, Chinese immigrants worked in
western agriculture and on the railroads under a contract-labor system, overseen by Chinese merchants in San Francisco, that in

many respects resembled indentured servitude.[43] California Indians could by statute be "apprenticed" out to work on local farms under conditions that hardly differed from formal slavery.[44] The objective conditions of the employment relation varied enormously. The law could force unpaid labor on convicts and paupers of any race, meanwhile, on the theory that these had manifested their inability to fend for themselves in society and would benefit from the industrial discipline that they got in penitentiaries and poorhouses.[45]

Wage bargains did not apply at all to the most typical antebellum economic unit, the family farm. Slave plantations represented a perversion of the form, but northern agriculture extracted labor even more efficiently from family members: the labor was "free" but took place within traditional families rather than under contract. Married women contributed enormously to their family economies through household maintenance or unpaid work on the farm, or by raising cash from keeping boarders or selling garden crops.[46] Even though nineteenth-century American courts tended to describe the act of marriage in contractual terms, the traditional common law doctrine of marital service still made wives' labor and its produce the property of husbands.[47] Marriage and the employment relation thus resembled each other in that people entered them through free bargains but, once in, occupied roles in a traditional hierarchy. Teenagers, likewise, had some power to refuse adoption into a family, but the law left them subject to the authority of their heads of household once they were in.[48]

Following the logic of free contract, mid-century reformers were able to advance married women's capacity to bargain on their own behalf to some degree. Some states enacted statutes that guaranteed wives title to whatever property they brought into their marriages, although control over those assets remained vested in husbands so long as the marriage lasted.[49] So-called "earnings statutes" gave married women property rights in their earnings from "separate" or "personal" labor, although any earnings that women contributed to the family economy remained in their husbands' hands.[50] As in the employment context, courts were quick to ratify traditional patterns of dominance and subordination when there was any doubt as to the reach of statutory reforms.[51] Husbands and wives could not even contract with each other to compensate the wife's contribution if they wanted to. In 1873 the New York Court of Appeals held such a promissory note from a deceased husband to his wife void for lack of consideration.[52]

Professional women, married or not, did somewhat better under American law than in England. There, the *Lumley* cases in the 1850s enjoined a stage actress who breached a performance contract from performing for any competing theater for the duration of the original contract. Anyone who did hire such a person was liable for common law enticement.[53] One American court rejected the *Lumley* rules in 1865, stressing that the right to quit a job was essential both to the worker's independence and to the community's interest in maintaining labor mobility.[54] States could, however, exclude women from whole professions: in 1873 *Bradwell v. Illinois* held that states had the authority to confine admission to legal practice exclusively to men.[55] Common law made married women incapable of making contracts without their husbands' consent: this, in turn, made them incompetent to practice law. Single women were an exception to the common law rule but, as Justice Bradley put it, "the rules of civil society must be adapted to the general constitution of things, and cannot be based upon exceptional cases."[56] Like children and slaves, then, women did most of their work in a realm that the law marked off as "private" and thus beyond the reach of freedom of contract.

The antebellum, free labor vision of contractarianism captured the imaginations of forward-thinking lawmakers and reformers because it incorporated both the individualistic ideals of the Revolution and the competitive, market-oriented ethos of economic progress. There were other visions that competed with it, however. Antebellum journeymen understood "free labor" to entitle them not only to a bargained-for wage but also to self-government inside the workplace.[57] Their vision of *Commonwealth v. Hunt* was a republican one: organized labor would manage its own part of the productive process and negotiate collectively with capital over working conditions and the division of profits. Some workers in skilled trades were, indeed, able to achieve some measure of control over production in the middle decades of the century.[58] These early unions, however, together with their particular vision of free contract, came under strenuous and effective assault after the Civil War.

Antebellum feminists likewise drew on the communitarian side of revolutionary republicanism to attack both the traditional economic structure of the family and the emerging, market-oriented vision of society. They demanded for women, not just control over their "separate" earnings in the wage-labor market but also joint ownership of family assets, half of which were the product of the wife's (albeit unpaid) labor.[59] Marriages and producers' associations were more than mere aggregations of contracting individuals; they were also self-governing communities within which people worked on other's behalf as well as their own. This alternative vision, however, made little impact on the formal law, either of labor or of families, in the period before 1880. It disappeared almost entirely in the decades that followed.

Nor did ideas of free contract, free labor, and free markets completely dominate the machinery of government in the period before 1880. Jacksonian ideology marked off a substantial realm in which individuals were free to pursue their own interests, but it also left legislatures with significant authority to regulate economic activity in the interest of the commonwealth. "All property," as Chief Justice Shaw put it, "derived directly or indirectly from the government, and [was] held subject to those general regulations, which are necessary to the common good and general welfare."[60] Promoting the release of economic creativity thus did not necessarily imply a minimalist, laissez-faire state.[61] Courts were the agencies most directly involved in administering labor relations in the nineteenth century; that they did so in the language of free contract and through the medium of common law does not gainsay the reality of their intervention in the market. Labor regulation by statute and administration did not become the dominant tradition until after the 1930s, though even then the courts retained a great deal of authority over labor relations and nineteenth-century ideas about work retained a great deal of power in spite of their formal repudiation in the New Deal.

Free contract ideology thus marked off different legal spheres in which productive labor took place. Where freedom of contract most completely held sway, labor was "like any other commodity in the market," as President Lincoln put it in 1862, bought and sold according to the laws of supply and demand.[62] Once inside an employment relation, however, wageworkers took subordinate places in a hierarchical system to which they had not agreed specifically but which courts read into their hiring contracts by impli-

cation, drawing from common law rules that had traditionally governed relations between masters and servants. In families and on
plantations, women, children, and slaves did their work without
benefit of contract. Women and children occupied a private space,
outside the realm of free contract, by virtue of the common law
and Justice Bradley's "general constitution of things"; slaves occupied that same space by virtue of being someone else's property.
The law made wageworkers free to sell their labor power by individual contract, just as it increasingly described marriage and adoption in contractual terms. Aside from a few skilled trades, however,
work generally took place under conditions in which equality and
voluntarism had little meaning.

The Civil War and Reconstruction marked the end of the first
stage of the free contract ideology's development in the United
States. To Lincoln and the congressional Republicans, emancipation accomplished not only the end of legal slavery but a "new
birth of freedom" for all Americans. To put that freedom into effect, Republicans passed the Civil Rights Act of 1866, which put
equal rights "to make and enforce contracts" first among the liberties that it guaranteed.[63] The original purpose of the Fourteenth
Amendment, indeed, was to remove any doubt as to the constitutionality of the act and its civil rights formula.[64] Interestingly
enough, the first test of the Fourteenth Amendment's meaning
came in 1873, at the suit not of former slaves but of free New Or-
leans butchers who claimed that a Louisiana statute creating a
regulated monopoly in their trade violated their rights to free labor
under the new constitution. *The Slaughterhouse Cases* occasioned
the clearest statement, albeit in dissent, of the free labor ideology
that had been developing since 1800.

The Supreme Court dismissed the butchers' claim in *Slaughterhouse*, holding that the purpose of the Thirteenth and Fourteenth Amendments was to enfranchise the freed slaves, not to
create new rights in already-free tradespeople.[65] For Justice Field,
however, "the right to pursue a lawful calling" was among the fundamental rights of free citizens and certainly came within the
guarantees of the Fourteenth Amendment.[66] Quoting Adam Smith,
Field insisted that laws hindering a citizen's free disposal of "the
property which every man has in his own labor" violated the
rights, not only of the workers but of those who would employ

them.[67] A constitution that was "general and universal in its application," that prohibited "not merely slavery in the strict sense of
the term, but involuntary servitude in every form," certainly incorporated the freedom to contract for one's labor.[68] Justice Bradley,
meanwhile, believed that "a law which prohibits a large class of
citizens from adopting a lawful employment, or from following a
lawful employment previously adopted, does deprive them of liberty as well as property, without due process of law."[69] Field and
Bradley thus articulated the free contract ideology in terms that
both captured its development over the decades since 1800 and
presaged the next half century of its history.

≺ II ≻

Liberty of Contract, 1880–1937

The structure of the American economy changed rapidly in the last
decades of the nineteenth century. First in the railroads and later in
other core-sector businesses, new management strategies substituted rational planning and bureaucratic, command-and-control
hierarchy for market bargaining in an effort to escape the uncertainties of vastly more powerful market forces and, not least, to
break the power of workers' associations over production.[70] Many
more industrial jobs than before required only minimal skills, and
massive immigration from Europe and Asia brought armies of
workers to fill them. Unions, nonetheless, grew significantly in
membership and power, first in the skilled trades and, after the
turn of the century, among the unskilled. Conflict between capital
and labor thus became the prime mover behind the development of
free contract doctrine in the second phase of its history.

Although it began the period in dissent, Justice Field's vision of
the Fourteenth Amendment won over a majority of the Supreme
Court by the turn of the twentieth century. Incorporation into the
Constitution transformed the "free labor" of the *Slaughterhouse*
dissents into the "liberty of contract" of *Lochner v. New York*.[71] As
freedom of contract became constitutional law, however, it took on
an increasingly defensive role. Courts used the doctrine to resist
fiercely government interference in the wage bargain. While they
allowed a great deal of factory-reform legislation to pass constitu-

tional scrutiny, their tolerance evaporated when reforms threatened the norm of formal equality between workers and employers. Free contract formalism, meanwhile, continued to support private control over family and plantation labor during the period. As labor's critique of the free contract regime developed in the early twentieth century, it laid the foundation for yet another transformation of the political economy in the New Deal.

The "liberty of contract" theory of *Lochner v. New York* synthesized two lines of jurisprudence, both of which developed in the 1880s and 1890s. First was the notion, key to the *Slaughterhouse* dissents, that the due process clause of the Fourteenth Amendment put substantive limits on the extent to which government could police economic relationships. The Supreme Court upheld state controls over pricing in such industries as transport and grain storage at first, following antebellum precedent.[72] In 1890, however, it held that a Minnesota statute empowering a state agency to set maximum rates for rail freight "deprived (the company) of the power of charging reasonable rates for the use of its property . . . and thus, in substance and effect, of the property itself, without due process of law."[73] Justice Bradley parted company with the majority at that point, claiming that the theory of the *Slaughterhouse* dissents did not go so far as to authorize the courts to substitute their judgment on regulatory policy for that of the legislature.[74] Substantive due process, then, developed in defense of businesses' free use of their *property*: freedom of contract was something else.

Free contract as a constitutional right developed first in the state courts, in parallel with federal due-process cases and motivated by the same natural-rights jurisprudence that had driven the *Slaughterhouse* dissents. In Pennsylvania, *Godcharles v. Wigeman* reasoned entirely from natural-law principles to invalidate a state law prohibiting the payment of wages in kind rather than in cash.[75] The Illinois Supreme Court voided a statute limiting the hours of women factory workers in similar terms in 1895.[76] Finally, *Lochner v. New York* invalidated a New York statute regulating the working hours of bakers on the ground that it violated the right to free contract, made substantive by the due process clause of the Fourteenth Amendment. Legislatures could limit hours in dangerous occupations like underground mining on acceptable public-safety grounds; they could also regulate the terms under which contractors could hire labor for public projects because here the legislature was itself the employer.[77] The bakers' law, however, invaded the realm where freedom of contract was supreme: it was, purely and simply, an effort to regulate bargaining between individuals in a private business and as such could not stand.[78]

Other contributors to this volume have treated Lochnerism in detail. Charles McCurdy traces its roots in the "free labor" ideology of the antebellum period and discusses the efforts of reformers and intellectuals to justify wage-and-hour, accident compensation, and other social-welfare legislation in the face of the courts' refusal to recognize real-world inequality as a legitimate motive for regulation.[79] James Gordley suggests that European countries were able to enact social reforms in the late nineteenth and early twentieth centuries, despite opposition from free-contract theorists, in part because European courts had no power to void legislation on constitutional grounds; that American courts can do so was crucial to the development of labor politics in the United States.[80] Much of Lochnerism's emphasis on contractualism and self-help survives in American social-welfare law to this day, in spite of the New Deal's putative overthrow of the "liberty of contract" regime.

The courts' iron determination to preserve formal equality in the wage bargain had enormous practical consequences for wage labor. Wage and hour statutes were particularly suspect because they implied legal recognition of inequalities in bargaining power between workers and employers. Such laws occasionally did survive constitutional scrutiny when advocates could argue that their beneficiaries were particularly vulnerable to oppression and thus proper objects for state paternalism. They did so in *Holden v. Hardy*, which sustained an hours law for underground miners, and in *Muller v. Oregon*, which upheld an Oregon statute mandating a ten-hour day for women in factory jobs on the ground that women's fragile constitutions and their roles as mothers of the race justified state intervention in the wage bargain.[81] As with hours, so also with respect to minimum wages: In 1916 the Supreme Court divided evenly over the constitutionality of an Oregon minimum-wage law for women and thus let it stand; state courts, also, were more likely after the turn of the century to allow minimum wages for women.[82] As in the case of statutes regulating working conditions, courts departed from formal equality and free contract only when reform efforts converged with well-established notions that women and children properly belonged in the home and were less than fully capable of holding their own in the marketplace.

Still, it was in a 1923 case overturning a congressional statute mandating a minimum wage for women and children in the District of Columbia that the Supreme Court delivered one of its most strenuous affirmations of free contract in the wage bargain. *Adkins v. Children's Hospital* denounced the wage measure as "purely a price-fixing law," one that took "account of the necessities of only one party to the contract," viz., the worker.[83] Although there was, "of course, no such thing as absolute freedom of contract . . . freedom of contract is, nevertheless, the general rule and restraint the exception."[84] Without any showing of "exceptional circumstances," the wage law amounted to no more than charity arbitrarily forced upon the employer.[85] As in *Lochner*, a statute designed solely to redress inequalities of bargaining power in the wage relation was "so clearly the product of a naked, arbitrary exercise of power that it cannot be allowed to stand under the Constitution of the United States."[86]

Laws designed to enhance the bargaining power of workers by prohibiting so-called "yellow-dog" contracts, which pledged workers to refrain from joining a union as a condition of employment, triggered judicial opposition even more surely than did wage and hour laws. The Supreme Court invalidated a state "yellow-dog" statute in the 1915 case of *Coppage v. Kansas* and a similar congressional law for railway workers in *Adair v. United States* in 1908.[87] The *Adair* opinion was the work of Justice John Marshall Harlan the Elder, who had thought the bakers' hour law at issue in *Lochner* a legitimate public health measure; here, however, the only possible justification for the statute was to redress inequalities in the wage bargain, and free contract would not allow this.[88] Justice Pitney made clear that inequality of bargaining power was precisely the issue in his opinion for the court in *Coppage*: "there must and will be inequalities of fortune . . . it is from the nature of things impossible to uphold freedom of contract and the right of private property without at the same time recognizing as legitimate those inequalities."[89]

Nowhere did conflict over the constitution of the labor market focus more sharply in the courts than over the issue of the unions' organizing tactics. *Commonwealth v. Hunt* had created a regime of limited judicial tolerance for union efforts to set terms for the wage bargain. Through the 1870s, then, union organizing was an acceptable market tactic like any other. Employers could hire and fire workers, employees could work for whom they wished, and unions could try to organize workers to act collectively if they could. All of these tactics were perfectly compatible with free contract under the *Hunt* regime.[90] After 1880 this tolerance evaporated. Prosecutions for labor conspiracy, which had never disappeared, became sharply punitive: penalties increased, while the range of activities that could support allegations of force and duress against employers broadened to include peaceful picketing and boycotting.[91] By 1890 many courts had come to believe that union strikes and boycotts were fundamentally subversive.[92] In the name of economic freedom they began looking for new remedies that would prevent such activities from interfering with employers' business activities.

They found it in the labor injunction. The tactic first appeared in the 1870s, when many of the nation's railroads were bankrupt and under the management of federal receivers. These, impatient with local officials who sympathized with the strikers and were thus slow to initiate conspiracy prosecutions, began to sue for injunctions against union activity on the ground that it posed a threat to employers' property for which no adequate legal remedy existed. In the 1880s the practice spread from the railroads to other industries.[93] In a process that paralleled the growth of substantive due process as a defense against state regulation of business, courts broadened the scope of employers' property rights that could be threatened with irreparable injury even by peaceful union activity and thus protectable through injunction and contempt.[94] One Supreme Court case went so far as to deem an employer's yellow-dog contracts as a property interest protectable by injunction against union interference.[95] So flexible and so powerful was the equity injunction that by the 1890s it eclipsed conspiracy prosecution as the weapon of choice in capital-labor struggles. Limiting the courts' power to issue labor injunctions became one of labor's key political goals after 1890.

The 1880s thus marked a sea change in the legal administration of the wage bargain, under the influence both of intensifying capital-labor conflict and of the legacy of Emancipation. So long as

there was a wage bargain, the law would characterize any employment relation as the product of free contract, protected by the Fourteenth Amendment as courts increasingly interpreted the latter in
substantive, common law terms. Inside the employment relation,
likewise, late nineteenth-century judicial formalism sanctioned
growing inequalities in ways that increasingly made free contract a
mask for oppression. One index of this change was the employment-at-will rule, which, like the labor injunction, emerged in the
1880s. When the term of employment became an issue in antebellum labor cases, courts looked to the parties' implied agreement as
to the duration of the contract—in agricultural cases, typically a
year. After the Civil War, however, the focus shifted to the kinds of
notice that either party had to give before terminating the relationship.

English courts generally required reasonable notice of intent to
terminate.[96] American courts, however, took an approach that gave
employers much more power to fire workers at will. The earliest
cases tended to involve salaried employees trying to save their jobs
from peremptory termination. In one, the New York Court of Appeals interpreted an insurance executive's contract to work for ten
thousand dollars a year to mean that the employee would be paid
at the *rate* of ten thousand per year, not that his contract guaranteed him employment for the full year. The insurance company
discharged him with two weeks' notice, and the court denied his
claim for the remainder of his year's salary: even though the parties
originally intended the contract to run for a full year, "the hiring of
the plaintiff was a hiring at will and the defendant was at liberty to
terminate the same at any time."[97] The manifest will of the parties
thus took a back seat to employer authority to manage the workplace, particularly with regard to discharging workers when business conditions required.[98] The at-will doctrine also strengthened
employers' power to impose productivity standards on their workers on pain of peremptory discharge.[99]

Employer prerogative over the workplace also limited the extent to which states could regulate safety and working conditions
during the *Lochner* era. Employers resisted such laws strenuously:
Congress did not make airbrakes and automatic couplers mandatory on interstate railroads until 1893, fully a quarter century after
they became available for use. Until that time the roads argued

successfully that such safety devices were unreliable, that they were too costly, but first and foremost that the law had no place interfering with their internal operations.[100] What factory reforms did go into force typically lacked mechanisms for effective enforcement.[101] By the turn of the century industrial accidents were a serious social problem.[102] New York moved first to investigate and then to regulate factory conditions in a meaningful way, but only after the disastrous fire at the Triangle Shirtwaist factory in 1911 dramatized the problem and catalyzed enough political energy to generate reform.[103]

Liability for industrial accidents continued to follow the outlines of *Farwell v. Boston and Worcester Railroad* until the World War I decade. Congress abrogated the employers' defenses for interstate railroads in the Federal Employers' Liability Act of 1908, which specifically voided any employer attempt to contract out of liability in the employment bargain.[104] State courts tended to uphold such waivers, however, instinctively resisting the idea that they could represent anything but voluntary agreements between workers and employers.[105] New York enacted the nation's first compulsory workers' compensation plan in 1910, but that state's highest court voided it the next year on substantive due process grounds.[106] New Yorkers specifically amended their constitution so as to permit such a scheme in the wake of the Triangle Shirtwaist fire.[107] Factory laws and worker's compensation threatened the Lochnerian free contract regime only indirectly because neither reached the wage bargain itself: at least some factory laws were justifiable on traditional police-power grounds, while employer contributions to workers' insurance schemes simply became a fringe benefit to the wage bargain.

As before Reconstruction, free contract principles served to keep certain classes of people outside the legally-constituted market for wage labor and thus in a private domain, subject to private authority with little or no legal supervision. Southern states did their best to reenact as many incidents of the slave regime as they could, only now as legislated terms to the annual labor contracts that all freed people were required to have on pain of arrest and imprisonment for vagrancy.[108] Army and Freedmen's Bureau officials cooperated with planters in tying poor farmers to the land and punished as vagrants those who refused to sign in to the contract-labor system.[109] Sharecroppers worked under a crop-lien system that gave their creditors complete authority over how their farms were to be run; landless farm laborers under the shadow of vagrancy laws and any number of criminal statutes that prescribed forced labor on county gangs.[110] The system survived into the 1930s, even though federal courts declared an Alabama vagrancy statute and others like it unconstitutional under the Thirteenth Amendment.[111]

Unemployed people were subject to vagrancy laws in all parts of the country. Industrial maturity meant that most people found jobs in the wage-labor market; coupled with the employment-at-will rule, meanwhile, business cycles of increasing severity meant that wage laborers could end up on the street without warning. Northern philanthropists and reformers devised model vagrancy laws to deal with the problem, using the Freedmen's Bureau's approach as a model. Massachusetts enacted the first such law in 1866, and other states followed. Relying on principles of exchange and free contract, these statutes made vagrancy—"having no visible means of support," in the common parlance—a crime punishable by imprisonment and forced labor. The indigent could receive public support, but only in return for labor given in consideration.[112] The United States lagged far behind other industrialized countries in developing a social-welfare system, although pre–New Deal efforts included a pension scheme for Civil War veterans and a number of Progressive-era plans for assisting mothers with children. While these were significant experiments, none of them linked poverty to the labor market even though most poor people, in the *Lochner* era as now, were neither chronically nor constitutionally indigent but rather drifted in and out of employment in response to forces over which they had little control.[113]

Protective schemes for mothers and other working women, indeed, were as much as anything designed to keep them *out* of the labor market; at a minimum, their underlying premise was that women properly belonged in the private sphere and were constitutionally unsuited for the wage-labor market. *Muller v. Oregon* limited the reach of Lochnerian principles over women, but only because protective laws for women guaranteed their primary role as mothers while allowing them to supplement the family wage to a limited extent.[114] Where such laws came too close to core free contract principles, as in *Adkins v. Children's Hospital*, courts did not hesitate to strike them on free contract grounds.[115] Professional women, meanwhile, lost ground as American courts in the 1890s finally adopted the British rules that allowed them to enjoin actresses from working elsewhere for the duration of a breached performance contract.[116] In different ways, then, liberty of contract worked to keep women, the unemployed, and southern farmers beyond the pale of the labor market to which the law deemed them somehow unsuited, whether by virtue of sex, race, or character.

So powerful was the hold of free contract theory over American law in the late nineteenth and early twentieth centuries that it eventually transformed the politics of some of its most ardent opponents. Organized labor, for example, largely abandoned its efforts to secure gains from the legislatures and adopted a "voluntaristic" strategy that stressed direct action to secure through collectively-bargained contracts what it could not through politics.[117] Organizations that maintained a cooperative, republican view of the labor struggle, such as the National Labor Union in the 1870s and the Knights of Labor in the 1880s, spoke to workers as citizens as well as producers when they advocated the nationalization of monopolies, the abolition of private banking, and factory reform.[118] By 1900 these organizations were defunct, crushed by conspiracy prosecutions, the labor injunction, and judicial usurpation of whatever legislative gains they were able to make.[119]

Despairing of its ability to capture the machinery of state, organized labor repudiated its social contract for a kind of laissez-faire outlawry: it abandoned its legislative program, save only a continued effort to limit the power of courts to issue labor injunctions, and concentrated on using whatever raw power it could muster to force employers to make concessions on their own.[120] In New York and California, Samuel Gompers of the American Federation of Labor joined the medical profession and the insurance industry in opposing state-guaranteed health insurance, preferring instead to push for the inclusion of health insurance for union members in collective bargaining agreements.[121] The AFL likewise opposed state-sponsored workers' compensation, preferring equal treatment for labor under a tort law shorn of the employers' defenses, such as was achieved in the Federal Employer's Liability Act.[122] Labor thus took up market ideology, free contract language, and street tactics, in a strategic choice made necessary by its inability to defeat Lochnerism in politics. Where older labor groups interpreted free labor to mean the abolition of the wage labor system, for the AFL free labor meant a remarkably pure version of free, albeit collective, contract.[123]

Turn-of-the-century feminists, likewise, abandoned the republican notions of work and family that had informed their advocacy of joint-property laws in the antebellum period. As Reva Siegel has argued, by 1880 women's advocates had ceased their pursuit of shared ownership in marital assets and no longer emphasized that domestic work was real work that deserved economic reward. Thereafter, they concentrated instead on measures that would enable women to work outside the home, as equals to men in the wage labor market, and to retain their earnings from such work.[124]

The issue of protective labor legislation seriously divided organized women's organizations after the turn of the century. Some demanded that women be allowed to work on the same basis and under the same legal protections as men, while others continued to endorse protection as a shield for women's traditional role in the family. In the course of the struggle over *Adkins v. Children's Hospital*, some feminists came to oppose protective labor laws for women entirely. The women's movement thus split into two wings, neither of which challenged the free contract vision of labor in the way that their predecessors had. One wing, identified with Alice Paul and Charlotte Perkins Gilman, pushed for economic freedom in the marketplace and an equal rights amendment while disparaging the value of domestic labor; the other, identified with Florence Kelley, concentrated on political suffrage, protective legislation, and upholding the value of the traditional family.[125]

A theoretical critique of Lochnerism came from writers in the Progressive and Legal Realist traditions and the significant minority of judges who followed them. Justice Holmes, a leader both as theoretician and as judge, outlined the position in his dissent to *Lochner*. Liberty of contract was no abstract theory derived from objective, common law principles, he wrote; instead, it was a mask behind which courts legislated policy on the basis of "an economic theory which a large part of the country does not entertain."[126] Holmes insisted that it was the job of legislatures, not courts, to "embody their opinions in law."[127] All sorts of laws interfered with liberty of contract in one way or another: reasonable people might think the bakers' law a legitimate health measure, while others might legitimately "uphold it as a first instalment of a general regulation of the hours of work."[128]

Other Progressive-era judges and writers developed Holmes's insight that the free contract principle, by itself, had neither theoretical nor constitutional power to decide cases. Roscoe Pound denounced liberty of contract as a fabrication without foundation in the common law, as a mask that kept judges ignorant of social reality and contemporary social theory, and ultimately as a threat to the courts' continued legitimacy.[129] In 1940 Robert Hale pointed out that the distinction between consent and coercion was an artificial one in any case: all market activity was coercive, he wrote, at a minimum because all contracts are agreed to under each party's threat to take its business elsewhere. Politics, not doctrine, dictated which agreements the law deemed "consensual" and which "coercive."[130] Justice Brandeis said as much in his dissent to *Hitchman Coal & Coke v. Mitchell*, a 1917 labor injunction case: if it was coercive for the union to threaten a strike, it was equally coercive for the employer to withhold employment or threaten to fire workers if they joined the union.[131] The mere fact of coercion gave no clue as to the case's proper legal disposition; what drove the court's ruling was not law but a political preference for the employers.

If unionists and feminists came to accept the basic tenets of free contract, their practical opposition to the liberty-of-contract regime remained powerful nonetheless. Labor conflict grew steadily in scale and intensity through the early 1930s. Women took the lead in translating the Triangle Fire disaster into a comprehensive system of protective labor legislation in New York, the nation's leading industrial state.[132] From within the temple, Progressive judges and legal writers exposed the liberty-of-contract theory's conceptual incoherence.[133] At the peak of its authority, then, the doctrine of *Lochner v. New York* began to collapse under the political attacks of unionists, the theoretical critiques of lawyers, and not least its own weight.

The mature industrial economy of the late nineteenth and early twentieth centuries generated huge imbalances in bargaining power, not only between labor and capital but between farmers and

those who marketed their products and between businesses, large
and small, so much so that free-market capitalism seemed to be on
the verge of destroying itself.[134] Most violently contested, however,
was the division between capital and labor. American courts took
up this struggle with a vengeance, under a free contract ideology
inherited from antebellum legal culture but transformed by Emancipation, the Civil War amendments, and a vision of social compact that made people equal before the law simply because they
possessed formally equal, common law rights to property and contract. This vision, which matured in the constitutional "liberty of
contract" of *Lochner v. New York*, demanded uncompromising defense of the marketplace in which employers and workers came together to make the wage bargain. Here, the courts tolerated no interference with free contract and on principle ignored the growing
inequalities of wealth and power that had by 1905 turned the free
labor idealism of the *Slaughterhouse* dissents into a cruel and
deadly joke.

Principled blindness to inequality in the wage bargain meant
tacit acceptance of oppressive working conditions, both within the
wage-labor relationship and in the private realm outside the labor
market. Political efforts to improve the lot of wageworkers had little impact, except where reformers could describe the beneficiaries
as particularly vulnerable, as in the case of women or men in ex-
ceptionally dangerous jobs such as underground mining. Liberty of
contract did not fully apply to people whom the law viewed as
somehow less than fully competent, such as women, the indigent,
and the freed slaves. The last worked under an imposed contractual
regime, but the formality of labor contracts and credit agreements
did little more than reinstate many of the material conditions of
slavery under a new name. So pervasive was the formalistic liberty-
of-contract ideology and so powerful was its hold over the legal
system at the turn of the century, indeed, that feminists and labor
advocates abandoned their principled opposition to it and, accepting its major premises, sought instead to do the best they could
under the wage-labor system.

If formal equality in the wage bargain was the linchpin of the
Lochnerian regime, the Supreme Court repudiated it in 1937, when
judicial opposition to New Deal efforts to lift the economy out of
the Great Depression brought the nation to a constitutional crisis

not unlike that which it had experienced during the Civil War.[135] Reversing course in the face of Roosevelt's effort to change its composition, the Court disavowed the theory of *Lochner* and *Adkins* and let pass regulatory and labor legislation that it had denounced only the year before. The New Deal also brought labor such key gains as an anti-injunction law, the right to organize and bargain collectively, guarantees against unfair labor practices, and federal arbitration of disputes with employers. In so doing, the New Deal ratified a critique of free contract that Progressives and Legal Realists had been developing since the turn of the century. It did so, however, in such a way as to preserve crucial elements of the free contract ideology and bring them forward, albeit modified, into the latter half of the twentieth century.

≺ III ≻

Collective Bargaining, 1937 to the Present

The New Deal worked a fundamental transformation in the American political economy. Laissez-faire, under which government could do much to promote but little to administer economic activity, gave way to an integrated, mixed capitalism in which regulation and contract, public and private activity blended together thoroughly. First and foremost, New Deal constitutionalism permitted intensive government regulation of private economic activity: common law rights to property and contract no longer stood as constitutional barriers, even to efforts to redress economic inequality. Next, as Justice Stone suggested in *U.S. v. Carolene Products*, the courts would henceforth balance constitutional license for "regulatory legislation affecting ordinary commercial transactions" with intensified judicial protection for Bill of Rights freedoms, political liberties, and "discrete and insular minorities" so as to guarantee the integrity of "those political processes which can ordinarily be expected to bring about the repeal of undesirable legislation."[136] Finally, the New Deal committed the state to providing some level of social insurance, many years after European countries had done so.[137]

Key to the New Deal was the state's accommodation to the labor unions that had grown up in spite of their outlawry under the

Lochnerian regime. Congress passed labor's key legislative demand even before Roosevelt took office: the Norris-LaGuardia Anti-Injunction Act of 1932 limited the power of federal courts to intervene in labor disputes.[138] During Roosevelt's first hundred days, the National Industrial Recovery Act guaranteed unions the right to organize and to bargain collectively "through representatives of their own choosing."[139] At the height of the confrontation between Roosevelt and the Supreme Court, the National Labor Relations Act of 1935 established a federal agency to arbitrate disputes and to ensure the integrity of union organization and collective bargaining.[140] Finally, after the court-packing incident and the Supreme Court's change in course, the Fair Labor Standards Act of 1938 established a minimum wage.[141] The FLSA brought to fruition a half-century's struggle for protective labor legislation, and finally in gender-neutral terms.[142] These reforms accommodated the most militant, well-organized sectors of the labor movement: they brought labor in from the outlawry of the preceding decades and gave it a place in the newly-stabilized political economy.[143]

While the New Deal may have transformed the classical regime, it by no means overthrew its basic principles. Ultimate control over production and investment remained in the hands of employers. Contractual voluntarism remained the organizing principle of capital-labor relations after the New Deal as before. New Deal constitutionalism thus amounted to a translation of freedom of contract into terms more compatible with twentieth-century political economy and legal theory. In practice, though, many of the traditional restraints on workers' power continued to rule the labor market from their graves. The new regime left large sectors of the workforce outside the newly-reconstituted, collective labor market. By the 1980s many of labor's gains had evaporated under the force of economic, technological, and political change, and a new critique of New Deal constitutionalism emerged that, once again, upheld the common law and free contract as fundamental principles of social order.

Congress's authority to premise legislation on inequality between parties to the wage bargain was the focus to which the struggle between Roosevelt and the Supreme Court came in the early 1930s, just as the issue of authority to legislate on slavery in the territories had drawn a broad range of constitutional issues to a focus in the 1850s.[144] In the wake of Roosevelt's court-packing scheme of 1937 and the shift of the Court's two centrist votes to the New Deal's favor, the Supreme Court repudiated several core tenets of the Lochnerian philosophy, chief among which was formal equality in the employment relation. *West Coast Hotel v. Parrish* explicitly overruled *Adkins v. Children's Hospital*, noting at the outset that "the Constitution does not speak of freedom of contract."[145] Contrary to *Adkins*'s description of the minimum wage as forced charity, *West Coast Hotel* affirmed that "the community is not bound to provide (through public relief made necessary by low wages) what is in effect a subsidy for unconscionable employers."[146] With the central pillar of Lochnerism thus overthrown, legislatures secured comprehensive power to allocate "the benefits and burdens of economic life in a manner that secures an average reciprocity of advantage to everyone concerned."[147]

Labor won fundamental guarantees for its rights to organize and bargain collectively, even if *Carolene Products* did not list them among the "preferred freedoms." Congress directly premised the National Labor Relations Act on the "inequality of bargaining power between employees who do not possess full freedom of association nor actual liberty of contract, and employers who are organized in the corporate or other form of ownership association."[148] As Chief Justice Hughes put it, the political freedom of labor unions was "essential to give laborers an opportunity to deal on an equality with their employer."[149] Building on the Realist insight that legal rules constitute markets in ways that have significant distributional consequences, the NLRA shifted power from employers to workers by reconstituting the labor market as a collective one. Collective bargaining became the foundation for American labor law in the post–New Deal period.

As it developed, however, the NLRA lost much of its potential for altering the balance of power in capital-labor relations. By collectivizing and equalizing the labor market, NLRA brought the structure of power inside the employment relation within the range of state intervention. It also meant, however, that labor would have to pursue *its* goals under the supervision of a government agency.[150] The National Labor Relations Board soon came under the control of "industrial pluralists," whose vision of the Act extended only to encouraging bargaining between groups and not to guiding the substance of the bargains themselves. The main goal was to promote productivity, economic growth, and above all industrial peace rather than to promote the rights of labor.[151] In 1947 a Republican Congress passed the Taft-Hartley Act, which narrowed the NLRB's authority, expanded the list of union activities that amounted to "unfair labor practices," and required cooling-off periods before unions could strike in some circumstances.[152] The courts, meanwhile, interpreted the NLRA so as to focus it narrowly on collective bargaining alone, rejecting any claims that it abolished private ordering as the basic framework of workplace governance or that it warranted any state inquiry into either the substantive fairness of the bargains reached or day-to-day management in the workplace.[153]

Labor re-negotiated its social contract during the New Deal. In return for formal recognition of their rights to participate in labor politics, however, the unions once again consented tacitly to the basic structure of capital-labor relations and gave up much of their power to affect the politics of the workplace. NLRB sponsorship both narrowed the range of potential union goals and sharply limited efforts to achieve them outside the formally-recognized negotiating and arbitration processes. Most aspects of working conditions and even the wage bargain itself remained primarily the subject of private—albeit collective—bargaining, and inevitably reflected inequalities in the bargaining power of parties to the contract.[154] In the words of one commentator, the New Deal regime created "a precarious island of due process surrounded by a constantly threatening sea of class power."[155] The New Deal may have collectivized the labor market, but freedom of contract remained the organizing principle of capital-labor relations as before.[156]

The collective bargaining regime worked an enormous benefit to workers in core-sector industries who were well enough organized to gain admission to the newly-reconstituted labor market. A detente of sorts prevailed between management and the unions in these industries, at least until the 1970s: collective bargaining agreements typically ran for three years with wage increases tied to inflation, although generally tied also to increases in worker productivity and premised on mutual commitment to binding arbitration. Retirement pensions, health insurance, job security, and other benefits that the European democracies guaranteed their citizens by statute became incidents to the wage bargain in the United States.[157] This relatively narrow core of union power failed to expand after the early 1950s, however, as unions concentrated on securing economic benefits for their members at the expense of unionization in other sectors.[158] Even while the postwar detente lasted, however, organized labor's power to control the terms of the wage bargain remained sharply limited.

Occasionally the law provided positive guarantees for fair dealing in the labor market; restrictions on child labor are a prominent example. Under pressure from A. Philip Randolph and the Pullman Car Porters' Union, President Roosevelt ordered all defense contractors to guarantee nondiscrimination in hiring in the crucial years before the United States entered World War II.[159] Later, civil rights laws mandated fair treatment of women, minorities, and the disabled in hiring, although these statutes may work more often to protect their beneficiaries from unfair dismissal once they are inside an employment relation than to guarantee equal access to jobs in the first place.[160]

For the most part, freedom of contract remained the norm in employment bargaining, regulatory requirements notwithstanding. The NLRA, so the Supreme Court said in its first review of the statute, "does not interfere with the normal exercise of the right of the employer to select its employees or to discharge them."[161] It might count as an unfair labor practice to fire workers for belonging to a union, but employers remained free to discriminate against union members in hiring if they could.[162] Courts very early interpreted the NLRA to preclude government review of the substantive fairness of employment bargains, as opposed to the process of working them out: the Act, wrote Justice Frankfurter, "leaves the adjustment of industrial relations to the free play of economic forces but seeks to assure that the play of those forces be truly free."[163] Collective bargaining agreements frequently contain no-strike clauses, "management's rights" clauses, and other provisions that waive what rights workers do have under applicable statutes.[164] Organized labor clearly benefited from state recognition and sponsorship, but gave up much of its freedom to act in return.[165]

The law's unwillingness to go beyond guaranteeing the process of collective bargaining to the substantive fairness of the bargains themselves meant that the workplace itself remained largely under the command of employers under the New Deal regime.[166] Collective bargaining law distinguishes between "mandatory" and "permissive" subjects of negotiation. The "permissive subject rule" permits employers to refuse negotiation over issues that are, in Justice Stewart's words, "fundamental to the basic direction of a corporate enterprise" or "which lie at the core of entrepreneurial control."[167] These were left to whatever concessions labor could wrest from business outside the purview of the NLRA. Courts, moreover, can and do refrain from enforcing the terms of valid labor agreements when doing so would limit employers' ability to run their businesses as they wish.[168] Workers remain under a "duty of loyalty" to obey the commands and operational directives of their employers, just as they did in the nineteenth century.[169]

Termination at will remains a powerful weapon in the hands of employers in the United States, even under the New Deal regime.[170] European economies afford a great deal of protection to job security, whether by statute, judicial ruling, or union agreement.[171] Civil rights laws nominally protect some classes of American workers from arbitrary firing, while some states provide tort remedies against wrongful discharge. American employers nonetheless retain a great deal of power to inflict wholesale losses on their workers by eliminating jobs altogether, with or without business reasons for doing so and even in retaliation for efforts to unionize.[172] Courts have consistently upheld the authority of employers to replace striking workers permanently in spite of legislative and administrative efforts to curtail it.[173] Remedies against wrongful discharge have done little to enhance job security in the United States, given the weakness of the unions and structural changes in the economy that have led employers to decrease their workforces, particularly in unionized sectors.[174]

The collective bargaining regime, finally, left intact much of the employer's traditional authority over safety and working conditions.[175] Congress enacted comprehensive schemes for environmental protection and workplace safety in the 1970s, although the agencies charged with administering them remained chronically overburdened and understaffed. Environmental and worker-safety laws drew especially strong opposition from business because they interfered so pervasively with management's control over day-to-day operations.[176] The Occupational Safety and Health Act of 1970 was a particular target.[177] Courts have interpreted the OSHA more conservatively than similarly-structured environmental statutes, reading into the Act a mandate to "balance the need of workers to have a [safe] and healthy work environment against the requirement of industry to function without undue interference."[178] In general, American labor, safety, and environmental regulations all work on businesses from the outside, at arm's length, and not as an integral aspect of business constitution and governance. Constitutional changes since the 1930s have thus left largely intact the presumption that the space inside the employment bargain is a private one, presumptively under the command of the employer and subject to worker control only indirectly, through the wage bargain.[179]

The New Deal reconstituted the wage labor market by allowing those labor organizations that had enough power to do so to cartelize their sectors of it under government sponsorship and supervision. After 1970 the proliferation of international free-trade agreements seriously undercut union membership and power in the core sectors, in effect "hollowing out" the collective bargaining regime from within.[180] Outside the core manufacturing sectors and the heavily regulated industries where unions were most powerful, a great many workers continued to meet employers as formally equal, individual bargainers. In one sense, these workers occupied a newly-delimited private realm, beyond the pale of the New Deal's collectivized labor market. The unorganized—domestic workers, many agricultural workers, immigrants, and disproportionate numbers of women and minorities—remained trapped in a turn-of-the-century free contract regime, increasingly insecure economically and largely unable to avail themselves of the protection of labor law.

Coherent critiques of the collective-bargaining regime established under the New Deal more commonly emerged from the left during the 1930s, when the regime was taking shape, and from the right after 1980, when it began to break down. One alternative, much debated in Congress during the early years of the New Deal, was the Workers' Unemployment and Social Insurance Bill sponsored by Representative Ernest Lundeen of Minnesota with the support of the AFL and a variety of local governments.[181] The Lundeen bill would have set up a federal insurance system guaranteeing a social wage for all workers left unemployed by layoffs, sickness, accident, old age, or maternity. Locally-elected workers' committees were to administer the system on a non-discriminatory basis with money from general government revenues. Part of the strategy behind the bill was to promote union organization by ensuring that no one would have to work at less than union wages: unemployment, social insurance, and industrial democracy were tightly linked goals under the plan.[182]

In place of the Lundeen bill, Congress enacted the NLRA and later the Social Security Act of 1938. NLRA focused, not on encouraging union membership but on guaranteeing the formal rights of established unions to bargain on behalf of their members. Social Security guaranteed not a social wage but individualized pensions funded through payroll deductions and a payroll tax that employers could pass on to consumers as part of their product costs.[183] The legacy of that choice has included, on the one hand, a divided and ultimately weakened union movement; and, on the other, an approach to social insurance that relies primarily on means-tested entitlement programs and eschews generic entitlements to welfare, health insurance, work leave, and the like.[184] In thus focusing on collective bargaining and in making social insurance almost exclusively an incident of employment, the New Deal labor regime preserved an important aspect of the Lochnerian social compact that it ostensibly overthrew. Modern left-wing critiques of New Deal labor law stress more than anything else this continuity with the classical regime and its ongoing commitment to free contract formalism in the labor market, on the one hand, and its tolerance of oppression inside the employment relationship and in work that goes on within households or otherwise outside the formally-constituted labor market, on the other.[185]

Right-wing critiques of New Deal constitutionalism have grown more numerous and articulate since 1980. Generally they echo the laissez-faire, common law formalism of the *Lochner*-era, but with the important difference that they justify liberty of contract, not in *a priori*, natural-rights terms but in pragmatic or consequentialist ones. One variant of the modern conservative critique argues from efficiency: labor cartels misallocate resources like any other market-defeating device. Richard Epstein, for example, has argued in favor of undoing "the mistakes of 1937" and returning to the rules of *Lochner v. New York* and *Adkins v. Children's Hospital*. The bakers' law at issue in *Lochner* was merely an anticompetitive weapon wielded on behalf of one group of bakers against another, with German immigrant workers the losers.[186] The opinion in *West Coast Hotel v. Parrish* failed to explain how workers could be helped by "rules that reduce their opportunities to contract *ex ante*"; Epstein's argument against minimum wage laws is that they represent "an inferior set of social arrangements to those routinely available when freedom of contract was an appropriate constitutional norm."[187]

Efficiency arguments thus capture the common law fundamentalism of the classical era, but they also incorporate the Legal Realist insight that legal rules cannot be correct or incorrect per se. Some external value, moral or instrumental, must justify the choice of one over another. For many conservatives, allocative efficiency is the most objective, apolitical such value available. One interesting variant of this argument holds that liberty of contract sometimes worked to the *advantage* of disenfranchised workers who suffered from discrimination by powerful but racist labor unions. Judicial cooperation with New Deal labor policies merely acquiesced in the cartelization of the labor market by union monopolists. One of the legacies of the New Deal, then, comes to us in the form of persistently high unemployment among African Americans and the emergence of a marginalized "underclass" of urban minority workers.[188]

Another variant of the neoclassical critique of New Deal labor law stresses the libertarian functions of common law formalism. For Epstein, one of the "mistakes of 1937" was to discard the Founders' commitment to "entrench individual rights against all levels of the state,"

not because we believe the rights are natural, but because we know that if usable property rights aren't made definite and permanent, then political actors will have far more power over the fortunes of citizens than is necessary for the maintenance of public order.[189]

The competing arguments about "forced charity" in *Adkins* and "subsidies to unconscionable employers" in *West Coast Hotel* were "misplaced," according to Epstein. Under liberty of contract, owners of labor and owners of capital engaged in "mutually advantageous" wage bargains: *West Coast Hotel* offered no coherent reason why the common law "baseline" was inappropriate. Minimum wage laws thus hamper both utility and liberty, and Epstein could find "no intellectual or practical reason" why the case "should not be overruled, even today."[190]

Freedom of contract thus remained a powerful norm in the late twentieth-century United States, in spite of the New Deal's effort to loosen the doctrine's stranglehold over the legal system. In the end, the New Deal accommodated critical elements of the Progressive attack on Lochnerism, chief among them being Holmes's insistence that no constitutional principle prevented legislatures from recognizing real inequality between parties to the wage bargain. New Deal legislation overcame 50 years of judicial resistance to enable labor unions to organize and to bargain collectively with employers. By accommodating labor within a regulated collective bargaining regime, the New Deal arguably saved American capitalism from collapse. It also preserved voluntaristic, contractual private ordering as the organizing principle of labor relations, thus leaving employer prerogative over production itself more or less intact.

The long-term result was that New Deal labor law ultimately preserved much of the inequality that pervaded the labor market since antebellum judges incorporated elements of the traditional master-servant relation into the emerging, contractarian law of labor relations. This was particularly true outside those sectors of the economy where union organization was strongest, although even in their core sectors the unions failed to stave off technological and structural changes that undermined their postwar detente with capital. The workplace itself remained fundamentally the property of employers and firmly under their command, massive bodies of civil rights, safety, and environmental law notwithstanding. A large and growing share of workers remained unenfranchised in the collective bargaining regime, while social insurance provisions for those unable to work remained inextricably linked to the employment relation and thus far less adequate to the task of maintaining a social wage than are welfare schemes in other industrialized countries. By the 1980s critics from both the left and the right increasingly found fault with the New Deal legacy: the left because it preserved too much of the Lochnerian tradition, the right because it had foolishly cast too much of Lochnerism aside.

≺ IV ≻

Conclusion

In the end, rumors of free contract's demise appear to have been somewhat exaggerated. P. S. Atiyah wrote in 1979 of the "decline of free choice and consent" in English law over the previous hundred years.[191] Grant Gilmore understood what he called "the decline and fall of the general theory of contract and, in most quarters, of laissez-faire economics" as reflections of the transition from nineteenth-century individualism to an age in which "we are all cogs in a machine, each dependent on the other."[192] Yet, as Lawrence Friedman noted, freedom to make choices, particularly in one's working life, has remained a powerful value in Anglo-American legal culture since Locke first articulated it in political-philosophical terms at the end of the seventeenth century. Life in an advanced, interdependent industrial economy is by no means incompatible with self-determination, nor is life under the regulatory-welfare state that such an economy makes necessary. In fact, insofar as technology, wealth, and socioeconomic development extend the range of choices available to individuals, Friedman argued that "individualism is not only not dead, but in fact much more vital and alive than it was in the nineteenth-century heyday of 'freedom of contract.'"[193] Classical-era liberals may have grounded an entire jurisprudence on common law rights to property and contract but, as Justice Holmes observed in his *Lochner* dissent, the Constitution did not bind Congress or the state legislatures to that jurisprudence for all time.

To be sure, the meaning of choice and consent has changed over time, both in response to changes in the material environments in which people make their livings and, withal, to the free contract doctrine's own developing logic. In the early nineteenth century American lawmakers reshaped what in Locke's and Jefferson's hands had been primarily a notion of political philosophy into one of economics and exchange—the free labor principle—the better both to explain and to channel the powerful currents of progress that were carrying the nation forward at the time. Having conquered slavery in the name of free labor and written free contract principles into the Constitution so as to make real the promise of universal emancipation, late nineteenth-century ideologues re-

formed freedom of contract again, this time into a shield to protect
the nation's core principles from what they honestly believed were
threats of socialism and class warfare. As the Lochnerian fiction of
common law equality increasingly became not only transparent
but self-defeating as well, those who eventually created the New
Deal argued for a new understanding of choice and consent; one
that captured the reality of life in the twentieth century better than
the now-empty formalisms of classical liberalism.

Crucial aspects of the free contract doctrine persisted over time,
however. One was the fact that the wage bargain remained the instrument of social contract between capital, labor, and the state. In
Lockean terms, whether articulated individually or collectively, it
transmitted labor's "tacit consent" to the basic structure of power
relations in the workplace. This is why it was "somehow special,"
as McCurdy put it, not only to the formalist judges of the "liberty
of contract" period but to antebellum judges like Lemuel Shaw and
to the New Deal collective bargaining regime.[194] Throughout, the
employment bargain served both as the measure of legal equality in
the labor market and as the foundation of real inequality inside the
workplace and in the "private" realm beyond the reach of labor
law.

On the other hand, freedom of contract has throughout its history also entailed an ideological commitment to genuine self-
determination, no matter who claimed authority to interpret it or
to what ends they did so. Because the idea has so much power in
Western culture, free contract has had a limited shelf life in the
possession of any particular faction. However the law articulated
it, the doctrine simultaneously sanctioned and challenged the hierarchy of real power in American labor relations. Ultimately, as
Friedman noted, free choice remains a fundamental value in
American culture, though its meaning has changed over time with
the repeated confrontation between changing material reality and
contemporary understanding of the legal culture's ground norms.

A third ongoing characteristic of free contract in labor relations
has been that at different times in its history lawmakers have used
the doctrine to divide the world of work into the three social
spaces discussed at the beginning of this chapter. These include a
public realm—the labor market—in which workers and employers
meet to forge productive relationships; here, the law has consis-

tently maintained its strongest commitment to voluntarism, whether lawmakers understood the concept in free labor, common law formalist, or collectivist terms. Once consented to, whatever the degree of coercion behind the consent, the employment relation creates a second space inside the first—the workplace—in which the law translates real inequalities in the wage bargain into varying degrees of real subordination in the performance of the work itself. Outside the legally-constituted labor market, finally, is a "private" realm of families, slave plantations, and other productive organizations in which the law perceives hierarchy to be so essential to the natural order of things that it hardly conceives the work that goes on there—by mothers, children, or chattel slaves—as constituting "labor" in any meaningful sense at all. Boundaries between these spaces have shifted over time, especially when social change and the logic of voluntarism combine to make the inequalities that configure them seem unjust, unnecessary, and eventually intolerable.

The final persistent feature in the history of free contract is the dynamic, creative tension that inheres in the notion itself. This tension is, on the one hand, intrinsic or conceptual: it embodies the contradiction between consent and coercion that necessarily inheres in the social life of any individual. People work voluntarily because it fulfills them at some level, but also because they must do so in order to feed themselves and those who depend on them. The tension is also historical: agreements that appear consensual enough in one context may appear more or less coerced in the future, particularly as the circumstances surrounding the original agreement change over time. Working relationships that seem immutable, traditional, or merely useful in one context may come to seem arbitrary and exploitative in the light of social, economic, or cultural development. That work is both transformative in capitalist economies and the central aspect of public life in capitalist societies is likely the main reason for its historical force in driving development of the free contract ideology.

Natural Resources and Economic Liberty in American History

DONALD J. PISANI

THE HISTORY OF THE United States is, in large part, the product of individual freedom and autonomy acting upon abundant natural resources within a decentralized nation of vast size. Land, water, forests, minerals, and wildlife served as incipient capital; ingenuity and labor transformed them into valuable commodities. Freedom of contract facilitated that process. By making economic risks as predictable as possible, it encouraged individual self-interest to shape the market. In the nineteenth century, economic actors bought, sold, and traded with few constraints; freedom of contract placed most bargaining beyond the purview of government. Powerful forces of localism—such as the absence of a hereditary aristocracy, national church, civil service, ideological political parties, and a large standing army—encouraged individual acquisitiveness. Capitalism suffered few constraints, but the state was far from passive. Government at all levels played a vital role in privatizing the commons. Nevertheless, until the twentieth century, it did little to preserve or to conserve natural resources, or to regulate their use. And until the 1960s, few Americans considered nature's value beyond its ability to generate new wealth.

Freedom of contract was more than a legal construct. It was a set of ideals and values that permeated American society and included a pervasive faith in economic liberty. This chapter is more concerned with public policies than with case law, legal doctrines, or abstract concepts of property. It focuses mainly on the public domain and on the national government rather than the states. Natural resource policies defined "Americanism." They were part of a continuing revolt against Europe; a revolt against class, privilege, and elitism; and against remote, arbitrary, overgrown governments.

The American preoccupation with economic freedom owed much to English law and political theory. Chapter 1 reminds us that modern English property law, including "fee simple" ownership, was fully formed by the American Revolution. The law can be "dynamic" even in an agricultural society; in England, it responded to the enclosure movement and the desire to consolidate small, inefficient farms. Limitations on the transfer of property, including various forms of entail, did not constrain the market for land. Nevertheless, the *motives* for buying and selling land were not as powerful in England as they would become in the United States. Put simply, where political power and social standing depended on the possession of land, there were more reasons to retain it than to sell it.

In the United States, the distribution of property had more to do with getting ahead than with social status, and William Blackstone's concept of property as "despotic dominion" better applied there than in England. Still, we should not forget that economic freedom was not unlimited. Economic growth depended on an active state, and Americans wrestled with the same dilemma as the English: how to balance the rights of the individual against the needs of the community. Chapter 5 discusses the legal order's attempts to reconcile vested rights with equal opportunity, and to protect established wealth at the same time it encouraged the creation of new wealth. My story touches upon the same themes, especially the tension between freedom of contract and government regulation. Rooted in the events of the middle and late eighteenth century, the Jeffersonian, anti-feudal vision of America exhibited great resilience and persistence. In a modified form, it has survived into the 1990s. My discussion comes full circle—from the Jeffersonian vision of property as independence to the neo-conservative "property rights" campaign of the 1980s and 1990s.

≺ I ≻

Land and Liberty

In the middle of the eighteenth century, dangerous strains appeared in the English colonies of North America. These included an enormous increase in population and in the number of poor in eastern cities; transients who wandered from village to village and job to job; soaring land prices; huge land grants to proprietors; widespread speculation; and an increasing number of adult males who held no land and had dim prospects of acquiring any. By the Revolution, between one-third and one-half of adult white males in western Pennsylvania, Kentucky, and parts of Massachusetts were landless. In many places farms were too small to provide a subsistence. The land shortage touched off one of the largest migrations in the colonial period as residents of Massachusetts and Connecticut moved into northern Maine, New Hampshire, Vermont, Nova Scotia, the Susquehanna and Wyoming valleys of Pennsylvania, and even West Florida. Between 1760 and 1776, 164 new towns were established in northern New England. By the end of the eighteenth century, 40 percent of the population of the United States lived in counties that had had little or no population in 1760. The frontier grew four or five times faster than the seaboard.[1]

The American Revolution was fought, in part, to insure access to land. American settlers believed that they had a sacred right and responsibility to tame the wilderness. God had given the earth to human beings in common, their religion taught them, and they did not need John Locke to remind them that labor gave land most of its value. Land taken from England on the field of battle belonged to Americans in common, and the Revolution had been fought for natural rights to life, liberty, and property.[2] As Thomas Jefferson put it in a 1785 letter to James Madison:

Whenever there is in any country uncultivated lands and unemployed poor, it is clear that the laws of property have been so far extended as to violate natural right. The earth is given as a common stock for man to labour and live on. If for the encouragement of industry we allow it to be appropriated, we must take care that other employment be furnished to those excluded from that appropriation. If we do not the fundamental right to labour the earth returns to the unemployed. It is too soon yet in our country to say that every man who cannot find employment but who can find uncultivated land, shall be at liberty to cultivate it, paying a moderate rent. But it is not too soon to provide by every possible means that as few as possible shall be without a little portion of the land. The small landholders are the most precious part of the state.[3]

In 1784–85, Congress debated how to populate the surplus land secured from England. Federalists considered taming the frontier as a dangerous phase in the economic development of the nation. Too many frontier farmers were indolent, satisfied with a subsistence economy that represented a step back from the market-oriented agriculture of the seaboard. In the eyes of the Federalists, the first white settlers were "savage" in appearance and disposition. They incited the Indians to violence and frightened away sober, industrious, responsible farmers. "The lawless West released the selfish impulses held in check in the 'civilized' East," historian Peter Onuf has remarked, "thus representing the negation of republican liberty." The goal of the American Revolution was to blend private and public interests by organizing law-abiding settlers into compact settlements that would transform individual acquisitiveness into a social good.[4]

The Federalists won the debate of 1784–85. Congress decided that Ohio's population should be concentrated rather than scattered and that public land should sell for as much as possible to retire the national debt as rapidly as possible. The federal government would survey land *before* opening it to settlers, and settlement would be orderly rather than pell-mell. As soon as seven ranges of townships had been surveyed—each range was about 50 miles square—that land would be thrown on the market for the minimum price of one dollar an acre. Settlers concentrated in compact communities would find it easier to govern themselves, to create commercial and transportation ties with the East, and to develop a sense of allegiance to the national government. In 1785, the first seven ranges were surveyed and Fort Harmar was established to provide military protection to the surveyors and to the Indians. To encourage prosperous farmers to buy land and to discourage impoverished and improvident frontiersmen from moving west, Congress purposely located the first land offices in the East, rather than on the frontier.[5]

In the Ohio Country, squatters rendered the best-laid plans of Congress moot, as they would on subsequent frontiers of the United States. Claiming a God-given right to enter vacant land and to tame the wilderness, they also invoked powerful legal principles to justify their actions. "I do certify that all mankind, agreeable to every constitution formed in America, have an undoubted right to pass into every vacant country," one squatter proclaimed in 1785, "and there to form their constitution, and that . . . Congress is not empowered to forbid, neither is Congress empowered . . . to make any sale of the uninhabited lands to pay the public debts."⁶ In 1786, the colonel in charge of military forces in the Ohio Country reported that trespassers on public land north of the river were, in his words, "averse to federal measures," and eager "to throw every obstacle in the way to impede the surveying of the Western territory, agreeably to the ordinance of Congress." Repeated attempts to evict the trespassers were unsuccessful. On one occasion, 100 soldiers burned the cabins and crops of 30 settlers near present-day Steubenville. The squatters used flatboats to ferry themselves and their possessions across the river into Virginia, but quickly returned once the soldiers had left. National land laws would be made on the ground, not in Washington.⁷

The first federal land auction, held in 1787, resulted in the sale of only 73,000 acres and the return of a scant $117,000 to the financially-strapped central government. Many members of Congress now believed that the government could raise more money by selling land in large blocks to land companies. Private enterprise, they reasoned, would speed up the process of settlement by offering land on credit and providing improvements such as roads, towns, and mills.⁸ Subsequently, Congress sold 1.5 million acres to the Ohio company, which established the region's first major settlement at Marietta in April 1788. In the years from 1787 to 1795, several other companies also acquired more than one million acres apiece in the Ohio Country.⁹

Frontier families favored a Jeffersonian society characterized by small-scale agriculture, community autonomy, and equal opportunity—including for those who lacked capital. The promoters of land companies, on the other hand, valued order, civic responsibility, intensive agriculture, and commerce above liberty and independence. In the words of the historian Andrew Cayton, investors in the Ohio Company

wanted to fully integrate the Ohio Country into the Atlantic cultural and commercial community. Unlike the squatters, they sought interdependence not independence, urban as much as agrarian development, manufactures as well as farms, social stratification instead of egalitarianism—all overseen by a firm national authority and secured by institutions like churches and schools. And they expected the gradual coordinated expansion of an urban, commercial society to bring to the frontier not just trade and cities, but glorious achievements in art, architecture, literature, science, and gentility. The howling American wilderness would become the heart of a great empire, the apex of Atlantic civilization. The key to the success of this western vision was the easy exchange of goods, ideas, and people between London and Pittsburgh, Boston and Cincinnati.

The Ohio Company established Marietta in the hope that it would be the first of many western cities to unify agriculture and commerce, binding both farm and city to the Atlantic economy. "Americans would not regress into the disorganization, laziness, selfishness, and parochialism so often associated with the frontier," Cayton has written, "but would progress across space and time into a world of commerce and manufactures, canals and cities, science and order, blending interests in national harmony." The Ohio country would become "the garden of the universe."[10]

Yet private companies had no better luck creating a stable frontier society than the national government had. Prosperous eastern farmers refused to move to Ohio, and those already there were strapped for cash; soldiers' scrip and ginseng were Marietta's most common forms of currency in 1789. The cost of surveys, taxes, and other expenses imposed a substantial burden on the land companies, and land buyers demanded credit over an extended period. To make matters worse, many settlers preferred to take up land in Ohio's Virginia Military District and, after 1800—when Congress adopted its own credit policy and opened four land offices in the Ohio country—from the federal government. Planned settlement was not popular on the frontier, where freedom meant access to land for yourself and your children, the right to use it as one saw fit, and the privilege of buying and selling for speculative profit.[11]

In the early nineteenth century, land policies were driven by the relentless pressure of population on the frontier and intense competition between the states and federal government. Kentucky's population tripled between 1790 and 1800, then doubled again in the first decade of the nineteenth century. Ohio's population increased thirteenfold between 1800 and 1820. Six new states entered the Union in the six years following the end of the War of 1812 as settlers poured over the Appalachian Mountains to Indiana (1816), Mississippi (1817), Illinois (1818), Alabama (1819), Maine (1820), and Missouri (1821). From the creation of the American nation to the end of the 1830s, 4.5 million people crossed the mountains—more than the entire population of the United States in 1789. Ten new states entered the Union during that period. The population increase averaged an astounding 35 percent per decade in the years from 1790 to 1860, as the nation expanded from 3.9 to 31.4 million. By 1820, the "western" states held one-third of the seats in the United States Senate.[12]

The states that owned surplus land in the West relinquished most of it to the central government, but that process took more than a decade—from 1791 to 1802. Meanwhile, they flooded the market. Virginia and Connecticut retained large tracts in Ohio and Kentucky. North Carolina ceded its holding in present-day Tennessee, but only after most of it had passed into private ownership. Moreover, Massachusetts, New York, and Georgia included vast tracts of vacant land when their borders were redrawn.[13]

By the beginning of the nineteenth century, most state land had passed into private ownership and the public domain began to sell. Pressure from the frontier reduced the minimum amount of land that could be purchased along with the price. An 1800 land law permitted minimum sales of 320 acres at $2 an acre with four years to pay. The credit system proved to be a disaster. Many defaulted on their payments, forcing Congress to enact twelve relief measures; the law was abolished in 1820. Nevertheless, in that year the minimum parcel was reduced to 80 acres and the price to $1.25 an acre.[14] An average 350,000 acres of public lands passed into private ownership each year during the first decade of the nineteenth century. The War of 1812 weakened the Indians' hold on the West and eliminated the British entirely. Land sales peaked in the 1830s, when the government auctioned off nearly 43 million acres.[15]

Nineteenth-century federal land policy rested on a series of interlocking economic assumptions and values. The central government was never expected to serve as a landlord—for example, by leasing its own grazing lands—nor was it expected to profit from the public lands by cutting and selling timber or digging up its mineral wealth. The paramount goal of American land policy was the creation of a middle-class society, a class of independent freeholders which would serve as the bulwark of the republic. A large dependent laboring class stifled civic virtue and laid the foundation for despotism.[16] Therefore, agriculture should take precedence over all other activities on the public domain. Forests should be cleared for farms rather than maintained as a permanent supply of lumber. Swamps and overflowed areas should be drained and cultivated even if the supply of fish and game suffered. The new states wanted to build their tax base as quickly as possible. Rapid growth was more likely than slow growth to create towns, factories, and commerce. And the capital needed to buy land could be raised only if lenders believed that the land could be readily and rapidly resold.

The central government never drafted an economic plan for western development. Nevertheless, it granted the states large amounts of land to encourage the drainage of swamps and the construction of schools, roads, and canals—without exercising any control over how those lands would be used.[17] It deeded over 150 million acres to the states—an expanse of land about one and one-half times the size of California—to encourage railroad construction alone.[18]

The triumph of the principle of preemption in the 1830s and the adoption of the Homestead Act in 1862 demonstrated once again that land policy was made in the West.[19] By 1880 settlers or speculators could parlay a homestead, preemption, and timber-culture claim into an estate of 480 acres—far more land than the average settler could cultivate, especially if that land required irrigation. (By purchasing railroad land, even larger estates were possible.) Federal land laws were inconsistent and worked at cross purposes. For example, the Timber Culture Act of 1873 granted millions of acres to farmers in such states as Iowa, Kansas, Nebraska, and Minnesota as an incentive to plant trees, while other laws encouraged the destruction of forests to prepare land for cultivation. For decades after Congress passed the Homestead Act, the United States continued to sell land at auction, which reduced both the amount and the quality of available "free" land.[20]

From 1870 to 1890, over 430 million acres passed from public to private hands, more than in all of American history prior to 1870. The last great land rush occurred on the northern Great Plains in Montana and the Dakotas, where over 50 million acres were taken from 1900 to 1917. By World War II, the nation had disposed of more than one billion acres. Of that amount, 419 million acres were purchased, 285 million acres were homesteaded, and 94 million acres were given directly to the railroads by the central government; and the states received over 230 million acres to aid education and to construct railroads, canals, and wagon roads.[21]

The consequences of this giveaway were enormous. Land policies were partly responsible for a population that doubled every 25 years by natural increase. Americans married relatively early—four to five years younger than people in Europe—and bore more children. In 1800, only 5 percent of the population lived in cities, and Americans were far less urbanized than Europeans. And while the Constitution created federalism, it was the nation's vast size and the fact that land and other resources were dispensed with no strings attached that permitted state and local governments to become relatively autonomous.[22]

There was also a dark side to the story. Cheap or free land encouraged settlers to claim far more than they could use and attracted poor farmers who had little chance of success. On the frontier, fluctuating prices reduced the value of land as collateral for bank loans; therefore, it was difficult to raise money at reasonable rates of interest. Farmers grew crops that required a minimum of labor and capital, mining the land and moving on instead of practicing soil conservation. The abundance of land encouraged litigation because settlement preceded survey. It isolated people, forcing them to live at a subsistence level for lack of markets and transportation. It deprived them of churches and schools, reduced social interaction, and divided their communities. It drove up the cost of roads and schools because random, scattered settlement did not provide an adequate tax base. It contributed to a proliferation of land offices, colleges, county seats, and other expensive institutions, often to serve a very sparse population. It nullified the national Indian policy because preemption encouraged white settlers to invade Indian land before formal cession treaties could be negotiated. It contributed to deep sectional divisions in Congress between East and West, as well as North and South.

In the 1780s, the Federalists had dreamed of using the public domain to create a planned economy and compact settlements, a stable society that valued civic virtue above frontier individualism. But Congress had little control over those who settled the frontier—men and women who resented any limitations on their acquisition, use, and disposal of property. Little wonder that Congress and the states disposed of other natural resources with similar disregard for their real or potential value. For example, originally the doctrine of riparian rights reserved the use of water to those who lived along a stream. Riparian rights were correlative; no

one could use the water to the exclusion or injury of another riparian owner. Industrialization introduced the concept of "prior appropriation"—or first in time, first in right. Those who built the
first factories dammed streams with the legal assurance that they
could use the water to drive looms and spindles. Chronological priority protected them from the ambitions of those who built mills
later, as they were protected from the extortionate damage claims
of those whose land was flooded.[23] But the greatest change came in
the far West, where federal inaction permitted the states to grant
water not just to the first person to put it to productive use, but to
people who diverted the water far from the living channel—even to
those who dried up the stream. In the West, Anglo-American law
displaced Mexican laws that had a very different objective from the
production of new wealth.[24]

The California Gold Rush made water far more valuable. Initially, most miners worked placer deposits adjoining streams, and
they worked for themselves rather than for private mining companies. The water needed to exploit a claim, they reasoned, should be
part and parcel of that claim—not a separate commodity. If water
could be bought and sold independently from the act of mining,
then outside capital would soon monopolize the water supply of
entire mining districts—and exclude independent operators. By the
mid-1850s, however, the gold adjoining streams had been ex-
hausted. Hydraulic mining companies began searching for gold in
ancient streambeds far removed from existing watercourses. They
could attract investors only if they had a reliable water supply.
They demanded, and got, absolute rights based on chronological
priority. In California and other mining districts in the West, the
scale of mining demanded that prior appropriation replace riparian
rights.[25]

It is a myth that prior appropriation triumphed in the American
West because that system of allocating water was the most efficient, just, or equitable. Inevitably, it spread from mining to agriculture and became as popular with land speculators as with mining companies. Nothing did more to drive up the value of agricultural land than supplying it with water, as the citrus orchards of
southern California—carved out of grazing land once considered
relatively worthless—demonstrated in the 1870s and after. In addition, prior appropriation did not require a large state bureaucracy to

administer. Its eventual cost would be enormous, but apportioning water by chronology was so simple that the record of claims could be maintained by existing county recorders.[26]

By the end of the nineteenth century, the weaknesses of prior appropriation were all too apparent. Twenty-five times more water had been claimed from the Salt River than its average annual flow, and the San Joaquin River had been claimed 172 times over. The law encouraged farmers to waste water rather than to save it. Throughout the West legal conflicts erupted between junior (later in time) and senior appropriators. It did not matter that a junior appropriator worked better land, raised higher value crops, or used the water for a purpose that created greater wealth. Junior users were generally restricted to the heavy spring runoff when the snow melted, and their water supply disappeared in the early summer. Weaknesses in water law, not an absolute shortage of water, led to the crusade to build storage reservoirs in the West beginning in the last decades of the nineteenth century. The construction of reservoirs by-passed the need to reform the system of water rights by augmenting the existing supply rather than reallocating it. The courts rarely questioned a "beneficial use," and since most western states lacked state engineering offices in 1900, judges relied almost entirely on testimony from interested witnesses. Claimants received the benefit of the doubt. During the 1880s, for example, Colorado water decrees promised as much as five times the water ditches were capable of carrying.[27]

The doctrine of prior appropriation had profound consequences for the American West. The national government became a pathetic giant. It spent huge sums to erect such dams as Hoover, Shasta, and Grand Coulee, but remained the prisoner of powerful local interests.[28] In interstate water cases, the Department of Justice argued that the federal government possessed inchoate rights to interstate streams, if not to all the *surplus* water in western rivers. But the Supreme Court consistently upheld state administrative control over water, and the federal government filed for rights under state law like any other water user—in the name of individuals rather than particular federal agencies or the central government.[29] Even when the high court recognized a "timeless" right outside state law—as it did in 1908 by acknowledging a special Indian water right to irrigate reservation and allotted land—Congress and the states blocked the implementation of that right.[30]

By the Civil War, water had been separated from the public domain in large parts of the American West; entrepreneurial imperatives transformed it into a separate species of property that could be bought, sold, and transported long distances from its natural channel. Because the public lands had never been classified, however, the law failed to distinguish between land whose primary potential use was to produce crops, and land that would produce grass, or minerals, or timber. Settlers did that themselves. Except for small tracts that produced oak for naval vessels, until 1878 timberland was treated the same as agricultural land. It could be acquired by auction, under the Homestead Act, under the Preemption Act of 1841, and with bounty warrants or agricultural college scrip.[31]

As settlers streamed onto the relatively treeless Great Plains in the 1850s and after, the nation came to realize that the forests of the public domain were not inexhaustible. Still, little was done to protect them, and opposition to federal regulation underscored the continuing American hostility to "feudalism." White Americans cast land law and policy as a stark choice between freedom and bondage, individualism and aristocracy. History offered an extended lesson in the dangers of land monopolies—from Rome, to medieval Europe, to eighteenth- and nineteenth-century Ireland, to the nations of South and Central America. Debates over land policy, the historian Mary Young has pointed out, were haunted by "the ghosts of monarchy, aristocracy, and feudalism."[32] The public domain came to be seen as the wellspring of American uniqueness; widespread landownership became essential to the experiment in liberty and balanced government. Without an abundance of readily accessible land, the United States would become a nation of landlords and tenants, rich and poor. It would come to exhibit the same poverty and class divisions as Europe. That was the troubling implication of Frederick Jackson Turner's famous essay, "The Significance of the Frontier in American History," delivered at the Chicago meeting of the American Historical Association in 1893. Could the United States survive as a democratic nation without an expanse of free or cheap land? In its absence, the family farm would wither and die, and the manufacturing corporation would exert absolute dominion over its workers.[33]

By the end of the nineteenth century, social critics warned that the United States was becoming a nation of tenants. In 1886, one writer observed: "Everywhere, amongst all nations, so records of the past seem to testify, there has been exhibited the same tendency to slow aggregation of estates in land; then to the acquisition of privileges; and, with accelerated velocity, to the movement of all wealth and all power into the hands of a few; and, finally, to the inevitable catastrophe of blood-shed and social confusion." Such was the law of history, if not of human society. In 1892, another student of American land policy warned that "the child is now living who will perhaps see in the fertile portions of the United States a population almost equal in density to that of England or France. Our statesmen can find no greater field than this for the exercise of statesmanship."[34]

≺ II ≻

Conservation and Reservation

The federal government and the nation's legal system worked hard to transform nature into marketable property, but there were many forces that limited the acquisitive impulses unleashed by American capitalism. Property rights were never absolute, and the law attempted to serve a "common good," not just individual rights. As Harry Scheiber has noted, the power of government has not simply been "a residuum—what is left over, in effect, after vested rights and constitutional limits on state action have been accounted for."[35]

While it differed from time to time and place to place, many Americans shared a common vision of material progress. The construction of bridges, turnpikes, canals, and railroads required the confiscation of private property through eminent domain and taxation. Without eminent domain, indirect damages would require compensation, and benefits to property not taken—the increase in value resulting from public works—could not be deducted from the value of the condemned property. By the end of the nineteenth century, the definition of "public interest"—and the justification for

using the police power of the state to benefit private companies—
expanded to include many businesses not directly involved in
transportation, including mining and irrigation companies.[36]

Some legal scholars argue that there was also property "affected
with a public interest." Navigable streams, fisheries, harbors, sea-
shores, and highways could not be converted into private property.
They had to be used for the common good and kept open to the
public. In the late nineteenth and early twentieth centuries, this
"public trust doctrine" expanded at the state and local level to include municipal water and sewage systems. At the national level,
it embraced inalienable federal land ranging from bird and wildlife
refuges to national parks. After World War II, the courts stretched
the definition to cover recreational land.[37]

The conservation movement that began in the late nineteenth
century split land, timber, minerals, and wildlife apart. It was the
first major limitation on the use of public resources; and in some
cases, notably soil conservation and fire protection, it extended to
private land. Conservation resulted from many inconsistent impulses. Some conservationists rejected the materialism of late nineteenth-century America and sought to perpetuate the values of a
pre-industrial, rural, agricultural America by leaving the West as
Nature's museum. Others feared that the United States was running out of vital natural resources. These included specialists in
such new sciences as hydrology and silviculture, who supported
conservation as the "gospel of efficiency," to use historian Samuel
P. Hays's apt phrase. A third group, composed of westerners, hoped
that greater national control over natural resources would stimulate an economic revival in the wake of the devastating depression
of the 1890s. Finally, some nominal friends of conservation expected that an increase in federal regulatory power would protect
their privileged access to natural resources and exclude their competitors.[38]

The meaning of land ownership changed from the end of the
Civil War to World War I.[39] The labor theory of value—the creature
of an agrarian society—made less sense in an economy dominated
by cities, corporations, giant factories, and elaborate transportation
systems. After the Civil War, the public domain remained an important part of the business of Congress, but new issues related to
industry, immigration, trade, money, and banking commanded

more and more attention. For adult white males, the franchise had
became almost universal, breaking the link between land and liberty. As time passed, the definition of opportunity changed from a
freehold to a good education and job. By 1920 the city became the
symbol of opportunity and, increasingly, the small farm represented backbreaking labor, isolation, loneliness, and a bare subsistence. Improvement in the conditions of many factory workers during the first decades of the twentieth century allowed them to
make higher salaries and enjoy a more comfortable life than most
small farmers.

In 1890, virtually the entire public domain was open to entry;
by 1940 it was closed. In 1950, the federal government still owned
and managed nearly one in four acres within the United States.
That land had been withdrawn from entry after 1891, when Congress gave the president the power to designate national forests. In
little more than half a century, 180 million acres were set aside as
national forests—19 million from the purchase of private lands in
the eastern half of the nation. An additional 14 million acres became national parks and monuments; 10 million acres were reserved for government use, such as military posts and gunnery
ranges; and Indian reservations covered an additional 55 million
acres. Theodore Roosevelt protected nearly 200,000,000 acres as
national forests, potential hydroelectric power sites, mineral lands,
parks, monuments, and bird and wildlife refuges.[40] Franklin D.
Roosevelt put the rest of the public domain—an additional
200,000,000 acres—off limits in 1934. In one of the most abrupt
public policy changes in American history, disposal gave way to
protection—though not before the nation's best farmland had been
taken.[41]

Conservation administered the "wise use" of natural resources;
it did not place those resources in cold storage. The break with the
nineteenth century was more apparent than real, and even the
creation of national parks was ambiguous. As Joseph Sax has written, "If the government had a plan for the parks it was establishing,
it was certainly casual about it. No bureau existed to manage these
places until 1916, forty-four years after the Yellowstone reservation
[in 1872]. Yellowstone, in fact, was run by the United States Cav-
alry, and the others were pretty much left to themselves and to a
few hardy innkeepers and adventurous tourists."[42]

If the conservation movement represents to some extent the expansion of regulatory authority and the attempts of the regulated to regulate the regulators, the park system was something quite different. Because each park was independent and poorly funded until 1916, it is likely that many in Congress expected that land devoted to recreation would be administered by state or local authorities, not the federal government.[43] Congress designated these largely inaccessible parks only after determining that they were worthless for farming, mining, stock raising, and other commercial purposes. It was slow to provide the money needed to administer or improve them. It dawdled for more than a decade before approving a superintendent and paid staff for Yellowstone. Private companies provided roads, hotels, restaurants, camping facilities, and tours. These companies also protected some of the sights, in exchange for the right to charge tourists for the privilege of seeing them. From 1886 to 1916, Congress cut expenses by using the United States Army to protect and administer the parks.[44]

Wildlife conservation was another new concern. It arose not just because of urbanization, the romanticization of the passing frontier, the destruction of buffalo and other big game, and the desire to manage nature. With the help of the refrigerated railroad car, domestic animals displaced wild game in the diet of most Americans during the late nineteenth century. Simultaneously, cheap factory-made textiles reduced the demand for hides and furs. By 1900, the age of the commercial hunter was over.

Until well into the twentieth century, limitations on hunting and fishing fell entirely within the police powers of the states. American law followed a policy of free taking; no title to land conferred ownership of the wildlife on that land. Game was plentiful in the United States, and Americans resented English laws which restricted hunting to an aristocracy or elite. In the United States the taking of game was open to all, and the privilege generally extended even to unfenced or unplanted private land.[45]

The first attempt at federal regulation came in 1900. The Lacey Act sought to protect egrets, herons, terns, and other rare birds used to decorate women's hats, but it applied only to the *interstate* shipment of birds and mammals taken in violation of *state* law.[46] In the first decades of the twentieth century, drought, the drainage of swamps, and a spectacular increase in the number of sport hunters exacerbated jurisdictional conflicts between the central government and the states. Congress gave the Secretary of Agriculture power to set seasons for migratory bird hunting in 1913, but some states questioned the constitutionality of that law until the ratification of a treaty with Canada in 1918. In 1929, at the urging of sportsmen, Congress enacted legislation to expand migratory bird refuges and in 1934 the Migratory Bird Hunting Stamp Act provided the first money to acquire *new* land for national bird refuges.

As in many other policy areas—such as the construction of highways—Congress used the power of the purse to shape state conservation policies. The Pittman-Robertson Act (1937) earmarked proceeds from a federal excise tax on firearms and ammunition for the use of state fish and wildlife agencies—on condition that the states put up one dollar for every three dollars raised by the federal tax. To take advantage of Pittman-Robertson, a state had to dedicate all money from hunting licenses to fish and wildlife. This prevented the states from using the revenue for schools, roads, and other government services during the darkest years of the Great Depression. Pittman-Robertson money was used for many purposes, including restocking cutover forests and abandoned farmland with deer, bear, and other game animals. However, all funds went to protect a few species, even when their expanding populations encroached on the habitats of other animals. Federal law ignored those creatures not coveted by hunters. Since these funds came from licenses and other taxes—rather than from general taxation—it was difficult to counter the influence hunters enjoyed within state fish and wildlife agencies. Wildlife conservation was one of the first issues to appeal to the public, but picnickers, hikers, birdwatchers, specialists in fish and wildlife management, and other "nature lovers" had little say in federal policies until after World War II.[47]

Regulating hunting underscored the dilemma Congress faced in its primitive efforts at land use planning. It could not administer resources held in common without exercising some control over private lands. The federal irrigation program encountered the same challenge. At the turn of the twentieth century, the remaining public land was largely arid or semi-arid; it had little value without water.[48] In an attempt to revive the family farm and salvage the lives of the poor and the unemployed trapped in burgeoning eastern cities, Congress in 1902 promised up to 160 acres to each settler willing to live on the land and repay over a ten-year period, interest-free, the cost of watering it. As the first generation of farmers paid off its debt to the government, money would become available to build more dams and canals. Eventually the West's entire stock of arable public land could be reclaimed.

In theory, this was a bold program to create new homes. The depression of the 1890s had stalled the flow of capital and settlers into the western half of the nation; federal reclamation promised to revive the land boom of the late 1870s and 1880s. But the Reclamation Act served established rather than new farmers, and private more than public land. The Reclamation Service had no choice but to accommodate those who had long owned the land adjoining the West's major streams. More than 50 percent of the land within the original 24 projects was privately owned, and the strongest support for federal reclamation came from those who hoped to sell their surplus land once the federal government had primed the pump. Rampant speculation and soaring land prices crippled most of the original projects in their infancy and set the stage for the vast water projects of the post–World War II era—schemes that proved a boon to agribusiness, particularly in California.[49]

Forest policy also regulated common resources in the name of private interests. Westerners resisted the creation of a bureau to administer the forested public domain. In 1875, for example, the commissioner of the General Land Office proposed that the United States forever reserve all remaining government timberland from entry and lease cutting rights. In that way, sufficient trees could be preserved for shade, to maintain the earth's moisture, and to protect against erosion. Such a policy, he conceded, would not be popular. "[I]t will at once be perceived that to make it in the smallest degree effective would require the constant presence and intervention of agents of the Government," the commissioner advised, "involving an expenditure for their support, and furnishing opportunities for fraudulent collusion and unjust exactions, which might well be considered as overbalancing the possible good to be attained." The fear of an abusive, expensive, and expansive central government—the pawn of monopoly and special privilege—died hard.[50]

The settlement of the Great Plains demonstrated that much of the West would not be able to supply its own timber—which would have to be imported from great distances. Nevertheless, in 1891—when Congress permitted the President to designate national forests—there were even more pressing needs in the West. Most timber on the public domain was inaccessible. The forest "reserves"—which the national forests were called until 1907—were created in response to the drought and fires of the late 1880s and early 1890s. Many scientists saw a direct correlation between the preservation of trees and the maintenance of steady, even flows in the nation's rivers. Forests were portrayed as nature's reservoirs, capable of preventing floods, increasing the water supply of western farmers, and protecting the navigability of eastern rivers.[51]

Initially, the national forests were closed to entry—or used only by those who lived near them.[52] But once Gifford Pinchot, head of the Forestry Bureau in the Department of Agriculture, took charge of them in 1905, that policy changed. The forests were more valuable for grazing and watershed protection than for lumber, and Pinchot, in the words of historian James L. Penick, "shamelessly courted the leading grazing interests." He favored cattlemen at the expense of sheepmen and large operators at the expense of small.[53]

Stockmen dictated public lands policy into the 1930s, in part because the price of cattle and sheep plummeted during the early years of the Great Depression. In 1934, the Taylor Grazing Act sought to drive up the price of livestock by limiting the number of animals pastured on the national commons. It set aside 80 and later 142 million acres as grazing districts. As Franklin D. Roosevelt explained in a letter to Secretary of the Interior Harold Ickes, the "most noteworthy feature of the program . . . is the unique coordination of local and Federal effort whereby fifteen thousand stockmen have participated successfully in the policy of the Department of the Interior to give local autonomy in the administration of the new law."[54]

Nominally, the Secretary of the Interior determined how many animals would be pastured within each district. But the Taylor Act granted preference to those already using the land and allowed them to renew any grazing permit if the livestock had been used as collateral for a loan and their value would suffer if the right was rescinded. District "advisory boards" determined how many animals each stockowner was permitted to pasture, and those boards were

dominated by the largest cattle and sheep owners. Seven percent of
the permit holders owned nearly half the cattle within the districts, and virtually all permit fees were used to maintain the range
or as payments to the counties in which the districts were located.
The Taylor Act represented the triumph of one set of rangeland users over another through the use of federal power. The real owners
of the public lands received nothing.[55]

The states administered forested land. They jealously guarded
their power to regulate health and safety on private lands, but most
lacked the financial resources to pay the full cost of protecting that
land from fire, insects, soil erosion, and other dangers. The Weeks
Act (1911) encouraged cooperative federal-state protection of private land within the watersheds of navigable streams, including
the suppression of fires. It was an alternative to the expansion of
direct federal regulatory power, which the states and many private
landowners resisted. The Weeks Act authorized the Forest Service
to buy forested land in the East on the pretext of watershed protection. The land had to be located at the headwaters of navigable
streams—such streams were clearly under federal control. But it
also laid the foundation for joint programs to eradicate insects and
diseases that preyed on trees, to control floods, and to reduce soil
erosion. Between 1911 and 1927, the Forest Service purchased
nearly three million acres in the East.[56]

The Clark-McNary Act of 1924 expanded cooperation. It authorized the federal government to enter cooperative agreements
with the states to control fires and reforest cutover lands. The Forest Service was restricted to the watershed of navigable streams, as
it had been under the Weeks Act, and it could purchase no more
than one million acres of land in each state. But the forests no
longer had to be located at the headwaters of such streams. As long
as the land was located within the watershed, it could be purchased
for timber production as well as for the protection of navigation.
The states participating in the Weeks, Clark-McNary, and Mc-
Sweeney-McNary[57] programs increased from 11 in 1911 to 38 by
the end of 1927. Federal expenditures rose from $37,000 to
$710,000 during this period, but state and private spending climbed
even more—from $220,000 to $3,450,000. The Forest Service set
guidelines, but conditions varied too much from state to state for it
to impose uniform standards. Cooperative forestry laws encouraged

the states to enact new restrictions on logging and burning. By 1933, half the forested land in the United States was under some form of organized protection, usually through the states, and the line between federal, state, and private policy was extremely blurry. By the early 1950s, the federal government paid 50 percent of the cost of forest fire protection on state and private lands.[58]

Cooperative programs appeased a West that was antagonistic to conservation. Conservationists had mixed feelings towards the pioneer. They regarded him as a vandal rather than the celebrated conquerer of the wilderness and carrier of civilization; he was selfish and irresponsible, conscious only of the present, cognizant only of the values of his local community, and heedless of the needs of future generations.

Whatever their motives, the opponents of conservation articulated an old and hallowed view of the state and natural resources policy. The first national forests were created as much to protect watersheds as to protect timber; they inevitably locked up a great deal of land that could have been farmed. The national forests were widely perceived as the abandonment or reversal of U.S. land policy from the 1780s into the 1890s. The central government appeared to have become a permanent landlord. Once control over the national forests passed from Interior to Agriculture in 1905, Gifford Pinchot dressed his Forest Rangers in what settlers took to be military uniforms. Few of the original rangers were from the region they served. In states with a great deal of forested land, it was natural to wonder where the process of reservation would end and whether that process symbolized a change in the relationship between Washington and the frontier states.[59]

In the West, opposition to conservation came from many quarters. Westerners resented any policy that permanently consigned a large part of the region to wilderness. Letting resources "go to waste"—even for the sake of future generations—was unthinkable, almost sinful. The forest reserves prevented small settlers from cutting timber for buildings and fences and from grazing their animals on the public lands. In 1909 Senator Henry Teller of Colorado observed: "I would rather have an American home, with an American family, than to have a forest as big as all out doors. I believe that the natural wealth of this country belongs to the people who go and subdue it. I do not believe that there is either a moral or any other claim upon me to postpone the use of what nature has given men, so that the next generation or generations yet unborn may have an opportunity to get what I myself ought to get."[60]

Westerners feared that the creation of national forests would permit huge non-resident corporations to monopolize the timber and dominate the economies of the western states. Healthy economic development, they believed, began with small-scale agriculture. Therefore, the creation of national forests—particularly in such states as Colorado, Idaho, and Wyoming—would prevent those states from competing on equal terms with their older rivals. Conservation, many westerners argued, put the region's future in the hands of "outsiders" who did not understand its problems. The administration of the reserved land would necessarily be political— subject to change with each new administration.[61]

On September 20, 1908, Denver's *Rocky Mountain News* published a political cartoon entitled "Czar Pinchot and His Cossack Rangers Administering the Forest Reserves." As the child of a wealthy, "aristocratic" eastern family, with a forestry education obtained in Germany, Pinchot was an easy target. The chief forester sat on a throne, wearing a crown and an ermine cape, holding a scepter. Behind him stood a line of forest rangers mounted on horseback. A cowering crowd faced him. Its members were labelled "stockman," "irrigationist," "miner," "new settler," and "pioneer." Newspapers likened the reservation policy to serfdom in Russia, English landlordism in Ireland, and the gigantic estates of Latin America. The message was always the same: the federal government was attempting to replace the American system of property law with a neo-feudal regime. In Colorado, newspaper after newspaper likened the Roosevelt-Pinchot reservation policy to "special privilege" and "bureaucratic tyranny." A Leadville paper complained that the national forests treated settlers "like serfs of English landlords instead of like decent, law-abiding, God-fearing, industrious, honest and honorable citizens of free America and the great commonwealth of Colorado." The *Denver Times* asked, "Will you turn over this land to a prince [Pinchot] under a system as foreign to our principles as is the government of Russia?" A Steamboat Springs, Colorado, paper put it concisely: "If Uncle Sam owns the forest reserves, so does he own you and me." The marriage of government conservation bureaus and private corporations threatened a tyranny that would rival any in Europe's history.[62]

In the 1930s, the West's heavy dependence on federal relief spending all but eliminated such criticism. Nevertheless, even during the Depression decade, when the "business civilization" of the 1920s came under withering criticism and droughts, dust storms, and major floods demanded conservation on a scale unprecedented in the Progressive era, limitations on private property were few. The federal government bought millions of acres of "marginal" land on the Great Plains to retire it from cultivation, and the Forest Service purchased over sixteen million acres of private land in the eastern United States—in large part to create national forests that could be used as CCC camps close to population centers on the eastern seaboard.

As in all New Deal conservation programs, the ambitions of science exceeded the limits of politics. The Soil Conservation Service, created in 1935 at the height of the dust storms, established districts within which farmers pursued land use plans that included crop rotation, drainage, contour plowing, tree planting, and flood control. The program suffered from two major limitations, however. It served private land under cultivation, not the most abused land (most of which had been abandoned); and it was largely confined geographically to the southern Plains. It never became a nationwide program, and it did not advance federal planning. Most European nations had adopted land use plans, but in the United States only the National Resources Planning Board (1934–44) proposed such plans, and Congress ignored its recommendations.[63]

Even during the Depression, public policy did little to limit private control of natural resources. To be sure, much changed between 1900 and 1940, and part of the foundation for the environmental movement of the 1960s and 1970s was laid during the 1930s. Environmental science, which did not exist in 1900 or 1920, rapidly advanced during the 1930s, in part because of the federal government's wildlife policies. The advent of paid vacations and cheap automobiles, as well as wildlife programs tailored to hunters and fishers, made recreation an increasingly important part of conservation, drawing the masses into the political arena as they had not been involved during the Progressive era.

At the turn of the twentieth century, conservation was limited to a small group of specialists in and out of government. Economic growth transcended the aesthetic value of natural resources, and "nature" served little purpose except to provide a backdrop to the Darwinian struggle for survival portrayed in the works of such writers as Jack London and Frank Norris. But by the 1930s, the national parks were no longer an anomaly of conservation policy, and the advent of federal water projects—which transformed the western half of the nation during the 1930s and World War II—set the stage for a backlash. In the 1960s and 1970s, the health of the environment became more important than the "mastery of nature."

≺ III ≻

The Environmental "Revolution" of the 1960s and After

In the last 35 years, environmental issues have captured the attention of middle-class America. The Santa Barbara oil spill, the wreck of the Exxon Valdez, and the nuclear catastrophe at Three Mile Island highlighted corporate irresponsibility as well as the limits of human foresight and judgment. Science and technology uncovered medical risks to human beings that were either unknown or incapable of measurement in 1900 or 1940, and television easily and vividly captured the degradation of the environment.

The conservation movement of 1900 to 1940 emphasized natural resources for use—the greatest good for the greatest number. Nationalizing control over nature, it was hoped, would prevent corporate monopolies. It was important to protect the grasslands so that Americans could have cheap meat; to protect farmland so that they could enjoy inexpensive grain and vegetables; and to protect forests so that homes remained affordable. Public control over natural resources would improve the standard of living and help maintain democratic political institutions. The national parks represented different values, but the "preservationist" impulse was far less important than the ethic of "wise use" and efficiency.

In the decades after World War II, the historian Samuel P. Hays has argued, environmental protection resulted from profound changes in American values and attitudes towards nature. From

1945 to 1970, per capita income in the United States doubled, higher education became accessible to the masses, and the relentless process of urbanization continued. A larger, more politically active middle class emerged, with values rooted in the expanding consumer culture rather than the "counterculture" or the "neo-primitivism" of hippies who wanted to return to nature. As income rose, so did discretionary spending, and middle-class Americans began to integrate "nature" into their lifestyle. "Quality of life as an idea and a focus of public action lay at the heart of what was new in American society and politics," Hays concludes, and "environmental affairs were an integral element."

Americans wanted more automobiles, television sets, and houses; but they also wanted better health, more leisure time, and greater access to land beyond the cities. As their worlds expanded, the old line between city and country, tame and wild, faded. The fading was evident in public opinion polls as well as in the number of visitors to national parks and monuments, wilderness areas, wetlands, and other recreation sanctuaries. Poll after poll reflected the shift in values. A 1973 survey conducted in the Pacific Northwest found that 95.6 percent of the sample agreed with the statement that "humans must live in harmony with nature in order to survive" and 84.7 percent disagreed with the proposition that "humans need not adapt to the natural environment because they can remake it to suit their needs." Even more significant, over 75 percent of the poll group agreed with the statement that "there are limits to growth beyond which our industrialized society cannot expand."[64]

Nevertheless, the environmental movement of the 1960s and 1970s demonstrated continuity as well as change. It reflected a chronic, pervasive suspicion of corporate America that had animated reformers since the late nineteenth century. After World War II, corporations placed unprecedented pressure on the public lands, and both Democratic and Republican administrations sympathized with the demands of business—the "pro-production" values of the past. For example, from 1964 to 1967 the leasing of public coal lands increased sharply, but the government received on average only 19 cents per ton for coal that energy companies sold for 20 dollars or more. Five companies, led by Exxon, captured 31 percent of all federal coal leases awarded during these years. In the early 1970s, the same businesses bought up uranium leases at bargain-basement prices. Simultaneously, large timber companies won the right to clear-cut the national forests. Timber harvested from the public lands increased in volume by 300 percent from 1950 to 1966.[65]

For most of the twentieth century, conservation policies originated within federal bureaucracies or specialized advocacy groups, such as wildlife societies. Conservationists outside government regarded "pet" federal resource agencies, such as the Forest Service and Reclamation Bureau, as guardians of the "public interest." By the 1960s and 1970s, however, Congress and the courts also formulated natural resource policies, and agencies created under the two Roosevelts lost much of their autonomy.[66]

As the public's interest in recreation increased, the older resource bureaucracies were squeezed between environmental organizations, Congress, and the courts. The Multiple-Use Sustained-Yield Act of 1960 was a case in point. A child of the Forest Service, MUSY promised that the national forests would be administered for recreation, range, watershed, and fish and wildlife protection as well as for timber. Many of the act's proponents outside government expected the law to increase recreational use of the national forests, and the Forest Service hoped it would pacify critics who claimed that the agency had been captured by large timber companies. Instead, it increased public criticism and led to the Wilderness Act of 1964. Since the 1920s, the Forest Service had taken the lead in designating primitive or wilderness areas, but in 1964 Congress reserved that power to itself.[67]

The pollution control laws of the 1960s and 1970s demonstrated Congress's new interest in the environment. They transferred much of the responsibility for environmental protection from the states to the national government. Environmental laws were far less effective at the state than the federal level, in part because the states were highly sensitive to the demands of the industries within their borders. Nevertheless, environmental agencies, commissions, and boards proliferated at all levels of government. Not surprisingly, environmental law grew rapidly during the 1970s and 1980s. In 1970, environmental statutes filled less than 30 pages in the *Environmental Law Reporter*, but by 1989 they took up over 800 pages.[68]

Simultaneously, the role of the courts expanded. Lawyers who represented environmental groups were far more likely to achieve their objectives in a federal court than by pursuing separate actions in a multitude of state courts. Moreover, the concept of "standing" changed as the result of a series of suits pressed by the Environmental Defense Fund against pesticide manufacturers and another set of suits against federal agencies under the National Environmental Policy Act (1970), which mandated environmental impact statements. As Harry Scheiber has noted, this legislation explicitly "recognized government itself as a force that generated environmental damage." More than one-third of the cases pressed in federal courts during the 1970s involved "action relating to the content and implications of environmental impact statements of government [agencies]." Traditionally, environmental suits pitted one private interest against another, or a private interest against a regulatory agency of government. The tendency of the courts to defer to administrative agencies of government, as they had since the New Deal, disappeared; the courts became the watch-dogs of the natural resource agencies.[69]

Prior to the 1970s, the courts required plaintiffs to demonstrate physical or economic injury before they could sue.[70] This requirement limited the effectiveness of environmental organizations because those organizations were rarely threatened directly. So did a narrow definition of injury. Traditionally, the law ignored injuries to scenic beauty and wildlife. It was difficult to find a human "victim" and difficult to translate the damage into monetary losses. During the 1970s, the courts transformed environmental law in two ways: by increasing the number of people eligible to bring suit and by expanding the concept of injury to include "nature," not just people. These changes had an impact far beyond the courtroom. For example, they transformed environmental organizations from tax-exempt educational foundations composed of volunteers and amateurs into professional advocacy groups with large paid staffs of lawyers and experts.[71]

The "environmental movement" drew the interest of many different groups—those interested in population control, in public health, in urban planning, and in preserving scenic beauty and wilderness, to name just a few.[72] In 1945, the Fish and Wildlife Service counted 56 non-governmental groups devoted to animal protection.

Thirty years later, there were six times that number, including the Foundation for North American Wild Sheep, the North American Bluebird Association, and the Desert Tortoise Preservation Committee. Moreover, the established organizations broadened their legislative agendas. During the 1960s, three of the leading environmental organizations—the Sierra Club, the Wilderness Society, and the National Audubon Society—quadrupled their membership and were joined by such new organizations as the Environmental Defense Fund (1967) and Friends of the Earth (1969). By the 1970s the Sierra Club had added pollution, pesticides, population, nuclear power, and even the danger of nuclear war to its list of concerns.[73]

Many new academic journals appeared, including *Environmental Ethics*, the *Environmental History Review*, *Ethics and Animals*, and *The Deep Ecologist*. In addition, Congress enacted a multitude of environmental protection laws, including the Wilderness Act (1964), the National Wildlife Refuge System Administration Act (1966), the Endangered Species acts (1966, 1968, 1973), the Laboratory Animal Welfare Act (1966), the National Wild and Scenic Rivers Act (1968), the National Forest Management Act (1976), the Fish and Wildlife Conservation Act or "Non-Game Act" (1980), and the Alaska National Interest Lands Conservation Act (1980).[74]

Francis Bacon, the sixteenth- and seventeenth-century English philosoper, argued that "man, if we look to final causes, may be regarded as the centre of the world insomuch that if man were taken away from the world the rest would seem to be all astray, without aim or purpose."[75] That view was at the heart of the Progressive conservation program. Progressives emphasized the protection of large game for moral reasons; they had no understanding of ecosystems. To men and women who exalted order, purpose, and rationality, predators were an embarrassment. It was hard to square nature's brutal appearance with social evolution and the idea of Progress. In 1904, the naturalist William Hornaday described wolves as the most "despicable" of the continent's wild animals: "There is no depth of meanness, treachery, or cruelty to which they do not cheerfully descend. They are the only animals on earth which make a regular practice of killing and devouring their wounded companions, and eating their own dead." In the absence of an ecological perspective, the value of wolves as one of nature's garbage collectors could not be appreciated. During the 1920s, the Bureau of Biological Survey poisoned an average of 35,000 coyotes per year, and in the following decade 75 percent of the bureau's budget went to the war against predators. Even the Park Service practiced predator control until the mid-1930s.[76]

Until after World War II, most animal rights advocates were "man-centered." Animals were property like land and water—or at least potential property. In the early twentieth century, a handful of wildlife champions argued that animals deserved protection because they had a capacity to feel pain and to suffer, but only those animals whose suffering human beings could understand received attention. In the 1960s and 1970s, scientists demonstrated that mammals carried on complicated social lives and lived in complex communities. Animals cooperated as well as competed. Television series such as Marlon Perkins's "Wild Kingdom," which represented a leap forward in nature photography, enjoyed great popularity during the 1960s and 1970s. They treated predators as a vital part of nature rather than as villains in thinly disguised morality plays.[77]

The Endangered Species Act of 1966 directed the Secretary of the Interior, in the words of the legislation, to "carry out a program in the United States of conserving, protecting, restoring and propagating selected species of native fish and wildlife." It gave the secretary authority to purchase land but did not list those species to be protected or provide a method to select them. Control over the taking of animals remained with the states. In 1969, Congress asked the secretary to determine which species were threatened, outside the United States as well as within. The department could now prohibit the importation of endangered species into the country. An even bigger change came in 1973, when Congress required the protection of *all* creatures above microscopic size (except pest insects), not simply favored mammals and birds. The health of the land and habitat protection now concerned the lawmakers as much as the welfare of particular species concerned them.

The 1973 Endangered Species Act required the Secretary of the Interior to reject all public works that threatened an endangered group of animals. Americans soon learned about snail darters, bald eagles, spotted owls, and red-cockaded woodpeckers. Congress exempted from the law certain projects—including the Tellico Dam on the Little Tennessee River. But the law's significance extended far beyond ecological balances or animal rights. It cut deeply into private property rights and the state police power. "Only the Marine Mammal Protection Act [1972] had been so sweeping in its preemption of state power," historian Thomas Dunlap has written, "and it had dealt with an area and a set of resources remote from most Americans' concerns. The new law would strike much closer to home." By arguing for the interdependence of *all* life, the science of ecology suggested that wildlife should fall under federal rather than state law.[78]

Wildlife and habitat protection prompted demands for national land use planning. Beginning in 1970, Congress considered several bills to reduce federal funding of highways, water projects, and public works in states that refused to prepare land use plans. A Nixon administration bill passed the Senate in 1972 and 1973, but failed in the House. The National Chamber of Commerce feared that such bills would undermine traditional property rights and lead to federal zoning and the taking of property without compensation. Other legislation—including the Coastal Zone Management Act (1972) and the Surface Mine Control and Reclamation Act (1977)—represented limited land use planning, but no comprehensive plan was enacted.[79]

Nevertheless, the spectre of federal control remained. In 1985, Bruce Babbitt, then governor of Arizona, proclaimed that

[t]he old concept of multiple use no longer fits the reality of the New West. It must be replaced by a concept of public use. From this day on, we must recognize the new reality that the highest, best and most productive use of western public land will usually be for public purposes—watershed, wildlife and recreation. Mining entry must be regulated, timber cutting must be honestly subordinated to regeneration and restoration of grasslands. It is time to replace . . . multiple use with a statutory mandate that public lands are to be administered primarily for public purposes.[80]

Such declarations raise profound questions about the power of the state to seize private property and limit freedom of contract. Private property has always been subject to taxation, eminent domain, and other restrictions. Many students of the law and politics argue that property rights derive from the state rather than from nature; that "private" property's ultimate justification is the common good; and that no right is absolute. Nevertheless, the libertarian perspective has become increasingly powerful, in part because it is so simple, in part because it serves as a cloak for corporate interests, and in part because it reinforces the contemporary antagonism to government. Twenty or thirty years ago, critics of eminent domain wondered how individual liberty could be protected in an increasingly interdependent society dominated by a centralized state and gigantic institutions. Powerful *business* corporations, they feared, would force government to confiscate the property rights of one group and transfer them to another—all in the name of the public good. Today champions of property rights see the "environmental movement," invested with the power of the state, as the primary threat to liberty.

Not surprisingly, anti-feudalism revived in the 1970s and 1980s. The takings issue has focused on the extent to which private property needed to protect the environment should be subject to eminent domain and the police power. "It is ironic," Ellen Frankel Paul has written, "that today many environmentalists explicitly reject . . . Lockean notions of land as an absolute dominion in favor of a nostalgic vision of duties, obligations, and a sense of community supposedly exemplified by the feudal land tenure system." Environmentalists, she charges, think of themselves as progressive, but defend a reactionary land tenure system.[81] During a 1992 debate over wetlands legislation, Don Young, a congressman from Alaska, warned against "the slide toward government imposed environmental Marxism." "What is the difference between Karl Marx and the environmental movement?" he asked. "If you can understand the practical difference between the central government managing the land for the collective benefit of the masses as Karl Marx suggests or for the collective benefit of the 'environment,' please explain it to me. I see no real difference. They both place virtually unlimited power in the hands of Federal bureaucrats at the expense of individual rights."[82]

Where the environmental revolution will end remains to be seen, but the implications for the law, private property, and freedom of contract are immense. The legal scholar A. Dan Tarlock puts it well: "The thrust of environmental or eco-ethics has been to collapse the historical duality between man and nature by assigning equal (or in some cases paramount) rights to nonhuman systems. This ethic is a radical departure from past ethical traditions because it both challenges the western liberal idea of property and strips the quasi- or perhaps pseudospiritual basis from environmental protection." Our legal system is built on concepts of human rights and duties that focus on the individual, and much of environmental law is inconsistent with these traditions.[83]

Centuries ago, European revolutionaries countered the absolutist state and church by creating individual rights to liberty and property. As Tarlock notes: "Constitutional doctrines such as equal protection, procedural due process, and prohibitions against takings without due compensation [must] apply to environmental regulation as they apply to all administrative action. However, the fundamental principles of environmental protection—protection from [toxic] risk and biodiversity protection—do not fit into our constitutional jurisprudence. The most striking feature of environmental law is that it has thrived at all. Environmental law sprouted almost overnight with almost no jurisprudential, ethical, or religious underpinning, but this is both its strength and its weakness." To be successful, environmental law will have to redefine the relationship between individual human beings and nature, if not our species and nature.[84]

If much of environmental law rests on a shaky foundation, so does environmental science. The comforting notion that nature represents order, purpose, and direction is at least as old as Plato and Aristotle, but over the last twenty or thirty years it has crumbled. The Earth is neither a set of rational, predictable ecosystems nor a "superorganism." There is no way to let nature be nature. The scientist Daniel Botkin has argued that three views of the Earth have dominated human history—nature as divine creation, nature as organism, and nature as machine. The machine model that prevailed into the 1970s, and upon which the environmental movement was built, has been around for several centuries. It assumes a world where "undisturbed populations and ecological communities (sets of interacting populations) . . . achieve constancy in abundance." Botkin sees nature as a complicated musical score rather than a machine: "Nature undisturbed by human influence seems more like a symphony whose harmonies arise from variation and change over every interval of time."[85]

Among the multitude of problems involved in defining environmental rights are how to calculate injuries to individual plants or collections of organisms organized into ecosystems (such as rivers, oceans, marshlands, or the planet); how to rank environmental rights against those of human beings; and how, if human beings are part of nature, to separate their acceptable from their unacceptable acts. The legal system that can accommodate individual rights, public rights, and the rights of nature will be quite a creation in its own right.

Globalization of Freedom of Contract

MARTIN SHAPIRO

A S OTHER CHAPTERS in this volume have indicated, the expression "freedom of contract" means different things in different contexts. In American constitutional history freedom of contract is a constitutional icon of laissez-faire having nothing particularly to do with contract. In this context, freedom of contract stands for a substantive due process right of entrepreneurs to be free of government regulation in all their business activities, contractual and otherwise, or at least free of unreasonable government regulation. It was particularly invoked against government wages and hours regulation.[1] In contexts other than the American constitutional one, and particularly in the context of nineteenth-century civil law, freedom of contract was the banner of a theory of contract law, and of private law more generally, that emphasized the free will of individuals and the role of law in facilitating and supporting the freedom of individuals to make whatever social and economic arrangements among themselves they wish to make.[2] In the twentieth century the civil law world and the common law as well speak more of contract than freedom of contract. And contract law is seen not only as facilitative and supportive of freedom of contract but as regulative of contractual behavior as well.[3] In this sense contract law is subtractive from as well as additive to the "natural" freedom to contract.

The regulative aspects of contract law are particularly important when we move to something referred to as the "globalization" of freedom of contract. So is the distinction between the legal practice of contracting and contract law. I will treat contract law as a form of government regulation of contract practice. Most forms of regulation actually involve the government in both fostering and restricting the regulated activity; we can certainly see "globalized" contract law as both fostering and restricting the freedom of contract.

If "freedom of contract" contains a number of ambiguities and cross currents, "globalization" contains even more. "Globalization" is a current catch phrase apparently coined either for sheer glamour or because someone thought that "international" and "internationalization" were, in their very announcement of the transcendence of nation, still redolent of our obsolescing fascination with the nation-state.[4] The globalization of contracts would mean contracting behavior that, more or less, treated national boundaries as irrelevant. And the globalization of contract law would produce a body of law that, more or less, operated without reference to national legal systems.

≺ I ≻

The Law of Merchants

The globalization of contract—not contract law but the practice of contracting—is a fairly easy matter to get a handle on. There is, of course, a very long history of international trade and of the invention by merchants, bankers, and carriers of forms of agreement to facilitate that trade. Perhaps in this area of human endeavor, more than most, the sequence of chicken and egg involving social practices and law is clear. Here, the social practice comes first and the law comes tumbling after. The endlessly recalled merchants and money lenders of the medieval fairs, the Hanseatic navigators, and so on created business customs, usages, practices, and written instruments that the law subsequently absorbed. Much of the law, indeed, is not nationally enacted statutory law, but the mere recognition and adoption of business practices by courts called upon to settle disputes between merchants.[5] Furthermore many of the courts that do the adopting are not themselves purely organs of national or other governments but rather are pie powder or fair courts—courts in which the judges are themselves merchants to whom government powers are delegated to enforce their own practices.[6]

Given the history, the notions of globalization of freedom of contract or contract law then are fairly easy to follow. First markets become global, and businesses become transnational. The transnational businesses engaging in global transactions perforce must enter into global agreements or local agreements that are globally similar. The law then globalizes to meet these practical business needs. Globalization of law in this context is simply the story of the law merchant all over again. We can expect that the globalization of contract law will simply be the writing into court practice of whatever business practices the global economy throws up. The legal materials, that is, the statutes, treaties, judicially and academically announced legal doctrines, model codes will simply formalize what the entrepreneurs and their customers have freely arrived at. Freedom of contract comes first and the law of contracts comes after.

Only one black mark seems to mar this historical picture. Historically the *lex mercatoria*, the international body of trade law, derived from merchant practice, came to be enforced mostly by regular national courts, not special merchant courts.[7] "Private international law" did not come to include a substantive body of contract law. Instead private international law responded to international contracting practices by evolving a huge body of procedural law, "conflict of laws," designed to shove disputes arising under international commercial agreements into one or another of the national court systems and under one or another of the national bodies of contract law.[8] It is true that national courts hearing such disputes would take into account all sorts of particular and peculiar international trade practices and the various legal materials that encapsulated them, but ultimately they remained national courts enforcing national law. Indeed much of the current concern with globalizing, harmonizing, or unifying contract law (or all three) arises from the palpable inconveniences that continue to arise when transnational business disputes must be resolved by national courts applying national law.

Beyond this one little cloud, there is another and larger problem that causes some disturbance to the picture of pure freedom of contract—that is, to business evolving its own agreements practices with the law merely following on to confirm them. Throughout its history in the Western world a fundamental tension has existed between contract as signifying the free will of the parties and contract as achieving a just, fair, or equitable exchange.[9] Particularly in the first half of the twentieth century, by court decision and often by statute, new contract law was created that did not simply reflect evolving contracting practices. Instead this new law was specifically designed to counter practices that increasingly favored the more over the less economically powerful. Labor contracts, consumer credit contracts, leases became the targets of law reform that demanded that contracts be fair even when the parties were "willing" to enter into unfair ones. Thus by the time we begin to speak of the globalization of contract law, contract law itself involves not only facilitating the freedom of contract but impinging on that freedom in the name of fairness.[10]

As we all know, most of these regulative aspects of contract law are conceived as attempts to remedy unfairness arising from radical disparities in the economic power of certain classes of contracting parties, such as creditors and debtors. Globalization of contract law particularly involves contracting between business enterprises, so that the context is not one of radical disparities between the parties. Nevertheless where globalization takes the form of transnational harmonizations or unifications of existing bodies of national contract law, the regulative aspects already introduced into those bodies of national law are likely to be introduced into the global law as well, simply because they are there. Moreover the "north-south" or "developed-developing" dimensions of the international economic arena are likely to trigger fairness concerns and thus interest in the regulative as well as the supportive aspects of contract law. Even where most of the contracting parties are corporations and governments, on the current international scene some contracting parties are clearly more equal than others.[11]

To the extent that the globalization of contract law is about harmonization or unification of national contract law—or both—and also about the further development of the traditional *lex mercatoria*, the story to be told is fairly simple. Globalizing markets lead to global contracting. Global contracting practices then call forth global contracting law. But as contract law globalizes, it concerns itself not only with fostering and facilitating contracting across national boundaries but also with insuring that such contracts will be fair.

The story is not as simple as this, however, because the globalization of contract practice involves not only the projection of former domestic contract practices onto a global screen, but also a more or less radical change in contracting practices themselves. To put the matter crudely, globalization of contract practices is, to a very great degree, the spread of the American style of long, detailed contracts, concocted by large American law firms for a very high fee, to the rest of the world. This contract gigantism is further aggravated by, or indeed perhaps even caused by, the increasingly complex interrelationships that business enterprises have invented. The more complex the relationships, the necessarily more complex the contracts governing them—at least so it can be argued.

≺ II ≻

Conflict of Laws, Lex Mercatoria, General Principles, and Arbitration

Legal scholarship has always found it easier to note and describe what legislatures and courts do, and what legal scholars themselves do, than to describe what lawyers and clients do. Accordingly I will go at contract matters backward, first looking at globalizing tendencies in contract law, doctrine, and jurisprudence, where it is relatively easy to pin down what is going on; and then moving to globalizing tendencies in contract practice, where what I have to say is far more speculative and unsupported by scholarly studies.

Contract law is, first and foremost, an authorization or acknowledgment of a realm of private law-making in which by mutual agreement parties create their own law to govern some mutual undertaking.[12] Precisely because the realm is one of private law-making, it has always seemed appropriate that the parties also structure a private mechanism for resolving conflicts that arise under the private law and within the private endeavor they are jointly undertaking.

The base line from which recent globalization tendencies can be measured is conflict of laws.[13] Much of the body of legal doctrine we know as conflict of laws has been engendered in the context of contract litigation. Where contracting parties or contracted transactions straddle legal jurisdictional boundaries, to the courts of which jurisdiction and which state or national body of contract law should contract litigation be assigned? Conflict of laws is a set of nonconsensual responses to this problem. The law itself, not the parties, chooses the jurisdiction for litigation. Conflict of laws is a great traditional and continuing mode of facilitating cross-boundary contracting. Conflict of laws, however, runs against the grain of the consensual nature of contracting. Thus contracting parties frequently seek to substitute their own consensual choices of jurisdiction for those imposed by conflict of law.

The most familiar form of such jurisdiction by agreement is the contract provision that explicitly provides that litigation concerning the contract shall take place in the courts and under the law of a specified state. Here is the paradox that parties contracting across boundaries can, to a degree, defeat the boundary problem by themselves localizing the dispute resolution process. But parties may choose to push even further along the private and consensual route. Thus mediation or arbitration clauses frequently appear in contracts. If we conceive of triadic conflict resolution as arranged along a continuum from go-between through mediator to arbitrator and judge,[14] contract provisions invoke a rather broad range of the continuum. Some contracts invoke more or less pure mediation, in which the triadic figure is substantively unbound by the law of the contract and simply proposes or assists the parties in proposing various alternative resolutions until one is struck to which both parties will agree. Further up the spectrum towards judging, we encounter arbitration clauses in which the arbiter is bound by the substantive law of the contract but, by the terms of the contract, is placed in a "paternal" relationship to the parties required to impose a resolution that will be benevolent to both the conflicting parties. Contracts may provide that the arbitrator act as an *amiable compositor* guided by equity.[15] Next comes the arbitrator who is in reality merely a privately employed judge who is required to enforce upon the parties the substantive law of the contract. And, of course, finally we encounter contracts that deviate from a regime of free litigation by the parties only to the extent of constraining them to bring their lawsuits within a particular jurisdiction.

Where pure mediation is involved, it may be argued that contract law as such, globalized or otherwise, is irrelevant because the mediator is concerned only with eliciting the consent of the parties, not with enforcing legal obligations upon them. In the language sometimes used for labor contracts, this is pure interest mediation. Even here, however, the more widely accepted various principles and doctrines of contract law become, the more easily the two parties may come to a common understanding of what is fair under the contract. And, of course, if such mediation is done "under the shadow of the law" or "under the shadow jurisdiction of a court," that is if it is done under the threat of future litigation if the mediation fails, then such principles may loom even larger for the parties. Where we move to amiable compositor-style arbitration, shared principles and doctrines may play an even larger role because arbitrators often find citation of shared principles to be a successful route to benevolent conflict resolution. Where arbitration is private judging, such shared principles are even more powerful, indeed more powerful than they are for state judges. For the private judge is likely to feel somewhat less bound by the particulars of any one state's formal contract law than is the judge on the state's payroll.

All this is preliminary to saying that the *lex mercatoria* often plays a substantial part in the resolution of contract disputes, particularly where arbitration is involved. A strong argument can be made that the *lex mercatoria* has been acquiring growing status among arbitrators[16] and even that "general principles" of contract law are increasingly employed by arbitrators.[17] The more conservative position is that the *lex mercatoria* or general principles of law may only be employed in conjunction with and as a supplement to some national system of contract law. The more globalized perspective would hold that arbitrators may consider some contracts to be totally stateless and appropriate for arbitral judgments derived entirely from non-national sources.[18]

Whatever the theory, in actual practice a large number of international contracts with arbitration clauses now either remain entirely silent about the choice of substantive law or invoke the *lex mercatoria* or general principles of law without invoking any particular national law of contract or specifing some national law or body of conflict of law rules that can be used to choose the appropriate national substantive law. They may or may not then go on to specify *lex mercatoria* or general principles of law as a supplementary source of substantive law for the arbitrator. Perhaps the increasing popularity of such non-national government or globalized substantive law has its origins in the many situations where one of the parties is private and the other is a government or one of its instruments. The private party does not wish the contract governed by either the national law or the national courts of the national contracting party. The national government finds it beneath its dignity to submit to the law and courts of another nation-state. Arbitration under the *lex mercatoria* or general principles of law may then be appealing to both parties.

In general even in arbitrations, and even where the parties have remained silent or explicitly sought to avoid all national law, the decision-maker will employ some rather traditional choice of law process to implicate some national body of substantive contract law, or perhaps the sum of several bodies of such law. The decision-maker will do so because the *lex mercatoria* and general principles are both rather uncertain and incomplete bodies of law. Nevertheless, particularly where the parties themselves have given prominence to these bodies of law in their contract provisions on substantive law or have chosen an amiable compositor style for arbitration, arbitration is likely to involve a legal technique that is far more global than national.

A further complexity is added of course by the need to achieve the enforcement of arbitral awards by national courts.[19] Presumably no national court will enforce an arbitral award that violates strong national public policy, whether it is based on non-national or national law. Some national courts, most notably those of France, will enforce arbitral awards based solely on the *lex mercatoria*. While the courts of some other states may explicitly decline to do so, the general tendency of courts to avoid searching review of an arbiter's substantive judgments, together with the arbitral practice of mixing global and national sources in various ways, means that arbitrators may rely fairly heavily on non-national law without much fear that their awards will be unenforceable. For instance where arbitrators interpret contract provisions or a provision of national contract law itself "in the light of" the *lex mercatoria* or as incorporating certain general principles of law, national courts are unlikely to refuse enforcement of awards on that ground.

In the broad picture of globalization here there is an obvious tension not so much between globalization and nationalism as between certainty and equity. And that tension runs along two contrary vectors. *Lex mercatoria*, trade practices, and general principles promise the parties and the arbitrators some flexibility in achieving fair outcomes where explicit national contract rules might do otherwise in a particular fact situation. The potential for fairness, however, is bought at the cost of increasing uncertainty of the law as we move from the specificity and relative completeness of national contract law to the vagaries of "general principles." Along a quite different vector the movement is the opposite. When contracting with certain governments, private parties may believe that the *lex mercatoria* yields greater certainty and fairness then the law of host state, even when applied by a outside arbitrator.

In spite of the uncertainties it creates, movement towards the *lex mercatoria* or general principles, particularly in contracts with arbitration clauses, is fueled both by the general international inclination to give the parties the broadest freedom in choosing the substantive law of their contracts and by the appeal of "lottery" solutions to the bargaining problems encountered by certain contracting parties in certain situations. Where any national law chosen appears to give undue advantage to one or the other of the parties, and both wish to avoid the high transaction costs of seeking to write a whole scheme of fundamental contract law into the contract itself, invoking an arbitrator and the *lex mercatoria* or general principles allows the contract to be completed now with legal questions deferred to a future black box. The two parties share the uncertainty costs and hope that future legal costs will never be incurred. The extreme solution of this sort is, of course, the provisions for an amiable compositor.

It should also be noted that the desire of some academics and arbitration specialists to emphasize the *lex mercatoria*, like the various European and United Nations efforts to draft model contract laws, constitutes a countercurrent to the Americanization of transnational contract practice and contract law that appears to be a major feature of globalization. If the *lex mercatoria* achieves a central importance in the law that international commercial arbitrators employ, that is really to say that an essentially civilian, continental body of learning largely cultivated by European academics becomes a central source of law.[20]

<< III >>

Trans-State Harmonization of Contract Law and Doctrine

The pattern that emerges from the development of the *lex merca-toria*, particularly at the least judge-like end of the arbitration range but even at the more judge-like end and in the work of national judges themselves, is one of relatively general principles of contract law along with some specific practices that have developed into such settled expectations that they can be used as legal rules. Either alternative to, or growing out of, or formalizing the *lex mercatoria* are various formal bodies of written trans- or multinational contract law enacted or announced by various trans- or multi-national bodies, governmental or otherwise. The United States Uniform Commercial Code is the most familiar of these. Composed by a quasi-official body, the Commission on Uniform State Laws, it is a model code which state legislatures were free to adopt. Eventually most states did adopt it in whole or in part, and it has been highly influential in judicial law-making as well. It consists in part of relatively specific legal formalizations of particular commercial practices and in part of much more general principles and rules. Its companion is the Restatement (Second) of Contracts, the product of the private American Law Institute. These two bodies of law play out the globalization theme in miniature—if something as large as the United States can ever be called miniature. Contract law remains state law. Contract disputes remain subject to conflict-of-laws assignment to one state or another. But trans-state models for parallel or harmonized state contract law are offered and widely accepted.

Since World War II a spate of international endeavors of a comparable kind has been launched. There was the Uniform Sales Law of the Hague of 1964, which was subscribed to almost exclusively by western European states. It was followed by the 1986 Hague Convention on the Law Applicable to Contracts for the International Sale of Goods, which has been joined by a wider range of states.[21] The United Nations Commission on International Trade Law has produced the Uncitral Legal Guide on Drawing Up International Contracts for the Construction of Industrial Works.[22] There is a Uncitral Model Law on International Commercial Arbitration.[23] The European Communities produced a convention on the Law Applicable to Contractual Obligations.[24] An array of model contract provisions of various specialized kinds such as the Conditions of Contract for Works of Civil Engineering Construction has been produced by private groups.[25] The European Community funds a project by the International Institute for the Unification for Private Law that prepared a number of drafts of "Principles for International Commercial Contracts."[26] The Institute has now completed a major project on principles of European contract law.

From all of these endeavors certain basic strands emerge. First there appears to be no inclination to create larger-than-traditional jurisdictions to match the increasing geographic reach of contracting. The American states and the nation-states of the rest of the world are to remain the basic jurisdictions for the resolution of contract disputes at least when the resolutions take place in formal courts. Globalization only means a multiplication of model provisions, international conventions, and so on, which individual states may choose to adopt in total or in part or particular parties may choose to introduce into their contracts. Only if and when particular contracting parties choose to bind themselves by arbitration clauses that establish an arbitrator not bound by the contract law of a particular state would we have something like a conflict resolution jurisdiction that ran as wide as the contract runs.

Second, all of the attempts to do contract law on a larger scale incorporate the basic tensions, dialectics, and antinomies that surface within particular states when contract restatement, codification, or systematization is in the wind. While much effort is spent in careful collection and systematization of existing law, elements of reform or change are also present. The usual debate rages about whether contract law should merely formalize successful business practices or accept some and reject others. The familiar tension is evident between "meeting of the minds" and "fairness" theories, and between "moral" or "keeping promises" theories and "economic" or "risk bearing" or "efficient breach" theories of contract. Some approaches to contract emphasize the goal of each party fully understanding exactly what he is promising and being promised. Others emphasize a normative concern for fairness even if the parties seem to have clearly agreed to some things that are unfair. Some emphasize a moral norm of keeping the promises made in contracts. Others see nothing wrong in promises being broken so long as the breaker compensates the other party for any injuries he suffers from the failure to keep the promise.

Thus some bodies of contract law are especially concerned that the contract be objectively fair to both sides while others are especially concerned that the contrast accurately express what each party wants and attain subjective agreement between the two. One approach emphasizes the facilitative side of contract. If the parties really wanted something and truly understood what they were getting, then it is the business of government to assure they get it even if it is actually unfair to one of them. The other emphasizes the regulative role of government. The government ought not to enforce unfairness even if the parties seem to have wanted it. Along another dimension, some contract regimes place great emphasis on what was promised actually being done. They incline towards authorizing judges to order the parties to do what they have promised to do. Other regimes are inclined towards allowing parties not to keep their promises when it would cost them more to keep the promise than to compensate the other party for their failure to do so. They incline towards authorizing judges to award money damages against those who break promises but not authorizing judges to order promise breakers to do what they promised to do. The differences between the two approaches rest in part on a disagreement about morality. Should the state enforce a morality of promise keeping? Or should it pursue economic efficiency as the primary value behind contract law? In part the difference arises out of differing estimates of the long-term public interest. Will the society flourish best if the government intervenes to enforce promises or intervenes to assure efficiency? Because common law generally has been loath to require specific performance, instead favoring money damages, and civil law has been much more favorable to performance remedies, these debates over fundamental contract questions are often expressed as differences between civil law and common law theories or between performance and damage remedies. But the basic tensions are to be found within as well as between the common law and civil law families.

Third, partly as a result of these tensions and partly as a result of the universal consciousness that the details of contracting and broader commercial practices are complex and constantly changing, all the efforts at composing harmonized or globalized contract law tend to run heavily towards a mix of rather generally stated principles and what amounts to capsules of well-settled particular practices. There seems to be fairly widespread agreement that a detailed international code of contract law cannot and should not be written.[27]

Fourth, these attempts at harmonized law tend to vest judges with a good deal of discretion. In part such judicial discretion is inevitable if harmonized law is to be a set of general principles. In part, however, the resort to judicial discretion represents a rather strong current in legal scholarship, or at least among the scholars who pursue these efforts towards an increasingly moral theory of contracts. No doubt because of the preponderance of civil lawyers involved, the emphasis tends to be on *pacta sunt servanda*, that is, that contract promises must be kept. Theories of risk allocation or efficient breach which, in effect, say that you may break contract promises if you are willing to pay the costs to others generated by your doing so are banished.[28] Therefore specific performance is typically incorporated parallel to money damages. The very same academic lawyers, however, do not subscribe to a pure meeting of the minds theory of contract. Instead they are much concerned with reasonableness, equitableness, and fairness. These concerns increase if those in breach cannot even choose to pay and walk away. As a result, the new drafting efforts are full of escape hatches for situations in which the words of the contract seem to compel or would result in grave injustice to one of the parties. Given the complex and changing circumstances attendant on contemporary contracts, these escape hatches tend to be written as discretions vested in judges to mitigate contract-compelled injustices rather than as detailed rules for escaping from obligations created by the contract. The result necessarily is not only judicial discretion for individual cases but a kind of declaration by drafters that in spite of their best efforts much of the law will continue to be judge-made case law.[29]

Perhaps the most interesting feature of the globalization efforts flows directly from those already noted. There is the strong sense, based on historical knowledge, that whatever the law written by legislators, judges, and lawyers, actual business practices will be the principal source of contract law. To the extent that certain of those practices become global, the law will follow suit as to both geographic reach and substance. On the other hand, there is the strong sense that if global contract law is to be a set of general principles and a call for just and fair results, then judges of different national or subnational legal cultures will decide contract cases to a significant degree in the light of those differing cultures. Perhaps it takes a good deal of optimism to engage in transcultural law-making efforts, but there certainly is a kind of Pollyannish quality to what is going on. In spite of the endless debates one would expect among academic lawyers, there is the almost open declaration that no matter what we do we cannot do any real damage, because business practice will overwhelm any mistake we make in formal law writing and judges will prevent the law we write both from generating serious injustice in individual cases and from excessively disturbing longstanding national contract law expectations.[30]

The two central attempts at creating model laws of contract have been the European Convention on Contracts for the Sale of Goods and the UN Convention on Contracts for the International Sale of Goods, which succeeds it.[31] Both have been subscribed to by a substantial number of states. Here, rather than the Americanization that we encounter in much contract practice and arbitration, we encounter a slight Europeanization of contract law. Specific performance remedies are much more available than under the Uniform Commercial Code. The civil law concepts of "avoidance" for "fundamental breach" rather than "revocation of acceptance" are employed. Failure of the buyer to pay probably cannot trigger as rapid a response from the buyer as may occur under the UCC. And the seller's failure to perform promptly may be cured by a further agreement between buyer and seller extending the time for performance. In an explicit compromise between common and civil law traditions, "good faith" is mentioned only in the interpretation provisions of the UN Convention and not in its performance and enforcement provisions.

Both Conventions also exhibit a particular dedication to freedom of contract, to the belief that law should follow practice, and to stating the law in terms of general principles, leaving room for much spontaneous growth in practice. The Conventions are even more liberal than the UCC or the Restatement (Second) of Conflict of Laws[32] in allowing the parties autonomy in choosing the law applicable to their contract. The UN Convention offers a very broad

opt out clause from almost any or all of its particulars. Many of the
UN Convention rules are default rules that only govern in the absence of specific agreement between the parties. Article 9 provides
that trade usages and the prior practices of the parties derogate
from the rules of the Convention. The Convention specifically
does not cover validity. It conspicuously avoids regulatory provisions such as reasonableness and unconscionability. (But it must
be noted that much of the new UNIDROIT drafting of Principles
for Commercial Contracts and that of the Principles of European
Contract Law project place considerable emphasis on "reasonableness."}[33] And it provides that matters "governed by" but "not expressly settled in it" are to be decided in conformity with "the general principles on which it is based." One could hardly encounter a
more favorable balance of freedom of contract over regulation of
contract than is to be found in the two Conventions. Both are, of
course, aimed primarily at the contractual relationships between
business firms and so we would expect to encounter less concern
for regulation than might be encountered in consumer sales or
credit contract law. The European Union has recently issued a
major harmonization directive on some aspects of consumer contracts that does take a much more regulatory stance but is very
limited in scope.[34]

≺ IV ≻

The American-Style Contract

The most obvious globalization phenomenon of contract law, and
the one most easily observed by its detritus of law review articles,
conference reports, yearbook volumes, and circulated draft codes, is
this flourishing industry of model contract, model statute, and
model code writing. The next phenomenon I wish to note is far
more difficult to document from traditional scholarly sources. It
should, however, be very evident to both transnational contracting
parties and to their lawyers. It is the global spread of the American-
style contract.

For quite a long time now there appears to have been
a relatively distinct style of American contracting among large business enterprises. No doubt it arose gradually, but it must go back

at least as far as the turn of the century. American contracts tended to be long, detailed, and designed—as much as humanly possible—to anticipate the possible vicissitudes of future business relationships under the contract. One can argue that such a development is inevitable in a capitalist, free enterprise (but regulated), large scale, rapidly growing economy deploying huge amounts of capital and labor and enjoying rapid technological progress. If the same development was not occurring in Europe, for instance, in the same time frame, the explanation might be more cartelized economies with lesser geographic reach.

The growth of the long, detailed American contract style also has two chicken and egg aspects particularly related to the American scene. Long detailed contracts might be written because the lawyers involved saw litigation as frequent and inevitable and were writing contract provisions to provide and close off defenses at trial. Or, frightened by the ever present spectres of litigation, contract writers might be seeking to anticipate and avoid every possible misunderstanding that might trigger litigation. One way or another, long detailed contracts, in some mixture of cause and effect, are probably related to the American style of litigation.

Related to the connection between contracts and litigation is a connection between contracts and law firms. Big law firms have the resources to write long, detailed contracts and to litigate issues that arise under them if necessary. Big law firms also have strong economic incentives to persuade clients to such contracts. And, of course, the inclination to such contracts, from wherever the inclination is derived, fuels the growth of large law firms.

American businessmen often can be heard wondering at how "what used to be done with a handshake" now requires an army of lawyers and how legal expenses have somehow grown into a significant part of their business expenses. It makes little difference to my argument whether the American businessmen are right or wrong in complaining about all this having happened recently. It is important to my argument that long, detailed contracts became prevalent far earlier in America than elsewhere. If I am wrong about that then much of my subsequent argument about globalization fails.

The simplest way to tell my globalization story would be to say that, for whatever reasons, a certain American style of contracting arose and then spread to Europe and the rest of the world as American companies doing business abroad insisted on contracting that business in the style to which they had become accustomed. I think that story is essentially true at least in some sectors of business, a point I will illustrate later with world wide developments in franchise law. An alternative story would be that transnational business, American based and otherwise, began to encounter world wide the same phenomena that had earlier fostered American-style contracting, and that as it encountered these phenomena it was also aware of the existence of American contracting practices and so borrowed from that ready-made body of contract technology. Perhaps this story is best illustrated by developments in large-scale mineral development agreements that I will turn to later.

≺ V ≻

Franchising Law

The world wide development of the business format, that is the McDonald's-style, franchise contracting practice illustrates many of the features of the globalization of freedom of contract.[35] Franchising flourished in the United States for many years; and most American states produced special franchise contract law. The simplest story would be that as American franchising traveled around the world it took the American franchise law with it. The real story is a little more complex but not essentially different. First of all the French went into franchising in wedding, maternity, and children's clothing quite early and many of the European legal responses are to this French rather than American franchising. Second, although between 1988 and the present the number of nations with explicit franchising laws has gone from one (the United States) to eighteen, most nations still do not have much explicit franchising law. Yet the pattern of working law among the rest is basically the same as that among the eighteen, and a general description of what has occurred can be offered.

In general, at least in the realm of contract law, most nations and the European Community have adopted a stance of benevolent neutrality towards business format franchising. They have recognized its economic benefits in the United States and allowed the market to decide its fate in their own domestic economies. Opposition to franchising, and particularly to American franchising, has expressed itself not in contract law but in such arenas as local land use planning and business licensing.

The most typical pattern in contract law has not been rapid response of law to practice. Particularly as American franchisors expanded abroad, they offered foreign franchisees their American-form franchise contracts. These contracts are the most American of the American-style contracts. That is, in contemplation of long continuing business relationships, they seek to nail down every last contingency that could arise in such situations and thus are extremely long and detailed, often incorporating a whole operations manual into the contract itself. In addition, and this is not so American perhaps, the very essence of their success is that they are uniform and dictated by one of the parties, the franchisor, to the other on a more or less take it or leave it basis. The response of academic lawyers throughout the world to this huge new contract phenomenon has been the usual response of academic contract lawyers to anything new. For as long as they could they studiously ignored it, continuing to slice thinner and thinner the dozen or so traditional topics of contract law scholarship. The initial response of law makers has been that to the 2,000 pound gorilla—they let it sit anywhere it wants. More specifically, the response largely has been to treat the business format franchise contract as an "innominate" or "mixed" contract having features of a number of kinds of contract previously known by particular legal systems and thus to be dealt with under the general law of contract or by analogy to the existing variety of contracts that its various parts resemble. Some countries then eventually enact a statute that in effect systematizes this application of general contract principles. With or without statutes, what most national law has done is essentially to normalize the American-style contract practice.

Thus the globalized contract law has been almost entirely supportive of the private contract practices developed by the franchisors. The new franchise law has been regulative, in the sense of seeking to impose government policies on contracting parties, only in a few areas. Among the few specific regulatory responses to franchising is a French decree requiring that French language endings rather than English be coupled to the root terms. Earlier we noted that modern contract law has been particularly regulatory with regard to situations in which standardized contract language is imposed by a stronger party and repeat player on a weaker, sporadically playing party. The franchise contract seems to provide one of those situations. Yet there are several good reasons for staying the regulatory hand here. First and foremost, uniformity is precisely the valuable economic good being created and sold to the public by the whole franchise arrangement and the public, the ultimate consumer, seems to benefit greatly from it. Boilerplate, which may appear to be a vice in other contract settings, is the very heart of virtue in this one. Second, the franchisee is not exactly a consumer who needs the special guardianship of the state. The franchisee is presumably a knowledgeable entrepreneur in his or her own right.

Therefore, in both the statutory and the nonstatutory states, the regulatory thrust to the extent that it has developed at all, largely has taken the form not of limiting form contracting, but of being meticulous about disclosure requirements. The franchisor is in a far better position than the franchisee to know the significance of each uniform bit of the contract and is placed under an appropriate burden to disclose.

Several areas of noncontract law are far more likely to impede business format franchise contracting than is contract law itself, at least as it is being construed today in most of the world. Business format franchising collides with the antitrust or competition law of many nations and most notably of the European Union. The response of the EU was to issue a "block exemption" from its competition laws for business format franchising along with a special individual waiver process for franchises that could not qualify for the block exemption. The response of most nations and of the European Union has been to mute competition law in favor of franchising. Business format franchise contracts typically contain numerous anti-competitive provisions, but the provisions usually can be successfully defended as essential to protecting the trademark or other economic efficiencies of the basic franchise arrangement.

Trademark is a second area of law to which special attention must be paid in writing global franchise contracts. Here the general movements towards internationalizing or globalizing trademark law itself have tended to ease the path of the global franchisor.

Thus the basic story is that American plus franchise contracting practices have been accepted largely by inaction in most of the legal systems of the world and by special accommodation when inaction would not have been enough. Franchise contracting is, of course, subsumed under the general contract law of the particular state, but the only major, specific regulatory move has been the beefing-up of disclosure requirements. Indeed the most typical move of those political entities that have made a special law-making effort to confront franchising has been the enactment of statutes or regulations which allow or require private associations of franchisors-franchisees to write voluntary codes of ethics for their sector.

Business format franchising can no doubt be cited as a great story in which globalizing contract law has been essentially supportive of globalizing contract practice. Certainly an enormous amount of contract language and an enormous number of contract provisions first developed in the United States have been exported around the world. And certainly such business format franchising contracts tend to be long and detailed.

≺ VI ≻

Mineral (Non-Oil) Development Contracts

The much touted flexibility of contract as a legal instrument is dramatically shown in a range of international contracts that deviate sharply from the standard repertoire because a sovereign state is one of the parties.[36] Perhaps among the most interesting of these deviations is the joint venture agreement for mineral development. In such agreements one regulatory potential of contract law comes to the fore and, as is often true, regulation is exercised in behalf of the "weaker" party. In older times mineral development in developing states by first-world investors usually took the form of a "concession" agreement. At least from the point of view of the developing states such concession agreements were not very complex. The cost of luring job- as well as tax revenue-creating projects into destitute countries was the grant of nearly sovereign powers to foreign investors to exploit a particular stretch of land in return for a small share of the profits. In more recent, post-colonial, days, the opposite extreme has been the service contract in which the out-side investor merely contracts with the host state to provide man-agement of the day-to-day mining operations at a government-owned site. Such arrangements have flourished in the oil industry where competition among oil companies and high market demand give the governments for the oil states an overwhelming bargaining advantage. In solid minerals, however, the situation is less advan-tageous to the host states, which must give potential exploiters of mineral resources a better deal.

The better deal that has evolved is essentially relatively long-term management control to the investors but a far greater share in management, and in management-acquired information, to the host country than occurred under the concession arrangement, or even under the service contract. Most interesting is that much of the increased host state control can be achieved either through state mining, tax, environmental, health, and corporation law or through contractual agreements between the state and the foreign investors. Contracts and regulatory statutes become alternative modes of increasing state control.

This balance of interests between investors and host states is achieved through mining agreements that create joint venture cor-porations to conduct the actual mining operations. Many alterna-tive corporate structures, decision-making processes, and share-holding patterns are available through such agreements. The host state may be the majority or minority shareholder. Whoever is the minority shareholder may or may not be given a veto over the cor-poration's management decisions. The basic agreement may pro-vide very detailed provisions of exactly what the management of the joint venture may do or not do, may do with or without the authorization of the board of directors, may do or not do with or without the authorization of an executive committee of the board whose voting is structured differently than the board itself. Nearly any mix of investor and host government day-to-day and long-term control of management can be achieved through a series of com-plex, legally binding documents. Those documents may include a detailed delineation of the joint venture's corporate structure and decision-making processes, a master contract, articles of incorpora-tion, and a project management contract.

A key element of the master contract may be an extremely

complex specification of the powers and the boundaries between a set of managing directors and a board of directors. In addition, the master contracts may provide for renegotiation of various specific goals of the joint venture over time. And these mixes can be very subtle. They are not only about who has the final say but about who gets to participate how much before the final say is said and who gets how much of the information on which the final say is based.

Here we have a contract that establishes a substantive exchange between the investors and the host state; it also establishes the details of the organization of an operating corporation that finally meshes investor and host country interests and management participation. Here contracts are used to fashion ongoing structures of state regulation of private endeavors and private participation in state enterprises. Joint participation is seen as an optimum mode of adjusting the interests of the two parties both because it can lead to a regime of reciprocal influence rather than all or nothing vetoes and because it assures each side access to the information necessary to protect its interests. Such joint participation contracts are necessarily quite long and detailed.

≺ VII ≻

Business Organization and the Law

Somehow attendant on both the franchising and mineral development stories is also a story about the worldwide evolution of business organization which can also be seen as either American diffusion or parallel development.

If we are interested in the globalization of commercial contracting practice and law, or simply in business law, obviously we must be concerned about developments in both business and law institutions and their ways of thinking and doing. My argument here in brief is that the theory and practice of business organization has moved towards the externalized complex big deal as central to success and that American law practice has moved towards the large law firm bent on manufacturing large, complex law. The result of the two movements is a globalization of the long, extremely complex and detailed "American" form of business contracting.

To turn first to the business side, business theory and practice at one time heavily favored the vertically integrated, oligopic firm. In such firms most relationships of production and distribution are internalized, the firm ideally touching the outside world only in its employment of labor, its purchase of sites, and its ultimate sale to consumers. Norms are enunciated in internal directives and manuals. Disputes among individual executives or units are administrative problems to be solved by administrative techniques. Relations with rival oligopolists were to be handled by secret and direct contact at the highest executive levels.

More recently business theory and practice has tended towards a view of the firm as a bundle of capital and intelligence, seeking profit by whatever arrangements will yield profit. Rather than the rigidities and clear boundaries between the internal and external of the vertically integrated firm, the new firm proactively seeks every sort of joint venture, minority or majority participation, lead- or sub-contractor, licensing franchising, leasing, concession, management, pooling, spin-off, subsidiary, partnership, or other arrangement that may be most feasible for meeting a particular business goal. The boundary between internal and external constantly shifts and is sometimes blurred. Many essential business relationships are externalized. As a result norms must be stated in contracts. Disputes become less a matter of internal administration and more a matter of bargaining, bargaining under the shadow of potential litigation and arbitration. More relationships are handled through lawyers rather than executive-to-executive.

Added to this general tendency of business is a phenomenon that has particularly marked international business. The vertically integrated firm tended to ignore national boundaries in a classic "imperialist" pattern of reaching abroad to secure its raw materials or its ultimate sales—or both. In the post-imperial world, many large businesses found that their international business relationships could not be internalized. Third-world governments nationalized major economic activities within their boundaries or demanded for themselves a major role in business activity. Often this role was played by way of intense regulatory regimes in which government acted as government. Just as often, as we have seen in the minerals area, third-world governments demanded a place as business participants or partners. Big firms found many of their overseas activities externalized and legalized because third-world governments had become their collaborators in business activities and these collaborations were defined by contract between the firm and the host state.

On the law side the story is equally familiar. Where business consists of complex, often long-term, ongoing relationships between two or more entities in economic, legal, political, social, and technological environments that are rapidly changing, those entities can maintain their relationships either by intimate, fluid, constant, and highly discretionary collaborations among their principals or by highly detailed legal, contractual provisions that are carefully tailored to their particular current situations and fully anticipate future changes in those situations. Any mix of the two is also possible. The large American law firm has the resources to provide the extremely complex, detailed, and particularized contracts needed if the second option is chosen and also the resources to provide the large-scale, fact- and procedure-oriented, litigation services necessary if trouble should arise under such contracts. Everyone is, of course, familiar with the paradox that the more carefully and fully contracts seek to anticipate every potential nuance that may arise in a complex, ongoing business relationship, the more massive the litigation is likely to become if the anticipation fails.

Just as the size of litigations and the size of law firms grew in some interlocked way in the U.S. business world, one would expect a similar growth internationally if for no other reason than because large American firms play a very large part in international business life and were likely to export their style. Even when American operating firms are not involved, American investment capital often is. American firms were likely to want the same kind of contracts with foreign firms that they had with domestic ones. American law firms representing American businesses were certainly ready, willing, and able to provide them. As we have noted, certain special features of the international business environment also seemed to require longer, more complex contracts.

And, at least once the resources and the habit were established, contracts were a natural place to pile all sorts of organizational and substantive rules and procedures that in another world would have gone into company manuals. The rules for cooking hamburgers get piled into the franchise contract. The rules for voting on the executive committee get piled into the mineral development contract. The contracts that govern bank financing agreements for large, new enterprises are notoriously long and detailed. But it can be argued that their great complexity is far less a result of the work of lawyers seeking to avoid problems that lead to litigation or seeking to gain advantage for their clients should litigation arise than it is the result of bankers writing into the contracts themselves the internal manuals that are to guide bank employees administering the loans.[37]

In any event, it may well be that a disproportionately large share of international contracting business now goes to large American law firms to write large American-style contracts. Perhaps most revealing is the situation within Europe. The customs and mores of the legal professions of most European countries have always made it difficult for continental lawyers to provide the legal services that large corporations need, and until very recently there were essentially no large European law firms. For reasons peculiar to the evolution of the English legal profession, there have been large solicitors' firms in London for a long time. Continental lawyers are now experiencing considerable angst at what they see as a flow of European contract business to London, because the large firms there can give the customers what they want. What is most notable, however, is that although the English firms traditionally were accustomed to writing relatively brief, "heads of agreement"–style contracts, they have now shifted to writing far more detailed contracts and their new continental business is often attributed to that shift. It may be that here we encounter a situation of globalization as Americanization in which English lawyers gain an advantage over their European Union competitors because they are better placed to quickly adopt American practices and are willing to Americanize.

While no hard quantitative evidence exists, it is clear to practitioners that the typical big deal contract is long, is drafted in New York or London by big firms that can "pick" the contract provisions "off the shelf," and provides for arbitration or litigation under New York or English contract law. It should be underlined, however, that the whole story of the globalization of the complex, detailed, litigation-oriented, American contract style is very weakly documented in empirical studies or even studies of the spread of doctrine. Wolfgang Wiegand's writing on the Americanization of European law is certainly pioneering[38] and Yves Dezalay has done a major empirical study of European law practice that certainly supports this story.[39] But until a great deal more real work is done, the notion of a globalized American-style contract law remains a hypothesis that I am pleased to offer but can barely begin to confirm.

Luckily Dezalay and Bryant Garth have now published their in-depth empirical study of international contract arbitration.[40] As they argue, arbitration clauses have become nearly universal in international business contracts and international contract arbitration has been growing by leaps and bounds. So international contract arbitration is clearly at the very center of whatever globalization of contract law is occurring. Along one dimension what they discover is a globalization of contract law in the sense of the creation of a global forum or set of institutions and a global set of arbitral practices or a global arbitration style and a relatively small, relatively coherent community of global arbitrators. And global here means not only all European (including Eastern Europe) and trans-Atlantic but also north-south (developed and developing nations) and to some degree even east-west. Along another dimension, however, what they depict is a conflict between Europeanization and Americanization of the globe with Americanization winning the upper hand.

Their story begins as one of Europeanized globalization. A small group of very senior, highly esteemed European academic lawyers and judges of particularly scholarly bent establish an intellectual discourse or body of legal lore of international arbitration and a number of European centers for the conduct of an international arbitration practice. While few of the initiators of this movement probably consciously saw it this way, this move to arbitration largely consists of a set of anti-Americanization moves. First it offered contracting parties the choice of specifying a European site of dispute resolution in order to counter the increasing tendency of international contracts, particularly those in which one firm was American, to explicitly choose New York law and either New York courts or the well-developed arbitration system in New York as the site of resolution. Second it sought to substitute a more informal, less adversarial mode of resolution for more formal, adversarial litigation. Third it sought to move the resolution process away from elaborate procedural maneuvering, and more particularly the complex wrangling over conflict of laws problems that had come to characterize much international contract litigation, towards a simple and direct confrontation with the basic substantive issues.

Fourth it sought to reduce the degree to which the parties' lawyers controlled the resolution process and to increase the degree of control of the third member of the triad—the arbitrator. The arbitrator was to be a person of far greater knowledge and far greater prestige than the lawyers, the true master of the transnational law of contract, and the wise old man devoted to substantive justice rather than the referee between two contesting lawyers. In part this enhanced role for the triadic figure stems from the very choice of arbitration over litigation which can be taken as implying a certain rejection by the parties themselves of the excessive legalism and accentuated adversarialism of the regular courts. In part it is a function of the specific historical circumstances. International contract arbitration was largely created by a small community of academics and judges closely allied to academics and was based on their uniquely vast grasp of both the most erudite and universal theories of contract and of comparative law. International arbitration was built up on this charisma of scholarly prowess. The environment created was one in which the "grand old man" doing the arbitrating knew everything. The very legitimacy of the arbitration rested on his knowledge that had in effect created the whole arbitrating institution. And the arbitrator was a repeat player legitimating his work partly by reference to his own previous experience. The lawyers for the parties, on the other hand, were mere parochial technicians, occasional interlopers into this scholarly realm from their mundane, professional, parochially national law practices.

Fifth because international contract arbitration grew up as a European movement, it tended towards the very limited discovery practices common in Europe. Thus arbitration was far, far less involved in the enormous machinery of fact gathering, organization, analysis, and presentation than is American corporate litigation. Sixth the leaders of this European arbitration movement were, for the most part, boosters of the *lex mercatoria* and some sort of modern version of the *ius gentium*. They much preferred to decide

cases by reference to general legal principles and common principles discerned by comparative analysis of national legal traditions
than by reference to the particular law of a particular state. And as
we have already seen, the *lex mercatoria* and the various European
and U.N. contract conventions that are seen as growing out and
becoming a part of it tend to adhere to European rather than American traditions and theories of contract law.

Having depicted this Europeanized origin of the globalization of
contract arbitration, Dezalay and Garth go on to depict a stage of
Americanization. Large American law firms become deeply involved in the arbitration sites in European cities and bring with
them their hard ball style and their capacity to marshall facts.
There arises a generation of practitioners who specialize in representing clients in international arbitration and then themselves
begin to replace the grand old men who are, after all, not only
grand but old. As the lawyers for the parties also become repeat
players and possessors of high levels of knowledge of transnational
contract law, the relative power of the triadic figure and the lawyer
for the parties shifts in favor of the lawyers. As a result of all these
phenomena there is a shift back towards concern for conflict of
laws and a renewed preference for finding concrete legal rules
rather than relying on general principles, theory, and comparative
method. Arbitration comes to look more and more like litigation,
and indeed litigation American style. The arbitrator looks less and
less like mediator and more and more like privately hired judge. As
international contract arbitration becomes more and more dominant and globalized, it comes more and more to look like American-style adversarial legal litigation.

As Dezalay and Garth emphasize, their findings are even harder
to support directly than would be findings about contract litigation
in regular courts. For most contract arbitration clauses contain secrecy provisions that prohibit the publication of arbitral awards
and the opinions supporting them. Of course this practice not only
hampers the researcher but also must, to some but unknown degree, favor the European over the American style. For the secrecy
cuts off the American-style lawyer from one of his favorite practices, searching out cases almost exactly the same on their facts to
the one being decided and citing those cases in precedential arguments. Where case particulars are hard to come by, academic writ-

ings and the theories and general principles they propound, in other words the world of the European grand old men, almost necessarily play a disproportionate role. Of course, those wedded to the American style will respond by treating published court precedents as authoritative for arbitrations and so drive arbitration further into the litigation mode.

If we put together the business firms externalizing many of their relationships and the penchant of large law firms to write long, detailed contracts that seek to anticipate every imaginable factual situation that may arise over a long future time span and then threaten to fiercely litigate every detail, we arrive at the crux of the modern debate about what the world of contract law is really like. In one story the large law firm and its extreme adversarial legal practices have themselves been created by the needs and demands of business. Society calls and the law responds. In the other story, the lawyers have been busily constituting legal practice to their own advantage, creating business for themselves rather than serving the needs of business. The lawyers say they are serving the clients. And the businessmen say that they have become the prisoners of law firms that complicate their lives and take an enormous ransom for doing so.

These two stories, so often told for the American scene, now seem to be equally at large in the global context. In one the contracting parties are more and more free to make the law that governs themselves. In the other contracting parties are freer and freer to subject themselves to the pathologies of the American legal profession.

≺ VIII ≻

Conclusion

Most students of law would agree that there has been an enormous growth in contracting between firms sited in different countries. There is a great deal of documentation of the growth of a body of model transnational contract principles, rules, and statutes; and of international contract arbitration institutions, processes, and personnel. I have insufficiently documented the spread of the long, detailed, litigation-oriented–"American"-style contract as a major

feature of the globalization of contract practice; but nonetheless I
assert it with some confidence until contradicted by contract specialists. Dezalay and Garth are at least on the way to documenting
an Americanization of the international arbitration processes that
clearly are a major feature of the globalization of contract practice
and law.

All of this may lead to either some very straightforward or some
rather paradoxical conclusions about the globalization of freedom
of contract, depending on one's point of view and on a number of
wild guesses unsupported by hard data. If freedom of contract is entirely a matter of how free *governments* allow private enterprises
to be in making contracts, then globalization is surely a story of increasing freedom. There is a growing body of practice and law that
makes it possible for private parties resident in different states to
make and anticipate enforcement of contracts with relatively few
barriers created by national sovereignty itself. There may even be a
growing capacity for private parties to make contracts with governments that enjoy a strong chance of performance. There is considerable growth in a global law of contracts and global forums for
the enforcement of that law that provide the legal support for
global growth in contracting. Leaving aside the waxing and waning
of government regulations that constrain the choices of contracting
parties,[41] the capacity to contract and the practice of contracting
freely across the globe have certainly increased since World War II.

If, however, we look at the world as containing not just two
players, those who wish to contract and governments, but instead
three players, those who wish to contract, governments, and the
legal profession, the freedom picture may not be as clear. It is here
that the arguable, but not proved, thesis of globalization as Americanization becomes relevant. To the extent that the American
style of contract writing and disputing is becoming global, global
freedom of contract may be, along a certain dimension, illusory, or
purchased at a very high cost. The lawyers may have become far
freer than the contracting parties.

REFERENCE MATTER

≺ ≻

Notes

INTRODUCTION

1. Friedrich Kessler and Malcolm Pitman Sharp, *Contracts: Cases and Materials* (Boston, 1951), 3.

CHAPTER I

1. There is a large literature on the evolution of the English land law, but no single major historical treatment exists. My *A History of the Land Law* (2d ed. Oxford, 1986) attempts to provide a concise readable account and includes a bibliography. Modern British treatises contain much historical material; the best is R. E. Megarry and H. W. R. Wade, *The Law of Real Property* (5th ed. London, 1984)—for present purposes any edition will serve. Other significant studies are W. R. Cornish and G. de N. Clark, *Law and Society in England 1750–1950* (London, 1989) esp. chap. 2; K. E. Digby, *An Introduction to the History of the Law of Real Property with Original Authorities* (5th ed. Oxford, 1897); J. H. Baker, *An Introduction to English Legal History* (3d ed. London, 1990), esp. chaps. 1–6 and 13–17; L. Bonfield, *Marriage Settlements 1601–1740, the Adoption of the Strict Settlement* (Cambridge, 1983); H. J. Habbakuk, *Marriage, Debt and the Estates System: English Landownership 1550–1950* (Oxford, 1994); S. F. C. Milsom, *The Legal Framework of English Feudalism* (Cambridge, 1976); G. E. Mingay, *English Landed Society in the Eighteenth Century* (London, 1963); E. Spring, *Law, Land and Family: Aristocratic Inheritance in England 1300–1800* (Chapel Hill, NC, 1993); F. M. L. Thompson, *English Landed Society in the Nineteenth Century* (London, 1963).

2. A justice of the Court of Common Pleas from 1466, and knighted in 1475.

3. See A. W. B. Simpson, ed., *Biographical Dictionary of the Common Law* (London, 1984) at 315–17, entry by J. H. Baker.

4. See, for example, among the currently used law school case-books, J. Dukeminier and J. E. Krier, *Property* (3d ed. Boston, 1993), at 201; and J. W. Singer, *Property Law. Rules, Policies and Practices* (Boston, 1993), 277–78, 508–9, 513.

5. O. W. Holmes, *The Common Law* (Boston, 1881), 1–2.

6. The classic analysis is that of A. M. Honoré, "Ownership," in A. G. Guest, ed., *Oxford Essays in Jurisprudence* (1st ser. Oxford, 1961), chap. 5. For modern discussion see J. E. Penner, "The 'Bundle of Rights' Picture of Property," *UCLA Law Review* 43 (1996): 711. However, Honoré did not conceive of property as comprising a bundle of rights, but rather, in the paradigm case, a relationship between a person and a thing recognized by law which commonly exhibited a set of standard incidents; for discussion see Penner, "Bundle of Rights."

7. There may be various exceptions and qualifications. For an analysis of what he calls the standard incidents of the paradigm case of ownership in liberal thought see Honoré, "Ownership," 112–24, where he argues for nine such incidents—the right to possess, the right to use, the right to manage, the right to the income, the right to the capital, the right to security, the incident of transmissibility, the incident of absence of term, and liability to execution.

8. E. Plowden, *Commentaries* (London, 1571), 555.

9. It may be impossible to locate one, in which case the property "escheated" to the feudal lord, and today to the State.

10. There were different sorts of entail—some could be inherited by both male and female heirs, though males always trumped females. Some could be inherited only by males. Some could be inherited only by descendants by a particular wife. But in all cases the entail could come to an end if the blood line ran out.

11. I do not go into all the complexities.

12. Once called "feoffees," persons to whom a fee had been transferred.

13. The common law courts were the Courts of Common Pleas, the Court of King's Bench, and the Court of Exchequer. The law they applied was the common law—the law available throughout the land.

14. See J. Davis, *Concepts in Social Thought. Exchange* (Minneapolis, 1992), esp. chap. 2.

15. *Commentaries on the Laws of England* (Chicago, 1979, facsimile repr. of the 1st ed., 1765–69), 2:2. At 1:134 he describes the right of property as "the third absolute right, inherent in every Englishman . . . which consists in the free use, enjoyment and disposal of all his acquisitions, without any control or diminution, save only be the laws of the land." An absolute right is one vested in an individual by the immutable laws of nature.

16. Ibid., 1:107.

17. Ibid., 2:14.

18. The reference is to the royal forests, which were appropriated by the monarch as hunting preserves, and which came to be covered by their own peculiar body of law.

19. Where a vessel was lost at sea, and goods or cargo came ashore, but no living creature survived, the property became wreck and vested in the Crown; the right was often granted by the Crown to local lords of the manor. Originally the owner's property right was ended by the loss of the

ship, but later it was provided that the Crown retained the property only if no owner turned up after a stated period. See Blackstone, *Commentaries* 1:280–84.

20. An estray is a domestic animal found wandering without its owner being discoverable; title vested in the Crown or, as was usually the case, in the local lord of the manor by grant from the Crown. See ibid., 1:287.

21. In general wild creatures were regarded by Blackstone as remaining in common, by which he means the same thing as owned by nobody, but available for the first taker. Blackstone at *Commentaries* 2:411 indeed says that they are "the property of nobody." In the case of creatures which were regarded as suitable for hunting the Crown acquired the sole right of pursuing and taking them, and any right vested in a subject was viewed as derivative only. See ibid., 2:410–19. Elaborate criminal penalties were developed to protect the rights of those entitled to take game.

22. The quotation is from a report of the West African Lands Commission of 1917; I have been unable to obtain access to a copy so as to give a more precise reference.

23. See K. A. Busia, *The Position of the Chief in the Modern Political System of Ashanti* (Oxford, 1951), at 42; and R. S. Rattray, *Ashanti* (Oxford, 1923), at 229. R. C. Ellickson in his "Property in Land," *Yale Law Journal* 102 (1992): 1344 and following discusses some modern communes, Hutterite colonies, and Israeli kibbutzim.

24. See E. Kerridge, *The Common Fields of England* (Manchester, 1992); G. E. Mingay, *The Agricultural Revolution, 1750–1880* (London, 1966); C. S. Orwin, *The Open Fields* (3d ed. Oxford, 1967). For a valuable modern account arguing that the inefficiency of the old system has been overstated see J. M. Neeson, *Commoners: Common Right, Enclosure and Social Change in England 1700–1820* (Cambridge, 1993).

25. For fuller explanation see A. W. B. Simpson, "Entails and Perpetuities," *The Juridical Review* 24 (1979): 1–20, repr. in *Legal Theory and Legal History. Essays on the Common Law* (London, 1987), chap. 8.

26. Blackstone, *Commentaries* 2:9.

27. Thomas Littleton, *Tenures* (London, 1481), sec. 1 and sec. 11.

28. Blackstone, *Commentaries* 2:103–5.

29. Ibid., 1:134.

30. See ibid., 2:282–83.

31. See my *A History of the Land Law*, chaps. 3 and 4, for discussion and references.

32. The term dates from the nineteenth century; *The Oxford English Dictionary* vol. 4 records a first use in 1839.

33. For discussion see S. F. C. Milsom, *Legal Framework*, and for discussion see R. C. Palmer, "The Origins of Property in England," *Law and History Review* 3 (1985): 1–50.

34. Special rules applied however to the Crown's tenants-in-chief.

35. Females could inherit land, but only if there were no males of equivalent degree. Females of equal degree took jointly as co-parceners;

however, there could be single female heirs, known as "heiresses" and viewed in aristocratic circles as highly desirable brides.

36. The critical legislation comprised the Wills Act of 1540 and the Statute of Tenures of 1660.

37. See my *A History of the Land Law*, chap. 1, for a brief account.

38. See Blackstone, *Commentaries* 4:411–31.

39. Ibid., 2:105.

40. For an account see my *A History of the Land Law*, chap. 7.

41. Blackstone, *Commentaries* 1:135.

42. Blackstone gives an account of the law of nuisance in ibid., 3:216–22 and 4:167–69. For discussion see J. P. S. McLaren, "Nuisance Law and the Industrial Revolution—Some Lessons from Social History," *Oxford Journal of Legal Studies* 3 (1983): 155; and A. W. B. Simpson, *Leading Cases in the Common Law* (Oxford, 1995), chap. 7.

43. There were qualifications—for example legitimate trade competition, rationalized around the idea that such competition did not deprive the victim of anything to which he was legally entitled.

44. Blackstone, *Commentaries* 3:216.

45. Ibid., 4:167.

46. For discussion see Cornish and Clark, *Law and Society*, 151–66.

47. See Simpson, *Leading Cases in the Common Law*, chap. 7, and in particular 172–75, discussing *Hole v. Barlow* (1858) 4 C.B. (N.S.) 334, 140 E.R. 1113 and *Bamford v. Turley* (1863) 3 B. & S. 62, 66, 122 E.R. 25.

48. *Case of the King's Prerogative in Saltpetre* (1607) 12 Co. Rep. 12.

49. J. Chitty, *A Treatise on Law of the Prerogatives of the Crown and the Relative Duties and Rights of the Subject* (London, 1820), 175.

50. 4 B. & S. 608, 616, 122 E.R. 588, 591, XI H.L.C. 642, 11 E.R. 1483, 1 chap. Alp. 66. See Simpson, *Leading Cases in the Common Law*, chap. 7, for discussion.

51. At 115.

52. "Privilege, Malice and Intent," *Harvard Law Review* 8 (1894): 10.

53. F. Pollock, *The Law of Torts*, 135–38.

54. See Simpson, *Leading Cases in the Common Law*, 72–75.

55. Holt K.B. 14, 17, 19, 90 E.R. 906 and elsewhere; see Simpson, *Leading Cases in the Common Law*, 45 n. 2 for reports, and chap. 3 generally for discussion.

56. [1895] A.C. 587. For a fuller discussion see A. W. B. Simpson, *Victorian Law and the Industrial Spirit* (London, 1995).

57. The relevant cases were *Chasemore v. Richards* (1859) 7 H.L.C. 349; and *Acton v. Blundell* (1843) 2 M. & W. 324 152 E.R. 1223.

58. For accounts see Neeson, *Commoners*; G. E. Mingay, *Land and Society in England 1750–1980* (London, 1994); J. D. Chambers and G. E. Mingay, *The Agricultural Revolution, 1750–1880* (London, 1966); E. C. K. Gonner, *Common Land and Enclosure* (London, 1966).

59. I have given accounts of these Acts and their significance in *Leading Cases in the Common Law*, 169–70 and 218–22.

60. Blackstone, *Commentaries* 1:134.

61. For an account of the system in operation see R. W. Kostal, *Law and English Railway Capitalism 1825–1875* (Oxford, 1994).

62. 4 B. & Ad. 30, 110 E.R. 366.

63. This is a major theme in Habbakuk's massive study of landowner-ship, *Marriage, Debt and the Estates System.*

64. Blackstone, *Commentaries* 2:10. He goes on to explain that a kind of secondary law of nature permits testamentary disposition and inheri-tance.

65. J. P. Dawson, *Gifts and Promises: Continental and American Law Compared* (New Haven, CT, 1980) is one of the few general analytical dis-cussions of gifts by a common law writer in modern times; unfortunately Dawson paid virtually no attention to gifts of landed property and appears to have been unfamiliar with the anthropological literature. The anthropo-logical literature is massive; see in particular B. Malinowski, *Argonauts of the Western Pacific. An Account of Native Enterprise and Adventures in the Archipelagoes of Melanesian New Guinea* (London, 1922); M. Mauss, *The Gift. Forms and Functions of Exchange in Archaic Societies* (London, 1954); M. D. Sahlins, *Stone Age Economics* (Chicago, 1972). J. Davis, *Concepts*, has a valuable bibliography.

66. See this explained in Simpson, "Entails and Perpetuities."

67. Blackstone, *Commentaries* 2:109.

68. See Simpson, *History of the Land Law*, chaps. 4 and 9, for the tech-nicalities; and "Entails and Perpetuities" for general discussion.

69. For discussion see Simpson, *Leading Cases in the Common Law*, chap. 4.

70. See Cornish and Clark, *Law and Society*, 166–72, for an account. Adam Smith in *The Wealth of Nations* expressed hostility to entails in bk. 3, chaps. 2 and 4.

71. See J. C. W. Wylie, *Irish Land Law*, para 1.42 and Simpson, *History of the Land Law*, 285, for details.

CHAPTER 2

1. A. V. Dicey, *Lectures on the Relation between Law and Public Opinion in England during the Nineteenth Century* (London, 1905), 152. On Dicey's mischaracterization of Benthamism, see J. B. Brebner, "Lais-sez-Faire and State Intervention in Nineteenth Century Britain," *Journal of Economic History* 8, supp. (1948): 59–73.

2. A. V. Dicey, "The Combination Laws as Illustrating the Relation be-tween Law and Opinion in England during the Nineteenth Century," *Harvard Law Review* 17 (1903): 511–32; Dicey, *Law and Opinion*, 271–73. As Dicey defined it, the term "combination law" included the legal rules concerning wage-setting by combinations on either side of the industrial divide, by employers as well as by employees.

3. A. V. Dicey, *Law and Opinion*, 2d ed. (London, 1914), xxii–xciv.

4. 198 U.S. 45 (1905) (invalidating statute restricting bakers' hours of labor to no more than sixty hours a week or ten hours a day, but upholding various hygienic and structural standards for bakeries).

5. See William S. Holdsworth, *A History of English Law*, 4th ed. (London, 1936), 2:355 ("In a feudal state where property and office are confused, under a primitive legal system which has a highly developed land law, but no theory of contract, the list of incorporeal things tends to expand, and to follow the most highly developed branch of the law").

6. 13 Edw. I, c. 25 (1285). The assize of novel disseisin was the form of action generally used by one who complained of having been wrongfully ejected from his land.

7. Glanvill xiii, 33 in *The Treatise on the Laws and Customs of the Realm of England Commonly Called Glanvill*, G. D. G. Hall, ed. (Oxford, 1993), 167–68.

8. Frederick Pollock and Frederic William Maitland, *The History of English Law*, 2d ed. (Cambridge, 1899), 2:135.

9. See *Manning's Case*, 8 Co. Rep. 94b, 77 Eng. Rep. 618 (K.B., 1609); *Lampet's Case*, 10 Co. Rep. 46b, 77 Eng. Rep. 994 (K.B., 1612). See also A. W. B. Simpson, *A History of the Land Law*, 2d ed. (Oxford, 1986), 249–50. In the distribution of the estates of deceased persons at common law, leases passed with personal property to the personal representative, not with real property to the heir.

10. See Marcel Planiol, *Treatise on the Civil Law* (St. Paul, MN, 1959), 2: § 1663 et seq.; 11 La. Civil Code, art. 2669 (1995).

11. See *American Law of Property*, A. James Casner, ed. (Boston, 1954), 1: § 3.11, pp. 202–3.

12. Ibid., § 3.50, p. 278.

13. Pollock and Maitland, *English Law* 2:131.

14. See Robert Kratovil, *Real Estate Law*, 5th ed. (Englewood Cliffs, NJ, 1969), § 364, p. 210.

15. The law of equitable mortgages illustrates the insignificant role played by agreement: "A mortgage may arise in equity, out of the transaction of the parties, without any deed or express contract for that special purpose." James Kent, *Commentaries on American Law*, 12th ed., O. W. Holmes, Jr., ed. (Boston, 1873), 4: 150.

16. See *Paine v. Meller*, 6 Ves. Jr. 349, 31 Eng. Rep. 1088 (Ch. 1801).

17. 2 W. Bl. 1078, 96 Eng. Rep. 635 (K.B., 1775).

18. When James Kent last revised his *Commentaries on American Law* in 1840, it still seemed possible that the rule in *Flureau v. Thornhill* would be generalized as the measure of damages for the breach of all contracts: Kent, *Commentaries* 2: 480 n. b. By the time Holmes prepared the notes for the twelfth edition, it was plain that *Flureau* would be treated as exceptional and confined to real estate contracts: Kent, *Commentaries* 2:479 n. 1.

19. See *Javins v. First Nat'l Realty Corp.*, 428 F.2d 1071, 1075 (D.C. Cir. 1970) ("leases of urban dwelling units should be interpreted and construed

like any other contract"); *Brown v. Southall Realty Co.*, 237 A.2d 834, 836 (D.C. Ct. App. 1968); North Carolina's Residential Rental Agreements Act, codified at *N.C. Gen. Stat.*, §§ 42-38 to §§ 42-46 (1994).

20. *N.C. Gen. Stat.*, § 42-41 (1994).

21. See Kratovil, *Real Estate Law*, § 364, p. 210.

22. See C. C. Langdell, "A Brief Survey of Equity Jurisdiction," *Harvard Law Review* 1 (1888): 355, 373–80; Samuel Williston, "The Risk of Loss After an Executory Contract of Sale in the Common Law," *Harvard Law Review* 9 (1895): 106–30; Samuel Williston, *The Law of Contracts* (New York, 1920), 2: § 940, pp. 1784–85; Harlan F. Stone, "Equitable Conversion by Contract," *Columbia Law Review* 13 (1913): 369–88; Benjamin N. Cardozo, *The Nature of the Judicial Process* (New Haven, CT, 1925), 38–39.

23. Law of Property Act, 15 & 16 Geo. 5, c. 20, § 47 (1925).

24. Uniform Vendor and Purchaser Risk Act, *Uniform Laws Annotated* 14 (St. Paul, MN, 1979): § 1, pp. 469, 471 (shifting risk of loss due to accidental destruction or taking by eminent domain on occurrence of change of possession or transfer of legal title, whichever occurs first, in the absence of express agreement to the contrary).

25. E.g., *Bleckley v. Langston*, 143 S.E. 2d 671, 672 (Ga. Ct. App., 1965) (admitting the "inaccuracy" of the theory of equitable conversion and its "inconsistency with natural justice, practical advantage, and the principles of law in analogous cases" but applying it anyway).

26. See Dan B. Dobbs, *Law of Remedies*, 2d ed. (St. Paul, MN, 1993), § 12.11 (1), p. 822 ("something less than half of the American states seem to accept it, and the number may be declining"). See also Lawrence V. Berkovich, "To Pay or to Convey? A Theory of Remedies for Breach of Real Estate Contracts," *Annual Survey of American Law* 1995, 319.

27. J. H. Baker, book review, *Law Quarterly Review* 43 (1980): 468.

28. An executory contract is an enforceable agreement that has not yet been fully performed; it is contrasted in contract law with an executed contract, that is, one that has already been fully performed. Kent, *Commentaries* 2:450, gives a simple illustration: "If, for instance, one person sells and delivers goods to another for a price paid, the agreement is *executed*, and becomes complete and absolute; but if the vendor agrees to sell and deliver at a future time, and for a stipulated price, and the other agrees to accept and pay, the contract is *executory*."

29. A. W. B. Simpson, intro., William Blackstone, *Commentaries* (Chicago, 1979), 2:xiii–xiv.

30. See Cardozo, *Judicial Process*, 38–39.

31. Herbert Butterfield, *The Origins of Modern Science, 1300–1800*, rev. ed. (New York, 1957), 19; Thomas S. Kuhn, *The Structure of Scientific Revolutions*, 2d ed. enlarged (Chicago, 1970), 85.

32. Lawrence M. Friedman, *Contract Law in America: A Social and Economic Case Study* (Madison, WI, 1965), 29. The equation of deeds and contracts was not limited to the nineteenth century. See, e.g., *Sakansky v.*

Wein, 169 A. 1, 3 (N.H., 1933) (referring to a deed with easement of right of way as "a contract which not only gave the dominant owner a way across the servient estate . . . but also gave that way definite location upon the ground"). The "contractual" aspect of deeds has become more pronounced in the last half of the twentieth century as restrictive covenants and equitable servitudes in deeds have proliferated.

33. F. W. Maitland, *Equity, Also the Forms of Action at Common Law: Two Courses of Lectures*, A. H. Chaytor and W. J. Whittaker, eds. (Cambridge, 1909), 342.

34. Adam Smith, *An Inquiry into the Nature and Causes of the Wealth of Nations*, Edwin Cannan, ed. (New York, 1937), 141 (1st ed. 1776). Parliament continued to legislate for "particular trades in particular places" through the end of the eighteenth century, as described below.

35. 23 Edw. 3 (1349); 25 Edw. 3, st. 1 (1350). The first enactment is commonly called an ordinance rather than a statute since it was issued by the king without the concurrence of Parliament, unable to meet because of the plague.

36. 5 Eliz. 1, c. 4 (1563).

37. See W. E. Minchinton, *Wage Regulation in Pre-Industrial England* (New York, 1972), 9–36, 206–35.

38. Otto Kahn-Freund had to struggle to write a whole lecture on Blackstone and the contract of employment: "Blackstone's Neglected Child: The Contract of Employment," *Law Quarterly Review* 93 (1977): 508. See John W. Cairns, "Blackstone, Kahn-Freund and the Contract of Employment," *Law Quarterly Review* 105 (1989): 300.

39. William Blackstone, *Commentaries on the Laws of England* (Oxford, 1765–69), 1:410.

40. Ibid., 421.

41. For the development over time of trusts for the sole and separate use of married women, see Holdsworth, *A History of English Law* 5:312–15; 6:644–45; 12:275–76.

42. The spouses cannot by agreement alter the rules concerning child custody. See *People ex rel. Barry v. Mercein*, 3 Hill 399 (N.Y., 1842). They cannot even choose the law that will apply to their new relationship. See *Bourcier v. Lanusse*, 3 Mart. 581 (La., 1815) (holding that contract of marriage entered into in Louisiana cannot provide that the rights of the spouses shall be governed by the law of France).

43. See Casner, ed., *American Law of Property* 6: § 26.15, p. 429.

44. Blackstone, *Commentaries* 1:413.

45. Ibid.

46. Ibid., 414, citing 5 Eliz. 1, c. 4 (1563).

47. See Morris S. Arnold, "Towards an Ideology of the Early English Law of Obligations," *Law and History Review* 5 (1987): 511 ("The law of landlord and tenant and of master and servant had at bottom nothing at all to do with promise: These were hierarchical relationships and they

gave rise to obligations based on status, not on what we would call contract").

48. Blackstone, *Commentaries* 1:417.

49. See John V. Orth, *Combination and Conspiracy: A Legal History of Trade Unionism, 1721–1906* (Oxford, 1991), 124. See also Holdsworth, *A History of English Law* 4:384 ("In this way a cause of action, introduced into the common law by the fourteenth century legislation which had created a special status for the servant or workman in relation to his employer, gradually came to be considered, as the contractual aspect of that relation assumed greater prominence, first as a peculiar incident annexed to the contract of service, and then as an incident annexed to all contracts").

50. See Daphne Simon, "Master and Servant," in *Democracy and the Labour Movement: Essays in Honor of Dona Torr*, ed. John Saville (London, 1954), 160; Brian W. Hanes, "English Labour Law and the Separation From Contract," *Journal of Legal History* 1 (1980): 262–96.

51. See 13 Geo. 3, c. 68, § 7 (1773) (limiting apprentices in silk-weaving to two per master); 17 Geo. 3, c. 55, § 2 (1777) (requiring master hatters to employ one journeyman for each apprentice).

52. The Combination Acts of the eighteenth century are analyzed in detail in Orth, *Combination and Conspiracy*, chap. 2, where it is demonstrated that many of the acts' most significant features concern criminal procedure, a subject not discussed here.

53. 7 Geo 1, st. 1, c. 13 (1721).

54. Ibid., § 1 ("all contracts, covenants or agreements in writing, or not in writing, heretofore made or entered into, or hereafter to be made or entered into, by or between any persons brought up in, or professing, using, or exercising the art or mystery of a taylor, or journeyman taylor, in making up men's or women's work, in the cities of London and Westminster, or either of them, or within the weekly bills or mortality, for advancing their wages, or for lessening their usual hours of work").

55. Technically, only maximum wages and hours were set. The justices of the peace were authorized to alter the terms according to the "plenty or scarcity of the time." Ibid., § 5.

56. 12 Geo. 1, c. 34 (1726).

57. Ibid., § 3. See George W. Hilton, *The Truck System, Including a History of the British Truck Acts, 1465–1960* (Cambridge, 1960), 75–76.

58. 29 Geo. 2, c. 33 (1756).

59. See C. R. Dobson, *Masters and Journeymen: A Prehistory of Industrial Relations, 1717–1800* (Totowa, NJ, 1980), 76.

60. 30 Geo. 2, c. 12, § 1 (1757).

61. Sidney Webb and Beatrice Webb, *The History of Trade Unionism*, rev. ed. (New York, 1920), 51.

62. 30 Geo. 2, c. 12, § 2 (1757) ("all or any contracts or agreements made, or hereafter to be made and entered into, between any clothier or

maker of mixed, medley or white broad cloth, and the weaver or weavers employed by such maker, in respect to any wages to be paid to such weaver or weavers, shall, from and immediately after the first day of May one thousand seven hundred and fifty seven, be, and are hereby declared to be good, valid and effectual, to all intents and purposes; any rate made or to be made in pursuance of any law, statute or usage, to the contrary thereof in any wise notwithstanding").

63. 8 Geo. 3, c. 17 (1768).

64. 13 Geo. 3, c. 68 (1773); 32 Geo. 3, c. 44 (1792).

65. 17 Geo. 3, c. 55 (1777).

66. 36 Geo. 3, c. 111 (1796).

67. Compare 7 Geo. 1, st. 1, c. 13, § 2 (1721) (setting maximum wages at 2 shillings a day from March 25 to June 20, 1 shilling eight pence at other times, and setting maximum hours as from 6 A.M. to 8 P.M. with an hour off for dinner) with 8 Geo. 3, c. 17, § 1 (1768) (setting maximum wages at 2 shillings seven pence a day all the year round and setting maximum hours as from 6 A.M. to 7 P.M. with an hour off for refreshment). The latter act stipulated a higher rate for times of general mourning.

68. 8 Geo. 3, c. 17, § 1 (setting maximum wages at 5 shillings one and one-half pence a day at times of general mourning). For the costume required for mourning, see C. Willett Cunnington and Phillis Cunnington, *Handbook of English Costume in the Eighteenth Century* (Boston, 1951), 218, 317–19; for an analysis of the economic impact of mourning on the clothing industry, see Smith, *Wealth of Nations*, 59, 116.

69. John Rule, *The Experience of Labour in Eighteenth-Century English Industry* (New York, 1981), 179.

70. 13 Geo. 3, c. 68, § 7 (1773).

71. 17 Geo. 3, c. 55, § 2 (1777).

72. 36 Geo. 3, c. 111, § 3 (1796). For a description of the early techniques of papermaking, including an explanation of the statutory terms, see D. C. Coleman, *The British Paper Industry, 1495–1860* (Oxford, 1958), 262–64, 272.

73. See ibid., 179–93.

74. F. W. Maitland, *The Constitutional History of England* (Cambridge, 1955), 383.

75. *R. v. Journeymen Tailors of Cambridge*, 8 Mod. 10, 88 Eng. Rep. 9 (K.B. 1721).

76. 33 Edw. 1, st. 2 (1304).

77. Edward Coke, *Third Institute* (London, 1641), 143. "Appeal" is used here in its older sense of a legal complaint brought by one private person against another for damages caused by a private wrong or tort; an indictment lay for the offense against the public.

78. Edward Coke, *Second Institute* (London, 1641), 562.

79. Blackstone, *Commentaries* 4:136 (listing conspiracy as the fifteenth of twenty-two "offenses against public justice"); see also ibid., 3:126 (concerning tort of malicious prosecution).

80. William Hawkins, *A Treatise of the Pleas of the Crown*, 7th ed., Thomas Leach, ed. (London, 1795), bk. 1, chap. 72, sec. 2 (1st ed. 1716).

81. 8 Mod. 10–11, 88 Eng. Rep. 10. Refusing to work was in fact an offense under the Statute of Artificers and other statutes concerning the law of master and servant.

82. That agreement was the gist of conspiracy had been established as early as the *Poulterers' Case*, 9 Co. Rep. 55b, 77 Eng. Rep. 813 (Star Ch., 1611); that an agreement to demand certain wages was a conspiracy was established by the *Journeymen Tailors' Case*.

83. *Rex v. Eccles*, 1 Leach 274, 276, 168 Eng. Rep. 240, 241 (K.B., 1783). See *The Mansfield Manuscripts and the Growth of English Law in the Eighteenth Century*, James Oldham, ed. (Chapel Hill, NC, 1992), 2: 1317–20.

84. 1 Leach 276–77, 168 Eng. Rep. 241.

85. *Commons Journal* 54 (1798–99): 405.

86. Ibid., 412–13.

87. *Parliamentary Register* 8 (1799): 323.

88. *The Times*, June 18, 1799.

89. 39 Geo. 3, c. 81, § 1 (1799) ("all contracts, covenants, and agreements whatsoever, in writing, or not in writing, at any time or times heretofore made or entered into by or between any journeymen manufacturers or other workmen, or other persons within this kingdom, [1] for obtaining an advance of wages of them, or any of them, or any other journeymen manufacturers or workmen, or other persons in any manufacture, trade, or business, or [2] for lessening or altering their or any of their usual hours or time of working, or [3] for decreasing the quantity of work, or [4] for preventing or hindering any person or persons from employing whomsoever he, she, or they shall think proper to employ in his, her, or their manufacture, trade, or business, or [5] for controlling or anyway affecting any person or persons carrying on any manufacture, trade, or business, in the conduct or management thereof") (numbers in brackets added).

90. 39 & 40 Geo. 3, c. 106, § 17 (1800) ("all contracts, covenants, and agreements whatsoever, in writing or not in writing, made or to be made by or between any masters or other persons, [1] for reducing the wages of workmen, or [2] for adding to or altering the usual hours or time of working, or [3] for increasing the quantity of work") (numbers in brackets added).

91. Ibid., § 1. Throughout the eighteenth century the word "manufacturer," true to its Latin roots, meant a person who produced goods manually. Thomas Jefferson used the word in this sense in an 1805 letter: "As yet our manufacturers are as . . . independent and moral as our agricultural inhabitants, [and] they will continue so so long as there are vacant lands for them to resort to; because whenever it shall be attempted by the other classes to reduce them to the minimum of subsistence, they will quit their trades and go to labouring the earth." Letter from Thomas Jefferson to Mr. Lithson (Jan. 4, 1805), repr. in *The Writings of Thomas Jef-*

ferson, Albert Ellery Bergh, ed. (Washington, 1907), 11:55. In the nineteenth century the word crossed the divide between capital and labor and became the common name of one who employed handworkers.

92. See S. E. Finer, "The Transmission of Benthamite Ideas 1820–50," in *Studies· in the Growth of Nineteenth-Century Government,* Gillian Sutherland, ed. (London, 1972), 13. The campaign began with an act in 1824, 5 Geo. 4, c. 95, repealed and replaced the following year.

93. 6 Geo. 4, c.129, § 2 (1825).

94. For an analysis of the repealed statutes, see Orth, *Combination and Conspiracy,* 77–78 and app. 2, 162–65.

95. 6 Geo. 4, c. 129, § 4 (1825) (exempting from prosecution for conspiracy workmen "who shall enter into any agreement, verbal or written, among themselves, for the purpose of fixing the rate of wages or prices which the parties entering into such agreement, or any of them, shall require or demand for his or their work, or the hours or time for which he or they will work, in any manufacture, trade, or business").

96. See Orth, *Combination and Conspiracy,* chap. 8; Michael Lobban, "Strikers and the Law, 1825–51," in *The Life of the Law,* Peter Birks, ed. (London, 1993), 211–33.

97. See John V. Orth, "The Legal Status of English Trade Unions, 1799–1871," in *Law-Making and Law-Makers in British History,* Alan Harding, ed. (London, 1980), 195, 207.

98. *Comm. v. Pulis* (Phila. Mayor's Ct., 1806), pamphlet report reprinted in *A Documentary History of American Industrial Society,* ed. John R. Commons and Eugene A. Gilmore (New York, 1910–11), 3:60–248.

99. 35 Mass. (4 Metc.) 111 (1842).

100. The 1825 English Act limited collective agreement to wages and hours; Shaw extended the permitted scope to include the closed shop. See Orth, *Combination and Conspiracy,* 95.

101. *Farwell v. Boston & Worcester RR,* 45 Mass. (4 Metc.) 49 (1842). See also *Priestley v. Fowler,* 3 M & W. 1, 150 Eng. Rep. 1030 (Exch., 1837). On the latter case, see A. W. B. Simpson, *Leading Cases in the Common Law* (Oxford, 1995), chap. 5.

102. 3 Macq. 266 (H.L. 1858).

103. See Horace G. Wood, *A Treatise on the Law of Master and Servant* (Albany, NY, 1877) § 134, p. 272. See also Jay M. Feinman, "The Development of the Employment at Will Rule," *American Journal of Legal History* 20 (1976): 118–35; Mayer G. Freed and Daniel D. Polsby, "The Doubtful Provenance of 'Wood's Rule' Revisited," *Arizona State Law Journal* 22 (1990): 551–58; Jay M. Feinman, "The Development of the Employment-at-Will Rule Revisited," *Arizona State Law Journal* 23 (1991): 733–40.

104. 6 A. 354, 356 (Pa. 1886).

105. See Roscoe Pound, "Liberty of Contract," *Yale Law Journal* 18 (1909): 471 (describing *Godcharles* as "the pioneer, and, so far as influence upon the later decisions is concerned, the leading case").

106. See chapter 6 for details.

107. For example, a truck act was denounced as an attempt "to do what, in this country, cannot be done; that is, prevent persons who are *sui juris* [i.e., legally competent] from making their own contracts. The act is an infringement alike of the right of the employer and the employe [sic]. More than this, it is an insulting attempt to put the laborer under a legislative tutelage, which is not only degrading to his manhood, but subversive of his rights as a citizen of the United States. He may sell his labor for what he thinks best, whether money or goods, just as his employer may sell his iron or coal; and any and every law that proposes to prevent him from so doing is an infringement of his constitutional privileges and consequently vicious and void." *Godcharles v. Wigeman*, 6 A. 354, 356 (Pa., 1886). For further discussion of this case, see chapter 6 below. See also Lawrence M. Friedman, *A History of American Law* (New York, 1973), 574 ("there was a time, mostly in the 19th century, when formal equality seemed to satisfy the working class and the lower orders.").

108. Smith, *Wealth of Nations*, 142.

109. See Orth, *Combination and Conspiracy*, 128–29.

110. See Catherine Fisk, "Still 'Learning Something of Legislation': The Judiciary in the History of Labor Law," *Law and Social Inquiry* 19 (1994): 156–57.

111. A sample "document" may be found in *Walsby v. Anley*, 3 El. & El. 516, 517, 121 Eng. Rep. 536, 536 (Q.B. 1861): "I declare that I am not now, nor will I during my engagement with you become, a member of, or support, any society which directly or indirectly interferes with the arrangements of this or any other establishment, or the hours or terms of labour; and that I recognize the right of employers and employed individually to make any trade engagements on which they may choose to agree."

112. *Adair v. United States*, 208 U.S. 161 (1908) (invalidating federal statute); *Coppage v. Kansas*, 236 U.S. 1 (1915) (invalidating state statute).

113. Dicey, *Law and Opinion*, 64. See John V. Orth, book review, *Michigan Law Review* 80 (1982): 753, 759 n. 34.

114. J. Willard Hurst, *Law and the Conditions of Freedom in the Nineteenth-Century United States* (Madison, WI, 1956), 7. See also Friedman, *Contract Law*, 32 ("Free contract was seen not as an end in itself, but as a method of releasing economic energy"); Friedman, *History of American Law*, 157 (describing the first half of the nineteenth century as "a period of promotion of enterprise, of release of creative energy").

115. *Printing & Numerical Registering Co. v. Sampson*, L.R. 19 Eq. 462, 465 (1875).

116. Cardozo, *Judicial Process*, 67.

117. See *Penn Central Transp. Co. v. City of New York*, 438 U.S. 104 (1978) ("a state statute that substantially furthers important public policies may so frustrate distinct investment-backed expectations as to amount to a 'taking'").

118. The Uniform Premarital Agreement Act, 9B *Uniform Laws Annotated* 369, permits the prospective spouses to contract specifically with

respect to the "modification or elimination of spousal support" and generally with respect to "[a]ny other matter including their personal rights and obligations, not in violation of public policy or a statute imposing a criminal penalty." § 4(a)(4) & (8). See Elizabeth S. Scott, "Rational Decisionmaking about Marriage and Divorce," *Virginia Law Review* 90 (1990): 9.

119. See J. H. Baker, *Introduction to English Legal History*, 2d ed. (London, 1979), 296: "In the twentieth century, parliament has taken to imposing unexcludable 'implied terms' in order to confer minimum standards upon persons entering into certain classes of contract. Of course, such terms are fictitious. The object is to protect classes of persons who are thought incapable for economic reasons of protecting themselves when making contracts. Protection was extended first to leasehold tenants, then to employees, and now to consumers. The result is that the law of contract is diminishing in importance as regards the ordinary non-commercial man; all the important transactions he is likely to make are governed not by the common law of contract but by the statutory law of landlord and tenant, labour law, or consumer law." See also John V. Orth, "Who Is a Tenant? The Correct Definition of the Status in North Carolina," *North Carolina Central Law Journal* 21 (1995): 81 ("As a practical matter residential leases today contain no terms, aside from the dates of occupancy and the amount of the rent, that derive their force solely from the agreement of the parties").

120. S. F. C. Milsom, "The Nature of Blackstone's Achievement," *Oxford Journal of Legal Studies* 1 (1981):7.

121. P. S. Atiyah, *Promises, Morals, and Law* (Oxford, 1981), 202–12. See also id., *The Rise and Fall of Freedom of Contract* (Oxford, 1979), 754–64.

122. See Ian R. Macneil, "Relational Contract: What We Do and Do Not Know," *Wisconsin Law Review* 1985: 483–525; P. S. Atiyah, *An Introduction to the Law of Contract*, 5th ed. (Oxford, 1995), 50–53.

CHAPTER 3

1. Chapter 4.

2. This is usually dated from *Slades Case*, 1602, 4 Coke 92b.

3. James Gordley, "Contract in Pre-Commercial Societies and in Western History," § 28, chap. 2 of vol. 7, *Contracts in General*, in U. Drobnig, ed., *International Encyclopedia of Comparative Law* (Tübingen, 1997); Reinhard Zimmermann, *The Law of Obligations* (Cape Town, 1990), 539–40.

4. Chapter 1.

5. Marcel Garaud, *La Révolution e la propriété foncière* (Paris, 1958), 17.

6. Ibid., 31; Felix Olivier-Martin, *Histoire du droit français des origines à la Revolution* (Paris, 1951), 647–48; François-Alphonse Aulard, *La Révolution française et le régime féodal* (Paris, 1919), 37.

7. William Blackstone, *Commentaries on the Law of England* 2 (London, 1769): 2.

8. Robert Pothier, *Traité du droit de domaine de propriété*, in J. J. Bugnet, ed., *Oeuvres de Pothier* 9 (Paris, 1861): § 4.

9. E.g. Grant Gilmore, *The Death of Contract* (Columbus, OH, 1974).

10. E.g., Morton Horwitz, *The Transformation of American Law 1870–1960: The Crisis of Legal Orthodoxy* (Oxford, 1992), 145 (arguing that pre-nineteenth century common lawyers had a "'physicalist' definition of property derived from land" which disappeared with the "abstraction of the legal idea of property").

11. Patrick S. Atiyah, *The Rise and Fall of Freedom of Contract* (Oxford, 1979), 37.

12. Ibid., 84–85.

13. Italo Birocchi, *Saggi sulla formazione storica della categoria generale del contratto* (Cagliari, 1988), 25; Paolo Cappellini, "Schemi contrattuale e cultura theologico-giuridica nella seconda scolastica: verso una teoria generale" (thesis, Univ. of Florence, 1978–79); Malte Diesselhorst, *Die Lehre des Hugo Grotius vom Versprechen* (Cologne, 1959), 6; Hans Thieme, "Qu'est-ce que nous, les juristes, devons à la seconde scolastique espagnole?" in Paolo Grossi, ed., *La seconda scolastica nella formazione del diritto privato moderno* (Milan, 1973), 20; Hans Thieme, "Natürliches Privatrecht und Spätscholastik," *Zeitschrift der Savigny-Stiftung für Rechtsgeschichte Romanistische Abteilung* 70 (1953): 230; James Gordley, *The Philosophical Origins of Modern Contract Doctrine* (Oxford, 1991), 69–133.

14. Leonard Lessius, *De iustitia et iure, ceterisque virtutibus cardinalis libri quatuor* (Paris, 1628), lib. 2, cap. 17, dubs. 1, 3; cap. 18, dub. 2; cap. 21, dubs. 2, 4; Luis de Molina, *De iustitia et iure tractatus* (Venice, 1614), disps. 252, 259, 348; Domenico Soto, *De iustitia et iure libri decem* (Salamanca, 1553), lib. 3, q. 5., a. 3; lib. 4, q. 1, a. 1; lib. 6, q. 2, aa. 1, 3.

15. Hugo Grotius, *De iure belli ac pacis libri tres* (Amsterdam, 1640), II.xii.1–7 ; Samuel Pufendorf, *De iure naturae et gentium libri octo* (Amsterdam, 1688), V.ii.8–10.

16. Jean Domat, *Les Loix civiles dans leur ordre naturel* (Paris, 1713), liv. 1, tit. 1, § 1, nos. 5–6; § 5, no. 13; Robert Pothier, *Traité des obligations*, in *Oeuvres* 2: § 42.

17. Thus according to Grotius: "Nor is it enough for anyone to say that what the other party has promised more than equality is to be regarded as a gift. For such is not the intention of the contracting parties, and is not to be presumed so, except it appear." Grotius, *De iure belli ac pacis*, II.xii.11.1.

18. Soto, *De iustitia et iure*, lib. 6, q. 2, a.3; Molina, *De iustitia et iure*,

disp. 348; Lessius, *De iustitia et iure*, lib. 2, cap. 21, dub. 4; Grotius, *De iure bellis ac pacis*, II.xii.4; Pufendorf, *De iure naturae*, V.i.6; Pothier, *Obligations*, § 33.

19. Molina, *De iustitia et iure*, disp. 353; Lessius, *De iustitia et iure*, lib. 2, cap. 21, dub. 11; Grotius, *De iure bellis ac pacis*, II.xii.9.1; Pufendorf, *De iure naturae*, V.iii.1–3.

20. Domat, *Les Loix civiles*, liv. 1, tit. 1, § 2.

21. Gordley, *Philosophical Origins*, 109–11.

22. Grotius, *De iure belli ac pacis*, II.xii.11.1.

23. Lessius, *De iustitia et iure*, lib. 2, cap. 5, dubs. 1–2; Molina, *De iustitia et iure*, disp. 20; Soto, *De iustitia et iure*, lib. 4, q. 3, a. 1; Grotius, *De iure belli ac pacis*, II.ii.2; Pufendorf, *De iure naturae*, II.vi.5; IV.iv.4–7.

24. Lessius, *De iustitia et iure*, lib. 2, cap. 12, dub. 12; Molina, *De iustitia et iure*, disp. 20; Soto, *De iustitia et iure*, lib. 5, q. 3, a. 4; Grotius, *De iure belli ac pacis*, II.ii.6–7; Pufendorf, *De iure naturae*, II.vi.5.

25. Grotius, *De iure belli ac pacis*, II.ii.11.

26. E.g. Christopher C. Langdell, *A Summary of the Law of Contracts*, 2d ed. (Boston, 1880), 1–21; Stephen Leake, *Elements of the Law of Contracts* (London, 1867), 7–8; Frederick Pollock, *Principles of Contract* (London, 1885), 1–9; Charles Demolombe, *Cours de Code Napoléon*, 3d ed., 24 (Paris, 1882): § 12; Léon Larombière, *Théorie et pratique des obligations* 1 (Paris, 1857): § 41; François Laurent, *Principes de droit civil français*, 3d ed., 15 (Paris, 1875): §§ 424–27; Georg Friedrich Puchta, *Pandekten* (Leipzig, 1844); §§ 49, 54; Friedrich Carl von Savigny, *System des heutigen römischen Rechts* 3 (Berlin, 1840): § 134; Bernhard Windscheid, *Lehrbuch des Pandektenrechts* 1 (Frankfurt, 1891): § 69. See generally Gordley, *Philosophical Origins*, 161–213.

27. Valérie Ranouil, *L'Autonomie de la volonté: naissance et évolution d'un concept* (Paris, 1980), 71–72.

28. E. Gounot, "Le Principe de l'autonomie e la volonté en droit privé: contribution à l'étude critique de l'individualisme juridique" (thesis, Paris, 1912), 129, quoted in Ranouil, *L'Autonomie*, 72 n. 31.

29. Puchta, *Pandekten*, § 58.

30. Laurent, *Principes* 16: § 182.

31. Siegmund Schlossmann, review of Ernst Zitelmann, *Irrthum und Rechtsgeschäft*, *Zeitschrift für das Privat- und öffentliche Recht der Gegenwart* 7 (1980): 562.

32. E.g. Christopher Columbus Langdell, "Classification of Rights and Wrongs," pt. 1, *Harvard Law Review* 13 (1900): 537–38; Frederick Pollock, *A First Book of Jurisprudence for Students of the Common Law* (London, 1896), 160; Charles Aubry and Charles Rau, *Cours de droit civil français d'après la méthode de Zachariae*, 4th ed., 2 (Paris, 1869): § 190; Laurent, *Principes* 6: § 101; Demolombe, *Cours* 9: § 543; Windschied, *Lehrbuch* 3: § 167.

33. Chapter 2.

34. A. W. B. Simpson, "Innovation in Nineteenth Century Contract Law," *Law Quarterly Review* 91 (1975): 262.

35. Ibid., 247; Gordley, *Philosophical Origins*, 135–46.

36. Gordley, *Philosophical Origins*, 154–58.

37. A. W. B. Simpson, "The Horwitz Thesis and the History of Contracts," *University of Chicago Law Review* 46 (1979): 533, 569. John Newland, *A Treatise on Contracts Within the Jurisdiction of Courts of Equity* (Philadelphia, 1821), 358–59; John Powell, *Essay Upon the Law of Contracts and Agreements* 2 (London, 1790): 157–58; Joseph Story, *Commentaries on Equity Jurisprudence as Administered in England and America*, 14th ed., 1 (Boston, 1918): 341; William Wentworth Story, *A Treatise on the Law of Contracts Not Under Seal*, 3d ed. (Boston, 1851), 437–38.

38. Joseph Chitty, *A Practical Treatise on the Law of Contracts Not Under Seal and Upon the Usual Defences to Actions Thereon* (London, 1826), 7; Leake, *Elements*, 311–12; Theron Metcalf, *Principles of the Law of Contracts as Applied by Courts of Law* (New York, 1878), 163; Newland, *Treatise*, 357; Pollock, *Principles*, 172; John Smith, *The Law of Contract in a Course of Lectures Delivered at the Law Institution* (Philadelphia, 1847), 96; J. Story, *Commentaries* 1:337, 339; W. W. Story, *Treatise*, 135; William Taylor, *A Treatise on the Differences Between the Laws of England and Scotland Relating to Contracts* (London, 1849), 17. Curiously, Langdell was an exception. He said that in theory the law did require consideration to be adequate although it shut its eyes in practice. Langdell, *Summary*, 70–71. See Gordley, *Philosophical Origins*, 147–48, 205–6.

39. The Roman text (Cod. 4.44.2) said the seller must receive less than half the just price; the French Civil Code (art. 1674) changed the fraction to five-twelfths.

40. Law of July 8, 1907, D.P. 1908.IV.173, as amended by Law of July 8, 1937, D.P. 1938.IV.168 (buyers of fertilizer, seeds, and fodder who pay a quarter more than their value); Law of April 29, 1916, art. 7, D.P. 1919.IV.IV. 285, current version Law of July 7, 1967, art. 15, D.S.L. 1967.258 (victims of sea accidents who pay too much for rescue); Law of May 31, 1925, art. 57, 1925 D.P.IV.41, 45, current version in Civil Aviation Code (Code de l'aviation civile) art. L. 142–1, Decree of March 31, 1967, D.S.L. 1967.184 (victims of aviation accidents who pay too much for rescue).

41. Antoine Marie Demante and Edouard Colmet de Santerre, *Cours analytique du Code Civil* 5, 2d ed. (Paris, 1883), § 28 bis. (by Colmet de Santerre); Alexandre Duranton, *Cours de droit français suivant le Code civil* 10, 3d ed. (Paris, 1834), § 200–201; Victor Marcadé, *Explication théorique et pratique du Code Napoléon*, 5th ed. (Paris, 1859), 357–58. Similarly, Glasson thought that, although relief violated the "principle of freedom of contract," it was justified for reasons of "humanity." Ernest Glasson, *Eléments du droit français considéré dans ses rapports avec le droit naturel et l'economie politique*, 2d ed. (Paris, 1884), 550, 553.

42. Demolombe, *Cours* 24: § 194; Laurent, *Principes* 15: § 485.

43. Landtagsabschiedes of Nov. 10, 1861, § 282.4 [1861–62] Gesetzblatt, quoted in Max Danzer, *Das Bayerische Landrecht (Codex Maximilianeus Bavaricus Civilis) vom Jahre 1756 in seiner heutigen Geltung* (1894), 229–30 (Bavaria); Bürgerliches Gesetzbuch für des Königreich Sachsen, § 864 (Saxony); Allgemeines deutsches Handelsgesetzbuch, art. 286 (commercial matters).

44. Karl von Vangerow, *Leitfaden für Pandekten-Vorlesung* 3 (Marburg, 1847): § 611.

45. Rudolph von Holzschuher, *Theorie und Casuistik des gemeinen Civilrechts* 3 (Leipzig, 1864): 729–30; Vangerow, *Leitfaden* 3: § 611 n. 1; Carl von Wächter, *Pandekten* 2 (Leipzig, 1881): § 207; Windscheid, *Lehrbuch* 2: § 396 n. 2.

46. *Rex v. Jordan*, cited in *Rex v. Pierce*, 89 Eng. Rep. 967, 2 Show. K.B. 327 (1683) ("for that such trades ought not to be in the principal parts of the city, but in the outskirts"); *Rex v. Neville*, 170 Eng. Rep. 102, Peake 125 (1791) ("where manufacturers have borne within a neighbourhood for many years, it will operate as a consent of the inhabitants to their being carried on").

47. Blackstone, *Commentaries* 3:217–18 ("for it is incumbent on him to find some other place to do that act, where it will be less offensive").

48. Bartolus de Saxoferrato, *Commentaria Corpus iuris civilis* to Dig. 8.5.8.5, in *Omnia quae extant opera* (Venice, 1615) ("Sometimes the owner of the lower premises makes fire in the usual way for the ordering of his family, and then he may do it lawfully, and he is not liable if the smoke ascends unless he acts with an intention to injure . . . But if the owner of the lower premises wants to make a shop or inn where he is continually making a fire and a great deal of smoke, he is not allowed to do so, as in this text [D. 8.5.8.5]").

49. Domat, *Les Loix Civiles*, liv. 1, tit. 12, §§ 4, 9–10 ("the interference must be suffered or may be hindered according to the character of the location and that of the interference").

50. Robert Pothier, *Traité du contrat de société* app. 2, *Du voisinage*, § 241, in *Oeuvres* 4 ("one is not allowed to do anything on one's land that would send into a neighboring house smoke that is too thick or too much of an interference").

51. *Bliss v. Hall*, 7 L.J.C.P. 122 (1838); *Hole v. Barlow*, 140 Eng. Rep. 1113, 4 C.B. (NS) 334 (1858); *Bamford v. Turnley*, 122 Eng. Rep. 25, 3 B. & S. 62 (1862); *St. Helen's Smelting Co. v. Tipping*, 35 L.J.Q.B. 66 (1865). See Joel Franklin Brenner, "Nuisance Law and the Industrial Revolution," *Journal of Legal Studies* 3 (1973): 408 ("the black letter law changed little").

52. E.g. *Gilbert v. Showerman*, 23 Mich. 447 (1871); *Campbell v. Seaman*, 63 N.Y. 568 (1876); *Hurlbut v. McCone*, 55 Conn. 31 (1887); *Price v. Grantz*, 118 Pa. 402, 11 A. 794 (1888). The absence of change in the rules governing nuisance, at least before the Civil War, is noted by Morton

Horwitz, *The Transformation of American Law, 1780–1860* (Cambridge, MA, 1977), 74.

53. Laurent, *Principes* 6: § 144. Apparently through oversight, the drafters of the French Civil Code did not include a provision on what common lawyers called nuisance. Nevertheless, beginning in the early nineteenth century, French courts filled the gap by allowing an action for *troubles de voisinage*. E.g. Req., 16 mai 1827, S. 28.2.159 (laundry operator recovered when smoke from a factory discolored the wash).

54. See Rudolph von Ihering, "Zur Lehre von den Beschränkungen des Grundeigenthümers im Interesse der Nachbarn," *Jahrbücher für die Dogmatik des heutigen römischen und deutschen Privatrechts* 6 (1863): 81.

55. According to Wood, each owner had rights which, nevertheless, he could not use. "It is part of the great social compact to which every person is a party ... that every person yields a portion of his right of absolute dominion and use of his own property, in recognition of, and obedience to the rights of others, so that others may enjoy their property without unreasonable hurt and hindrance." Horace Wood, *A Practical Treatise on the Law of Nuisances in their Various Forms; Including Remedies Therefore at Law and in Equity* (Albany, NY, 1875), § 1, pp. 1–2. Horwitz notes the "logical difficulties": "Not until the 19th century did it become clear that, because [an absolute] conception of ownership necessarily circumscribed the rights of others to develop their land, it was, in fact incompatible with a commitment to absolute dominion." Horwitz, *Transformation 1780–1860*, 31. But he believes that this absolute conception of property was held by pre-nineteenth-century jurists, and difficulties were not observed because land use conflicts were rare.

56. Thus according to Aubry and Rau, the "respective rights of [the] proprietors" of adjacent land were in a "conflict [that] cannot be resolved except by means of certain limits imposed on the natural exercise of the powers inherent in property." Aubry & Rau, *Cours* 2: § 194. Similarly, Laurent thought that "[a]ccording to the rigor of the law, each proprietor would be able to object if one of his neighbors released on his property smoke or exhalations of any kind, because he has a right to the purity of air for his person and his goods." Laurent, *Principes* 6: § 144. If that were so, he admitted, the existence of towns would be impossible. Ibid. In a later volume of his work, Laurent finally decided that "[t]he Code was wrong to say that the owner has the right to enjoy and to dispose of his thing in the *most absolute manner.*" *Principes* 20: § 417. Nevertheless, he did not suggest any other way that property could be defined.

57. Ihering, "Beschränkungen des Grundeigenthümers."

58. Horwitz, *Transformation 1780–1860*, 181; Atiyah, *Rise and Fall*, 61–62.

59. Some societies have fixed exchange rates, in which so many physical units of commodity A must be exchanged for so many of commodity B: Elizabeth Cashdan, "Information Costs and Customary Prices," in E. Cashdan, ed., *Risk and Uncertainty in Tribal and Peasant Societies*

(Boulder, CO, 1990), 259–78; Raymond Firth, *Primitive Polynesian Economy*, 2d ed. (London, 1965), 347–48; Max Gluckman, *Ideas in Barotse Jurisprudence* (New Haven, CT, 1965), 189; Isaac Schapera, *A Handbook of Tswana Law and Custom* (London, 1938), 242. Some have an ideal exchange rate, which may not be the average rate at which people usually trade but is deemed to be the rate an honest person would demand. Cashdan, "Information Costs," 271; Leopold Pospisil, *Kapauku Papuan Economy* (New Haven, CT, 1963), 305.

60. Cashdan, "Information Costs," 264–67; Stuart Plattner, "Economic Behavior in Markets," in S. Plattner, ed., *Economic Anthropology* (Stanford, 1989), 214–16. See Gordley, "Contract Law in Historical Perspective," § 8.

61. Accursius, *Glossa ordinaria* to Dig. 35.2.63 to "funguntur"; to Cod. 4.44.2 to "auctoritate iudicis"; to Cod. 4.44.6 to "non est" (Venice, 1581). The *Glossa ordinaria* was the standard commentary on the Justinian *Corpus*. It was compiled in the first part of the thirteenth century by assembling glosses or short notes, many written by other jurists over the previous century.

62. Accursius, *Glossa ordinaria* to Dig. 13.4.3 [vulg. 13.4.4] to "varia"; to Cod. 4.44.4 to "auctoritate iudicis."

63. Accursius, *Glossa ordinaria* to Cod. 4.44.4 to "auctoritate iudicis."

64. Atiyah, *Rise and Fall*, 63.

65. Ibid. ("If everything had one just price, how was it possible for a person to buy at one price and sell at a higher?").

66. For example, Thomas put the case of a merchant who arrives with grain at a famine-stricken city having passed several other grain-bearing ships on the way. For Thomas, the question was not whether the famine level price was just but whether the merchant could sell at that price without revealing that the other ships would soon arrive and relieve the famine. Thomas answered that the merchant could remain silent and sell. *Summa theologiae*, 3d ed. (Madrid, 1963) (Leonine text), II-II, q. 77, a. 3 ad 4. On the identification of the just price with the market price in the Thomistic tradition, see John Noonan, *The Scholastic Analysis of Usury* (Cambridge, MA, 1957), 82–88; Raymond de Roover, "The Concept of the Just Price Theory and Economic Policy," *Journal of Economic History* 18 (1958): 418. But for Atiyah (who cites de Roover), if Thomas identified the just price with the market price, it merely shows he could not have been thinking of the world of trade. Atiyah, *Rise and Fall*, 63.

67. Horwitz, *Transformation 1780–1860*, 31.

68. *Aldred's Case*, 77 Eng. Rep. 816, 9 Co. Rep. 57b (K.B., 1611).

69. *Jones v. Powell*, Palm. 536 (K.B., 1628); *Rex v. Jordan*, cited in *Rex v. Pierce*, 89 Eng. Rep. 967, 2 Show. K.B. 327 (1683).

70. Ulpian, Dig. 8.5.8.5 ("Aristo states in an opinion given to Cerellius Vitalis that he does not think that smoke can lawfully be discharged from a cheese shop onto the buildings above it, unless they are subject to a servitude to this effect, and this is admitted.")

71. Blackstone, *Commentaries* 2:2.
72. Horwitz, *Transformation 1780–1860*, 31.
73. Ibid.
74. Blackstone, *Commentaries* 3:217–18.
75. Frederick Pollock, "The Nature of Jurisprudence Considered in Relation to some Recent Contributions to Legal Science," in Frederick Pollock, *Essays in Jurisprudence and Ethics* (London, 1882), 19–20.
76. Pollock, *A First Book*, 26–27.
77. Ranouil, *L'Autonomie*, 9, 53–55, 79.
78. Ibid., 70.
79. Savigny, *System* 1:331–32.
80. Ibid., 19; Friedrich C. von Savigny, *Vom Beruf unsrer Zeit für Gesetzgebung und Rechtswissenschaft* (Heidelberg, 1840), 8.
81. Savigny, *System* 3:102.
82. See René Savatier, *Les Métamorphoses économiques et sociales du droit privé d'aujourd'hui: l'Universalisme renouvelé des disciplines juridiques* (Paris, 1959), 6–8; André Tunc, "The Grand Outlines of the Code," in B. Schwartz, ed., *The Code Napoléon and the Common Law World* (New York, 1956), 40; Franz Wieacker, *Privatrechtsgeschichte der Neuzeit unter besonderer Berücksichtigung der deutschen Entwicklung*, 2d ed. (Gottingen, 1967), 249. Ranouil, *L'Autonomie*, 9, 17, 53–55.
83. André-Jean Arnaud, *Les Origines doctrinales du Code civil français* (Paris, 1969), 10–11, 183; Guy Augé, "Le contrat et l'évolution du consensualisme chez Grotius," *Archives de philosophie du droit* 13 (1968): 104; Jean-Louis Halperin, *L'Impossible Code civil* (Paris, 1992), 56–58; Martin Lipp, *Die Bedeutung des Naturrechts für die Ausbildung der Allgemeinen Lehren des deutschen Privatrechts* (Berlin, 1980), 133–41.
84. Cappellini, "Schemi," 138–40, 253, 529–30. See Paolo Grossi, "La proprietà nel sistema privatistico della seconda scolastica," in *La seconda scholastica*, 117.
85. *Nicomachean Ethics*, V.ii, iv–v.
86. Thomas Aquinas, *Summa theologiae*, II-II, q. 61, a. 3. For Aristotle, liberality meant disposing of one's wealth sensibly, giving "to the right people the right amounts and at the right time." *Nicomachean Ethics*, IV.i 1119^{b}–1120^{a}.
87. Thomas Aquinas, *Summa theologiae*, II-II, q. 77, a. 1, obj. 1 & ad. 1.
88. Ibid., q. 77, aa. 2–3.
89. *Politics*, II.v.
90. He was also borrowing from the medieval canon lawyers. Gratian's collection of authoritative sources contained a text in which Saint Ambrose admonished rich people who failed to provide for the needs of the poor: "Let no one call his own what is common." Gratian, *Decretum, Corpus iuris canonici*, ed. E. Friedberg, 1 (Leipzig, 1876), D. 47 c. 8. The *Ordinary Gloss* to this text, ascribed to the canon lawyer Johannes Teutonicus, suggested that this maxim applied literally in a state of necessity. *Glossa ordinaria* to Gratian, *Decretum* (Venice, 1595) to D. 47 c. 8 to *commune*;

to D. 1 c. 7, to *communis omnium; Glossa ordinaria* to *Decretales Grego-rii IX* (Venice, 1595) to 5.18.3 to *poenitaet.* It cited a Roman legal text that said all the passengers on a ship had a right to share the provisions if food ran short during a voyage. Dig. 14.2.2.2. Therefore, the owner's rights were limited in cases of necessity.

91. Loi de 9 avril 1898. It was eventually repealed by the Ordonnance of Oct. 19, 1945 and Oct. 30, 1946 which integrated work accidents into the social security system.

92. Chapter 6.

93. Richard Ely, *Studies in the Evolution of Industrial Society* (New York, 1903), 402.

94. Roscoe Pound, "Liberty of Contract," *Yale Law Journal* 18 (1909): 454.

95. J. Story, *Commentaries* 1:337.

96. 198 U.S. 45 (1905).

97. 300 U.S. 379 (1937).

98. 198 U.S. at 57–59. See chapter 6 for elaboration.

99. 198 U.S. at 75.

100. 198 U.S. at 57.

101. 272 U.S. 365 (1926).

CHAPTER 4

This chapter was written during a year's fellowship at the Center for Advanced Study in the Behavioral Sciences, Stanford, CA. I gratefully record my indebtedness to the Center and, for the financial support, to the Andrew W. Mellon Foundation.

1. The essentially "transitional" nature of the major legal changes of the period are stressed by James Oldham, *The Mansfield Manuscripts and the Growth of English Law in the Eighteenth-Century*, 2 vols. (Chapel Hill, NC, 1992), 2:213–44. See also the brief survey by Henry Horwitz, "Liberty, Law and Property, 1689–1776," in J. R. Jones, ed., *Liberty Secured? Britain Before and After 1688* (Stanford, 1992), 286–92.

2. *Law and Public Opinion* was first published in 1905 (in London), based on lectures Dicey delivered at Harvard in 1898.

3. William Blackstone, *Commentaries on the Laws of England*, 4 vols. (Oxford, 1765–69), facsimile reprint of the first edition (Chicago, 1979), 1:35.

4. See ibid., 2, chaps. 10 and 20.

5. Ibid., 1:410.

6. Ibid., 3:153.

7. Ibid., 2, chap. 30.

8. Ibid., 2:xiv.

9. William Jones, *An Essay on the Law of Bailments* (London, 1781), 2–3.

10. Henry Sumner Maine, *Ancient Law* (1861), ed. Raymond Firth (Gloucester, MA, 1970), 165.

11. Ibid., 295.

12. Maine immediately invokes the example following the passage cited above; *Ancient Law*, 295.

13. For a more general overview of the developments, see James Gordley, *The Philosophical Origins of Modern Contract Doctrine* (Oxford, 1991).

14. P. S. Atiyah, *Rise and Fall of Freedom of Contract* (Oxford, 1979), 399–400 (Atiyah here gives the definition in summary of Pothier's treatise on obligations).

15. Ibid., 398.

16. A. W. B. Simpson, "The Horwitz Thesis and the History of Contracts," *University of Chicago Law Review* 46 (1979): 533–601; id., "Innovation in Nineteenth-Century Contract Law," *Law Quarterly Review* 91 (1975): 247–78; and J. H. Baker's review of Atiyah, *Rise and Fall of Freedom of Contract*, *Modern Law Review* 43 (1980): 467–69. These contributions appeared in criticism of the interpretations advanced by Morton J. Horwitz and Atiyah which derived the doctrinal developments more directly from the imperatives of capitalist development. See Morton J. Horwitz, "Historical Foundations of Modern Contract Law," *Harvard Law Review* 87 (1974): 917–56, and *Transformation of American Law* (Cambridge, MA, 1977), chap. 7.

17. Philip Hamburger, "The Development of the Nineteenth-Century Consensus Theory of Contract," *Law and History Review* 7 (1989): 241–329. For other recent treatments which emphasize different procedural developments, see Michael Lobban, *Common Law and English Jurisprudence, 1760–1850* (Oxford, 1991), chap. 9; W. R. Cornish and G. de N. Clark, *Law and Society in England, 1750–1950* (London, 1989), 200–226; Clinton W. Francis, "The Structure of Judicial Administration and the Development of Contract Law in Seventeenth-Century England," *Columbia Law Review* 83 (1983): 35–137.

18. See also on this theme the important discussions by J. L. Barton in "The Enforcement of Hard Bargains," *Law Quarterly Review* 103 (1987): 118–47; and most recently by Michael Lobban in "Contractual Fraud in Law and Equity," *Oxford Journal of Legal Studies* 17 (1997): 442–76.

19. Baker, review of Atiyah, *Rise and Fall*, 467.

20. Henry Sidgwick, *Elements of Politics* (London, 1891), 78.

21. The contemporary political context for Dicey's *Law and Public Opinion* is considered in Stefan Collini's *Liberalism and Sociology* (Cambridge, 1979). For a parallel process in the case of U.S. law, see chapter 6 above.

22. Atiyah, *Freedom of Contract*, 234, 250, 263, 270, 271, 344–45.

23. Ibid., 293.

24. Ibid., 292, 324, 293, 294. Compare Dicey's earlier assessment of the "Period of Benthamism or Individualism": "Individualism as regards legislation is popularly, and not without reason, connected with the name and principles of Bentham . . . The influence even on law reform of Adam

Smith and his disciples ought, of course, not to be forgotten, but in 1830 the economists and the Benthamites formed one school," *Law and Public Opinion*, 126 and n.

25. Biancamaria Fontana, *Rethinking the Politics of Commercial Society* (Cambridge, 1985), 77. See also Donald Winch's discussion in Stefan Collini et al., *That Noble Science of Politics* (Cambridge, 1983), chap. 1.

26. Norman Gash, *Aristocracy and People: England 1815–65* (London, 1979), 46. For a recent survey of this much-traversed theme, see Stephen Conway, "Bentham and the Nineteenth-Century Revolution in Government," in Richard Bellamy, ed., *Victorian Liberalism: Nineteenth-Century Political Thought and Practice* (London, 1990), 71–90.

27. Boyd Hilton, *The Age of Atonement* (Oxford, 1988), 6–7; and see also his *Corn Cash and Commerce* (Oxford, 1977), especially 303–14. Hilton's general case for the impact of Christian political economy is sustained by Peter Mandler in his important work on the 1834 Poor Law; see "The Making of the New Poor Law Redivivus," *Past and Present* 117 (1987): 131–57, and "Tories and Paupers: Christian Political Economy and the Making of the New Poor Law," *Historical Journal* 33 (1990): 81–103.

28. Atiyah, *Freedom of Contract*, 466.

29. Ibid., 330. See also his comments on Smith, ibid., 303, and on Bentham, ibid., 325.

30. Ibid., 294.

31. Adam Smith, *The Theory of Moral Sentiments* (1759), ed. D. D. Raphael and A. L. Macfie (Oxford, 1976), 78–79, 82.

32. Ibid., 87.

33. Ibid., 340–41.

34. Smith promised publication of a work on law and government at the conclusion of *Theory of Moral Sentiments*. The lectures survive in the form of student notes; see the editorial introduction to Adam Smith, *Lectures on Jurisprudence*, ed. R. L. Meek, D. D. Raphael, and P. G. Stein (Oxford, 1978).

35. For Smith, the system of natural jurisprudence regarded perfect rights and attended to issues of commutative justice only; see *Lectures on Jurisprudence*, 9.

36. Ibid., 86. See also 12.

37. Ibid., 92–94.

38. See Atiyah, *Freedom of Contract*, 398.

39. *Theory of Moral Sentiments*, 341.

40. See, for illustrative examples, *Lectures on Jurisprudence*, 14, 16 (on the relationship between the complexity of property rules and the level of social development); 208 (on the introduction of government with the emergence of "shepherd society"); 49–62 (in condemnation of primogeniture); and 23 (in condemnation of game laws).

41. See, however, the important treatments by Donald Winch, *Adam Smith's Politics* (Cambridge, 1978), chap. 4; Knud Haakonssen, *The Science of a Legislator* (Cambridge, 1981); and Istvan Hont and Michael Ig-

natieff, "Needs and Justice in the Wealth of Nations," in Istvan Hont and Michael Ignatieff, eds., *Wealth and Virtue* (Cambridge, 1983), chap. 1.

42. See Adam Smith, *An Inquiry into the Nature and Causes of the Wealth of Nations* (1776), ed. R. H. Campbell, A. S. Skinner, and W. B. Todd, 2 vols. (Oxford, 1976), 708–23. The Glasgow edition fully annotates the parallel discussions in the *Theory of Moral Sentiments and Lectures on Jurisprudence*.

43. *Wealth of Nations*, 412 and passim. The changing patterns of judicial organization were further treated in bk. 5, 708–23.

44. See a characteristic passage in Smith's discussion of the Tudor legislation against forestalling and engrossing: these "laws were evident violations of natural liberty and therefore unjust; and they were both too as impolitick as they were unjust," *Wealth of Nations*, 530.

45. Ibid., 687.

46. See *Freedom of Contract*, 302–3.

47. See ibid., 300, 315.

48. *Wealth of Nations*, 471.

49. See ibid., 322–29, 356–58.

50. This is one of the conclusions of Richard Teichgraber's study of Smith's first audience; see "'Less Abused Than I Had Reason to Expect': The Reception of The Wealth of Nations in Britain, 1776–90," *Historical Journal* 30 (1987): 337–66; see also his *"Free Trade" and Moral Philosophy* (Durham, NC, 1986).

51. See *An Introduction to the Principles of Morals and Legislation* (1789), ed. J. H. Burns and H. L. A. Hart (London, 1970), 4–5.

52. See *Defence of Usury*, in *Jeremy Bentham's Economic Writings*, ed. W. Stark, 3 vols. (London, 1952–54), 1:130, 169, 183–85.

53. *Defence of Usury*, 167.

54. See *Manual of Political Economy* (c. 1793–95), *Bentham's Economic Writings* 1:223–25, 233–37.

55. Bentham, *The Theory of Legislation*, ed. C. K. Ogden (London, 1931), 199–200. (*The Theory of Legislation* was first published, in French, in 1802; the work was based on manuscript materials of the 1770s and 1780s.)

56. Ibid., 171–72. See also his criticisms of the restraints on the alienation of real property, 175.

57. See Atiyah's comments on this theme, *Freedom of Contract*, 324–26.

58. *Theory of Legislation*, 194.

59. Ibid., 93–94.

60. Bentham's most famous rehearsal of this theme was contained in his critique of the 1791 French Declaration of the Rights of Man and of the Citizen; see Bentham, *Anarchical Fallacies*, in *Works of Jeremy Bentham*, 11 vols. (Edinburgh, 1838–43), 2:489–534. The thesis, though, was developed in his earliest jurisprudential explorations; see Douglas G. Long, *Bentham on Liberty* (Toronto, 1977).

61. Long, *Bentham on Liberty*, 109.

62. Ibid., 172–73, 201–9.

63. *Defence of a Maximum*, in *Bentham's Economic Writings* 3:257–58. Bentham in this section of the tract directly addressed the contrast with his *Defence of Usury*.

64. Blackstone (not without reason) is the exemplary candidate for such characterizations; for examples, see the introductory comments of A. W. B. Simpson in Blackstone, *Commentaries* 2:xii; Otto Kahn-Freund, "Blackstone's Neglected Child: The Contract of Employment," *Law Quarterly Review* 93 (1977): 508–14; and Atiyah, *Freedom of Contract*, 103.

65. See, for examples, Dicey, *Law and Public Opinion*, 112–15; Atiyah, *Freedom of Contract*, 219–20.

66. For a review of this literature, see David Cannadine, "The Past and the Present in the English Industrial Revolution 1880–1980," *Past and Present* 103 (1984): 131–72.

67. See *Works of . . . Edmund Burke* (1865–67), 8th ed., 12 vols. (Boston, 1884), 11:84; and Blackstone, *Commentaries* 3:325.

68. *Wealth of Nations*, 37.

69. For valuable surveys of this intellectual tradition and its many impacts, see Knud Haakonssen, "Hugo Grotius and the History of Political Thought," *Political Theory* 13 (1985): 238–65; and "From Natural Law to the Rights of Man: a European Perspective on American Debates," in Michael J. Lacey and Knud Haakonssen, eds., *A Culture of Rights* (Cambridge, 1991), 19–61.

70. See, for examples, John Kenyon, *Revolution Principles* (Cambridge, 1990); J. G. A. Pocock, *Virtue, Commerce and History* (Cambridge, 1985), chaps. 3 and 11; J. C. D. Clark, *English Society, 1688–1832* (Cambridge, 1985), chaps. 2–3.

71. Blackstone, *Commentaries* 3:159.

72. Robert Chambers, *A Course of Lectures on the English Law* (1767–73), ed. Thomas M. Curley, 2 vols. (Oxford, 1986), 2:224–25. See also the valuable discussion by Peter Birks and Grant McLeod, "The Implied Contract Theory of Quasi-Contract," *Oxford Journal of Legal Studies* 6 (1986): 46–85.

73. Paul Langford, *Public Life and the Propertied Englishman, 1689–1798* (Oxford, 1991), 1.

74. See John Locke, *Two Treatises of Government*, ed. Peter Laslett (Cambridge, 1964), 368–69 (*Second Treatise*, chap. 9, pars. 123–24).

75. *Wealth of Nations*, 715.

76. Blackstone, *Commentaries* 2:2.

77. See Horwitz, "Liberty, Law and Property"; and Robert W. Gordon, "Paradoxical Property," in John Brewer and Susan Staves, eds., *Early Modern Conceptions of Property* (London, 1995), 95–110.

78. Langford, *Public Life and the Propertied Englishman*, 14, 24, and passim.

79. Ibid., 46.

80. Neil McKendrick et al., *Birth of a Consumer Society* (London, 1982), 27. See also Lorna Weatherill, *Consumer Behaviour and Material Culture in Britain, 1600–1760* (London, 1988); Peter Earle, *The Making of the English Middle Class* (Berkeley, 1989); John Brewer and Roy Porter, eds., *Consumption and the World of Goods* (London, 1993).

81. McKendrick, *Birth of a Consumer Society*, 27.

82. Quoted in Roy Porter, *English Society in the Eighteenth Century* (Harmondsworth, 1982), 202.

83. Henry Fielding, *Enquiry into the Late Increase of Robbers* (1751), *Complete Works of Henry Fielding*, ed. William Ernest Henley, 16 vols. (London 1903), 13:14.

84. Philip C. Yorke, *Life and Correspondence of . . . Earle of Hardwicke*, 3 vols. (Cambridge, 1913), 2:554–55.

85. Blackstone, *Commentaries* 4:434.

86. Linda Colley, *Britons: Forging the Nation 1707–1837* (New Haven, CT, 1992), 100.

87. Bolingbroke, *Remarks on the History of England*, *Works of Lord Bolingbroke*, 4 vols. (London, 1844), 1:375.

88. Blackstone, *Commentaries* 3:267–68.

89. Grant Gilmore, *The Death of Contract* (Columbus, OH, 1974), 8.

90. *Perrin v. Blake* (1770), in Francis Hargrave, ed., *Collectanea Juridica*, 2 vols. (London, 1787), 1:297.

91. Ibid., 392.

92. *Spirit of the Laws*, bk. 20, chap. 7.

93. See Julian Hoppit, "The Use and Abuse of Credit in Eighteenth-century England," in Neil McKendrick and R. B. Outhwaite, eds., *Business Life and Public Policy* (Cambridge, 1986), 64–78; and Brewer, "Commercialization and Politics," in *Birth of a Consumer Society*, chap. 5.

94. See John Brewer, *The Sinews of Power. War, Money and the English State, 1688–1783* (New York, 1989), 231–49.

95. On the unprecedented growth of parliamentary legislation, see David Lieberman, *Province of Legislation Determined* (Cambridge, 1989), 13–16; and Langford, *Public Life and the Propertied Englishman*, chap. 3.

96. Langford, *Public Life and the Propertied Englishman*, 166.

97. See John V. Orth, "English Combination Acts of the Eighteenth Century," *Law and History Review* 5 (1987): 175–211; and *Combination and Conspiracy* (Oxford, 1991), chap. 2.

98. See Ralph Davis, "The Rise of Protection in England 1689–1786," *Economic History Review* 19 (1966): 306–17. See also D. C. Coleman, "Adam Smith, Businessmen, and the Mercantile System in England," *History of European Ideas* 9 (1988): 161–70.

99. Jessel MR, *Printing and Numerical Registering Co v. Sampson* (1875); quoted in A. H. Manchester, *Modern Legal History of England and Wales 1750–1950* (London, 1980), 267.

100. The mechanics of legislative procedure tended to encourage this blending of private and public initiatives in eighteenth-century parliamen-

tary law-making; see Sheila Lambert, *Bills and Acts: Legislative Procedure in Eighteenth-Century England* (Cambridge, 1971).

101. Robert J. Steinfeld, *The Invention of Free Labor. The Employment Relation in English and American Law and Culture, 1350–1870* (Chapel Hill, NC, 1991), 113.

102. Ibid., 108.

103. Susan Staves, *Married Women's Separate Property in England, 1660–1833* (Cambridge, MA, 1990), 164, 167.

104. Hamburger, "Development of Consensus Theory," 270.

105. See Yorke, *Life and Correspondence* 2:554–55.

106. In what follows I draw upon my discussion in *Province of Legislation Determined*, chaps. 5–6. The fullest assessment of Mansfield's career is now supplied by Oldham, *Mansfield Manuscripts*.

107. See Francis Buller in *Lickbarrow v. Mason* (1787) 2 *Term Reports* 73; and George Joseph Bell, *Commentaries on the . . . Principles of Mercantile Jurisprudence*, 2d ed. (Edinburgh, 1810), ix–x.

108. For these episodes, see Lieberman, *Province of Legislation Determined*, 131–40.

109. The development commonly has been described in terms of the common law courts acting to "incorporate" into English law a system of continental "law merchant." This conventional description, it now appears, mischaracterizes much of the historical process in question; see J. H. Baker, "The Law Merchant and the Common Law before 1700," *Cambridge Law Journal* 38 (1979): 295–322; and James Steven Rogers, *The Early History of the Law of Bills and Notes* (Cambridge, 1995).

110. See Henry Horwitz and James Oldham, "John Locke, Lord Mansfield, and Arbitration During the Eighteenth Century," *Historical Journal* 36 (1993): 137–59. The Arbitration Act was principally intended for the benefit of merchants, but merchants were not the only parties who utilized its provisions.

111. Langford, *Public Life and the Propertied Englishman*, 158–61. Blackstone's complaints against the legislative development appear at *Commentaries* 3:82.

112. Lewis Namier, *England in the Age of the American Revolution*, 2d ed. (London 1966), 32.

113. David Hume, "Of the Origin of Government," in *Essays Moral Political and Literary* (1741–42) (Oxford, 1963), 35.

114. David Hume, *Treatise of Human Nature* (1739–40), ed. L. A. Selby-Bigge (Oxford, 1888), 501–25.

115. Lawrence M. Friedman, *Contract Law in America* (Madison, WI, 1965), 24; Gilmore, *Death of Contract*, 8.

116. These points figured critically in the late nineteenth- and twentieth-century debates over "social legislation" and "freedom of contract." They continue to receive attention in recent scholarship on the "death of contract" (see Gilmore, *Death of Contract*, and Atiyah, *Freedom of Contract*, 681–779); on "contract law as ideology" (see Elizabeth Mensch,

"The History of Mainstream Legal Thought," and Peter Gabel and Jay M. Feinman, "Contract Law as Ideology," in David Kairys, ed., *The Politics of Law* (New York, 1982), 18–39, 172–84); and on the philosophical inadequacy of "modern contract doctrine" (see Gordley, *Philosophical Origins of Modern Contract Doctrine*, 230–48).

117. Blackstone's "conservatism" is more frequently invoked than analyzed, and deserves more careful elucidation than it frequently receives; see the discussion in my "Blackstone's Science of Legislation," *Journal of British Studies* 27 (1988): 117–49.

118. Blackstone, *Commentaries* 2:xii.

119. On this point I am indebted to the themes developed by S. F. C. Milsom, "The Nature of Blackstone's Achievement," *Oxford Journal of Legal Studies* 1 (1981): 7; and by John W. Cairns, "Blackstone, Kahn-Freund and the Contract of Employment," *Law Quarterly Review* 105 (1989): 300–314.

120. William David Evans, *A General View of the Decisions of Lord Mansfield* (2 vols., London, 1803), 1:9, v. In the introduction to his translation of Pothier, Evans praised the *Commentaries* as "a work allowed by general assent to afford a more beautiful specimen of elegant literature than has in any other instance been applied to a professional subject"; William David Evans, ed. and trans., *A Treatise on the Law of Obligations or Contracts by M. Pothier*, 2 vols. (London, 1806), 1:75.

121. There has been a wealth of recent, fruitful discussion of the structure of Blackstone's *Commentaries*; see especially Milsom, "The Nature of Blackstone's Achievement"; John W. Cairns, "Blackstone an English Institutist," *Oxford Journal of Legal Studies* 4 (1984): 318–60; Michael Lobban, "Blackstone and the Science of Law," *Historical Journal* 30 (1987): 311–35; and Alan Watson, "The Structure of Blackstone's Commentaries," *Yale Law Journal* 97 (1988): 795–821.

122. Blackstone supplied a summary of previous attempts at a summary of English law in his *Analysis of the Laws of England* (London, 1756), v–viii. See also John W. Cairns, "Eighteenth-Century Professional Classifications of English Common Law," *McGill Law Journal* 33 (1987): 225–44.

123. See Gordley, *Philosophical Origins of Modern Contract Doctrine*, chaps. 5–6.

124. Paley's career and influence is surveyed in D. L. LeMahieu, *The Mind of William Paley* (Lincoln, NE, 1976).

125. William Paley, *Principles of Moral and Political Philosophy* (1785) (Boston, 1818), vii, x.

126. See ibid., bk. 3, pt. 1, chaps. 1–5, esp. 84–85.

127. See ibid., 78–83.

128. See ibid., chaps. 11–14, 104–13. Paley also restricted his discussion of rules governing the household to the relations between parents and children; see bk. 3, pt. 3, chaps. 9–11.

CHAPTER 5

1. A vital element of the commonality of political culture in England and America, as Élie Halévy suggested, has been the willingness of labor and other progressive-left leaders to compromise rather than engage in the "fanatical" pursuit of ideological programs that appeared to have little support from a popular class-based constituency. Halévy, *The Era of Tyrannies: Essays on Socialism and War*, trans. R. K. Webb (Garden City, NY, 1965). A long line of studies of American labor and political history that consider the failure of socialism in American politics make the same point—from some writers' standpoint, in a regretful mode, or even accusingly as they regard labor leaders as having betrayed collectivist ideals and workers' "real" interests, and from the standpoint of others (for example, Louis Hartz) in a largely admiring mode. See chapter 7 for other citations of the most recent scholarship, especially the work of Christopher Tomlins.

2. Martin Shapiro deals with globalization in chapter 9 of this book; see also Wolfgang Wiegand, "Americanization of Law: Reception or Convergence?" in *Legal Culture and the Legal Profession*, ed. Lawrence M. Friedman and Harry N. Scheiber (Boulder, CO, 1996), 137–52. On European welfare state history and ideology, see Gosta Esping-Anderson, "The Three Political Economies of the Welfare State," *Canadian Review of Sociology and Anthropology* 26 (1989): 10–36; Hugh Heclo, *Modern Social Politics in Britain and Sweden* (New Haven, CT, 1974); and P. Flora and A. Heidenheimer, eds., *The Development of Welfare States in Europe and America* (New Brunswick, NJ, 1981).

3. What is "their own," when we speak of owners' claims to vested rights, is of course a much debated matter in the theory of property rights. In the technical legal sense, ownership is a matter for judgment at law. Thus Justice Jackson once wrote that "only those economic advantages [i.e., claims] are 'rights' which have the law back of them," so that when a litigant contends at the bar that his or her "vested rights" are being harmed by state action or by another private party, the claim is premature since the court itself determines what is "vested." *U.S. v. Willow R. Power Co.*, 324 U.S. 499, 502–3 (1945).

4. Although much of contemporary writing on positive versus negative liberty centers on the writings of Isaiah Berlin, the issue was well defined more than a century ago in the debates of English liberalism. See, e.g., T. H. Green, "Liberal Legislation or Freedom of Contract" (1881), in *The Liberal Tradition from Fox to Keynes*, ed. Alan Bullock and Maurice Shock (London, 1956), 180–83. A perceptive discussion of the negative/positive liberty issue is in the essays of Jeremy Waldron, *Liberal Rights: Collected Papers 1981–1991* (Cambridge, 1993), 39–43 and passim.

5. See chapter 6.

6. Tony Freyer, "Economic Liberty, Antitrust, and the Constitution 1880–1925," in *Liberty, Property, and Government: Constitutional Inter-*

pretation Before the New Deal, ed. Ellen Frankel Paul and Howard Dickman (Albany, NY, 1989), 205.

7. An excellent overview and critical analysis of these controversies, from the Founding period to nearly the present, are to be found in Donald Pisani, "Promotion and Regulation: Constitutionalism and the American Economy," *Journal of American History* 74 (1987): 740–68; see also Howard Gillman, *The Constitution Besieged: The Rise and Demise of Lochner Era Police Powers Jurisprudence* (Durham, NC, 1993); and id., "The Antinomy of Public Purposes and Private Rights in the American Constitutional Tradition, or Why Communitarianism Is Not Necessarily Exogenous to Liberal Constitutionalism," *Law & Social Inquiry* 21 (1996): 67–78.

8. See, inter alia, Michael Freeden, *Liberalism Divided: A Study in British Political Thought, 1914–1939* (Oxford, 1986).

9. James Willard Hurst, *Law and Social Order in the United States* (Ithaca, NY, 1977), 220. Hurst qualifies the concept of agreement on values, as follows: "Where law embodied general integrating ideas about public policy, there could be wide sharing of the basic concept, coupled with dispute over what the concept called for in particular activity"; for example, there was broad support for government's encouragement of material growth but significant disagreement over the appropriate types of intervention. Ibid., 21.

10. On legal culture, see Hurst, *Law and Social Order*, passim; Lawrence M. Friedman, "Legal Culture and Social Development," *Law and Society Review* 4 (1969): 29; Friedman and Scheiber, eds., *Legal Culture and the Legal Profession*, passim.

11. Hurst, *Law and Social Order*, 227.

12. Ibid., 226.

13. Id., *Law and the Conditions of Freedom in the 19th Century United States* (Madison, WI, 1956), chap. 1; see also Harry N. Scheiber, "At the Borderland of Law and Economic History: The Contributions of Willard Hurst," *American Historical Review* 75 (1970): 744–56.

14. Robert A. Dahl, "The American Oppositions: Affirmation and Denial," in *Political Oppositions in Western Democracies*, ed. Robert A. Dahl (New Haven, CT, 1966), 35–41.

15. John Phillip Reid, *Law for the Elephant: Property and Social Behavior on the Overland Trail* (San Marino, CA, 1980), 361–62.

16. Edward S. Corwin, "The Basic Doctrine of American Constitutional Law," *Michigan Law Review* 12 (1914): 247–76; cf. Stuart Bruchey, "The Impact of Concern for the Security of Property Rights on the Legal System of the Early American Republic," 1980 *Wisconsin Law Review*, 1135–58.

17. See, inter alia, William Graebner, *Coal Mining Safety in the Progressive Period: The Political Economy of Reform* (Lexington, KY, 1976); for a debate that similarly evidenced some shocking indifference to social dislocation and children's welfare, see Stephen B. Wood, *Constitutional Politics in the Progressive Era: Child Labor and the Law* (Chicago, 1968).

18. Robert Nozick's *Anarchy, State and Utopia* (Oxford, 1974) is exemplary of work on this line; see critical discussion in Waldron, *Liberal Rights*, 18ff. and passim.

19. Richard Epstein, *Takings: Private Property and the Power of Eminent Domain* (Cambridge, MA, 1986); see critical discussion in Harry N. Scheiber, "The Jurisprudence—and Mythology—of Eminent Domain in American Legal History," in Paul and Dickman, eds., *Liberty, Property, and Government*, 121–86.

20. Charles W. McCurdy, "Justice Field and the Jurisprudence of Government-Business Relations: The Parameters of Laissez-Faire Constitutionalism, 1863–1897," *Journal of American History* 61 (1975): 970–1005; Gillman, *The Constitution Besieged*, 98ff.

21. Hurst, *Law and the Conditions of Freedom*, 28; see also Hurst, *Law and Social Process in United States History* (Ann Arbor, MI, 1960), 234–53 and passim.

22. Harry N. Scheiber, "Public Rights and the Rule of Law in American Legal History," *California Law Review* 72 (1984): 217–51; id., "Law and the Imperatives of Progress: Private Rights and Public Values in American Legal History," in *Ethics, Economics and the Law*, ed. J. Roland Pennock and John W. Chapman (New York, 1982), 303–20; Paul Kens, "Liberty and the Public Ingredient of Private Property," *Review of Politics* 55 (1993), 85; William J. Novak, *The People's Welfare: Law and Regulation in 19th-Century America* (Chapel Hill, NC, 1996).

23. J. A. C. Grant, "The 'Higher Law' Background of Eminent Domain," *Wisconsin Law Review* 6 (1931): 67–85; Harry N. Scheiber, "Property Law, Expropriation, and Resource Allocation by Government, 1789–1910," *Journal of Economic History* 33 (1973): 232–51; Tony Freyer, "Reassessing the Impact of Eminent Domain in Early American Economic Development," 1981 *Wisconsin Law Review*, 1263.

24. Peter Onuf, "Anarchy and the Crisis of the Union," in *To Form a More Perfect Union: The Critical Ideas of the Constitution*, ed. Herman Belz et al. (Charlottesville, VA, 1992), 272–302.

25. Harry N. Scheiber, "Federalism and the Constitution: The Original Understanding," in Lawrence Friedman and Harry Scheiber, eds., *American Law and the Constitutional Order*, 2d ed. (Cambridge, MA, 1988), 85–98.

26. Madison, quoted in Edward G. White, *The Marshall Court and Cultural Change, 1815–1835* (abr. ed., New York, 1988), 601.

27. Adams, quoted in James W. Ely, Jr., *The Guardian of Every Other Right: A Constitutional History of Property Rights* (New York, 1992), 43.

28. See, e.g., John M. Murrin, "Fundamental Values, the Founding Fathers, and the Constitution," in *To Form a More Perfect Union*, ed. Belz et al., 1–37. Cf. Jennifer Nedelsky, *Private Property and the Limits of American Constitutionalism: The Madisonian Framework and Its Legacy* (Chicago, 1990).

29. *Van Horne's Lessee v. Dorrance*, 2 Dall. 304 (1795).

30. Ibid., at 310.

31. See Scheiber, "Public Rights and the Rule of Law," passim; Novak, *The People's Welfare*, 14ff.

32. Chancellor Kent's opinion, in *Palmer v. Mulligan*, 3 Cai. R. 308 (N.Y., 1805).

33. *Rodgers v. Bradshaw*, 20 Johns. 735, 740 (N.Y., 1832).

34. *Cooper v. Williams*, 4 Ohio Rep. 285–88 (1831).

35. Pennsylvania Declaration of Rights, 1776, reprinted in Bernard Schwartz, ed., *The Roots of the Bill of Rights* (5 vols., New York, 1971), 2:264, 266–67. Naturalization law would soon become an issue of major importance in the party politics of the era, brought to a head by the enactment of (and Republican reaction to) the 1798 alien and sedition acts.

36. Reprinted in Schwartz, ed., *Bill of Rights* 2.

37. Paine quoted in Jack P. Greene, "Values and Society in Revolutionary America," *Annals of the American Academy of Political and Social Science*, No. 426 (1976), 62 (an article dealing with the larger question of "happiness" in American rhetoric); see also William B. Scott, *In Pursuit of Happiness: American Conceptions of Property from the Seventeenth to the Twentieth Century* (Bloomington, IN, 1977).

38. Reprinted in Schwartz, ed., *Bill of Rights* 2.

39. Petition of Oct. 12, 1811, regarding the Tiger River, quoted in Harry Watson, "The Common Rights of Mankind: Subsistence, Shad, and Commerce in the Early Republican South," *Journal of American History* 83 (1996): 29. Watson's study works out in great detail from archival documentation the history of one state's law for protection of fisheries and the ideology that was expressed in the attendant debates. For a jurisprudential approach to the same theme, see Carol M. Rose, *Property and Persuasion: Essays on the History and Rhetoric of Ownership* (Boulder, CO, 1994), 105–62.

40. Lord Matthew Hale, *De Jure Maris*, as quoted and paraphrased in Kent's opinion in *Palmer v. Mulligan*, 3 Cai. 315, 319 (N.Y. 1805).

41. See Harry N. Scheiber, "The Road to Munn: Eminent Domain and the Concept of Public Purpose in the State Courts," *Perspectives in American History* 5 (1971): 329–402.

42. Curtis P. Nettels, "British Mercantilism and the Economic Development of the Thirteen Colonies," *Journal of Economic History* 12 (1952): 105–14; see also Marc Egnal and Joseph A. Ernst, "An Economic Interpretation of the American Revolution," *William and Mary Quarterly*, 3d ser., 29 (1972).

43. See chapter 4 above; and also the important work by David Konig and Carol Rose on how the ideal of "sociability" was incorporated into American legal and political ideology of the Founding period. Konig, "Jurisprudence and Social Policy in the New Republic," in *Devising Liberty: Preserving and Creating Freedom in the New American Republic*, ed. David Thomas Konig (Stanford, 1995), 184ff; Rose, *Property and Persuasion*, 146–50.

44. See note 67 below.

45. *Annals,* 1st Cong., quoted in E. A. J. Johnson, *The Foundations of American Economic Freedom: Government and Enterprise in the Age of Washington* (Minneapolis, 1973), 243.

46. "The Federalist," no. 26, in *The Federalist,* ed. Jacob Cooke (Cleveland, OH, 1961), 70.

47. See, inter alia, Scheiber, "Federalism and the Constitution"; Walton H. Hamilton and Douglass Adair, *The Power to Govern: The Constitution—Then and Now* (1937, repr. New York, 1972); Forrest McDonald, *Novus Ordo Seclorum: The Intellectual Origins of the Constitution* (Lawrence, KS, 1985). On how Madison himself had contributed to a neomercantilist policy move in Virginia in the Confederation period, see John E. Crowley, *The Privileges of Independence: Neomercantilism and the American Revolution* (Baltimore, 1993).

48. Thus while Gordon Wood is right, I think, in contending that the Federalists should not be understood as being "modern-day pluralists," still in Wood's own view they sought for a strong national solution to the problem of guiding and coordinating economic forces. See Gordon Wood, *The Radicalism of the American Revolution* (New York, 1991), 253; and ibid. for the quotation from Madison.

49. Crowley, *The Privileges of Independence,* 99–103. For an excellent analysis of Madison's views of national economic interests, see ibid., 94–116. Cf. Drew R. McCoy, *The Elusive Republic: Political Economy in Jeffersonian America* (Chapel Hill, NC, 1980).

50. Quoted in Jacob E. Cooke, *Tenche Coxe and the Early Republic* (Williamsburg, VA, 1978), 45.

51. Johnson, *Foundations,* 262–312.

52. Washington, First Annual Address to Congress, quoted in ibid., 163.

53. Senate reply, quoted in Johnson, *Foundations,* 163.

54. Annals, 1st Congress, I, 117 (Apr. 9, 1789).

55. Johnson, *Foundations,* 9, 21, and passim; see also John R. Nelson, Jr. *Liberty and Property: Political Economy and Policymaking in the New Nation, 1789–1812* (Baltimore, 1987), 66–99.

56. For analysis of Jefferson's report on the fisheries, see Crowley, *The Privileges of Independence,* 143ff.

57. Quoted in John C. Miller, *Alexander Hamilton, Portrait in Paradox* (New York, 1959), 223.

58. Merrill D. Peterson, *Thomas Jefferson and the New Nation: A Biography* (New York, 1970), 293.

59. Quoted in Crowley, *Privileges of Independence,* 136.

60. Madison to Edmund Randolph, May 20, 1783, in *The Papers of James Madison,* ed. William T. Hutchinson and William M. E. Rachal, vol. 7 (Chicago, 1971): 61.

61. Quoted in Johnson, *Foundations,* 259.

62. The phrase is Gordon Wood's from his essay "Interests and Disin-

terestedness in the Making of the Constitution," in *Beyond Confederation*, ed. Richard Beeman et al. (Chapel Hill, NC, 1987), 109.

63. Cooke, *Tenche Coxe*, 218.

64. See John Lauritz Larson, "A Bridge, a Dam, a River: Liberty and Innovation in the Early Republic," *Journal of the Early Republic* 7 (1987): 352–75; and Joseph H. Harrison, Jr., "*Sic et Non:* Thomas Jefferson and Internal Improvement," *Journal of the Early Republic* 7 (1987): 336–49.

65. Curtis P. Nettels, *The Emergence of a National Economy, 1775–1815* (New York, 1962).

66. The Jeffersonian opposition is treated insightfully in Isaac Kramnick, "The Great National Discussion: The Discourse of Politics in 1787," *William and Mary Quarterly*, 3d ser., vol. 45 (1988): 3ff; and Marshall Smelser, *The Democratic Republic, 1801–1815* (New York, 1968). On Jacksonian ideology, see, inter alia, Edward Pessen, *Jacksonian America: Society, Personality, and Politics* (rev. ed., Urbana, IL, 1985).

67. Jackson's Bank Message, quoted in Gillman, *Constitution Besieged*, 36–37. For excellent analyses of the anti-monopoly, egalitarian, economic-libertarian thrust of Jacksonian policies, see discussion in ibid., 33ff; and Pessen, *Jacksonian America*, passim. That there was also an important but seldom-remembered regulatory side to Jacksonian policy, manifested in the aftermath of the "Bank War," is shown in Harry N. Scheiber, "The Pet Banks in Jacksonian Politics and Finance," *Journal of Economic History* 23 (1963): 196–214.

68. Glyndon Van Deusen, *The Jacksonian Era, 1828–1848* (New York, 1959), 52.

69. See, inter alia, Charles Sellers, *The Market Revolution: Jacksonian America, 1815–1846* (New York, 1991).

70. Harry N. Scheiber, *Ohio Canal Era: A Case Study of Government and the Economy, 1820–1861* (2d ed. Athens, OH, 1987); id., "Public Rights and the Rule of Law," *California Law Review* 72 (1984): 420–23.

71. James Willard Hurst, *The Legitimacy of the Business Corporation in the Law of the United States, 1780–1970* (Charlottesville, VA, 1970), 22–30.

72. For the most recent analysis of Marshall Court jurisprudence on the Contract Clause, see White, *The Marshall Court*. Still of great value is the older study by Benjamin F. Wright, *The Contract Clause of the Constitution* (Cambridge, MA, 1938).

73. Hurst, *Law and Social Order*, 241; id., *Legitimacy of the Business Corporation*, 31–57.

74. This is not to say that there was no concern manifested about how giant corporations might dominate local or national markets; but debate centered more on the privileges and immunities required by corporations, and the regulations that ought to be imposed, than on the legitimacy of using this form of capital mobilization and enterprise. See Hurst, *Legitimacy of the Business Corporation;* Lawrence M. Friedman, *A History of*

American Law (2d ed., New York, 1985), 199–201. On free labor ideology, see chapters 6 and 7 of this work.

75. I have offered this term and sought to provide full documentation in several earlier studies; see, e.g., Scheiber, "Federalism and the American Economic Order, 1789–1910," *Law and Society Review* 10 (1975): 57–118.

76. The recent book by Novak, *The People's Welfare*, provides the fullest documentation in the entire scholarly literature, showing how wide ranging and deeply influential the regulatory interventionist regime was. Whether the regulatory concept should be denominated the "dominant" ideology or legal regime in the antebellum economy, as he argues, is another and more difficult question. See, on this point, Harry N. Scheiber, "Private Rights and Public Power: American Law, Capitalism, and the Republican Polity," *Yale Law Journal* 107 (1997): 832–61.

77. Scheiber, "The Road to Munn"; Charles M. Haar and Daniel William Fessler, *Fairness and Justice: Law in the Service of Equality* (New York, 1986).

78. Novak, *The People's Welfare*, 15–16 and passim.

79. Similarly, as A. W. B. Simpson has made clear, many of the innovations in the common law of contract in England during an earlier era were borrowed and assimilated from the civil law. Simpson, "Innovation in Nineteenth Century Contract Law," *Law Quarterly Review* 91 (1975): 247–78.

80. *Commonwealth v. Alger*, 61 Mass. 53 (1851). On the Shaw Court's important role in establishing the legitimacy of the regulatory power, see Leonard W. Levy, *The Law of the Commonwealth and Chief Justice Shaw* (Cambridge, 1954).

81. *Charles River Bridge v. Warren Bridge*, 36 U.S. 420 (1837).

82. *The License Cases*, 46 U.S. 504, 582 (1847).

83. Especially as Marshall framed the natural law argument in *Fletcher v. Peck* and other cases on state actions reversing former grants. See, inter alia, Wright, *The Contract Clause of the Constitution*, 17–61; and White, *Marshall Court*, 602ff. A detailed study of the case is provided in Peter C. Magrath, *Yazoo* (Providence, RI, 1966).

84. See Sidney Fine, *Laissez Faire and the General Welfare State: A Study of Conflict in American Thought, 1865–1901* (Ann Arbor, 1956); and compare discussion of the British debate in Michael Freeden, *The New Liberalism: An Ideology of Social Reform* (Oxford, 1978).

85. Levy, *Law of the Commonwealth and Chief Justice Shaw*, repr. in *American Law and the Constitutional Order*, ed. Friedman and Scheiber, 158–59.

86. Ibid. (with quotation from Roscoe Pound, in ibid.); see also Friedman, *History of American Law*, 285ff.

87. *Rupart v. Dunn*, 1 Reich. 101 (So. Carolina, 1844).

88. Grant Gilmore, *The Death of Contract*, 15–16.

89. For the English background in the combination laws and in doctrines of the common law, see discussion in chapter 2, above; see also

chapter 7, and Daniel R. Ernst, *Lawyers Against Labor: From Individual Rights to Corporate Liberalism* (Urbana, IL, 1995).

90. For a brief discussion comparing the history of antitrust doctrines in England and America, Freyer, "Economic Liberty, Antitrust," in *Liberty, Property, and Government*, ed. Paul and Dickman; see also William Letwin, *Law and Economic Policy in America: The Evolution of the Sherman Antitrust Act* (Chicago, 1965).

91. Kevin M. Teeven, *A History of the Anglo-American Common Law of Contract* (New York, 1990), 298ff.

92. The discussion in this paragraph owes much to the writings of my colleague Melvin Aron Eisenberg and follows closely in part from his landmark article, "The Responsive Model of Contract Law," *Stanford Law Review* 36 (1984): 1107–68 discussing the expectation principle and other postulates and corollaries of the basic terms of classical contract theory.

93. *Hotchkiss v. National City Bank*, 200 F. 287, 293 (S.D. N.Y., 1911), aff'd 231 U.S. 50 (1913).

94. Eisenberg, "Responsive Model," 1164–65.

95. Kevin M. Teeven, "A History of Legislative Reform of the Common Law of Contract," *University of Toledo Law Review* 26 (1994): 70.

96. Friedman, *History of American Law*, 540–41.

97. Ibid., 540–41.

98. Teeven, "History of Legislative Reform," 67–68 and passim; id., *History of the Anglo-American Common Law*, 175–216; and chap. 6, passim.

99. See, inter alia, Gillman, *Constitution Besieged*.

100. On Progressive era debates, see especially Arthur S. Link, *Woodrow Wilson and the Progressive Era, 1910–1917* (New York, 1954); and, on the courts, Melvin Urofsky, "Myth and Reality: The Supreme Court and Protective Legislation in the Progressive Era," *Yearbook of the Supreme Court Historical Society* (1983), 53–72; and Gillman, *Constitution Besieged*.

101. Lawrence M. Friedman, *Contract Law in America: A Social and Economic Case Study* (Madison, WI, 1965), 24.

102. See, on all these modern developments, Teeven, *History of the Anglo-American Common Law*; Melvin Aron Eisenberg, *The Nature of the Common Law* (Cambridge, MA, 1988); and W. David Slawson, *Binding Promises: The Late 20th-Century Reformation of Contract Law* (Princeton, NJ, 1996).

103. Acton, letter to Mary Gladstone, Apr. 24, 1881, in Alan Bullock and Maurice Shock, eds., *The Liberal Tradition from Fox to Keynes* (London, 1956), 125–26.

104. In ibid., 182.

105. Acton, "The History of Freedom in Antiquity" (1877), in ibid., 121.

106. Michael Freeden, *The New Liberalism*, 254.

107. The British debate is analyzed in Freeden, *New Liberalism*; on the American counterpart discourse, see chapter 6.

108. *Nebbia v. New York*, 291 U.S. 502 (1934); *Home Building and Loan Association v. Blaisdell*, 290 U.S. 398 (1934).

109. *United States v. Carolene Products Co.*, 304 U.S. 144 (1938).

110. *Wickard v. Filburn*, 317 U.S. 111 (1942). See also chapter 6 on the Parrish case and its significance.

111. William E. Leuchtenburg, *Franklin D. Roosevelt and the New Deal, 1932–1940* (New York, 1963); Harry N. Scheiber, "Redesigning the Architecture of Federalism: An American Tradition," *Yale Law and Policy Review* 14/*Yale Journal on Regulation*, Symposium Issue: *Constructing a New Federalism* (1996), 227–96.

112. Learned Hand, "Chief Justice Stone's Conception of the Judicial Function," *Columbia Law Review* 46 (1946): 698.

113. W. Beveridge, *Social Insurance and Allied Services*, Cmd. 86404 (London 1942); see discussion in Freeden, *Liberalism Divided*, 366ff.

114. Scheiber, "Redesigning the Architecture of Federalism." See also Michael Kammen, *Spheres of Liberty: Changing Perceptions of Liberty in American Culture* (Ithaca, NY, 1986) 127–74.

115. Bernard Schwartz, *A Commentary on the Constitution of the United States, Part II: The Rights of Property* (New York, 1965), 205. Some of the discussion in ensuing paragraphs follows the line of argument in an earlier study in which the evidence is set out much more at length and closely documented: see Scheiber, "Economic Liberty and the Constitution," in *Essays in the History of Liberty: Seaver Institute Lectures* (San Marino, CA, 1988), 75. Cf. Paul Kens, "The Source of a Myth; Police Powers of the States and Laissez Fair Constitutionalism, 1930–1937," *American Journal of Legal History* 35 (1991): 70–98.

116. Robert G. McCloskey, *The American Supreme Court*, 2d ed., rev. Sanford Levinson (Chicago, 1994): 148–205.

117. Charles Reich, "The New Property," *Yale Law Journal* 73 (1964): 733.

118. *Shapiro v. Thompson*, 394 U.S. 618 (1969).

119. *Goldberg v. Kelley*, 397 U.S. 254 (1970).

120. For example, in the March-May period of 1997, both the New Jersey and the Ohio supreme courts mandated radical revisions of state school finance in order to provide genuine equality of educational opportunity.

121. See, *inter alia*, Jeremy Waldron, *Liberal Rights*.

122. See the analysis of the adversarial style and its critics in various articles by Robert Kagan, most recently "American Lawyers, Legal Culture, and Adversarial Legalism," in *Legal Culture*, ed. Friedman and Scheiber, 7 et seq.

123. See generally Eisenberg, "Responsive Model"; and id., *Nature of the Common Law*.

CHAPTER 6

1. David Dudley Field, "American Progress in Jurisprudence," *American Law Review* 27 (1893): 643–45. For a splendid account of how these assumptions shaped behavior, see Robert W. Gordon, "Legal Thought and Legal Practice in the Age of American Enterprise, 1870–1920," *Professions and Professional Ideologies in America*, ed. Gerald L. Geison (Chapel Hill, NC, 1984), 70–110.

2. Richard T. Ely, *Studies in the Evolution of Industrial Society* (New York, 1903), 400, 402, 406, 410. For intensive analysis of the variations on Ely's story, see Dorothy Ross, *The Origins of American Social Science* (New York, 1991), chap. 4; James T. Kloppenberg, *Uncertain Victory: Social Democracy and Progressivism in European and American Thought, 1870–1920* (New York, 1986), chap. 7.

3. Ernst Freund, *Standards of American Legislation* (Chicago, 1917), 22. The best account of the drive for "social legislation" in a bellwether state is still Irwin Yellowitz, *Labor and the Progressive Movement in New York State, 1897–1916* (Ithaca, NY, 1965). The three opinions in which judges used the term "social legislation" prior to 1940, located thanks to LEXIS, were *People v. Charles Schweinler Press*, 163 App. Div. 620, 630 (N.Y. 1914) (sustaining statute barring night work for female factory workers); *Carroll v. Knickerbocker Ice Co.*, 218 N.Y. 435, 445 (1916) (ruling on admissibility of hearsay evidence in worker's compensation hearings); *Ohio Automatic Sprinkler v. Fender*, 108 Ohio St. 149, 174 (1923) (interpreting worker's compensation statute).

4. *Lochner v. New York*, 198 U.S. 45, 57–59 (1905).

5. Roscoe Pound, "Liberty of Contract," *Yale Law Journal* 18 (1909): 454–87. Compare S. Whitney Dunscomb, Jr., "The Police Power and Civil Liberty," *Columbia Law Review* 6 (1906): 93–101.

6. Michael Les Benedict, "Laissez-Faire and Liberty: A Reevaluation of the Meaning and Origins of Laissez-Faire Constitutionalism," *Law and History Review* 3 (1985): 293–331; Cass Sunstein, "Lochner's Legacy," *Columbia Law Review* 87 (1987): 873–919; Morton J. Horwitz, *The Transformation of American Law, 1870–1960: The Crisis of Legal Orthodoxy* (New York, 1992), chap. 1; Howard Gillman, *The Constitution Besieged: The Rise and Demise of Lochner Era Police Power Jurisprudence* (Durham, NC, 1993); Owen M. Fiss, *Troubled Beginnings of the Modern State, 1888–1910* (New York, 1993), chaps. 1, 6.

7. James Willard Hurst, "Freedom of Contract," *Encyclopedia of the American Constitution*, ed. Leonard W. Levy et al., 4 vols. (New York, 1986), 2:778–79. See also Lawrence M. Friedman, "Freedom of Contract and Occupational Licensing, 1890–1910: A Legal and Social Study," *California Law Review* 53 (1965): 487–534.

8. *Godcharles v. Wigeman*, 113 Penn. St. 431, 437 (1886).

9. *Powell v. State*, 114 Penn. St. 265, 296 (1887).

10. Eric Foner, *Free Soil, Free Labor, Free Men: The Ideology of the Re-

publican Party before the Civil War (New York, 1970), 16–17 and passim; James D. Richardson, ed., *Messages and Papers of the Presidents, 1789–1897,* 10 vols. (Washington, 1897), 6:30. See also Bruce W. Collins, "The Ideology of the Antebellum Northern Democrats," *Journal of American Studies* 11 (1977): 103–21; David Montgomery, *Citizen Worker: The Experience of Workers in the United States with Democracy and the Free Market during the Nineteenth Century* (New York, 1993), chap. 1.

11. Eric Foner, *Reconstruction: America's Unfinished Revolution, 1863–1877* (New York, 1988), chaps. 3–4, 6, 8, 11; Harold Woodman, *New South, New Law: The Legal Foundations of Credit and Labor Relations in the Postbellum Agricultural South* (Baton Rouge, LA, 1995), 93–94.

12. *New-York Times,* Feb. 22, 1869; John R. Commons et al., eds., *A Documentary History of American Industrial Society,* 10 vols. (Cleveland, 1911), 9:302–5. See also Daniel T. Rodgers, *The Work Ethic in Industrial America, 1850–1920* (Chicago, 1974), 30–50, 57, 155–57.

13. David Montgomery, *Beyond Equality: Labor and the Radical Republicans, 1862–1872* (New York, 1967), 249–60.

14. *New York Evening Post,* June 4, 1872.

15. Wisconsin, *General Laws,* chap. 87 (1867); John R. Commons, *History of Labor in the United States,* 2 vols. (New York, 1918), 2:169–70; Montgomery, *Beyond Equality,* 44, 303, 305. See also New York, *Laws,* chap. 856 (1867); Connecticut, *Public Acts,* 77 (1867); Illinois, *Laws,* 101 (1867); Missouri, *Laws,* 132 (1867); Pennsylvania, *Laws,* 99 (1868); California, *Statutes,* chap. 70 (1868). The act applied in Connecticut "unless otherwise agreed by the parties," in Illinois and Pennsylvania "where there is no special contract or agreement to the contrary," in California "unless otherwise expressly stipulated between the parties concerned." In Missouri the statute provided that "nothing in this act shall be so construed as to prevent parties to make any contract for work, services, or labor upon a longer or shorter time."

16. *Albany Evening Journal,* Apr. 6, 1867; *Sacramento Bee,* Jan. 8, 1868; *Drew v. Smith,* 38 Cal. 325 (1869).

17. William E. Forbath, *Law and the Shaping of the American Labor Movement* (Cambridge, MA, 1991), 37–58, 177–82.

18. See, generally, Christopher L. Tomlins, "'A Mysterious Power': Industrial Accidents and the Legal Construction of Employment Relations in Massachusetts, 1800–1850," *Law and History Review* 6 (1988): 375–438. The early Pennsylvania case is *Mitchell v. Pennsylvania R.R. Co.,* 1 American L. Reg. 717 (1853).

19. *Western & Atlantic R.R. Co. v. Bishop,* 50 Georgia 465, 470–71 (1873). On the emergence of the early employers liability laws, see Lawrence M. Friedman, *A History of American Law,* 2d. ed. (New York, 1985), 484.

20. Morton J. Horwitz, *The Transformation of American Law, 1780–1860* (Cambridge, MA, 1977), 204–7; Brief for Plaintiff in Error, *New York*

Central R.R. v. Lockwood, 17 Wall. 357 (1873), Records and Briefs, Supreme Court of the United States (microfilm), 21–22.

21. *New York Central R.R. v. Lockwood*, 17 Wall. 357, 379–80 (U.S., 1873).

22. *Western & Atlantic R.R. Co. v. Bishop*, 50 Georgia 465, 472 (1873).

23. Seymour D. Thompson, *The Law of Negligence*, 2 vols. (San Francisco, 1886), 2:1025; *American Law Review* 26 (1892): 404. For a biographical sketch of Thompson, see Arnold M. Paul, *Conservative Crisis and the Rule of Law: Attitudes of Bar and Bench, 1887–1895* (Ithaca, NY, 1960), 43.

24. *Lake Shore & Michigan Southern Railway Co. v. Spangler*, 44 Ohio St. 471, 479 (1886); *Little Rock & Fort Smith Ry. Co. v. Eubanks*, 48 Arkansas 460, 464 (1886).

25. *Holden v. Hardy*, 169 U.S. 366 (1898).

26. *Lochner v. New York*, 198 U.S. 45, 72–73 (1905); *Adair v. United States*, 208 U.S. 161, 174–75 (1908).

27. *Lochner v. New York*, 198 U.S. 45, 76 (1905); *Adair v. United States*, 208 U.S. 161, 192 (1908); Oliver Wendell Holmes, Jr., *The Common Law* (Boston, 1881), 41. For the jury/trial judge, legislature/appellate judge connection, see James Bradley Thayer, "The Origin and Scope of the American Doctrine of Constitutional Law," *Harvard Law Review* 7 (1893): 129–56; J. B. Thayer, *A Preliminary Treatise on Evidence at the Common Law* (Boston, 1898), 218–19.

28. *McClean v. Arkansas*, 211 U.S. 539, 550 (1909). See also *Knoxville Iron Co. v. Harbison*, 183 U.S. 13 (1901); *Rail & River Coal Co. v. Yapple*, 236 U.S. 338 (1915).

29. *Seymour v. Delancey*, 3 Cowen 445, 525 (N.Y. Ct. of Errors, 1824); Francis Bohlen, "Voluntary Assumption of Risk," *Harvard Law Review* 20 (1906): 22; James Gordley, *The Philosophical Origins of Modern Contract Doctrine* (Oxford, 1991), 202–8. See also John Norton Pomeroy, *A Treatise on Equity Jurisprudence*, 3 vols. (San Francisco, 1882), 2:428–33.

30. *Keokee Consolidated Coke Co. v. Taylor*, 234 U.S. 224 (1917); Alexander M. Bickel and Benno C. Schmidt, Jr., *The Judiciary and Responsible Government, 1910–1921* (New York, 1984), 298.

31. Ely, *Studies in the Evolution of Industrial Society*, 419–20.

32. *Johnson v. Philadelphia & Reading R.R. Co.*, 163 Penn. St. 127, 134 (1894). See also Annotation, "Validity of contract providing that acceptance of benefits from relief associations shall bar action against employer," 12 ALR 477–95 (1920); George E. Beers, "Contracts Exempting Employers From Liability for Negligence," *Yale Law Journal* 7 (1898): 352–61.

33. *United States Statutes at Large* 35:65–66 (1908); Edward A. Purcell, Jr., *Litigation and Inequality: Federal Diversity Jurisdiction in Industrial America, 1870–1958* (New York, 1992), 31–45.

34. *Chicago, Burlington & Quincy R.R. Co. v. McGuire*, 219 U.S. 549, 569, 572–73 (1911) (Hughes's emphasis).

342   NOTES TO PAGES 186–94

35. *Second Employers' Liability Cases*, 223 U.S. 1, 52 (1912); *New York Central R.R. v. White*, 243 U.S. 188, 207 (1917).

36. Alexander M. Bickel, *The Unpublished Opinions of Mr. Justice Brandeis* (Cambridge, MA, 1957), 74.

37. Edward S. Corwin, "Social Insurance and the Constitution," *Yale Law Journal* 26 (1917): 431–43.

38. Henry W. Farnam, *Chapters in the History of Social Legislation in the United States to 1860* (Washington, 1938), 6.

39. Ibid., 8–115, 119–26, 152–56, 231–52.

40. Henry W. Farnam, *The Economic Utilization of History and Other Economic Studies* (New Haven, CT, 1913), 49; *New State Ice Co. v. Liebmann*, 285 U.S. 262, 311 (1932). Ely called Farnam "the real founder" of the AALL. See Richard T. Ely to John B. Andrews, Aug. 29, 1909, AALL Collection, Andrews Papers, School of Industrial and Labor Relations, Cornell University. For an overview of the origins and development of the AALL, see Theda Skocpol, *Protecting Soldiers and Mothers: The Political Origins of Social Policy in the United States* (Cambridge, MA, 1992), 176–204.

41. Henry W. Farnam, book review, *Political Science Quarterly* 1 (1886): 683–87. For details on Farnam's career, see the obituary by Irving Fisher, a devoted friend, in *American Economic Review* 24 (1934): 175–77.

42. Farnam, *Economic Utilization of History*, 81–82, 88–89.

43. Ibid., 89–90.

44. Ibid., 85, 91–92. For an account of the toothless laws already on the books when Farnam wrote, see Herbert Schreiber, "The Majority Preference Provisions in Early State Labor Arbitration Statutes, 1880–1900," *American Journal of Legal History* 15 (1971): 186–98.

45. Victor S. Clark, "Introductory Note," in Farnam, *Chapters in the History of Social Legislation*, vii–xii; James Leiby, *Carroll Wright and Labor Reform: The Origins of Labor Statistics* (Cambridge, MA, 1960), 192–97.

46. Freund, *Standards of American Legislation*, 7, 22, 211–13; [Henry W. Farnam], "Constructive Factors in Legislation," *Nation* 106 (1918): 599–600. For a splendid account of the role First Amendment values played in the AALL campaign against the yellow-dog contract, see Barry Cushman, "Doctrinal Synergies and Liberal Dilemmas: The Case of the Yellow-Dog Contract," *Supreme Court Review* 1992: 235–93. For a serviceable biography of Freund, see Oscar Kraines, *The World and Ideas of Ernst Freund* (University, AL, 1974).

47. *West Coast Hotel v. Parrish*, 300 U.S. 379, 391–93 (1937). For a different reading of *Parrish*, identifying it as such a decisive break with the principle of neutrality that it marked a "constitutional revolution," see Gillman, *The Constitution Besieged*, chap. 4; Sunstein, "Lochner's Legacy," 876–83, 917. My view is the result of countless conversations with Barry Cushman. See his Ph.D. dissertation, "The Structure of a Constitutional Revolution: *Nebbia v. New York* and the Collapse of Laissez-Faire Constitutionalism" (Univ. of VA, 1995).

48. *West Coast Hotel v. Parrish*, 300 U.S. 379, 399–400 (1937).

49. *United States v. Carolene Products Co.*, 304 U.S. 144, 152 (1938).

50. Pound, "Liberty of Contract," 464; Harlan Fiske Stone, *Law and its Administration* (New York, 1915), 47–48, 153.

51. Alexis de Tocqueville, *Democracy in America*, ed. Phillips Bradley, 2 vols. (New York, 1945), 1:288–90.

52. James Willard Hurst, *Law and Markets in United States History: Different Modes of Bargaining Among Interests* (Madison, WI, 1982), 141.

CHAPTER 7

1. Charles W. McCurdy, "The Roots of 'Liberty of Contract' Reconsidered: Major Premises in the Law of Employment, 1867–1937," *Supreme Court Historical Society Yearbook*, 1984: 24; Lawrence M. Friedman, *The Republic of Choice: Law, Authority, and Culture* (Cambridge, MA, 1990), 2–3.

2. Clifford Geertz, *The Interpretation of Cultures: Selected Essays* (New York, 1973), 218–19.

3. Christopher L. Tomlins, "How Who Rides Whom: Recent 'New' Histories of American Labour Law and What They May Signify," *Social History* 20 (1995): 9.

4. Jay M. Feinman and Peter Gabel, "Contract Law as Ideology," in D. Kairys, ed., *The Politics of Law: A Progressive Critique*, 2d ed. (New York, 1990), 384.

5. Tomlins, "How Who Rides Whom," 5, 16; Fineman and Gabel, "Contract Law as Ideology," 377; Robert W. Gordon, "Critical Legal Histories," *Stanford Law Review* 36 (1984): 93–96, 109–13.

6. Betty Mensch, "Freedom of Contract as Ideology," *Stanford Law Review* 33 (1981): 759, 765.

7. Robert Hale, "Coercion and Distribution in a Supposedly Non-Coercive State," *Political Science Quarterly* 38 (1940): 472. See also P. S. Atiyah, *The Rise and Fall of Freedom of Contract* (Oxford, 1979), 50.

8. John Locke, *Two Treatises of Government* (1698), ed. Peter Laslett (Cambridge, 1960), 2: §§ 48, 119; see also Atiyah, *Freedom of Contract*, 46, 50.

9. Duncan Kennedy, "Form and Substance in Private Law Adjudication," *Harvard Law Review* 89 (1976): 1725–37; Mensch, "Freedom of Contract as Ideology," 757.

10. Gordon S. Wood, *The Radicalism of the American Revolution* (New York, 1992), 162–68.

11. Robert J. Steinfeld, "The *Philadelphia Cordwainers'* Case of 1806: The Struggle over Alternative Legal Constructions of a Free Market in Labor," in Christopher L. Tomlins and Andrew J. King, eds., *Labor Law in America: Historical and Critical Essays* (Baltimore, 1992), 24; Christopher L. Tomlins, "Law and Power in the Employment Relationship," in Tomlins and King, eds., *Labor Law in America*, 81; Raymond L. Hogler, "Labor

History and Critical Labor Law: An Interdisciplinary Approach to Workers' Control," *Labor History* 30 (1989): 169.

12. Karl Polanyi, *The Great Transformation* (1944; repr. New York, 1957), 156–57.

13. James Willard Hurst, *Law and the Conditions of Freedom in the Nineteenth-Century United States* (Madison, WI, 1956), 11–15, 18; id., *Law and Markets in United States History: Different Modes of Bargaining Among Interests* (Madison, WI, 1982); Christopher L. Tomlins, *Law, Labor, and Ideology in the Early American Republic* (Cambridge, 1993), xv.

14. Arthur Bestor, "The American Civil War as a Constitutional Crisis," *American Historical Review* 69 (1964): 327–52. See generally Eric Foner, *Free Soil, Free Labor, Free Men: The Ideology of the Republican Party Before the Civil War* (New York, 1970).

15. Elizabeth Mensch, "The History of Mainstream Legal Thought," in Kairys, ed., *The Politics of Law*, 17; Morton J. Horwitz, *The Transformation of American Law, 1780–1860* (Cambridge, MA, 1977), 111–14; Polanyi, *The Great Transformation*, 71.

16. Atiyah, *Freedom of Contract*, 524–28; Polanyi, *The Great Transformation*, 95–102.

17. Tomlins, "Law and Power in the Employment Relationship," 76–80.

18. Steinfeld, "The *Philadelphia Cordwainers'* Case," 21, 33–35; Tomlins, *The State and the Unions: Labor Relations, Law, and the Organized Labor Movement in America, 1880–1960* (Cambridge, 1985), 49.

19. Tomlins, *Law, Labor, and Ideology*, 215; Horwitz, *The Transformation of American Law*, 209.

20. Horwitz, *The Transformation of American Law*, 180–85.

21. Tomlins, "Law and Power in the Employment Relationship," 71; Horwitz, *The Transformation of American Law*, 209.

22. Locke, *Two Treatises of Government* 2: §§ 119–20.

23. Tomlins, "How Who Rides Whom," 14.

24. On the Cordwainers' case, *Commonwealth v. Pullis*, see Steinfeld, "The *Philadelphia Cordwainers'* Case," 20–43, 22–23, 36; Tomlins, *Law, Labor, and Ideology*, 131–37; Victoria Hattam, *Labor Visions and State Power: The Origins of Business Unionism in the United States* (Princeton, NJ, 1993), 47–56.

25. Atiyah, *Freedom of Contract*, 533.

26. 45 Mass. 111 (1842). On the *Hunt* case, see Leonard W. Levy, *The Law of the Commonwealth and Chief Justice Shaw* (Cambridge, MA, 1957), 185–206.

27. Quoted in Tomlins, *Law, Labor, and Ideology*, 209.

28. Karen Orren, *Belated Feudalism: Labor, the Law, and Liberal Development in the United States* (Cambridge, 1991), 122–35; Tomlins, *Law, Labor, and Ideology*, 210–16; Sean Wilentz, "Conspiracy, Power, and the Early Labor Movement: The People v. James Melvin et al., 1811," *Labor History* 24 (1983): 572–79; Tomlins, "Criminal Conspiracy and Early Labor Combinations: Massachusetts, 1824–1840," *Labor History* 28 (1987): 370–71.

29. Tomlins, *The State and the Unions*, 44–45.

30. *Commonwealth v. Hunt*, 45 Mass. at 134; Tomlins, *Law, Labor, and Ideology*, 215–16.

31. E.g., *M'Millan et al. v. Vanderlip*, 12 Johnson 165, 166–67 (N.Y., 1815); Tomlins, *Law, Labor, and Ideology*, 227–28; Peter Karsten, "'Bottomed on Justice': A Reappraisal of Critical Legal Studies Scholarship Concerning Breaches of Labor Contracts by Quitting or Firing in Britain and the U.S., 1630–1880," *American Journal of Legal History* 34 (1990): 229; Wythe Holt, "Recovery by the Worker Who Quits: A Comparison of the Mainstream, Legal Realist, and Critical Legal Studies Approaches to a Problem of Nineteenth Century Contract Law," 1986 *Wisconsin Law Review*, 678–79.

32. *Little Miami Railroad v. John Stevens*, 20 Ohio 416, 432–33 (1851).

33. Tomlins, *Law, Labor, and Ideology*, 227–28, 278–80.

34. 45 Mass. 49 (1842).

35. Ibid., at 57.

36. Ibid., at 59.

37. A good review of the historiographical literature on employers' defenses may be found in Eric Tucker, *Administering Danger in the Workplace: The Law and Politics of Occupational Health and Safety in Toronto, 1850–1914* (Toronto, 1990), 50–63; see also Arthur F. McEvoy, "Working Environments: An Ecological Approach to Industrial Health and Safety," *Technology and Culture* 36 (1995): S145–72.

38. Tomlins, *Law, Labor, and Ideology*, 303, 363–68; Tucker, *Administering Danger in the Workplace*, 38–44; Tomlins, "A Mysterious Power: Industrial Accidents and the Legal Construction of Employment Relations in Massachusetts, 1800–1850," *Law and History Review* 6 (1988): 415.

39. *Ryan v. Cumberland Valley Railroad Co.*, 23 Pa. 384, 386 (1854).

40. Ibid., at 387–88.

41. Ibid., at 388.

42. See, for example, *Latimer v. Alexander*, 14 Ga. 185 (1853); Paul Finkelman, "Slaves as Fellow Servants: Ideology, Law, and Industrialization," *American Journal of Legal History* 31 (1987): 269–305.

43. Charles McClain does not think the term "indentured servitude" fits the situation of nineteenth-century Chinese immigrant workers. McClain, *In Search of Equality: The Chinese Struggle Against Discrimination in Nineteenth-Century America* (Berkeley, 1994), 14–15. But see Lucy E. Salyer, *Laws Harsh as Tigers: Chinese Immigrants and the Shaping of Modern Immigration Law* (Chapel Hill, NC, 1995), 10, 259 n. 55.

44. 1850 *California Statutes*, ch. 133; 1860 *California Statutes*, ch. 231; Robert F. Heizer and Alan F. Almquist, *The Other Californians: Prejudice and Discrimination Under Spain, Mexico, and the United States to 1920* (Berkeley, 1971), 39–58.

45. See generally David Rothman, *The Discovery of the Asylum: Social Order and Disorder in the New Republic* (Boston, 1971).

46. Alice Kessler-Harris, *Out to Work: A History of Wage-Earning*

Women in the United States (New York, 1982), 71; Norma Basch, *In the Eyes of the Law: Women, Marriage, and Property in Nineteenth-Century New York* (Ithaca, NY, 1982), 165; see generally Jeanne Boydston, *Home and Work: Housework, Wages, and the Ideology of Labor in the Early Republic* (New York, 1990).

47. *Askew v. Dupree*, 30 Ga. 173 (1860) (common law marriage described in free contract terms). Reva Siegel, "Home as Work: The First Woman's Rights Claims Concerning Wives' Household Labor, 1850–1880," *Yale Law Journal* 103 (1994): 1076.

48. See, e.g., 1851 Mass. Acts. ch. 324 (child's consent required for adoptions at age 14 and over).

49. E.g., 1860 *N.Y. Laws* ch. 90.

50. E.g., 1869 *Ill. Laws* 440, 1872 *Wis. Laws* 218; Siegel, "Home as Work," 1077.

51. Siegel, "Home as Work," 1181–84.

52. *Whitaker v. Whitaker*, 52 N.Y. 368 (1873); Siegel, "Home as Work," 1184.

53. *Lumley v. Wagner*, 42 Eng. Rep. 687 (1852); *Lumley v. Gye*, 118 Eng. Rep. 749 (Q.B. 1853). See Lea S. VanderVelde, "Hidden Dimensions in Labor Law History: Gender Variations on the Theme of Free Labor," in Tomlins and King, eds., *Labor Law in America*, 102–4.

54. *Ford v. Jermon*, 6 Phila. 6 (1865); VanderVelde, "Hidden Dimensions in Labor Law History," 106–8.

55. 83 U.S. 131 (1873).

56. Ibid., at 141.

57. Hattam, *Labor Visions and State Power*, 76–111; Tomlins, "How Who Rides Whom," 14; Steinfeld, "The *Philadelphia Cordwainers'* Case," 35, 40.

58. David Montgomery, *The Fall of the House of Labor: The Workplace, the State, and American Labor Activism, 1865–1925* (Cambridge, 1987), 9–13; Daniel Nelson, *Managers & Workers: Origins of the Twentieth-Century Factory System in the United States, 1880–1920*, 2d ed. (Madison, WI, 1995), 37–39.

59. Siegel, "Home as Work," 1092, 1112, 1124–27.

60. *Commonwealth v. Alger*, 61 Mass. 53, 85 (1851).

61. Hurst, *Law and the Conditions of Freedom*, 7–8; see also Harry N. Scheiber, "Public Rights and the Rule of Law in American Legal History," *California Law Review* 72 (1984): 217–51; William J. Novak, *The People's Welfare: Law and Regulation in Nineteenth-Century America* (Chapel Hill, NC, 1996).

62. Abraham Lincoln, Second Annual Message to Congress (Dec. 1, 1862), in Roy P. Basler, ed., *Collected Works of Abraham Lincoln* (New Brunswick, NJ, 1953), 5:518–37, 535.

63. Civil Rights Act of 1866 § 1, 14 *Statutes at Large* 27 (1866) *codified* at 18 U.S.C. § 1981; Eric Foner, *Reconstruction: America's Unfinished Revolution, 1863–1877* (New York, 1988), 244–45.

64. *Slaughterhouse Cases*, 83 U.S. 36, 70–71 (1873); Foner, *Reconstruction*, 257.

65. *Slaughterhouse Cases*, 83 U.S. at 71–81 (1873).

66. Ibid., at 97 (Field, J., dissenting).

67. Ibid., at 110 and n. 39 (Field, J., dissenting).

68. Ibid., at 90 (Field, J., dissenting).

69. Ibid., at 118 (Bradley, J., dissenting).

70. Alfred D. Chandler, Jr., *The Visible Hand: The Managerial Revolution in American Business* (Cambridge MA, 1977), 81–82; Gabriel Kolko, *The Triumph of Conservatism: A Reinterpretation of American History, 1900–1915* (New York, 1963), 12–17. See generally Daniel Nelson, *Managers & Workers: Origins of the Factory System in the United States, 1880–1920*, 2d ed. (Madison, WI, 1995).

71. 198 U.S. 45 (1905).

72. *Munn v. Illinois*, 94 U.S. 113 (1877); see Harry N. Scheiber, "The Road to *Munn*: Eminent Domain and the Concept of Public Purpose in the State Courts," *Perspectives in American History* 5 (1971): 329–402.

73. *Chicago, Minnesota & St. Paul Railway Co. v. Minnesota*, 134 U.S. 418, 458.

74. Ibid., at 462–63.

75. *Godcharles v. Wigeman*, 113 Pa. 431 (1886).

76. *Ritchie v. People*, 155 Ill. 98, 103 (1895).

77. *Lochner v. New York*, 198 U.S. 45, 54–55 (1905). On dangerous employments, see *Holden v. Hardy*, 169 U.S. 366 (1898). On the constitutionality of laws limiting hours on public works, see *Knoxville Iron Co. v. Harbison*, 183 U.S. 13 (1901); *Atkins v. Kansas*, 191 U.S. 222 (1903); see also Melvin I. Urofsky, "State Courts and Protective Legislation during the Progressive Era: A Reevaluation," *Journal of American History* 72 (1985): 76.

78. *Lochner*, 198 U.S. at 64.

79. Chapter 6 above.

80. Chapter 3 above; William E. Forbath, *Law and the Shaping of the American Labor Movement* (Cambridge, MA, 1991), 201–30.

81. *Holden v. Hardy*, 169 U.S. 366 (1898); *Muller v. Oregon*, 208 U.S. 412 (1908). See Theda Skocpol, *Protecting Soldiers and Mothers: The Political Origins of Social Policy in the United States* (Cambridge, MA, 1992), 373–74.

82. *Stettler v. O'Hara*, 69 Or. 519 (1914), *affirmed*, 243 U.S. 629 (1916); Urofsky, "State Courts and Protective Legislation," 79, 83.

83. *Adkins v. Children's Hospital*, 261 U.S. 525, 555, 557.

84. Ibid., at 546.

85. Ibid., at 557–58.

86. Ibid., at 559.

87. *Coppage v. Kansas*, 236 U.S. 1 (1915); *Adair v. United States*, 208 U.S. 161 (1908).

88. *Adair v. United States*, 208 U.S. at 175; McCurdy, "Roots of Liberty of Contract," 25.

89. *Coppage v. Kansas,* 236 U.S. at 15.

90. Haggai Hurvitz, "American Labor Law and the Doctrine of Entrepreneurial Property Rights: Boycotts, Courts, and the Juridical Reorientation of 1886–1895," *Industrial Relations Law Journal* 8 (1986): 313–15.

91. Ibid., 321–24; Victoria Hattam, "Courts and the Question of Class: Judicial Regulation of Labor under the Common Law Doctrine of Criminal Conspiracy," in Tomlins and King, eds., *Labor Law in America,* 55–58.

92. Arnold M. Paul, *Conservative Crisis and the Rule of Law: Attitudes of Bar and Bench, 1887–1895* (Ithaca, NY, 1960), 61–81; see, e.g., the opinion of Judge Taft in *In re Phelan,* 62 F. 803, 821 (S.D. Ohio, 1894) ["Certainly the starvation of a nation cannot be a lawful purpose of a combination."]; William Howard Taft, *The Anti-Trust Act and the Supreme Court* (1914; repr. New York, 1970), 26.

93. Forbath, *Law and the Shaping of the American Labor Movement,* 66–79.

94. Arnold M. Paul, *Conservative Crisis and the Rule of Law: Attitudes of Bar and Bench, 1887–1895* (New York, 1960), 107.

95. *Hitchman Coal and Coke Co. v. Mitchell,* 245 U.S. 229 (1917).

96. Jay M. Feinman, "The Development of the Employment at Will Rule," *American Journal of Legal History* 20 (1976): 119–22.

97. *Martin v. New York Life Insurance Co.,* 148 N.Y. 117, 121 (1895).

98. Feinman, "Development of Employment at Will," 129.

99. Hogler, "Labor History and Critical Labor Law," 182–83.

100. Walter Licht, *Working for the Railroad: The Organization of Work in the Nineteenth Century* (Princeton, NJ, 1983), 188; Kurt Wetzel, "Railroad Management's Response to Operating Employees' Accidents, 1890–1913," *Labor History* 21 (1980): 351–52.

101. Forbath, "Law and the Shaping of Labor Politics," in Tomlins and King, eds., *Labor Law in America,* 209; Urofsky, "State Courts and Protective Legislation," 89.

102. Crystal Eastman, *Work Accidents and the Law,* vol. 2 of *The Pittsburgh Survey,* ed. Paul Underwood Kellogg (New York, 1910).

103. McEvoy, "The Triangle Shirtwaist Factory Fire of 1911: Social Change, Industrial Accidents, and the Evolution of Common-Sense Causality," *Law & Social Inquiry* 20 (1995): 641–48.

104. 35 *Statutes at Large* 65 (1908), *codified at* 45 U.S.C. §§ 51 et seq.

105. McCurdy, "Roots of Liberty of Contract," 30–33.

106. 1910 *N.Y. Laws* 1945; *Ives v. South Buffalo Railway Co.,* 201 N.Y. 271 (1911).

107. 1912 *N.Y. Laws* 1382; 1913 *N.Y. Laws* 2277; *New York Central Railroad Co. v. White,* 243 U.S. 188 (1917).

108. E.g., *Miss. Laws* ch. IV, §§ 5–9 (1865).

109. Foner, *Reconstruction,* 164–68; Amy Dru Stanley, "Beggars Can't Be Choosers: Compulsion and Contract in Postbellum America," in Tomlins and King, eds., *Labor Law in America,* 143–44.

110. William Cohen, "Negro Involuntary Servitude in the South, 1865–1940: A Preliminary Analysis," *Journal of Southern History* 42 (1976): 31–60; Gavin Wright, *The Political Economy of the Cotton South: Households, Markets, and Wealth in the Nineteenth Century* (New York, 1978), 177–78.

111. *Bailey v. Alabama*, 219 U.S. 219 (1911).

112. Stanley, "Beggars Can't Be Choosers," 129–30, 134, 149.

113. Udo Sautter, "North American Government Labor Agencies Before World War One: A Cure for Unemployment?" *Labor History* 24 (1983): 375–77; Stanley, "Beggars Can't Be Choosers," 133–34. On pensions for mothers and civil war veterans, see Skocpol, *Protecting Soldiers and Mothers*, passim.

114. Skocpol, *Protecting Soldiers and Mothers*, 33–34, 408–9; Susan Lehrer, *Origins of Protective Labor Legislation for Women, 1905–1925* (Albany, NY, 1987), 42.

115. Lehrer, *Origins of Protective Labor Legislation for Women*, 64.

116. VanderVelde, "Hidden Dimensions in Labor Law History," 110–16.

117. Forbath, *Law and the Shaping of the American Labor Movement*, 14–15; Hattam, "Courts and the Question of Class," 62–64.

118. Forbath, *Law and the Shaping of the American Labor Movement*, 12–14; id., "The Shaping of the American Labor Movement," *Harvard Law Review* 102 (1989): 1120–22.

119. Hattam, "Courts and the Question of Class," 62–64.

120. Forbath, *Law and the Shaping of the American Labor Movement*, 53–57.

121. Catherine Fisk, "Still 'Learning Something of Legislation': The Judiciary in the History of Labor Law," *Law & Social Inquiry* 19 (1994): 179.

122. James Weinstein, *The Corporate Ideal in the Liberal State: 1900–1918* (Boston, 1968), 41–43.

123. William E. Forbath, "The Ambiguities of Free Labor: Labor and the Law in the Gilded Age," 1985 *Wisconsin Law Review*, 769; Tomlins, *The State and the Unions*, 74–82.

124. Siegel, "Home as Work," 1161–84.

125. Lehrer, *Origins of Protective Labor Legislation for Women*, 95–114; Siegel, "Home as Work," 1209; Joan G. Zimmerman, "The Jurisprudence of Equality: The Women's Minimum Wage, the First Equal Rights Amendment, and *Adkins v. Children's Hospital*, 1905–1923," *Journal of American History* 70 (1991): 188–225.

126. *Lochner v. New York*, 198 U.S. at 75 (Holmes, J., dissenting).

127. Ibid., at 75.

128. Ibid., at 76 (Holmes, J., dissenting).

129. Roscoe Pound, "Liberty of Contract," *Yale Law Journal* 18 (1909): 455, 470, 487.

130. Hale, "Coercion and Distribution," 476; Klare, "Judicial Deradicalization of the Wagner Act and the Origins of Modern Legal Consciousness, 1937–1941," *Minnesota Law Review* 62 (1978): 277–79.

131. *Hitchman Coal and Coke v. Mitchell*, 245 U.S. at 271–72 (Brandeis, J., dissenting).

132. McEvoy, "Triangle Shirtwaist Fire," 645–47.

133. See chapter 6 above.

134. Hurst, *Law and Markets in United States History*, 20–21, 67, 88.

135. Bruce A. Ackerman, "The Storrs Lectures: Discovering the Constitution," *Yale Law Journal* 93 (1984): 1052–57; Ackerman, "Beyond *Carolene Products*," *Harvard Law Review* 98 (1985): 714.

136. *United States v. Carolene Products*, 304 U.S. 144, 152 and n. 4 (1937). See Robert Cover, "The Origins of Judicial Activism in the Protection of Minorities," *Yale Law Journal* 91 (1982): 1291–92.

137. Theodore R. Marmor, Jerry L. Mashaw, and Philip L. Harvey, *America's Misunderstood Welfare State: Persistent Myths, Enduring Realities* (New York, 1990), 33–35.

138. 47 *Statutes at Large* 70 (1932), *codified at* 29 U.S.C. §§ 101 et seq.

139. National Industrial Recovery Act § 7(a), 48 *Statutes at Large* 195, 198 (1933).

140. 49 *Statutes at Large* 449, *codified at* 29 U.S.C.A. §§ 151 et seq.

141. 52 *Statutes at Large* 1060 (1938), *codified at* 29 U.S.C. §§ 201 et seq.

142. Eileen Boris, "The Regulation of Homework and the Devolution of the Postwar Labor Standards Regime: Beyond Dichotomy," in Tomlins and King, eds., *Labor Law in America*, 262.

143. Hurst, *Law and Markets in United States History*, 76.

144. Ackerman, "Discovering the Constitution," 1053–54.

145. *West Coast Hotel v. Parrish*, 300 U.S. 379, 391; Cass R. Sunstein, "Lochner's Legacy," *Columbia Law Review* 87 (1987): 880–81. On the court packing episode and the Supreme Court's shift in view, see Charles L. Black, Jr., *The People and the Court: Judicial Review in a Democracy* (New York, 1960), 56–68.

146. *Adkins v. Children's Hospital*, 261 U.S. at 558; *West Coast Hotel v. Parrish*, 300 U.S. at 399; Sunstein, "Lochner's Legacy," 876.

147. *Lucas v. South Carolina Coastal Council*, 505 U.S. 1003, 1017 (1992) (citations omitted). The clearest statement of the principle of legislative deference is in *United States v. Carolene Products Co.*, 304 U.S. 144, 152 (1937).

148. National Labor Relations Act § 1, 29 U.S.C. § 151.

149. *NLRB v. Jones & Laughlin Steel Corp.*, 301 U.S. 1, 33 (1937).

150. Klare, "Judicial Deradicalization of the Wagner Act," 292–93; Tomlins, *The State and the Unions*, 147.

151. Daniel R. Ernst, "Common Laborers? Industrial Pluralists, Legal Realists, and the Law of Industrial Disputes, 1915–1943," *Law and History Review* 11 (1993): 79–84; Leon Fink, "Labor, Liberty, and the Law: Trade Unionism and the Problem of the American Constitutional Order," *Journal of American History* 74 (1987): 922; Katherine Van Wezel Stone,

"The Post-War Paradigm in American Labor Law," *Yale Law Journal* 90 (1981): 1565.

152. Labor-Management Relations Act, 61 *Statutes at Large* 136, codified at 29 U.S.C. §§ 141 et seq.; Tomlins, *The State and the Unions*, 284–90.

153. Tomlins, *The State and the Unions*, 238–41, 258–62; James B. Atleson, *Values and Assumptions in American Labor Law* (Amherst, MA, 1983), 113–15; Klare, "Judicial Deradicalization of the Wagner Act," 298–302. On Klare's "judicial deradicalization" thesis, compare Matthew W. Finkin, "Revisionism in Labor Law," *Maryland Law Review* 43 (1984): 23–92; and Klare, "Traditional Labor Law Scholarship and the Crisis of Collective Bargaining Law: A Reply to Professor Finkin," *Maryland Law Review* 44 (1985): 731–840.

154. Tomlins, *The State and the Unions*, 317–28; Atleson, *Values and Assumptions in American Labor Law*, 171–80.

155. Katherine Stone, "The Structure of Postwar Labor Relations," *New York University Review of Law and Social Change* 11 (1982–83): 131.

156. Klare, "Judicial Deradicalization of the Wagner Act," 293–95.

157. Friedman, *The Republic of Choice*, 107; Joel Rogers, "In the Shadow of the Law: Institutional Aspects of Postwar U.S. Union Decline," in Tomlins and King, eds., *Labor Law in America*, 289; Derek Bok, "Reflections on the Distinctive Character of American Labor Laws," *Harvard Law Review* 84 (1971): 1417–25.

158. Rogers, "Institutional Aspects of Postwar U.S. Union Decline," 288–89.

159. Executive Order 8802 (June 25, 1941), 3 CFR 957 (Comp. 1968); John Hope Franklin, *From Slavery to Freedom: A History of Negro Americans*, 3d ed. (New York, 1967), 578–79.

160. John J. Donohue III and Peter Siegelman, "The Changing Nature of Employment Discrimination Litigation," *Stanford Law Review* 43 (1991): 1015–21.

161. *NLRB v. Jones & Laughlin Steel*, 301 U.S. at 45.

162. *Phelps Dodge Corp. v. National Labor Relations Board*, 313 U.S. 177 (141).

163. Ibid., 313 U.S. at 183.

164. Atleson, *Values and Assumptions in American Labor Law*, 97–98.

165. Tomlins, *The State and the Unions*, 317–19.

166. Atleson, *Values and Assumptions in American Labor Law*, 91–96; H. W. Arthurs, "Labour Law Without The State," *University of Toronto Law Review* 46 (1996): 3.

167. *Fibreboard Paper Products Corp. v. NLRB*, 379 U.S. 203, 223 (1964) (Stewart, J., concurring).

168. *United Automobile Workers v. NLRB*, 765 F.2d 175 (D.C.Cir., 1985).

169. Atleson, *Values and Assumptions in American Labor Law*, 84–87.

170. Hogler, "Labor History and Critical Labor Law," 190; Kenneth Casebeer, "The Workers' Unemployment Insurance Bill: American Social Wage, Labor Organization, and Legal Ideology," in Tomlins and King, eds., *Labor Law in America*, 253.

171. Atiyah, *Freedom of Contract*, 579, 762.

172. Atleson, *Values and Assumptions in American Labor Law*, 136–42.

173. Ibid., 23–24.

174. Friedman, *The Republic of Choice*, 107–11; Fisk, "Judiciary in the History of Labor Law," 184.

175. Atleson, *Values and Assumptions in American Labor Law*, 91–96; Mark Barenberg, "Democracy and Domination in the Law of Workplace Cooperation: From Bureaucratic to Flexible Production," *Columbia Law Review* 94 (1994): 930–36.

176. David Vogel, "The 'New' Social Regulation in Historical and Comparative Perspective," in Thomas K. McCraw, ed., *Regulation in Perspective: Historical Essays* (Cambridge, MA, 1981), 155–85.

177. Occupational Safety and Health Act of 1970, 84 *Statutes at Large* 1590, *codified at* 29 U.S.C. §§ 651 et seq.; Thomas O. McGarity and Sidney A. Shapiro, *Workers at Risk: The Failed Promise of the Occupational Safety and Health Administration* (Westport, CT, 1993).

178. *Industrial Union Department, AFL-CIO v. American Petroleum Institute*, 448 U.S. 607, 668 n. 5 (1980) (Powell, J., concurring) [citing 116 *Congressional Record* 37342 (1970)]; see also *Gade v. National Solid Wastes Management Association*, 505 U.S. 88 (1992) (unlike pollution statutes, the OSHA does not permit states to institute standards more protective than federal ones). See Howard A. Laitin, "The 'Significance' of Toxic Health Risks: An Essay on Legal Decisionmaking Under Uncertainty," *Ecology Law Quarterly* 10 (1982): 339–95.

179. Hurst, *Law and Markets in United States History*, 48; Hurst, *The Legitimacy of the Business Corporation in the Law of the United States, 1780–1970* (Charlottesville VA, 1970), 162–64.

180. Arthurs, "Labour Law Without The State," 11–18.

181. H.R. 7598, 73d Congress, 2d Sess. (Feb. 2, 1934); see generally Casebeer, "The Workers' Unemployment Insurance Bill."

182. Casebeer, "The Workers' Unemployment Insurance Bill," 237, 245, 249.

183. Ibid., 252–53.

184. Rogers, "Institutional Aspects of Postwar U.S. Union Decline," 289.

185. E.g., Klare, "Judicial Deradicalization of the Wagner Act," 280; Atleson, *Values and Assumptions in American Labor Law*, 171–80.

186. Richard Epstein, "The Mistakes of 1937," *George Mason University Law Review* 11 (1988): 17.

187. Ibid., 19.

188. David E. Bernstein, "Roots of the 'Underclass': The Decline of

Laissez-Faire Jurisprudence and the Rise of Racist Labor Legislation," *American University Law Review* 43 (1993): 136.

189. Epstein, "Mistakes of 1937," 7.

190. Ibid., 19–20. Sunstein, on the other hand, argues that the "subsidy" issue was the core difference between *Adkins* and *West Coast Hotel*, as well as between the two constitutional regimes for which they stood. Sunstein, "Lochner's Legacy," 880–81.

191. Atiyah, *Freedom of Contract*, 726.

192. Grant Gilmore, *The Death of Contract* (Columbus, OH, 1974), 95–96.

193. Friedman, *The Republic of Choice*, 222 n. 20.

194. McCurdy, "Roots of Liberty of Contract," 20.

CHAPTER 8

1. Dennis P. Ryan, "Landholding, Opportunity, and Mobility in Revolutionary New Jersey," *William & Mary Quarterly* 36 (1979): 571–92; Alan Taylor, "Land and Liberty on the Post-Revolutionary Frontier," in David T. Konig, ed., *Devising Liberty: Preserving and Creating Freedom in the New American Republic* (Stanford, 1995), 87; Alan Taylor, "Agrarian Independence: Northern Land Rioters after the Revolution," in Alfred F. Young, ed., *Beyond the American Revolution: Explorations in the History of American Radicalism* (DeKalb, IL, 1993), 232; Gordon Wood, *The Radicalism of the American Revolution* (New York, 1991), 127, 129.

2. Alan Taylor, *Liberty Men and Great Proprietors: The Revolutionary Settlement on the Maine Frontier, 1760–1820* (Chapel Hill, NC, 1990).

3. As quoted in Eugene C. Hargrove, "Anglo-American Land Use Attitudes," *Environmental Ethics* 2 (1980): 136.

4. Peter Onuf, *Statehood and Union: A History of the Northwest Ordinance* (Bloomington, IN, 1987), 32, 42; Malcolm J. Rohrbough, *The Land Office Business: The Settlement and Administration of American Public Lands, 1789–1837* (New York, 1968), 9–10; Paul W. Gates, *History of Public Land Law Development* (Washington, 1968), 59–74.

5. Onuf, *Statehood and Union*, 30, 37–40.

6. Taylor, "Land and Liberty on the Post-Revolutionary Frontier," 89.

7. Andrew R. L. Cayton, *The Frontier Republic: Ideology and Politics in the Ohio Country, 1780–1825* (Kent, OH, 1986), 7, 9; Rohrbough, *The Land Office Business*, 162.

8. Onuf, *Statehood and Union*, 42–43.

9. Cayton, *The Frontier Republic*, 14–15.

10. Ibid., x, xi, 22, 32. In 1786 Benjamin Rush, one of the most influential politicians and scientists of his age, argued that frontier development passed through three phases. The first white settlers reverted to primitivism and spent much of their time hunting, fishing, and drinking. The second "generation" raised crops, but on land encumbered with debt. Like those first on the scene, these pioneers exhibited little sense of commu-

nity or civic virtue. Enterprising market farmers characterized the last stage. They looked to the future, not just the present, and supported government, schools, and churches—a society built on order and reason. The Ohio Company of Associates wanted to bypass the first two stages. (Cayton, *Frontier Republic,* 14–15.)

11. Timothy J. Shannon, "'This Unpleasant Business': The Transformation of Land Speculation in the Ohio Country, 1787–1820," in Jeffrey P. Brown and Andrew R. L. Cayton, eds., *The Pursuit of Public Power: Political Culture in Ohio, 1787–1861* (Kent, OH, 1994), 22, 25, 27.

12. David B. Danbom, *Born in the Country: A History of Rural America* (Baltimore, 1995), 75, 132; Rohrbough, *The Land Office Business,* 233.

13. Daniel Feller, *The Public Lands in Jacksonian Politics* (Madison, WI, 1984), 4–5.

14. Gates, *History of Public Land Law Development,* 121–43.

15. Rohrbough, *The Land Office Business,* 40, 187.

16. See, for example, "Republican Theory and Practice," in Harry L. Watson, *Liberty and Power: The Politics of Jacksonian America* (New York, 1990), 42–72.

17. One of the first monetary subsidies to the states—designed to encourage road-building—was 2 percent of the proceeds from public land sales. This began with the admission of Ohio into the Union in 1803 and established an important precedent. By the early twentieth century, virtually all proceeds from land sales went to assist the economic development of western states.

18. The best summary of the assumptions and values behind early U.S. land policy is still Thomas Le Duc, "History and Appraisal of U.S. Land Policy to 1862," in Howard W. Ottoson, ed., *Land Use Policy and Problems in the United States* (Lincoln, NE, 1963), 3–27. Also see the overview of land policy in James Willard Hurst, *Law and Economic Growth: The Legal History of the Lumber Industry in Wisconsin, 1836–1915* (Cambridge, MA, 1964), 1–61.

19. Preemption permitted squatters on the public lands to purchase, for $1.25 per acre, up to 160 acres they had occupied in advance of government surveys. The first preemption act that applied to the entire public domain passed Congress in 1841. Because Spain and France provided free land to settlers, and because the cost of setting up a farm increased as families moved farther and farther west, many settlers thought they were doing the nation a favor by taking up land on the frontier.

20. In addition to the standard works on land policy cited above, see Robert P. Swierenga, "Land Speculation and Its Impact on American Economic Growth and Welfare: A Historiographical Review," *Western Historical Quarterly* 8 (1977): 283–302.

21. Richard B. Morris, ed., *Encyclopedia of American History* (New York, 1961), 466.

22. Wood, *The Radicalism of the American Revolution,* 312.

23. On the transformation of water law in the East see Theodore Stein-

berg, *Nature Incorporated: Industrialization and the Waters of New England* (New York, 1991); and Morton Horwitz, *The Transformation of American Law, 1780–1860* (Cambridge, MA, 1977).

24. Freedom of contract was far more important to Anglo-American than to Mexican law. As David Langum puts it, "Rights [under Anglo-American law] were absolute entitlements and duties [were] their stern correlatives, owned unconditionally. No matter how onesided or unfair, a contract should be enforced strictly according to its terms. Courts should not rewrite agreements. If debts were owned or damages assessed, judgment should be rendered for immediate payment in cash, with no extensions and regardless of a defendant's personal needs or ability to pay. The common law would make the world safe for contract. Furthermore, at common law rights were defined in accordance with complicated but neutral rules . . . clearly stated and preferably written down for all to see. [T]he essense of Anglo-American law . . . was rugged individualism, let the chips fall where they might, and an attitude on the part of litigants and the law alike of whole hog or none." David J. Langum, *Law and Community on the Mexican California Frontier: Anglo-American Expatriates and the Clash of Legal Traditions, 1821–1846* (Norman, OK, 1987), 270–71.

25. Donald J. Pisani, *To Reclaim a Divided West: Water, Law, and Public Policy, 1848–1902* (Albuquerque, NM, 1992), 11–32.

26. In the 1870s, the California legislature toyed with the idea of condemning or purchasing private water rights and creating a state bureaucracy to rent or lease the state's water. Instead, the irrigation district—which allowed communities to bond land to raise money for dams and canals—became the preferred alternative. The district reflected the assumption that the state should encourage the expansion of irrigation but that local interests should operate their own water system, without outside interference. By bonding the land, the district, rather than non-resident land speculators, captured the "unearned increment" as land values rose. On the irrigation district—a neglected institution in the legal history of the American West—see Donald J. Pisani, *From the Family Farm to Agribusiness: The Irrigation Crusade in California and the West, 1850–1933* (Berkeley, 1984), 129–53 and 250–82.

27. Donald J. Pisani, "Enterprise and Equity: A Critique of Western Water Law in the Nineteenth Century," *Western Historical Quarterly* 18 (1987): 24–26.

28. For a different interpretation, see Donald Worster, *Rivers of Empire: Water, Aridity & the Growth of the American West* (New York, 1985).

29. Donald J. Pisani, "State vs. Nation: Federal Reclamation and Water Rights in the Progressive Era," *Pacific Historical Review* 51 (1982): 265–82.

30. Id., "Irrigation, Water Rights, and the Betrayal of Indian Allotment," *Environmental History Review* 10 (1986): 157–76.

31. On forestry laws see Jay P. Kinney, *The Development of Forest Law in America* (New York, 1917); James Willard Hurst, *Law and Economic*

Growth: The Legal History of the Lumber Industry in Wisconsin, 1836–1915 (Cambridge, MA, 1964); John Ise, *The United States Forest Policy* (New Haven, CT, 1920); and Samuel Trask Dana, *Forest and Range Policy: Its Development in the United States* (New York, 1956).

32. Mary E. Young, "Congress Looks West: Liberal Ideology and Public Land Policy in the Nineteenth Century," in David M. Ellis, ed., *The Frontier in American Development: Essays in Honor of Paul Wallace Gates* (Ithaca, NY, 1969), 91.

33. Young, "Congress Looks West," 74–112. An Illinois congressman observed in 1844: "The relation of landlord and tenant is not favorable to the growth or maintenance of free principles. The constant aim of monarchies is to build up a landed and moneyed aristocracy; to accumulate wealth and power in the hands of the few; to create distinctions and orders in society; to make the poor laborer a mere serf of his wealthy employer; and a policy precisely opposite to that should be adopted by us. The moment the citizen becomes a freeholder, his ties to his country and its institutions are increased. He has his home, his fireside, and his personal liberty and security, to protect and defend." (Young, "Congress Looks West," 92–93.)

34. Alexander G. Eels, "The Land Question Stated," *Overland Monthly* 7 (1886): 371; John N. Irwin, "A Great Domain by Irrigation," *Forum* 12 (1892): 749. See also Thomas P. Gill, "Landlordism in America," *North American Review* 142 (1886): 52–67; A. J. Desmond, "America's Land Question," *North American Review* 142 (1886): 153–58; and Humphrey J. Desmond, "The Last Resort of the Landless," *Forum* 6 (1888): 319–25.

35. Harry N. Scheiber, "Public Rights and the Rule of Law in American Legal History," *California Law Review* 72 (1984): 219.

36. Id., "Property Law, Expropriation, and Resource Allocation by Government: The United States, 1789–1910," *Journal of Economic History* 33 (1973): 232–51; id., "The Road to *Munn*: Eminent Domain and the Concept of Public Purpose in the State Courts," *Perspectives in American History* 5 (1971): 327–402; and id., "The Jurisprudence—and Mythology—of Eminent Domain in American Legal History," in Ellen Frankel Paul and Howard Dickman, eds., *Liberty, Property, and Government: Constitutional Interpretation Before the New Deal* (Albany, NY, 1989), 217–38.

37. Joseph L. Sax, "The Public Trust Doctrine in Natural Resource Law: Effective Judicial Intervention," *Michigan Law Review* 68 (1970): 473–566; Molly Selvin, "The Public Trust Doctrine in American Law and Economic Policy, 1789–1920," 1980 *Wisconsin Law Review*, 1403–42; Carol Rose, "The Comedy of the Commons: Custom, Commerce, and Inherently Public Property," *University of Chicago Law Review* 53 (1986): 711–81; and Scheiber, "Public Rights and the Rule of Law in American Legal History," 217–51.

38. The basic works on conservation in the late nineteenth and early twentieth centuries include Samuel P. Hays, *Conservation and the Gospel of Efficiency: The Progressive Conservation Movement, 1890–1920* (New

York, 1975); Elmo Richardson, *The Politics of Conservation: Crusades and Controversies* (Berkeley, 1962); John F. Reiger, *American Sportsmen and the Origins of Conservation* (New York, 1975); Donald C. Swain, *Federal Conservation Policy, 1921–1933* (Berkeley, 1963); James L. Penick, *Progressive Politics and Conservation: The Ballinger-Pinchot Affair* (Chicago, 1968); and J. Leonard Bates, "Fulfilling American Democracy: The Conservation Movement, 1907–1921," *Mississippi Valley Historical Review* 44 (1957): 29–57.

39. Kenneth J. Vandevelde, in "The New Property of the Nineteenth Century: The Development of the Modern Concept of Property," *Buffalo Law Review* 29 (1980): 325–67, has argued that during the nineteenth century the American conception of property as *things* gave way to a vision of *rights* defined by legal relations among individuals. At the same time, many forms of intangible property emerged, such as business goodwill, brand names, and trade secrets.

40. It is important to note that as much land was claimed under the Kinkaid Act of 1904, the Enlarged Homestead Act of 1909, and the Stock-Raising Homestead Act of 1916, as under the Homestead Act of 1862—perhaps more. Theodore Roosevelt attempted to placate powerful Republican senators in the West, trading access to public land on the northern Great Plains for that reserved in the national forests. See Donald J. Pisani, "George Maxwell, the Railroads, and American Land Policy, 1899–1904," *Pacific Historical Review* 63 (1994): 177–202.

41. Henry Clepper, ed., *American Forestry: Six Decades of Growth* (Washington, 1960), 217; Samuel Trask Dana, *Forest and Range Policy: Its Development in the United States* (New York, 1956), 325.

42. Joseph L. Sax, *Mountains Without Handrails: Reflections on the National Parks* (Ann Arbor, MI, 1980), 7. Sax denies that parks and wilderness areas are products "of the modern growth of regulatory government or of the expansion of the federal role in American life. They are, instead, elements of a peculiar byway of American government, an experiment in public ownership and management that has no significant counterpart in our national experience." Id., "Parks, Wilderness, and Recreation," in Michael J. Lacey, ed., *Government and Environmental Politics: Essays on Historical Developments Since World War Two* (Baltimore, 1989), 115.

43. See id., "Parks, Wilderness, and Recreation," 115.

44. On the national park policy see Alfred Runte, *National Parks: The American Experience* (Lincoln, NE, 1987); John Ise, *Our National Park Policy: A Critical History* (Baltimore, 1961); and Sax, *Mountains Without Handrails.*

45. *Geer v. Connecticut*, 161 U.S. 519 (1896), was widely interpreted as the foundation of state ownership of game, but *Hunt v. United States*, 278 U.S. 96 (1928), ruled that the power of the federal government to protect and administer the public domain was beyond question or doubt. See Michael Bean, *The Evolution of National Wildlife Law* (New York, 1983),

16–17, 22, 105–6; Thomas A. Lund, *American Wildlife Law* (Berkeley, 1980), 20–27.

46. James B. Trefethen has described women's hats at the turn of the twentieth century as "mobile habitat groups festooned with mounted warblers, cardinals, or blubirds arranged in lifelife poses." See his *An American Crusade for Wildlife* (New York, 1975), 129.

47. Ibid., 154–56, 228; Bean, *Evolution of National Wildlife Law*, 19–20, 120–21, 215–16. It is important to recognize that, as in road-building at the beginning of the twentieth century, the nineteenth century jurisdictional battle over the regulation of hunting and fishing was between the states, counties, and towns as well as the federal government and the states.

48. On western reclamation in the nineteenth century, see Pisani, *To Reclaim a Divided West.*

49. The most balanced overview of federal reclamation in the twentieth century is Gates, *History of Public Land Law Development,* 635–98. Two more polemical but still useful studies are Worster, *Rivers of Empire,* and Marc Reisner, *Cadillac Desert: The American West and Its Disappearing Water* (New York, 1986).

50. As quoted in Hurst, *Law and Economic Growth,* 99.

51. Donald J. Pisani, "Forests and Conservation, 1865–1890," *Journal of American History* 72 (1985): 340–59.

52. Congress considered the first bill to create national forests in 1876; that legislation confined the proposed forests to the watershed of navigable streams to minimize fluctuations in streamflow. Other unsuccessful bills were introduced in 1880, 1882, 1884–85, 1886, and 1888. See Jenks Cameron, *The Development of Governmental Forest Control in the United States* (Baltimore, 1928), 201–3; Ise, *United States Forest Policy,* 52–53, 112–14.

53. William D. Rowley, *U.S. Forest Service Grazing and Rangelands: A History* (College Station, TX, 1985), 32, 36–37, 47, 63, 81; Penick, *Progressive Politics and Conservation,* 4; Donald J. Pisani, "Forests and Reclamation, 1891–1911," *Forest & Conservation History* 37 (1993): 73–74.

54. Franklin D. Roosevelt to Harold Ickes, Jan. 3, 1936, in Edgar B. Nixon, ed., *Franklin D. Roosevelt and Conservation, 1911–1945* 1 (Hyde Park, NY, 1957): 463.

55. Richard Lowitt, *The New Deal and the West* (Norman, OK, 1993), 67; Clayton R. Koppes, "Efficiency, Equity, Esthetics: Shifting Themes in American Conservation," in Donald Worster, ed., *The Ends of the Earth: Perspectives on Modern Environmental History* (Cambridge, MA, 1988), 245; Frank Gregg, "Public Land Policy: Controversial Beginnings for the Third Century," in Michael J. Lacey, ed., *Government and Environmental Politics: Essays on Historical Developments Since World War Two* (Baltimore, 1989), 148.

56. Cameron, *Development of Governmental Forest Control,* 308.

57. The Forest Service established its first experiment station in 1908.

The McSweeney-McNary Act (1928) provided for the creation of forest research stations linked to state land-grant universities—institutions similar to agricultural experiment stations. The 1928 act made forest research one of the major activities of the Department of Agriculture.

58. William G. Robbins, *American Forestry: A History of National, State & Private Cooperation* (Lincoln, NE, 1985), 50–104; Harold K. Steen, *The U.S. Forest Service: A History* (Seattle, WA, 1977), 129–31, 173, 189–90, 193; Dana, *Forest and Range Policy*, 221–26, 237, 239, 282. The courts did not affirm the power of individual states to dictate forest policies on private land until 1949. During the 1930s, U.S. Supreme Court rulings suggested that the high court would acknowledge a federal regulatory power under the commerce or general welfare clauses, but the Forest Service was reluctant to follow this course.

59. For a fascinating view of U.S. forest policy in the early twentieth century from the ground up see Hal K. Rothman, ed., *"I'll Never Fight Fire with My Bare Hands Again": Recollections of the First Forest Rangers of the Inland Northwest* (Lawrence, KS, 1994).

60. As quoted in Hurst, *Law and Economic Growth*, 115.

61. Few historians take the arguments of westerners as more than a cover for special interests. See, for example, Hays, *Conservation and the Gospel of Efficiency*, 241–60; and Roy M. Robbins, *Our Landed Heritage: The Public Domain, 1776–1970* (Lincoln, NE, 1976), 343–63. A notable exception is G. Michael McCarthy, *Hour of Trial: The Conservation Conflict in Colorado and the West, 1891–1907* (Norman, OK, 1977).

62. As reprinted in McCarthy, *Hour of Trial*, 86, 87, 141, 179, 188, 192, 215.

63. Donald Worster, *Dust Bowl: The Southern Plains in the 1930s* (New York, 1979), 210–30; R. Douglas Hurt, *The Dust Bowl: An Agricultural and Social History* (Chicago, 1981), 69–71; Lowitt, *The New Deal and the West*, 59, 61.

64. Samuel P. Hays, *Beauty, Health, and Permanence: Environmental Politics in the United States, 1955–1985* (New York, 1987), 3–4, 32–33. Also see Hays, "Three Decades of Environmental Politics: The Historical Context," in Lacey, ed., *Government and Environmental Politics*, 19–79.

65. Peter Wiley and Robert Gottlieb, *Empires in the Sun: The Rise of the New American West* (Tucson, AZ, 1982), 47, 50; Frank Gregg, "Public Land Policy: Controversial Beginnings for the Third Century," 156–58.

66. Conservationists interested in recreation and wildlife have always been suspicious of some federal agencies, particularly the General Land Office, Soil Conservation Service, and Corps of Engineers. The Great Depression muted this criticism because dam-building projects put people to work. After World War II, however, the drainage of marshlands by the SCS, and the construction of flood control dams by the Army, profoundly affected fish and wildlife populations.

67. Paul W. Hirt, *A Conspiracy of Optimism: Management of the National Forests Since World War II* (Lincoln, NE, 1994), 151–92.

68. Philip Shabecoff, *A Fierce Green Fire: The American Environmental Movement* (New York, 1993), 134.

69. Harry N. Scheiber, "The Impact of Technology on American Legal Development," in Joel E. Colton and Stuart Bruchey, eds., *Technology, the Economy, and Society* (New York, 1987), 110–11. In 1974 environmental groups launched a successful suit to require the Bureau of Land Management to assess the impact of grazing on the 170 million acres it administered. Over the next decade, hundreds of environmental impact statements were drafted, resulting in sharp reductions in the number of animals pastured on about half of the land involved. This came on top of a reduction of 25 percent from 1950 to 1970 and contributed to the "Sagebrush Rebellion" and the unpopularity of the Carter Administration in the American West. Gregg, "Public Land Policy," 154–55.

70. See Christopher Schroeder, "The Evolution of Federal Regulation of Toxic Substances," in Lacey, ed., *Government and Environmental Politics*, 278, 280.

71. Sax, "Parks, Wilderness, and Recreation," 132–33.

72. Robert Cameron Mitchell, "From Conservation to Environmental Movement: The Development of the Modern Environmental Lobbies," in Lacey, ed., *Government and Environmental Politics*, 87, 88, 96–98.

73. Thomas Dunlap, *Saving America's Wildlife* (Princeton, NJ, 1988), 108–9.

74. Ibid., 142–55; Bean, *Evolution of National Wildlife Law*, 227–30. On the environmental movement see Shabecoff, *A Fierce Green Fire*; and Robert Gottlieb, *Forcing the Spring: The Transformation of the American Environmental Movement* (Washington, 1993).

75. As quoted in Shabecoff, *A Fierce Green Fire*, 136.

76. Lisa Mighetto, *Wild Animals and American Environmental Ethics* (Tucson, AZ, 1991), 85, 106; Dunlap, *Saving America's Wildlife*, 16 (Hornaday quote).

77. Tom Regan, "Animals and the Law: The Need for Reform," in id., *All That Dwell Therein: Essays on Animal Rights and Environmental Ethics* (Berkeley, 1982), 148–64.

78. Bean, *Evolution of National Wildlife Law*, 318–83; Thomas R. Dunlap, "The Federal Government, Wildlife, and Endangered Species," in Lacey, ed., *Government and Environmental Politics*, 210, 218, 222–23, 226–27.

79. Malcolm Forbes Baldwin, "The Federal Government's Role in the Management of Private Rural Land," in Lacey, ed., *Government and Environmental Politics*, 187, 197–99.

80. As quoted in Gregg, "Public Land Policy," 177.

81. Ellen Frankel Paul, *Property Rights and Eminent Domain* (New Brunswick, NJ, 1987), 9. Also see Dennis J. Coyle, "Feudalism and Liberalism," in *Property Rights and the Constitution: Shaping Society Through Land Use Regulation* (Albany, NY, 1993), 213–37. The perceived threat to property rights comes from both the federal government—in the form of

endangered species acts, NEPA, the Strip Mining Control and Reclamation Act, Superfund and many other laws—and the states. Beginning in 1961, Hawaii subjected all property to statewide zoning. A state commission classified all land as agricultural, conservation, urban, and rural; only the commission could issue variances. Other states have preempted local zoning for limited areas, as California has with its coastal and regional planning commissions. See Paul, *Property Rights*, 38–54.

82. *Takings, Compensation, and Pending Wetlands Legislation*, Hearing before the House Subcommittee on Fisheries and Wildlife Conservation and the Environment, May 21, 1992 (Washington, 1992), 3.

83. A. Dan Tarlock, "Environmental Law, But Not Environmental Protection," in Lawrence J. McDonnell and Sarah F. Bates, eds., *Natural Resources Policy and Law* (Washington, 1993), 181.

84. Tarlock, "Environmental Law," 167, 169.

85. Daniel B. Botkin, *Discordant Harmonies: A New Ecology for the Twenty-first Century* (New York, 1990), 33, 62.

CHAPTER 9

I wish to thank my colleague Richard Buxbaum for his assistance and hasten to add that he would be horrified to be held responsible for anything an interloper into his field such as myself has said.

1. See David Currie, "The Constitution and the Supreme Court: The Protection of Economic Interests, 1889–1910," *University of Chicago Law Review* 52 (1985): 324–88.

2. See chapter 3 above.

3. See Melvin Eisenberg, "The World of Contract and the World of Gift," *California Law Review* 85 (1997): 821–67.

4. See Jost Dellbruck, "Globalization of Law, Politics and Markets—Implications for Domestic Law—A European Perspective," *Indiana Journal of Global Legal Studies* 1 (1993): 5–36; Martin Shapiro, "The Globalization of Law," *Indiana Journal of Global Legal Studies* 1 (1993): 37–64; Wolfgang Wiegand, "Americanization of Law: Reception or Convergence," and Martin Shapiro, "The Globalization of Judicial Review," in Lawrence Friedman and Harry Scheiber, eds., *Legal Culture and the Legal Profession* (Boulder, CO, 1996).

5. See Leon Trakman, *The Law Merchant: The Evolution of Commercial Law* (Littleton, CO, 1983).

6. See Marianne Constable, *The Law of the Other* (Chicago, 1993); Paul Milgrom, Douglass North, and Barry Weingast, "The Role of Institutions in the Revival of Trade: The Law Merchant, Private Judges, and the Champagne Fairs," *Economics and Politics* 2 (1990): 1–36.

7. Berthold Goldman, "The Complementary Roles of Judges and Arbitrators in Ensuring That International Commercial Arbitration Is Effective," in International Chamber of Commerce, *Sixty Years of ICC Arbitration* (Paris, 1984).

8. See Philip Webb, *The Conflict of Laws and Contract* (Auckland, N.Z., 1985).

9. See chapters 1, 3, 4, and 5 above.

10. See Melvin Eisenberg, "Private Ordering through Negotiation: Dispute Settlement and Rulemaking, *Harvard Law Review* 89 (1976): 637–81.

11. See E. A. Laing, "Equal International Economic Access And Its Antidote: National Welfare As Legitimate Discrimination," *Emory International Law Review* 7 (1993): 337–455.

12. Charles Goetz and Robert Scott, "Enforcing Promises: An Examination of the Basis of Contract," *Yale Law Journal* 89 (1980): 1261–1312.

13. See "Conflict of Laws in the Global Village," *Vanderbilt Journal of Transnational Law* 28 (1995): 359–501.

14. Martin Shapiro, *Courts: A Comparative and Political Analysis* (Chicago, 1981), chap. 1.

15. Ole Lando, "*The Lex Mercatoria* in International Commercial Arbitration," *International and Comparative Law Quarterly* 34 (1985): 747–68.

16. Ibid.

17. Note, "General Principles of Law in International Commercial Arbitration," *Harvard Law Review* 101 (1988): 1816–34.

18. See Thomas Carbonneau, ed., *Lex Mercatoria and Arbitration* (Dobbs Ferry, NY, 1990).

19. See J. L. Volz and R. S. Haydock, "Foreign Arbitral Awards: Enforcing the Award Against the Recalcitrant Loser," *William Mitchell Law Review* 21 (1996): 867–940.

20. See Yves Dezalay and Bryant G. Garth, *Dealing in Virtue: International Commercial Arbitration and the Construction of a Transnational Legal Order* (Chicago, 1996), chap. 5.

21. See also The United Nations Convention on the Contracts for the International Sale of Goods (1980).

22. 1988.

23. 1985. Uncitral publishes an annual yearbook in which its various legal guides and model laws can be followed.

24. 1980.

25. Federation Internationale des Ingenieurs—Conseils, *Conditions of Contract for Works of Civil Engineering Construction*, 4th ed. (1987).

26. See "Contract Law in a Changing World," *American Journal of Comparative Law* 40 (1992): 541–728.

27. See Christian Joerges, "The Europeanization of Private Law as a Rationalization Process and as a Contest of Disciplines—An Analysis of the Directive on Unfair Terms in Consumer Contracts," *European Review of Private Law* 3 (1995): 175–207.

28. See Robert Cooter and Thomas Ulen, *Law and Economics* (Glenview, IL, 1988), chap. 6.

29. See Ole Lando, *Principles of European Contract Law* (Dordrecht, 1995).

30. See Arthur Rosett, "Unification, Harmonization, Restatement, Codification, and Reform in International Commercial Law," *American Journal of Comparative Law* 40 (1992): 683–97.

31. See Symposium: "Contract Law in a Changing World."

32. See section III above.

33. See e.g., "Principles for International Commercial Contracts" Art. 1.9(2), *American Journal of Comparative Law* 40 (1992): 705.

34. Joerges, "Europeanization."

35. This section draws heavily on Dennis Campbell, ed., *International Franchising Law*, 2 vols. (New York, 1994).

36. Most of the information for this section has been obtained from Erick Schanze, "Forms of Agreement and the Joint Venture Practice," in Christian Kirchner et al., *Mining Ventures in Developing Cultures, Part 2* (Frankfurt, 1981); and David N. Smith and Louis T. Wells, *Negotiating Third World Mineral Agreements* (Cambridge, MA, 1975).

37. I owe this point to Professor Buxbaum. See Wolfgang Peter, *Arbitration and Renogotiation of International Investment Agreements*, 2d ed. (Hague, 1995).

38. Wolfgang Wiegand, "The Reception of American Law in Europe," *American Journal of Comparative Law* 39 (1991): 229–59.

39. *Marchands de Droit* (Paris, 1992)

40. Dezalay and Garth, *Dealing in Virtue*.

41. See Steven Vogel, *Freer Markets, More Rules: The Paradoxical Politics of Regulatory Reform in the Advanced Industrial Countries* (Cambridge, MA, 1997).

Index

In this index an "f" after a number indicates a separate reference on the next page, and an "ff" indicates separate references on the next two pages. A continuous discussion over two or more pages is indicated by a span of page numbers, e.g., "57–59." *Passim* is used for a cluster of references in close but not consecutive sequence.

Library of Congress Cataloging-in-Publication Data
The State and Freedom of Contract / edited by Harry N. Scheiber.
   p. cm. – (The making of modern freedom)
Includes bibliographical references (p.   ) and index.
ISBN 0-8047-3370-8 (cloth : alk. paper)
   1. Contracts—United States.   2. Liberty of contract—United States.
I. Scheiber, Harry N.   II. Series
KF801.Z9S73   1998
346.7302—DC21
98-24281 CIP

This book is printed on acid-free, recycled paper.

Original printing 1998
Last figure below indicates year of this printing:
07   06   05   04   03   02   01   00   99   98

DISCARD